SPARTAN SEASONS

SPARTAN SEASONS

THE TRIUMPHS AND TURMOIL OF MICHIGAN STATE SPORTS

LYNN HENNING

MOMENTUM PUBLISHING
EDITORIAL OFFICES–BLOOMFIELD HILLS, MICHIGAN
BUSINESS OFFICES–UNION LAKE, MICHIGAN

SPARTAN SEASONS:
THE TRIUMPHS AND TURMOIL OF MICHIGAN STATE SPORTS

Jacket design by Deanna Kingins.
Photography editor: Stan Stein.

Manufactured in the United States of America.

Momentum Publishing
Business office:
865 Rachelle Drive
Union Lake, Michigan 48085
(313) 360-2426

ISBN 0-9618726-0-8

Momentum Books are published by the Momentum Publishing Company.
Its mark consists of the words "Momentum Publishing."

To Sandy—for caring, for coping.

ACKNOWLEDGEMENTS

Dozens of people inside and outside of Michigan State University assisted in putting together a book that was first discussed in May of 1986. The men who proposed that book, Bill Haney and Stan Stein, have earned special thanks for their constant attention and concern. Bill Haney is a dream publisher—a man with vast knowledge of the business whose integrity as an editor became one of the great benefits of taking on a project so enormous. Bill Haney is a professional worthy of a writer's complete confidence. No greater asset can a publisher bring to his profession.

Stan Stein's enthusiasm for the project was infectious, just as his intimate knowledge of Michigan State proved invaluable. Together, their phone calls, lunch discussions, and most of all their encouragement, enabled this book to develop and, ultimately, be completed. Craig Brown and Bob Beardslee also lent great support and enthusiasm, as did Danny McCarty, Monte Story and Max Hoffman Jr. Mark Haney's production and computer expertise eliminated a slew of potential headaches.

Equal thanks go to the scores of people associated with Michigan State University whose input, experiences, recollections—and trust—combined to provide the volumes of material needed for a comprehensive study of the MSU athletic program. It is difficult to express personal gratitude to all those who spoke so openly and honestly about the way in which Michigan State has functioned

viii   *Acknowledgements*

during these past 40 years. Many of them spoke about subjects and people that opened them to uneasiness or great pain. Many were motivated to speak because they wanted the truth, as they believed it to be, told. Some conflicts occasionally occurred, but it was the sources' lack of self-serving feedback that made the many months of interviewing so enlightening, and even gratifying.

Although some wish to remain anonymous, a special thanks to the many Michigan State executives, staffers and athletic directors, past and present, who assisted: Dr. John Hannah, John Fuzak, Jack Breslin, Jack Shingleton, Burt Smith, Joe Kearney, Doug Weaver, Fred Stabley Sr. (whose book, *The Spartans*, was of great help), Clarence Underwood, Jacob Hoefer, Mary Kay Smith and Sylvia Thompson.

Particular thanks to coaches, past and present, who gave freely of their time and memory: Duffy Daugherty, Muddy Waters, George Perles, Darryl Rogers, Gus Ganakas, Jud Heathcote, Mike Deane, Vern Payne, Sherman Lewis, Howard Weyers, Kurt Schottenheimer, Cal Stoll, Vince Carillot, Hank Bullough, Chuck Noll, Charlie Baggett, Joe Pendry, Danny Litwhiler, Tom Smith, Amo Bessone, Ron Mason and Bruce Fossum.

To players: Don Japinga, Steve Juday, Charley Thornhill, Skip Macholz, Rod Strata, Steve Smith, Kirk Gibson, Chuck Fusina, Bryan Clark, Randy Lark, Edgar Wilson, Magic Johnson, Scott Skiles, Jeff Tropf, Sam Vincent, Jim Morrissey, John McDowell, Terry Tanker, Jim Epolito, Joe Palamara, Arnie Mathews and Shane Bullough.

Many thanks also to Vera Munn, Blanche Martin, Ron Karle, Bob Jones, Bill Burgess, Doug Mintline, Tim Staudt, Edgar Hayes, Vito Stellino, Jim Teets, Joe Greene and Mike Doyle.

To sports information departments at Notre Dame, Ohio State, Purdue and the University of Michigan. And, particularly, to the Michigan State sports information team of Nick Vista and Mike Pearson for their hours of assistance and facts-checking, and for producing media guides so thorough they act as a window to 100 years of sports history at Michigan State.

PREFACE

The athletic program at Michigan State University has always had a knack for noise. It seems to prefer an extremist personality, where the good times are truly good, and the bad hours are incredibly dark and often tangled in a Shakespearian web of human tragedy. In short, Michigan State, newest member of the Big Ten Conference, has always been an incredible newsmaker.

The university at East Lansing has known its share of sports glory since the modern era began following World War II, when President John Hannah set into motion the development of a giant university that would need to diversify from its heritage as an agricultural school. Contained within Hannah's vision was the idea of a balanced program of athletics, centered on football, that would promote social interaction among students and alumni. Football games would be a binding activity, Hannah thought, and to that end he wanted Michigan State to pursue athletics with the same enthusiasm and desire for excellence with which he was fueling MSU's campus-wide growth and drive for national distinction.

He would bring to Michigan State a man named Biggie Munn. In his seven years as football coach at Michigan State, and during ensuing years as athletic director, Munn would help establish the game at East Lansing in much the way Knute Rockne had made it an institution at Notre Dame.

Munn would bring with him an assistant coach named Duffy

Daugherty, who would take over as football coach when Munn moved to athletic director. The Golden Era of football at Michigan State would continue, climaxing in the mid-1960s, when Daugherty's teams were for two consecutive years among the best that had ever played college football.

Six years later, Daugherty would resign amid the woe of another disappointing season—a debilitating, mystifying series of so-so autumns that had begun immediately following the glory years.

From college football's summit, to a new role as struggler, Michigan State had descended. And made news. Several years later, it had undergone a renaissance under Denny Stolz, and almost immediately, found itself enveloped in a NCAA investigation that would bring on the program's greatest strife in 100 years of athletics at Michigan State.

Two years later, it would finish as Big Ten co-champion.

Michigan State. Ever the newsmaker.

At about the same time, the university's basketball team made national headlines because of a player walkout a few hours before Michigan State was to meet the No. 1-ranked team in the country, Indiana. Two years later, MSU signed high school star Earvin Johnson. Big Ten championships and a national championship would follow—within four years of the walkout.

At Michigan State, the roller-coaster was never confined to football.

From 1968 until 1987, Michigan State's principal rival and its chief agitator, the University of Michigan, got along very nicely with one athletic director and one head football coach: The great tandem of Don Canham and Bo Schembechler had been together 19 years as of April 1987.

From 1971 to 1982—a mere 11 years—Michigan State employed at various times five athletic directors and five head football coaches. An athletic department born of the stability brought on by Munn-Daugherty had fallen into such unsettled ways that its turnover rate became at best, puzzling, and at worst, embarrassing. Michigan State throughout was maintaining its image as the Big Ten's uncontested leader in off-the-field headlines.

A young coach named Darryl Rogers arrived from California in 1976 and brought life to a devastated MSU football program by preaching an offensive philosophy geared around the forward pass. A year after his concepts helped bring MSU a football co-championship in 1978, Rogers—an East Lansing hero the previous year—was branded a traitor as he *and* Athletic Director Joe Kearney bolted for Arizona State in a stunning package deal.

In the Rogers-Kearney exodus, Michigan State not only was proving to be accomplished in abrupt turnarounds; it was again displaying its knack for finding novel ways to draw national attention.

The path would run differently for Michigan State's hockey team, a program that had gone from misery in the late 1970s to mid-'80s status as a college dynasty under Ron Mason. Michigan State's 1986 NCAA Championship gave MSU its fourth national title in three sports, all within 20 years.

If there was one constant through all the post-war decades at Michigan State, it was, above all, great talents and personalities. Michigan State was forever absorbing its share of celebrity athletes: Magic Johnson, Kirk Gibson, Terry Furlow, Lorenzo White, Scott Skiles—many of whom, like their university, specialized as much in controversy as in prominence. The same could be said for coaches like Munn, Daugherty, Rogers, Denny Stolz, Muddy Waters, Pete Newell, Gus Ganakas, Jud Heathcote and Amo Bessone. They, at times, were larger-than-life figures whose personalities, words and deeds away from competition exposed them to great acceptance or even greater rejection; to admiration and scorn; to victories and, occasionally, failures.

There endured through these past four decades an athletic department that was a reflection of mankind's strengths and weaknesses. Egos, aspirations, visions, delusions, foresight, blindness, triumph, turbulence—they were aspects that seemed always so pronounced as the Michigan State sports tapestry was woven in rich color.

When Michigan State was founded in 1855, the only path connecting it to major urban centers was a plank road that extended from Detroit to the bend of the Grand River in Lansing's "Lowertown." Michigan State was chopped out of thick wilderness growth, which Governor Austin Blair chided for its position "in the woods, as if our young men needed to be taught scientifically the business of chopping and logging." Even before its doors opened, Michigan State was fighting the rap as a hick school.

A field meet at Olivet College in 1884 was Michigan State's first intercollegiate athletic competition, and 64 years later, in December of 1948, Michigan State had graduated to the big time—to acceptance in the Big Ten Conference. John Hannah two years earlier had impressed the NCAA body when during an address he said:

"If intercollegiate athletics are defensible, they are defensible only because of their contribution as a part of the college's educational program." Membership in the Big Ten, Hannah realized, meant a school would be elevated as much in academic scope as in its athletic endeavors. Faculty and programs would all be influenced positively.

Hannah never lost sight of a philosophy in which academics and athletics not only coexisted smoothly, but in fact enhanced one another. With considerable success, Hannah's concepts were put into practice during his stewardship as MSU president. The school grew in stature and, not coincidentally, its sports program also developed into a national power.

It is on the modern era of Michigan State sports—the post-war period, with particular emphasis on athletics during the 1960s, '70s and '80s—that this book concentrates.

Lynn Henning
May 18, 1987

CONTENTS

One

AN EMPIRE FALLS

At the Daugherty home on South-lawn Street in East Lansing, and in the seventh-floor rooms at Kellogg Center, the concern that Saturday morning of November 19, 1966, was weather. It was mild and gray in East Lansing. Acceptable, as long as rain held off from a game they were calling the biggest in 100 years of college football in America.

Michigan State-Notre Dame hype had turned an otherwise peaceful campus and community into a circus, and gripped a nation that had yet to taste something called the Super Bowl. But since MSU's coaching staff and players checked into Kellogg Center for their standard Friday night stay, the Spartans had stayed calm. It was for most players a sweet break from hysteria. Classes had been attended that week even if attention spans were slight. It was worse at night when players returned to their rooms, walled off from the on-campus voltage until a group of students would collect beneath a window, shouting for that player, any player, to appear and say a few words. Say even one word. It didn't matter on a campus where mid-'60s passions and energy were choosing football as a channel.

That Friday night at Kellogg the MSU players ate a routine dinner of steak, split pea soup and salad, then adjourned to a meeting room for a war flick that would serve as this week's Game Eve team movie. By the time the movie had ended and the team gathered for its nightcap of hot chocolate—Hawaiians Bob Apisa, Dick

1

Kenney and Charley Wedemeyer, faithful to the shtick, always gulped Hawaiian Punch—the jitters were nearing.

An exception was the man who lived on Southlawn. Duffy Daugherty always slept peacefully the night before a game. It was after the game, when replays and second guesses raced through his mind, that he struggled until fatigue won out at 3 or 4 a.m. It was different at Kellogg the night before Michigan State and Notre Dame were to match their 9-0 records. Lights had been cut by 11, but the energy levels were too high, the anxiety too great, to slip smoothly into slumber. Most would say years later they slept five or six hours at best. Most were wide awake when shortly before 7 the sun began grappling with gray skies.

At 9:45 they met for team breakfast in an atmosphere growing more quiet by the moment. A 20-minute, post-meal team meeting was tense. Nerves were becoming more of a challenge than Notre Dame, especially as players caught drift of the noise and clatter outside Kellogg's windows on a campus that by mid-morning had turned volcanic.

At 11:45 they lined up for the traditional walk to Spartan Stadium. Across the bridge that spans the Red Cedar River, passing over sluggish brown water flanked by bare trees, past Jenison Field House and Demonstration Hall, the team walked while whistling *The Spartan Fight Song*—a game-day tradition.

By the time Daugherty's players reached the Men's Intramural Building, they were within 100 yards of Spartan Stadium. Clint Jones, the All-American halfback, had hit the brink. He stopped whistling and began singing the Fight Song—louder, louder, louder, until now the entire team was in chorus. Fans mobbed the pathway, screaming as the players rolled by and disappeared into the stadium's north tunnel. It was only 90 minutes until The Game of the Century, as the world had dubbed it, would begin.

Separated from the madness outside, players undressed in the quiet of MSU's dressing room. Nerves were keeping conversations at a minimum, although there had been moments where the pressure and tension burst, geyser-like, from a player. Jones that morning not only had broken dramatically into song, but at a pre-game meeting he grabbed a folding chair and let fly with it. Most players appreciated the outburst. It was brash. It was leadership.

Daugherty's pre-game words were calm and free of dramatics. It was a typical speech, businesslike, emphasizing execution and performance. By design he avoided anything evangelical or contrived.

Daugherty knew, absolutely knew, Michigan State had the better team and in no way would he risk anything hokey during this pre-game address, when the team's psyches were already overloaded.

Daugherty thought the team's temperament was perfect. There was potential to be too high or to be so caught in the dramatics of the moment that a good team might stumble. He had seen that happen a few times during 13 seasons at Michigan State. But if he needed any assurance MSU was ready for Notre Dame, there was Pat Gallinagh, the wild defensive lineman from Detroit, going into his usual war dance minutes before MSU was to take the field. Gallinagh was known to smash his head against a locker until blood flowed as he slipped into character in the pre-game dressing room. During the pre-Notre Dame minutes he got so worked up he grabbed hold of Daugherty.

"Alright," Daugherty yelled, "it's time to go."

Players from both teams tromped onto a football field that shook from the crowd thunder, a setting so electric players from both sides talked 20 years later about the psychotic look in each others' eyes. The crowd that day never took a break. On every play Spartan Stadium roared like overhead jet planes, until, late in the game, the score tied 10-10, boos came as Notre Dame began running into the line to kill the clock and escape East Lansing with a tie. With one more game to play at Southern Cal the Irish had a chance to steal the final No. 1 ranking. The Irish would play it smart.

Ara Parseghian's strategy was no hit with MSU players, nor did it go over well with a few of the Notre Dame players as college football's grand moment melted into one of sports' all-time let-downs and controversies. As the seconds ticked away players on both teams were crying.

Next with the tears was Duffy Daugherty. He kneeled on the locker room floor afterward and led the team in prayer, then wept over a game he told his players Michigan State should have won. The season was over for MSU. With the Big Ten locked into a Rose Bowl-only agreement, the Spartans were finished for 1966. And since they had gone to Pasadena the previous year, a Rose Bowl revisit was out because of the Big Ten's no-repeat rule.

An overcast November day had come and gone as the height of football might at Michigan State. What Daugherty never dreamed as he went home for the usual Saturday night gathering of coaches and friends, was that '66 would be his final big season at Michigan

State. What the players could not have imagined as they shuffled off to their dorm rooms was such an abrupt end to the glory Michigan State had known during '65-66.

The fall, in fact, was under way. Anyone studying social systems in the South could see it coming. Anyone familiar with the recruiting of Bubba Smith, George Webster, Gene Washington or Charley Thornhill realized Daugherty was about to run dry of the great Southern All-Americans who were MSU's underpinnings in '65 and '66. Alabama Coach Bear Bryant knew it better than anyone.

It was December 1962 when Bryant flew into Roanoke, Virginia, to attend an all-city banquet honoring Roanoke's top high school football players. The player selected as the area's best was a running back from Roanoke Addison High named Charley (Big Dog, later called Mad Dog) Thornhill, the first black player so honored at Roanoke. Bryant sat in the audience and listened to Thornhill's acceptance speech. The next day he was on the phone to Daugherty.

"I've got a kid at Roanoke, and I wish I could have him," Bryant said. "He could make it anywhere. I'm going to send him to you."

Daugherty and Bryant were close friends who watched out for each other. It was Daugherty who helped send Joe Namath to Alabama after Namath visited Michigan State (Namath had lost interest in MSU, and Daugherty would forever insist that Namath's failure to graduate in the upper half of his class—then an admission requirement at Michigan State—cost him a legendary quarterback).

Thornhill was typical of Southern athletes in the early '60s. Deep South universities were not admitting black players, and only recently had other Southern schools begun enrolling blacks. Maryland, Tulane and Notre Dame were after Thornhill, but the recruiting push consisted mostly of letters and infrequent visits—common in an era when Northern schools had clear paths to the South's best black athletes.

The phone rang several days later at the Thornhill home.

"Charley, this is Coach Bryant. You'll get a ticket in the mail to visit Michigan State. Coach Daugherty is a good man and you'll enjoy playing up there."

Thornhill had intended to play for Notre Dame. He knew of Michigan State, had heard of Daugherty, but his respect for Bryant was immense. When The Bear spoke, you listened, even if a racial system he at least tacitly supported kept you off his team.

There were similar episodes across the southern states in 1962 and '63, a year before the Civil Rights Act was to break up much of the South's institutionalized discrimination. At Beaumont, Texas, Daugherty was signing Bubba Smith to a MSU tender. At LaPorte, Texas, a wide receiver named Gene Washington was choosing Michigan State. Only 20 miles from Clemson, South Carolina, George Webster—who years later would be selected MSU's greatest player of all time—looked at a couple of recruiting letters, considered a minimum of options, and happily signed with the Spartans.

Rapidly unfurling in those old Southern homes were national-championship seasons at Michigan State. The Spartans had established themselves as kingpin in-state recruiters during the 1950s and '60s as Daugherty, picking up a Rose Bowl team Biggie Munn handed over to him in 1954, became one of the game's best recruiters. But while MSU was loading up with personnel capable of keeping a Big Ten school in regular contention, the Spartans were missing out on Rose Bowls and on the national prominence Daugherty, Munn and others wanted to restore at Michigan State.

They needed world-class skill athletes. More speed and size. Michigan's high school crop was insufficient, as were most cities in the industrial North which shared their loot with regional universities. The Spartan coaching staff decided in the early '60s that it needed to expand its territory. Daugherty knew there was gold to be had and nobody was better at finding it than an old Irish prospector raised hard by Pennsylvania's coal mines.

His style was unique, impossible for other coaches to duplicate. Daugherty had become a national figure during the '50s as he took the Spartans to the Rose Bowl in 1956 and in October of that year made the cover of *TIME*. His wit was his greatest ally, but in the homes, and at Kellogg Center when parents and recruits came for weekend visits to Michigan State, Daugherty's intelligence and charm won the parents. He knew when to quip, but more importantly, he knew in a split second when to be sincere and serious.

On the road he would fly into an area already scouted by an assistant coach who would pick him up at the airport. Once in the car the assistant would brief Daugherty on everything: the player, his classes, his hobbies, his parents, brothers and sisters, and any trivia that might prove irresistible when it came time to finish the deal. Daugherty's memory awed his assistant coaches.

"Well, Barbara," he would say to the recruit's nine-year-old sister. "Your birthday is May 20, isn't it?"

On a second visit to a coal miner's home in western Pennsylvania he would be chatting with the player's father. This was Daugherty's turf and he knew the social structure intimately.

"Jim, how's your brother Ralph?" he would ask, and the father, all but obliged to consider Daugherty family, would explain and later tell his son the man from Michigan State seemed awfully nice. He was even better if he could get mom isolated for a one-on-one chat as she served up coffee and apple pie. Mothers usually cast the final vote.

He also knew how to treat recruits when they visited Michigan State. In 1960 Namath and his high school receiver, Tom Krzemienski, came to East Lansing to see the campus and learn something about the head coach. Daugherty took them to dinner at Win Schuler's in Marshall, and Schuler, a great friend of Daugherty's, served a majestic meal.

Even had he decided on MSU, Namath was in jeopardy because of his lower-half graduating position—it was one of the Big Ten's former red-tape regulations that so irked Daugherty—although Krzemienski chose MSU and lettered two years at end. Three years later Bryant invited Daugherty to Alabama to speak at a team dinner. Halfway through the evening Namath came up to Daugherty, shook hands, and asked: "How's Mr. Schuler?"

If Daugherty had a knack for coming into a home, pulling up a stool, and within 10 minutes making player and parents feel as if they had known him for years, his recruiting was helped as much by strong assistant coaches. Bob Devaney, Bill Yeoman, Dan Devine and Sonny Grandelius were on his '50s staff before they moved on to head coaching jobs. Hank Bullough, Cal Stoll, Danny Boisture, George Perles and Vince Carillot were among the '60s gang that eventually took head college jobs or moved to the pros.

Daugherty and Michigan State rolled on. It had taken time for Daugherty to establish his own program away from the irritating shadow of Munn, but he was running a football team at MSU as distinctive as his personality. Missed trips to Pasadena was the problem.

The Spartans were 7-2 in 1956, 8-1 in '57, then had a 3-5-1 thud in '58. They came back, with players like the classy Dean Look, to finish second in the Big Ten in '59 and miss a Rose Bowl trip when Minnesota threw away a final-game upset it had all but wrapped up against Wisconsin. Daugherty had winning seasons from 1960-62, but again, no Rose Bowl. The best shot came in 1963 when the Spartans and Illinois met in a season-ender that would send the winner to Pasadena. The big names: Sherman Lewis, MSU's All-American halfback, vs. Illinois' monstrous linebacker-fullback combo of Dick Butkus and Jim Grabowski.

It was scheduled for November 23, 1963, at Spartan Stadium.

A game that by midweek had become a minor preview of the '66 MSU-Notre Dame commotion withered Friday afternoon when news exploded from Dallas that President John F. Kennedy had been shot. It was decided only two Big Ten games would be played Saturday: MSU-Illinois, and Michigan-Ohio State, but by Saturday morning political and public pressure forced the games to be postponed. MSU and Illinois would meet on Thanksgiving Day.

Illinois won, 13-0, as Butkus devastated the Spartans. For years afterward Michigan State players and coaches would say the postponement psychologically wrecked a Spartan team that Daugherty had motivated to perfection. Getting the rhythm back was Daugherty's challenge the following week. But it never developed. Practices were flat and Michigan State was no sharper on Thursday as Butkus starred and Illinois—which had contended with the same trauma—won a Rose Bowl trip.

It was early in the '63 season Daugherty may have come closest to taking another job. There had been regular offers along the way and there would be offers, college and pro, throughout his years at MSU. In 1957 Texas offered Daugherty a lifetime contract as athletic director and head coach at twice his MSU salary, with only one stipulation: that he stay at least 10 years. Daugherty turned it down and Texas hired Darrell Royal. When Bear Bryant left Texas A&M a year later, the Aggies offered Daugherty a raise, percentage of gate receipts, an interest in an apartment house and a new home if he would come to College Station. Again Daugherty said no.

The interested party in '63 was Notre Dame. Joe Kuharich had been fired the previous year and Hugh Devore was working as interim coach on a team looking for another Rockne or Leahy. The Irish needed an experienced football man who was both a winner and a personality. The obvious choice was Duffy Daugherty.

Late on the night of October 5, Daugherty and his team returned to the Sheraton Hotel in Los Angeles. Michigan State had just lost, 13-10, to Southern Cal and Michigan State President John Hannah invited Daugherty up to his suite to relax and talk.

"Been a long night," Hannah said as he ordered Daugherty a cold Heineken. The two men leaned back, propping their feet on a coffee table. Hannah delivered the news.

"Father Hesburgh called. He said it didn't matter whether you lost every game the rest of the way, they would like you to work for them after this season.

"But I can't let you go to Notre Dame."

Hannah acknowledged what Daugherty knew: Notre Dame was probably the best job in the country. It had the resources, the reputation and the financial backing to be an annual giant. Daugherty knew he would have a national television show and endless speaking dates that could be a financial and personal bonanza. The job was ideal.

Hannah sighed. He was smiling.

"I would like to think," he said, "the two men in this room have done more for Michigan State than any two men in history."

Daugherty, the quipster, looked to either side.

"I can think of one."

Hannah continued with the personal appeal. Daugherty, he said, had been such an ambassador for Michigan State. He had shaped so much of its image. What would it take? Money? More security?

Daugherty was a tenured professor and worked without a contract. Security was no concern. Nor was title.

"I don't want to be athletic director," he said. "I want to be responsible just to you."

Hannah proposed that Daugherty be made Head of Football at Michigan State—a title that would do nothing but give Daugherty added status and perhaps more clout against Munn. The Cold War between athletic director and head coach had been escalating, and when Munn learned of the Hannah-Daugherty hookup that would bypass his office, he made an "either he goes, or I go" threat that in November came dangerously close to being acted upon at a Board of Trustees meeting.

There was no raise or other incentives promised Daugherty in his chat with Hannah, but staying at Michigan State was the easy choice. It had been home for 16 years. Daugherty was comfortable in Michigan and enthused about a football team that would come within a game of going to the Rose Bowl. It seemed smarter to stick in East Lansing and enjoy the known quantities rather than trundle on down to South Bend where the Irish were now stumbling.

Daugherty was also enjoying being in control. Michigan State was now his production entirely, from the talent MSU was bringing in, to the way it performed. He was symphony director, and assistants could not help but notice his style versus Munn's on the practice field.

Munn had come from the "run it again" school of repetition. If a play was botched the whistle blew and everyone lined up and ran it until it was executed crisply. Assistant coaches, most of whom practiced the same philosophy, loved Munn's reinforcement.

Daugherty was more the counselor. If the pulling guard missed his block, Daugherty would talk with him, explain to him, appeal to him, attempt to inspire rather than intimidate. It could frustrate assistants who had just threatened to put the entire backfield through extra wind sprints. But it was Daugherty's way, and on offense, he was boss.

Differences between Munn and Daugherty extended far from MSU's practice field. They had been growing since Munn turned the team over to his top assistant following the 1954 Rose Bowl.

After taking over a modest independent football program known as Michigan State College in 1947, Munn built a team that paralleled Michigan State's physical and academic growth during the late '40s and early '50s. The Spartans debuted on the Big Ten schedule in 1953 and now were cleaning up on the conference bullies, Michigan included. With his team certified in the Big Ten and a Rose Bowl victory under his belt, Munn was ready for the AD's office.

He was not ready to back off entirely from the football team. Michigan State started 1-5 and finished 3-6 in 1954, its worst record in 14 years. After a 20-19 loss to Notre Dame in the season's fourth game, Munn told Daugherty he wanted to talk with his staff. Daugherty invited him to a meeting the next day at Spartan Stadium.

Munn did not have pleasantries in mind. He chewed on the assistants, wondering whether shoddy coaching might not explain close losses (four by 11 points) and such a miserable start by a team he had taken nine months earlier to a Rose Bowl.

Daugherty, expecting a pep talk or something consoling from Biggie, blew up.

"You've got no right to come in here and berate them," he yelled. "As far as I'm concerned, this meeting is over."

Daugherty walked out. Munn later tried to talk with the assistants individually, but the coaches backed Daugherty. It was the new coach who had scored—standing up to Munn in a way that moved Biggie out of the picture and cemented Daugherty as the man in charge.

But it also signaled 17 years of tension and bitterness between the two. Munn fired back later that year, on the Sunday following MSU's final game, when he called a meeting in Hannah's office between himself, Hannah, Daugherty and Ed Harden, Michigan State's faculty representative.

Munn railed about the 3-6 record. He wondered what could be done before Daugherty wrecked the program. Hannah, Harden and Daugherty listened, embarrassed and uneasy. After Munn and the others had spoken, the president signaled that Daugherty should stay. The door closed and Hannah turned to him.

"Well," Hannah said, "the Big Man wasn't too big today, was he?"

Hannah told Daugherty to forget about it, that he had confidence in him and Daugherty should call if ever there was a problem.

The next season Michigan State went 9-1 and beat UCLA in the Rose Bowl, 17-14, on Dave Kaiser's field goal. After Michigan State walloped Marquette, 33-0, in the regular-season finale, Daugherty, still smarting over the previous year's digs, evened the score against his old boss.

He called a meeting the next day in Hannah's office between himself, the president, Harden—and Munn.

Rose Bowls vanished from MSU's schedule for 11 years, although the '60s started brightly for Daugherty and MSU—winning seasons from '60-63 until a 4-5 finish against a brutal schedule ended the streak in 1964. But even the '64 team had enough talent to earn it a No. 20 ranking in the final UPI poll. What it may have lacked was heart.

It was a season of underachievement in East Lansing. Players whined. And so did the head coach, who complained that too many skilled players were performing at 80 percent. Daugherty was no more disgusted than a few of his players who were tired of the hollering. It only added to talk Duffy would need a big 1965 to ease the heat.

In fact, the groundwork was finished. Daugherty's best back-to-back recruiting classes were setting up two seasons of college football dominance at East Lansing; teams that would finish 19-1-1 and make Michigan State and Daugherty national attractions.

Daugherty never anticipated the '65 breakthrough. He and his staff thought '66 would be the year two great recruiting crops matured. Daugherty merely liked what he saw in '65: a defense built around Smith, Webster, Thornhill, Ron Goovert, Bob Viney and Don Japinga. An offense starring Jones, Washington, Apisa, Harold Lucas and a third-year quarterback, Steve Juday.

There weren't any holes. UCLA fell first in a 13-3 whipping at East Lansing. Penn State was next, and by the time MSU had ripped the Lions, 23-0, at State College, MSU was flying. Even Spartan players who had grown accustomed to grand hopes and two or three losses per season could feel the difference.

After the shutout at Penn State, Viney, the team firebrand, yelled to his teammates: "You've got to realize we've got a great football team!" It was significant. The inferiority complex was disappearing. By the time everyone was aboard the team plane it was sinking in that UCLA and Penn State had been crushed and the Spartans were unbeaten. Michigan State had more talent than even the players understood.

Daugherty's offense was becoming glamorous behind the running of Jones and Washington's flair for grabbing passes. But the Spartans' 1965 celebrity would be its defense. Especially Smith and Webster, whose size and speed were putting college defensive football at a new altitude.

It was personnel suited to a defensive general like Hank Bullough. He had played for Munn and Daugherty after coming out of Canton, Ohio and now as Daugherty's assistant, the defense was his. Bullough believed opponents should be shut out, held to zero yardage or less if you had the players. Beyond muscle it was a matter of discipline and drive, and Bullough was going to get the maximum from this bunch if it killed them. Some days it nearly did.

When one workout early in the season bothered Bullough, he lined up the defense for a ghastly night of wind sprints. They ran dozens of 30-yard sprints nonstop. Toward the end players were cramped up, nauseated, some of them falling out as their legs and lungs gave out. A few players seriously thought about jumping Bullough as the torture went on.

A few days later Michigan State was getting ready for Ohio State when Bullough said to the defense: "You remember those sprints? I guarantee if you don't play better this game, you'll do double on Monday." No one doubted him.

State won, 32-7, and held the Buckeyes to a minus-22 yards

rushing. It had been such annihilation that OSU in the second half stopped running. The Buckeyes threw 29 passes, a normal season's worth for Woody Hayes' old teams, and scored only once, when MSU went with its reserves.

At Monday night's practice Bullough reconvened the sprint squad. The starters protested. Benchwarmers had cost MSU its shutout.

"I don't care," Bullough roared. "You're all family. You play together." The session wasn't as bad as the previous week's. But it helped set the tone on a defense where pursuit and gang-tackling were the trademarks.

It wasn't only Bullough who could crack the whip at practice. Although Daugherty spent his hours with the offense, lecturing and counseling more than threatening, Bubba Smith put an end to his patience one night during a scrimmage.

Smith never thought he should be hit at the knees. He and blockers got into regular tiffs until the night he spit at a man who had hit him low. Daugherty was on Smith in a second, jumping on his chest, yelling: "Bubba Smith, if I ever catch you spitting on somebody again, you'll be back in Beaumont, Texas, tomorrow!" Smith could have thrown Daugherty into the adjacent soccer field, but kept quiet and went on with his All-American seasons.

Off the field Daugherty had likewise managed to keep peace and a racially mixed team from splitting or collecting in black and white cliques. Most Southern black players came to East Lansing half-terrified that the white society they had come to know would be at least as hostile in the North. Most discovered, to their surprise, it was far different. People treated them courteously, especially assistants like Vince Carillot. Arriving players found Daugherty gracious and friendly, and only rarely was he a screamer on the field.

The culture shock came in huge classrooms where competitive athletes were now expected to be competitive students. Segregated Southern schools had not always provided the strongest elementary or secondary educations, which for many athletes meant intense work with tutors during their freshman years, and even later, as they tried to catch up.

And whether one was dealing with it in a dormitory or at a drug store, racism could be found. Older black players told new recruits to avoid dating white women if they expected to play. Thornhill was studying in the lobby at Jenison Field House one day when a white coed sat down a few feet from him. He jumped from the sofa and left the lobby, hoping his playing chances hadn't been damaged by a two-second indiscretion.

Racism might have been a subtle part of campus life, but it was never sanctioned on the football team. Daugherty one night came into the post-practice dining room to see whites sitting with whites and blacks sitting by themselves at dinner. He exploded.

"You play together, dammit, you eat together!" It was the last time tables were segregated.

On the field the '65 team cruised as Juday, Jones and Washington piled up the points and Smith and Webster led a defense ruled by Bullough. He was the roughest and gruffest of Daugherty's assistants, the drill sergeant who would spin his baseball cap angrily and go one-on-one with Viney or Bubba when either slipped up. And often Bullough would win.

He also had brought a new defensive wrinkle to Michigan State's '65 team— the safety blitz. A new trick in the early '60s, Bullough worked it into MSU's scheme as the *coup de grace* on a defense that owned the line of scrimmage and could afford to free up its secondary. Within two seasons a blitz that figured in MSU's negative-yardage raids was a standard part of college defenses.

It was a team heading for the Rose Bowl in '65, a team that tore through everyone but Purdue as Bob Griese took the Boilermakers to a 10-0 halftime lead at West Lafayette before MSU came back to win, 14-10. A 12-3 cleanup of Notre Dame in the finale at South Bend sent Michigan State to Pasadena with a 10-0 record (11-game schedules did not arrive until 1971) and the No. 1 ranking in the land. It would be MSU vs. UCLA in the Rose Bowl—a replay of the opener MSU won, 13-3, at East Lansing.

By the time Michigan State arrived in California, the world was set for a New Year's Day slaughter at Pasadena. At least subconsciously, so were the Spartans.

Daugherty had told the team to have fun and treat the West Coast trip as a reward for one of the more spectacular seasons any college team had crafted. No one disobeyed. Chrysler was waiting for the team with chauffeur-driven cars ready to wheel players to Sunset Strip and Hollywood Boulevard, anywhere around town as long as they made curfew.

But MSU's football psyche was crumbling. There were girls around, and gluttonous dinners at Lawry's. There was an obsession to soak up California's delights and simply endure the practices at East Los Angeles Junior College. Another contributor was the local newspapers. Jim Murray, having his usual fun, wrote in the *Los Angeles Times* of the "Jolly Green Giants" and their front line which was "so big that when they ran a picture of it on the front page of the *Detroit Free Press*, they had to make it 'Continued on Page 11.' And even then, they only got to the left guard."

By midweek, Daugherty knew Michigan State was soft and set up for a New Year's Day disaster. On Wednesday, three days before the game, he collared Juday and Japinga.

"We're in trouble," he said. "What are we gonna do to get out of it?"

To steer their minds from the beach to football, Daugherty had planned to move the team into a monastery in the Sierra Madres a couple of days before the game. He decided on a quick check-in. But by now the partying and distractions had left Michigan State a mental wreck. It was UCLA, practicing without pressure for a game in which it was a laughable underdog, that had built momentum and prepared neatly behind Coach Tommy Prothro.

The monastery had done little to help Daugherty's team. In the pre-game locker room on New Year's Day there was less talk about football than about the priorities a team from East Lansing had put at the head of its agenda: Did parents get their tickets? Had girl-friends arrived on the train? Were their accommodations arranged?

After playing two miserable quarters marked by Japinga's fumble, Dick Kenney's missed 23-yard field goal and a game plan that UCLA devoured, Michigan State was down, 14-0.

Prothro had gone along merrily with the MSU hype, chuckling at the idea UCLA could stay in a game with the mighty Spartans. But he had been doing his homework. He studied five years of Michigan State films to get a grip on Daugherty's tendencies. State, he knew, would try and muscle UCLA by running from tackle to tackle. Prothro's only chance was to jam tackle holes and chop down the Spartan sweeps.

Michigan State stayed stubborn. Gene Washington had been crying for the ball but barely saw it until late in the game, when MSU put together two fourth-quarter touchdowns. On the first TD, a 38-yard run by Bob Apisa, Juday tried a two-point pass off a faked kick, but missed. Juday scored again late in the game on a plunge, which left State with a two-point try to tie. Apisa swept right, turning the corner and charging toward the end zone until Bobby Stiles flew from the secondary to cut him down. It was Michigan State's payback for all the partying, all the indulgence, all the abysmal preparation that would help bring on one of New Year's Day's classic upsets.

At the hotel after the game, steaks were served to players whose appetites had slipped since their visit to Lawry's. Chris Schenkel, the network sportscaster, stopped by for interviews and reflections but was told by at least one player to forget it.

The tough part, Daugherty and all realized, was the Rose Bowl was gone for at least two years because of the Big Ten's no-repeat rule. In an era when Big Ten champions could not make consecutive trips to Pasadena, at a time when conference teams could play in no bowl but the Rose, it added to the misery of a team that had missed its chance at greatness.

It meant 1966 would be played for pride and for the pros, who were anxious to get their hands on Daugherty's fabulous seniors. Also, as it would develop, there would be a meeting with Notre Dame that would dwarf anything college football had before seen in single-game buildup. And along the way there would be an understanding that the '66 team had even greater athletes than the '65 squad, not to mention a personality that was part battlefield bravado, part Old West in its shoot'em-up, free-spirited way.

On the day of the '66 opener against North Carolina State, Clint Jones, one of the genuine leaders, stood in the dressing room and shouted: "Don't let anybody come in here and whip your butts in front of the home fans!" It was a command more than a battle cry. Jess Phillips, the defensive back, was even more brash if less eloquent. He would skip across the tunnel to the opposing dressing room, stick his head in the door and yell: "You shouldn't have showed up! Don't you know you're gonna get killed?"

On the field Phillips liked to verbally blow-torch players such as Notre Dame's Jim Seymour. "If you catch the ball I will hurt you," he promised Seymour in the '66 game. "I will hurt you bad." Seymour had averaged six catches a game but never caught a pass in the 10-10 tie.

Bullough's style had been seeping steadily into the defense. There were times during the '66 season when the defense would huddle and someone would say cheerfully: "Hey, let's see how hard we can hit (ball carrier)." Or, "Hey, everybody just unload on somebody." It wasn't sadism as much as it was a defense amusing itself as routine football challenges vanished.

But the good times were about to end. Daugherty's Southern recruiting pipeline had closed off now that Deep South schools were admitting blacks. Washington, Smith, Jones, Webster, Thornhill, Apisa, Jimmy Raye and Phillips departed after the '66 season and now Daugherty had not only lost one of college football's great collections of talent, but also the team's leadership.

Bill Yeoman, his old assistant who now was head coach at Houston, arrived in East Lansing for the '67 opener and wiped out MSU, 37-7. Southern Cal visited the next week and won, 21-17. Later on, a five-game losing streak would ruin the Spartans, leaving them with a 3-7 record for MSU's worst finish since 1958. A dynasty had given way to middle-of-the-pack football that would stick with Daugherty for five more seasons.

It had threatened to get better in '68, when the Spartans started 3-0 but finished 5-5. They were 4-6-0 the next two seasons, and by now Daugherty's kingdom was slipping away as solid assistants left for new jobs. Danny Boisture went to Eastern Michigan following the '66 season. Carillot (Tulsa) and Stoll (Wake Forest) took head coaching jobs in '68, and Bullough left for the NFL the following year.

There were bigger problems away from the field. Administration problems. John Hannah had left Michigan State early in 1969 and a new president, Clifton Wharton Jr., a lover of the arts who had only a slight interest in sports, was installed in 1971. Daugherty had met once a week with Hannah to lunch and talk about everything, but he was now at odds with a man who avoided one-on-one sessions.

Daugherty was also growling about money. About red tape. And about his boss. He had evidence, never disproved, that MSU's was the lowest football budget in the Big Ten next to Northwestern. While Daugherty's budget was low, it was common for the university to quietly handle the football office's budget over-runs. It didn't mean either side was always making the smartest business decisions. In 1969 Daugherty and Jack Breslin, the university vice president who oversaw athletics, discussed expansion. Michigan State was installing a new basketball surface at Jenison Field House, and new surfaces for tennis courts and an indoor track. Football was to be included in the dress-up.

Daugherty had wanted artificial turf to replace Spartan Stadium's grass field, and he wanted an indoor facility that would give MSU a year-round edge in training and recruiting. Breslin told him turf was agreeable but MSU could fund only half a building immediately. Daugherty decided on turf. Wisconsin already was using it,

Michigan was in the process of installing it, and Daugherty believed artificial grass was the coming thing. It went in that summer but deteriorated steadily and was replaced five years later.

Administratively, Daugherty continued to gripe privately about John Fuzak, the MSU faculty representative who helped set academic policy for Big Ten athletics. Daugherty had complained for years that faculty reps were destroying the Big Ten's chances at being competitive. There had been grade-point requirements Daugherty thought inflexible . . . a provision that all financial aid be based upon "need," a cumbersome and idealistic measure, opposed by Fuzak, that sent many athletes scurrying to other schools . . . and Big Ten disapproval of "redshirting," which allowed an athlete to be held out of games for one year without a loss of eligibility.

Daugherty had fought continually with the Big Ten. And yet the feelings between Daugherty and faculty reps were mild compared with the Daugherty-Munn hostilities. They clashed constantly, and not always privately. A regular squabble involved who would fly on the team charter to away football games.

Daugherty would draw up his list which always contained a non-football coach, or a priest, or someone Munn thought expendable on a flight with limited seating. He would cross off names and replace them with his own until another spat would bring on Breslin to mediate. It was during another round of mid-week bickering that Breslin, exasperated, took the debate to Hannah for a final ruling. Hannah was fed up with the weekly wars.

"You handle it," he told Breslin, "or two people are going to be fired. And one of them will be you." Breslin told Munn that from now on Daugherty would decide the list. It led to a fight between Munn and Breslin, but Daugherty had won again.

His football team wasn't doing as well. There were losing seasons in '69 and '70 that made Daugherty's off-the-field headaches more miserable. A break came in 1971 when Eric Allen set a NCAA rushing record against Purdue (350 yards) and the 6-5 Spartans tied for third in the Big Ten. A team seemed revived, and so did a coach who had recruited well in-state, through Ohio and Pennsylvania, and now had his best core of talent in seven years as he, at age 57, got ready for 1972.

There was strength and depth in '72 even if Allen, the great halfback, had moved on to the pros. Joe DeLamielleure, Jim Nicholson, Billy Joe DuPree, Skip Macholz, Bob McClowry and Marv Roberts would give Daugherty one of his great offensive fronts. Brad

Van Pelt, Bill Simpson, John Shinsky, Paul Hayner, Gary Van Elst, Brian McConnell and Gail Clark were the center of an exceptional defense.

If the Spartans were short it was at skill spots. Quarterback had been a regular problem for Michigan State. Running back was a question now that Allen was gone, although Damond Mays, a spectacular junior college back from Phoenix, had promise. Daugherty was enthused. He had thought about retiring at various times during the past three years, but there was more talent in 1972 than he had seen in a half-dozen years.

It looked even brighter after the Spartans shut out Illinois, 24-0, at Champaign. But then came the collapse that would bring on Daugherty's dark days: Georgia Tech came to East Lansing and upset the Spartans, 21-16. Total destruction the next week at Los Angeles as Southern Cal won, 51-6. Then back-to-back shutouts, 16-0 against Notre Dame, and 10-0 at Ann Arbor.

Partly because he was Duffy Daugherty, partly because Michigan State had now grown almost accustomed to losing big games and finishing as a middle-runger, Daugherty dealt with only moderate heat. Munn had suffered a stroke the year before and no longer was over him. Burt Smith was only six months into his tenure as new athletic director and not about to take jabs at a man who had infinitely more support and influence. Wharton was busy with the academic world and not terribly bothered by what was happening on the football field. Administrators griped and grumbled privately but stayed out of Daugherty's way.

Daugherty's biggest troubles were internal. The old dynamism, the old magic, had been slipping away since the late '60s. Meetings were fuzzy. Practice-field organization was lacking. Recruiting, too, had begun to fade as Daugherty grew older, his assistants departed and Bo Schembechler took command at Michigan.

Worst of all was the backbiting among assistant coaches. Gordie Serr, who was a lineman under Munn and Daugherty in the early '50s, thought he was in line for the job when Daugherty left, and made it known he was ready for it.

Another problem was Denny Stolz. He had arrived in 1971 as a highly paid, all-hairs-in-place defensive coordinator fresh from the head coaching job at Alma College. Daugherty had hired Stolz at the request of his good friend, Alma oil man Harold McClure, who thought Stolz would make a superb assistant. The problem was salary: Stolz was making more than $15,000 at Alma and would have to be paid proportionately on a MSU staff where most assistants were lucky to make $12,000. Daugherty justified the pay by making Stolz MSU's defensive coordinator.

The title and money came as a slam to George Perles, who had taken over the defense when Bullough left following the '69 season. Stolz walked in on a staff that resented his paycheck and his position. Perles continued to run the defense and ignored the newcomer, who had much to learn about a system that had been in place since Bullough's days.

After Perles went to the Pittsburgh Steelers following the '71 season, Stolz kept his title but watched Ed Youngs, who had arrived the same time as Stolz, take control. Tension in Daugherty's staff offices grew. But it was on the field where matters were getting worse, with Michigan State's offense the problem.

Daugherty had an offensive line that would send five players to the pros, but the Spartans weren't scoring. There were backfield breakdowns as neither Damond Mays nor Arnold Morgado made anyone forget Eric Allen. But the great weakness was at quarterback, as it had been since 1968. Since Jimmy Raye had moved on, Daugherty had tried everyone—Bill Triplett, Bill Feraco, Frank Kolch, Mike Rasmussen—and none had sparkled. Daugherty understood that Brad Van Pelt, who finished as an All-American safety, would have been a great wishbone quarterback, but he threw a poor spiral and was left in the secondary.

The 1972 hope was River Rouge High's George Mihaiu, more mobile and better-suited to Daugherty's offense than Dan Werner. It was Werner who in 1969 had become MSU's first quarterback to throw for 300 yards as he got 314 against Purdue. But Werner, a devastating drop-back passer who needed time to throw, had nervous feet and was finished if he got sacked. Daugherty would stick with Mihaiu, although by the end of the season transplanted defensive back Mark Niesen would finish as State's quarterback.

The Spartans ended their five-game slide with a 31-0 rout of Wisconsin at East Lansing, and at 2-5 still had a shot at salvaging the season. There was no better place to start a winning streak than at Iowa City the following Saturday. The Hawkeyes were their usual sorry selves, a team that had not had a winning season in 11 years and in 1972 was headed for a 3-7-1 finish that would get Frank Lauterbur fired.

On October 28, 1972 at Kinnick Stadium, Michigan State lost one touchdown when the Spartans were flagged for having an ineligibile man downfield. An extra-point snap was fumbled by Werner on another touchdown and the Spartans had treated Iowa to a 6-6 tie—a worse embarrassment than the 51-6 disaster at USC.

Daugherty was quiet as the team charter flew back to Lansing. He was thinking. Despairingly. Whatever chance a good team had at making '72 a winner had collapsed against the sorry Hawkeyes.

The plane landed at Capitol City Airport and MSU's team party climbed down stairs onto the tarmac. Daugherty pulled Breslin to one side, beneath the wing of the jet.

"Jack, I think it's time for me to leave."

Breslin had never intended to ask for Daugherty's resignation, and even if he was more disgusted than any of MSU's execs over a football program that had been steadily unraveling—not to mention the lack of playing time his son, Jay, had received from 1968-70—he was careful with the coach.

"I think you better think about this," he told Daugherty. "We'll talk Monday or Tuesday."

There was nothing to discuss. Daugherty was bitter over budgets and some weak assistants who had replaced his old lieutenants. Recruiting had suffered— Daugherty would not acknowledge he had lost a step there—and he was ready to dump at least two coaches who, he maintained, had knocked MSU off players such as Reggie McKenzie and Billy Taylor, who had gone on to star at Michigan; and Mike Kadish and Clarence Ellis, who were signed by Notre Dame.

Daugherty went home that night, told his wife of his plans, then endured one of his toss-and-turn sleeping ordeals. The next morning he told his assistants he was quitting. They were ordered to keep quiet until he could make the formal announcement following Saturday's home game against Purdue.

The next night, before practice, he called his team together.

"Fellas, I want you to know I'm resigning at the end of the season," he began. "This is it. Now just go out and have fun during the next four weeks." He asked them to keep it secret, and then Daugherty told a joke, as he did every day before practice.

Daugherty's secret remained so for four nights. On Friday evening, Tim Staudt, sports director at Lansing's WJIM-TV, broke the story on his 6 p.m. telecast. Daugherty was forced into an evening press conference at a pre-game party at the MSU Faculty Club.

Michigan State the next day beat Purdue, 22-12. Then, looking finally like the team envisioned, the Spartans a week later got four field goals from a Dutch walk-on named Dirk Kryt as they popped Ohio State, 19-12.

But the next week Michigan State slipped again and lost, 14-10, at Minnesota. Daugherty's coaching finale would come at Spartan Stadium against Northwestern. On a cold afternoon two days after Thanksgiving, big snow mounds lay piled around the field as the Spartans beat Northwestern, 24-14, in front of 46,140 fans. At the end of a game, a 5-5-1 season, and an era marked as much by disappointment as by glory, his players carried Daugherty off the field on their shoulders.

Two

FROM REVIVAL CAME SCANDAL

It was Barry Switzer's job to lose as he, Johnny Majors, Lee Corso and Denny Stolz sat in the vice-president's office four floors above the cement paths and grassy banks that slope softly toward the Red Cedar River. Switzer had every reason to believe the interview session before MSU's top executives would be nothing more than a formalization of the appointment Burt Smith had tentatively made during their conversations a week earlier at Norman, Oklahoma, where Switzer was working as offensive coordinator under Oklahoma Coach Chuck Fairbanks.

Barry Switzer would be the first head football coach at Michigan State since Duffy Daugherty had taken over from Biggie Munn in 1954. Stunning longevity to this job, the top spot at MSU.

All it required was that Switzer impress the executives and interviewing panel in the same manner he had charmed Smith. There seemed little chance he would miss. Already, Bob Reynolds, sports director of Detroit radio station WJR, had broken the story that Switzer was coming to East Lansing.

It was December 1972, six weeks after Daugherty had resigned in the midst of a 5-5-1 season that had gone down as one more disappointment following the football grandeur of the mid-'60s. There appeared no sound reason for the fade at Michigan State which, by any measure, still ranked as one of the potentially best programs in the country. It simply needed new direction. New vigor. A new coach, perhaps, like the sharp, engaging director of an offense that had helped keep Oklahoma one of the giants of college football.

Among the Michigan State interviewers was President Clifton Wharton, Vice-President Jack Breslin, Faculty Representative John Fuzak, Smith—the MSU athletic director—and Assistant Athletic Director Clarence Underwood.

The three men sitting with Switzer before the panel came from different football backgrounds: Stolz had been Daugherty's defensive coordinator the past two seasons; Majors, who would go on to become head coach at Pitt and later at Tennessee, was head coach at Iowa State; and Corso was in charge of the football program at Louisville.

Wharton started the session by asking each man to make an opening statement, presenting background and reason for interest in the position at Michigan State. Switzer's problems began immediately, as soon as he got going on a windy, marathon spiel that sounded more like a Senate filibuster. It dragged on for so long that Wharton several times tried to interrupt the sandy-haired man with the Texarkana twang who was running the verbal equivalent of a wishbone offense—Switzer simply could not be stopped. Smith, athletic director only since May, was embarrassed, his head clasped in his hand as the new AD's personal candidate began slowly sinking from consideration.

Conversations between candidate and panel followed later in the session.

How many private jets or airplanes would the football program have access to for recruiting purposes, Switzer wondered?

Panel members shook their heads. There were no private jets or planes available.

Switzer was stunned that something so basic to building a national program would be lacking at a university with MSU's clout.

What about credit-card arrangements, Switzer next asked. What kind of system did the football program utilize for the convenience of coaching staffs who traveled so frequently?

Again, Breslin said there was no such credit card program.

Switzer's energy and mental sharpness were attractive, everyone agreed, but the perks that were obviously fundamental to Oklahoma's program were not—and would not be—established at Michigan State. The Switzer candidacy was crumbling by mutual consent.

Majors would also have problems, beginning with a sore throat that hurt his speaking voice. Like Switzer, Majors could be dynamic, but his question on how many non-predictors (athletes who did not qualify at minimum entrance levels) MSU would take, further bothered a panel aware that Majors had squabbled with Iowa State's faculty.

Corso asked no impertinent questions, made no unsavory requests, but failed to impress interviewers who thought he was overly slick. There was the great smile, the charm, the humor that made Corso a very appealing showman. But he was also wearing a fully loaded $200 suit at a time when $100 bought very nice attire. The panel's perception was that Corso, who would soon be named head coach at Indiana, needed more seasoning.

Michigan State was not of a mind in December of 1972 to name any entertainers or power brokers as its new head football coach. Daugherty, the administration believed, had become so powerful during his 19 seasons as coach that the program needed to be brought under control without sacrificing university commitment. Michigan State's executives wanted a bright, energetic football man who would keep things clean and re-establish the drive that MSU had been lacking during the decline of 1967-72.

Gaining more and more support from the center of MSU's screeners and interviewers was Daugherty's defensive coordinator, Denny Stolz, a 39-year-old former head coach at Alma College who had joined MSU's staff in 1971. Stolz was clean-cut, conservative, a winner at neighboring Haslett High School and at Alma, where he coached the son of John Fuzak, MSU's Big Ten faculty representative and one of the Selection Committee's foremost members.

Stolz had not been overwhelming during his interview, but that was just the point: Michigan State wasn't looking for a sharpie. It wanted stability and youth, and in Stolz, who had directed Daugherty's defense—the one aspect in which Michigan State had shined—it was getting a man already familiar with players and university procedures. The more the panel saw of others, the more Stolz was gaining in appeal, except in the eyes of Smith, who supported Switzer and wanted in his first year as AD to have his own man as head coach.

Stolz had grown up a few miles south of Lansing, in Mason, and for 30 years had dreamed of becoming Michigan State football coach. He didn't have the national clout so many of Michigan State's fans were looking toward as the decision drew near, but on December 13, 1972, he was named Michigan State's 16th head football coach at annual salary of $25,000. The Daugherty era had given way to a man Daugherty hired a year earlier at the behest of Daugherty friend Harold McClure, head of McClure Oil Company in Alma, Michigan, who thought the local small-college coach would be a terrific addition to a Big Ten staff. McClure and the world would now see whether or not Dennis Edward Stolz could make it as Daugherty's follow-up act. It was something even his old boss thought would be tough in 1973.

"I didn't leave Denny very many good players," Daugherty acknowledged. National Football League clubs would draft 11 players from a '72 team that for all its pro material had finished a mushy 5-5-1. Recruiting had been a problem since the Deep South pipeline was plugged in the mid-'60s and was even more of a problem regionally in the three years since Bo Schembechler had been working and winning at Michigan.

A head coach with no major-college credentials would combat Michigan's edge by working overtime, hiring a solid staff, and counting on MSU's tradition and supporters to help out until Stolz could establish his own momentum.

From the Daugherty staff Stolz would keep Sherm Lewis, Ed Rutherford, Jimmy Raye and Ed Youngs, who would run the defense. Outside additions would include ex-MSU lineman Dan Underwood, Charlie Butler and Andy MacDonald from Colorado State, Bill Davis from Adrian College, and Miami (Ohio) assistant Howard Weyers.

Stolz was proving himself no greenhorn when it came to sizing up coaches who would be technical pluses and, in most cases, effective recruiters familiar with the turf and the kind of athletes who could be major-college stars. Stolz had seen and been told how Daugherty's staff in his latter years had grown weaker due to infighting and inferior personnel. He intended to revamp his own staff by bringing in a majority of outsiders who would work well with the few Daugherty holdovers he was retaining.

Stolz was intent on making his administration separate from the Daugherty regime. He wanted neither to be compared with his old boss, nor did he want any of Daugherty's baggage that administrators also wanted to put behind, particularly the old-line boosters network that to Stolz looked like trouble.

George Perles, a Daugherty assistant who had left to join the Pittsburgh Steelers, got a taste of the new rules when he called his old friend, Rutherford.

"George," Rutherford said, "I'm not supposed to talk with you."

Stolz wanted his staff even to sever connections with old-school coaches who bore the Daugherty pedigree.

Stolz tended to see the dark side in people, the MSU circle was discovering as he set up shop in the football office at Jenison Field House. He had a taut, severe personality that didn't make him a bad guy, they thought—he was polite and not by any means humorless—but Stolz was definitely not a man who easily relaxed nor a man who tolerated any kind of loose end or nonconformity. To him, the world was something a man spent all his life trying to organize. His own world at Michigan State would reflect the control and careful grooming he worked so earnestly to make part of his own life.

There would be rigid office rules, an unwritten dress code, behavior and conduct expectations. If the president was coming by, then Stolz wanted all coffee cups off the desks. Stolz had been a high school biology and history teacher who ran a classroom as tightly as he now ran his football office.

It carried outside the office and into his home, where at night Stolz would work until midnight on piles of paperwork, letters to be dictated, any correspondence that would help keep this ultimate job in order and under control.

It all seemed to be paying off as the months between his appointment and his debut as head coach rolled by. Stolz had a clear, resonant voice and a poise about him that impressed audiences. You weren't going to get many jokes from him—Daugherty's legacy was certainly safe—but he could get to the point and speak in upbeat, encouraging tones that suggested to most of MSU's camp that the new guy was a winner.

First priority during spring drills was to settle on a quarterback who might steady the offense and eliminate instability the position so often had under Daugherty. The two frontrunners in '73 were Mark Niesen, who had switched from the defensive secondary to start at quarterback during the final weeks of the '72 season, and a sophomore transfer from North Carolina named Charlie Baggett.

Baggett had been a next-door neighbor to Jimmy Raye back in Fayetteville, North Carolina, when the Raye residence was located at 1610 Murchison Road and the Baggett home at 1612 Murchison. Although Raye was seven years older, Baggett considered him an idol and followed every step of his career when Raye went on to quarterback Daugherty's big teams of 1965-66. But in 1971 Baggett had decided to stay home and sign with North Carolina, whose head coach, Bill Dooley, assured Baggett he would become the Tar Heels' first black quarterback.

When Dooley told him following his freshman year—Baggett had led the frosh team to a 5-0 record—that he wanted to make him a wide receiver, Baggett called Raye. Daugherty was soon on the phone and Baggett was headed for Michigan State, where he would sit out the '72 season before gaining sophomore eligibility in 1973. Two weeks into spring drills, Stolz had determined that Niesen would be returning his talents to the secondary.

"You're gonna be our quarterback," Stolz said to Baggett. "We're starting a new era here and we think you're the man."

Baggett's and Michigan State's problem in '73 was that most of its returning talent was on defense: Bill Simpson, John Shinsky, Ray Nester, Terry McClowry, Otto Smith, Paul Hayner and Niesen would supply Ed Youngs' defense with enough core personnel to hold down opponents, but offense, again, would be Michigan State's headache. There were decent linemen in Charlie Ane and tight end Paul Manderino, a fleet receiver in Mike Hurd, running backs in Mike Holt, David E. Brown and Clarence Bullock. But Michigan State was going to play an option offense that ideally needed better personnel than Stolz was inheriting.

Daugherty, it soon became clear, had been right about the thin estate bequeathed Stolz. John Pont's Northwestern team beat MSU, 14-10, in Stolz' Michigan State debut. Stolz got his first victory a week later when the Spartans outlasted a poor Syracuse team, 14-8, in an appalling game televised by ABC that mainly showcased Baggett's running ability. Four consecutive losses —including a 31-0 home-field annihilation at the hands of Michigan—followed until the schedule eased up, helping MSU to victories in four of its final five games for a 5-6 finish.

Stolz had at least managed to win as many games in his first season as Daugherty, with more gifted players, had accomplished in his last. It was enough momentum to put some crackle into the post-season banquet at the Lansing Civic Center and, more critically, encourage all those recruits the Spartan staff already was targeting.

Stolz had survived his first year as head coach minus any castastrophes nor any loss of confidence from employers or fans. His staff was happy, although the assistants wished he would ease up on the Hammurabi Code that had made life within the office so rigid and unbending. They also, privately, thought he should worry less about whether one hair was out of place. Stolz insisted on wardrobes that were thoroughly coordinated, wrinkle-free and compatible with his position. Assistants smirked to themselves when Stolz decided on dressing them for games in matching outfits, but kept for himself an ensemble that was different—signifying him as head coach.

Players snickered at the way Stolz seemed always to be adjusting his hat, shirt and pants, keeping them crisp and in order, or, how he would flip his whistle if it were twisted backward so that he could smoothly bring it to his mouth. There were just so many appearance-related idiosyncrasies to a man most players liked, but few found truly inspiring.

What Stolz had managed to do very well in his first year as head coach was hire good assistants, at least a couple of whom were proving to be crackerjack recruiters. Howard Weyers, principally. Weyers was on the staff of Miami (Ohio) Head Coach Bill Mallory, with whom he had discussed the difficulty a Miami assistant faced in becoming a head coach. They agreed that working as an assistant at any of three different Big Ten schools—Michigan, Michigan State or Ohio State—was the best vehicle to a top job.

Michigan State in December of '72 was looking for a replacement for Duffy Daugherty, a spot that Mallory and Weyers heard would be filled by Oklahoma's Barry Switzer. Mallory and Switzer were friends. Mallory assured Weyers he would put a word in for him. When an assistant by the name of Denny Stolz, whom neither of them knew, was named MSU's new coach, Weyers called Stolz with his application.

"Well, I have all these commitments," Stolz answered, typical of head coaches who like to shop before they name a staff.

Weyers: "Do you plan to do much recruiting in Pennsylvania and Ohio?"

"Sure," Stolz answered.

Weyers: "Well, I hope you have someone who knows what the hell they're doing down here."

Weyers was a Pittsburgh native who had coached at Elwood City with former Detroit Lions assistant, and future NFL head coach, Chuck Knox. During a recruiting trip to Detroit, Stolz and Sherm Lewis ran into Knox, who gave Weyers an endorsement. A few days later Weyers was invited to interview in East Lansing.

He was disappointed by Michigan's flat terrain as he drove to East Lansing, and figured a campus he had never before seen probably resembled the University of Michigan's layout in Ann Arbor, which he had seen. But one pass around Circle Drive stunned him. The place was beautiful.

"With a campus like this," he told Stolz, "you should be able to dominate college football."

Weyers was later hired as defensive ends coach, but his familiarity with the talent-rich preplands of Ohio and western Pennsylvania would be the real strength of a man who liked the challenge, the sport, the gamesmanship of selling high school athletes on playing football at the school he represented. Doing it at Michigan State, he believed, would be a dream.

Weyers on his first day as MSU assistant teamed with another new hire, Bill Davis, on a recruiting trip in which they would work both sides of the Ohio Turnpike from Toledo to Pittsburgh. Among some of the excellent regional kids still uncommitted were Bob Brudzinski, Rob Lytle, Ross Browner, Gary Jeter, Mike Cobb, Tony Dorsett, Marvin Powell, Joe Hunt and Tom Hannon.

Brudzinski came close to signing with MSU but opted at the end for Ohio State . . . Powell visited but also signed with Ohio State . . . Browner decided finally on Notre Dame . . . Cobb and Hunt signed with Michigan State, while Hannon was still listening. When Weyers got to Massillon, Ohio, Bob Commings, the Washington High head coach who was to become University of Iowa head coach, had news:

"Howard, you're out of luck. Hannon committed to Jerry Hanlon today."

Hanlon was an assistant to Bo Schembechler at Michigan. Weyers, though, decided later that day to stop at the Hannon home, where Hannon confirmed he was going to Michigan. Weyers wished him good luck.

Later that week, Hannon's uncle from Detroit called Weyers with the message to "Go back and talk with Tom." Hannon, who had been declining visits to MSU, now wanted to take a look. A week later he was visiting the University of Michigan when on Saturday morning, suddenly, he left Ann Arbor to go to his uncle's home in Detroit. He later signed with MSU, sprouting suspicion among Michigan's coaching staff that the new assistant at Michigan State had pried Hannon loose with something other than conventional techniques.

Weyers' passion for recruiting made him that rarest of coaches who didn't mind 18-hour days or living-room socials with parents, grandparents and whomever else from the family happened to be taking in the sales pitch. He enjoyed the psychology and the intimacy of recruiting. He could kiss grandmothers and aunts. He could shake hands and shoot the breeze with hard-boiled dads, all because of his knack in most cases to establish immediate rapport and trust with a family. Pennsylvania players recruited by him agreed that Weyers was the best conversationalist next to the grand man himself, Penn State's Joe Paterno. They also marveled at how he knew every detail about the player, his likes, dislikes, a profile that was so thorough as to suggest Weyers had been part of the family.

It was not a recruiting style appreciated by competitors such as Ohio State coaches, who were suggesting that Weyers was buying local talent they once owned. But it was not only Weyers who was stocking MSU's shelves with the brand of material that would kick Stolz' teams into gear and clear the way for a Big Ten co-championship in 1978.

Jimmy Raye was recruiting the Southeast better than any MSU staff had managed since Daugherty's heyday. Larry Bethea and Tommy Graves were brought out of Virginia during a recruiting gold rush that had re-established Michigan State as a national talent picker and, according to some of its competition, as a program that should be inspected by the NCAA.

Stolz in 1974 assumed the program was at least operating efficiently. Recruiting was picking up and his system was now established in the minds of players and assistants nearly 18 months after he had become head coach. At a MSU golf outing in May of 1974, Stolz got a taste of how his program was playing among the alumni.

A graying, well-heeled grad stood among the banquet crowd and praised Stolz for a 1973 debut that in his estimation had shown the new coaching staff to be "imaginative"—better adjectives might have been used—and on the verge of becoming a winner. The audience nodded. Stolz thanked him, gave a five-minute address that was all business and reminded the gathering that, "We will be young."

He neglected to add "disciplined."

Players had learned that Stolz' somber, no-nonsense style shaped policies that said everything about the strict German's makeup. When running back Julius Askew, a junior college transfer, was caught by an assistant coach checking in late to the training-camp dormitory, Stolz put the entire team through sprints.

The discipline, the sprints, the straight-laced personality that became MSU's on-field personality helped push Stolz' team to a 2-0 start in 1974 as State whipped Northwestern, 41-7, and Syracuse, 19-0. Defense looked as if it might put Michigan State in the neighborhood of those two well-known roughnecks, Michigan and Ohio State, until a trip to UCLA produced a 56-14 massacre of MSU that put things back in perspective. MSU a week later lost to Notre Dame, 19-14, followed that with a 21-7 fall at Michigan, then lost a big lead the next week at Illinois to tie, 21-21.

Greg Croxton, a guard from Highland Park, afterward sat in the visitors' dressing room at Illinois, saying over and over: "This game's gonna cost us the Rose Bowl." With five weeks left in the season and MSU sitting with a 2-3-1 record, no one paid much attention to Croxton's prophecy. But three weeks later, after cleaning up on Purdue and Wisconsin, Michigan State—which had lost only once in the Big Ten—was lathering up for top-ranked Ohio State in a home game the players had been obsessed with since boarding the homeward-bound team plane at Wisconsin.

Defense wasn't Michigan State's concern as Woody Hayes and Co. rolled into East Lansing the first weekend of November. With Stolz' team it was still a matter of offense: Could State put a couple of touchdowns on the board against a team that was a four-touchdown favorite? That's what it would take to stay in a hunt in which MSU expected to have an enormous emotional edge.

The trick was to throw deep on an Ohio State secondary that loitered too close to the line because of its concentration on the run. The Buckeyes would be especially careful because of MSU's option offense that had made Baggett the team's leading rusher coming into November.

It was 3-3 at the half; 6-3, Ohio State, at the end of three quarters; and then 13-3 after Baggett set up a Buckeye touchdown by somehow dropping the ball during an open-field jaunt in front of the Spartan bench. What likely would have been a Michigan State TD had turned into seven points for the Buckeyes, who needed only to kill the remaining 10 minutes.

Baggett following the fumble was agonizing along the sidelines when Stolz came up to him and said: "Don't worry about it. You'll make it up."

Stolz wasn't always so clairvoyant. Baggett on the next series hit Mike Jones on the bomb MSU had been trying to drop all day, and now it was 13-9 after a two-point conversion pass missed. The crowd was screaming when Ohio State punted on its next possession, setting up Michigan State with a first-and-10 at its own 12. The play came in: Veer 44. Basic option football. Baggett was to take his read off the Buckeye defensive end. If the end closed on the play, Baggett was to keep and flow to the outside. If the end stepped out, Baggett would give to fullback Levi Jackson who would shoot through the hole between guard and tackle.

The defensive end stayed put, Baggett handed off to Jackson, who zipped past a cornerback and linebacker who had moved on Baggett. Jackson cutting to the outside, juking free safety Tim Fox, and blazing down the right sideline 88 yards on one of the more dramatic jaunts a college football game had produced. The game would become from that moment an exercise in surrealism: Nothing terribly defined, nothing approximating sanity taking place in the stands, and no resolution forthcoming even after Referee Gene Calhoun waved his arms as OSU's Brian Baschnagel disappeared at the MSU goal line amid confusion, and a fumble, that ended the game just as it appeared Ohio State would pull it out.

Forty-five minutes later it was verified that Michigan State had upset No. 1-ranked OSU (there had been no doubt among Calhoun's officials crew that the game was over, but because of goal-line confusion Big Ten Commissioner Wayne Duke ordered that no decision be announced until he conferred with the crew, which had escaped to its hotel).

More remarkable than the upset was that no one had been killed as the end zone's mammoth, steel goal posts came toppling down among the hordes below. There already was a party going on in the MSU dressing room that matched in intensity any of the off-campus keggers that turned East Lansing at nightfall into a sea of foam. The revelry stopped, instantly, when word came that Troy Hickman, MSU's assistant equipment manager, had been hit with a heart attack. Stolz led the team in prayer, barely finished when Hickman came waltzing into the dressing room, wondering what was going on.

Security personnel had ushered him out of the way as the goal posts fell, and as mobs flooded Spartan Stadium's turf, delaying Hickman's return trip to the dressing room. He was fine. And so was Stolz, who uncharacteristically hung in the MSU locker room, going over the game's great moments, soaking it all in more than an hour after Ohio State had pulled out of town.

"Tommy Graves," he yelled as his prized defensive back headed out the door, "you hit too hard for a freshman!"

It was considered in East Lansing as the greatest single-game drama since the '66 Notre Dame-Michigan State contest, and probably the most stirring finish in Michigan State football history. Stolz had swept the last of Daugherty's influence out the door and inaugurated in one, 88-yard run for the end zone an era of high-voltage football that most believed would push Michigan State into a customary place among college football's Top 20 teams. After a cleanup of Indiana the following week, and an awesome 60-21 romp over Iowa in the finale—another freshman, running back Claude Geiger from Charleston, West Virginia, broke loose against the Hawkeyes—MSU had a 7-3-1 season. The program Stolz inherited two years earlier was now blazing, and figuring to pick up another notch in the recruiting shootouts.

The previous winter's recruiting had been Michigan State's best since the bonanza years of the early '60s. Weyers and Raye, particularly, had gone berserk, pulling in Bethea, Graves, Geiger, Bill Brown, Eddie Smith, Al Pitts, and the most spectacular running back Ohio had produced in Ted Bell, a star at Youngstown Cardinal Mooney whom Weyers could see was a better runner than Tony Dorsett, a player he had also sought.

It was no secret among MSU's staff and recruits that Ohio State was aching to see Michigan State strung up for the way it was recruiting Ohio and Pennsylvania. Woody Hayes had even warned several recruits not to go to MSU because "Michigan State was going on probation," which became a definite possibility when, in April of 1975, the NCAA announced it was investigating the MSU football program.

The NCAA's focus became clear quickly: Recruits from Ohio, Pennsylvania and the South were being interviewed and examined for evidence of any illegal offers made by MSU recruiters or boosters. Stolz and his staff went about their business, taking an aloof attitude toward the probe, but Michigan State, at the executive level, was shaken. President Wharton planted a gag rule on all university employes and eventually announced the formation of a four-man Select Committee that would conduct an internal investigation simultaneously to the NCAA's. The committee would consist of John Bruff of the MSU Board of Trustees, and three of the university's most respected professors: Fred Williams, Charles Scarborough and Jacob Hoefer.

It was impossible on that humid Friday in April—a day when devastating flash-floods hit Lansing and East Lansing—to imagine the upheaval that would unfold during the next 11 months. But while mid-April spring drills moved along peacefully, a program already was coming apart as NCAA detectives went to work.

Weyers knew it could get very hot. Things had begun to break down during the 1973-74 recuriting season that had seen MSU score so well in Ohio and Pennsylvania as he got Bell, Al Pitts, Bill Brown, Eddie Smith, and nearly landed three players who would sign at Ohio State: Aaron Brown, Jeff Logan and Robert Robertson, a running back out of Barberton, Ohio.

Because Robertson had verbally committed to Weyers and Michigan State, Weyers on the day national letters could be signed proposed that he pick up Robertson and take him to meet Bell, the great runner who was coming to MSU and who figured, in time, to be Robertson's main competition. Weyers wanted Robertson with him and safe from any 11th-hour meddling by the OSU staff.

Weyers was told upon arriving that Robertson was at his girlfriend's. But at 1 a.m. Robertson still was neither at his girlfriend's nor at home. Ohio State soon got Robertson's signature, as it got Aaron Brown's, who turned from MSU to OSU when Robertson did.

OSU assistant coaches George Hill and Rudy Hubbard had been running against Weyers and weren't disappointed when Robertson and Brown told the OSU staff that Weyers had given them money and clothing. Weyers in fact had.

Robertson had a serious personal problem which required from $200 to $300 that Weyers believed he was obligated to provide a high school senior in a pinch—at least a needy one who had committed to him and Michigan State.

Brown had also called to ask a favor.

"You know, Coach, those green jackets you wear? I'd like one of those to wear to my team banquet."

Weyers liked Brown's mother and often stopped by to visit her at the grade school cafeteria where she worked. She, typical of so many parents whose sons were courted by Weyers, was fond of the MSU coach.

"You know," she said to him, "Aaron doesn't have a coat to wear to this banquet."

Brown soon got his green blazer.

The incidents were typical of a recruiting philosophy Weyers considered sensible, no matter how utterly in conflict it may have been with NCAA rules. He would not give money to recruits whose families were making ends meet, nor would he help recruits who had not verbally committed to Michigan State.

One Pennsylvanian who eventually signed at Michigan State heard it from Weyers early: "If you whore yourself out once, you'll whore yourself out the rest of your life."

Instead, other, less direct conveniences were mentioned: Long-distance phone calls between the player and his girlfriend back home could be handled. And, it was said, many of the good alumni at Michigan State could also help with jobs, and in helping families arrange travel to East Lansing. Various players became acquainted with those "helpful" alums at the MSU football banquet.

Weyers saw nothing unsavory about assisting basic player needs that did not involve direct cash handouts—unless it were a circumstance such as Robertson faced. He would help if a committed recruit needed football shoes, or a shirt, or equipment to play in an All-Star game, or if a recruit with no sport coat needed one for a banquet.

He was also a regular source of transportation for varsity players who stopped by the football office to borrow his car. If they needed to run errands or take care of personal business, a number of them grew accustomed to counting on the Weyers auto. You would do that for a lot of people, said Weyers. You surely would do it for a player in whose living room you had sat.

In all instances, the favors that Weyers found to whatever degree morally justifiable, were clear NCAA violations. It was a violation when, on his way to Cleveland, he saw Mel Land hitchhiking down Trowbridge Road and gave him a ride to Campbell, Ohio, just as it was an infraction when he gave other players rides home during his trips through Ohio and Pennsylvania.

It was an infraction, too, the NCAA said, that T. Michael Doyle's credit card had been used by two players to purchase articles during 1974 and '75. It remained an infraction to the NCAA even after evidence showed that the card had been stolen, and even as the offending players admitted their guilt and paid restitution to Doyle.

It was the way the card was discovered that the NCAA considered part and parcel to the unacceptable ways of Howard Weyers.

The friendship between Weyers and Doyle—an East Lansing attorney, Notre Dame graduate and Michigan State booster—began shortly after Weyers was hired in December of 1972. A MSU booster group, the Fightin' 50, was hosting a reception for the new coaching staff at the Michigan Automobile Dealers Association, where Weyers became acquainted with Doyle, whose wife was a Miami graduate and surprised to meet someone with a Miami background.

Doyle and Weyers in November of 1973 were having a drink at Dagwood's following the MSU Football Bust at Lansing's Civic Center when the subject of salary came up. Weyers mentioned that he was making $14,000. Doyle was shocked. Weyers was considered the staff's hardest worker—he regularly ran four miles in the morning and was at work no later than 7:30—as well as the coaching staff's best dresser, his cuffs always hanging a perfect inch beneath his jacket sleeve. The wardrobe and coach's lifestyle were possible only because his wife was a schoolteacher.

Doyle knew that Weyers the next day was going on the road, on his usual paths to cities and hamlets across Ohio and Pennsylvania. He was driving an old Oldsmobile with poor tires.

"You got any extra money on you?"

Nothing heavy, Weyers answered.

"They give you a credit card you can use on the road?"

No way.

Doyle was aghast.

"Here's my credit card," Doyle told Weyers. "If you're out and the car breaks down, you can at least use this."

Weyers kept the card in his wallet which he routinely kept locked in his car glove compartment. Weyers on that trip did use the card to charge a tire, repaying Doyle when he returned. Doyle, though, did not religiously keep track of his charge accounts only because the monthly balances were handled by his secretary. A year later, Doyle ran into Weyers at a MSU basketball game.

"You're giving that credit card to the kids," Doyle said.

Weyers shook his head.

"No I didn't."

By the summer of 1975, Doyle's credit card was only one of the matters NCAA investigator David Berst wanted explained as he arrived in East Lansing. Berst to those who observed him during his days on campus was a model organizer who could cut through red tape and paperwork in a snap. He brought a James Bond-like aura to his work, a politeness he displayed around executives that could turn to viciousness when he brought in a player for questioning.

During his first campus visit, Berst requested to see athletic department folders from which he took files and phone numbers on about 20 athletes. A week later he was back on campus, anxious to visit various East Lansing businesses. Berst wanted access to records that MSU athletic department personnel could help him gain.

He called on several businesses: Sibley's Shoes, MSU Bootery, Redwood & Ross clothiers, a record store, all of them businesses at which Berst intended to get specific copies of charges made during the previous year.

Could you check your Master Card records for this particular date, he asked a clerk? A receipt for a $35 pair of boots charged to the Doyle account appeared. Berst obtained a copy of the charge for himself and one to be retained by the MSU athletic department, just as he did at several other businesses. Several purchases that would benefit a college-age man—the boots, a jacket, record albums—bore Doyle signatures that clearly fit the handwriting of MSU defensive back Joe Hunt.

In questioning Hunt later, Berst again showed himself to be direct and tough. Here was the evidence. Here was the signature. Unless you cooperate with me 100 percent, he told Hunt, you will never play football again.

"All I want to do," Hunt said, very scared, very plaintive, "is play football."

Also implicated in the credit card abuses was tight end Mike Cobb, a close friend of Hunt's, who admitted being involved not long before the bogus charges were discovered. It had been obvious to Weyers that Doyle's credit card had been taken from the car's glove compartment. Hunt and Cobb were frequent borrowers of his car and would have had easy access to the locked glove compartment in which Weyers always kept his wallet.

Hunt and Cobb admitted to Weyers, and to investigators, that the card had been stolen. MSU later reported to the NCAA that Cobb had made complete restitution to Doyle for any expenses incurred, and that Hunt was in the process of paying off his debt. The NCAA would view the credit card misdeeds—and the fact Weyers' car was involved directly in MSU's defense that Weyers had not given them the card—as one of the centerpieces in its probe.

Other allegations were surfacing regularly during the spring and summer of 1975 as newspaper stories centered on many of the same people in whom the NCAA was taking an interest. Baggett, the quarterback returning for his senior season in 1975, purchased in the spring of 1975 a new Buick through John Demmer, his summer employer who co-signed the bank loan. The loan would be paid back via earnings Baggett and Demmer anticipated from a pro football contract. After the purchase was made public, Wharton called Baggett to his office and asked him to return the $5,898 auto, which Baggett did at a personal loss of $329.

The NCAA said Baggett's co-signed loan was an infraction and further evidence of players obtaining advantages not available to other students. It was the same charge leveled against players like Eddie Smith and Jim Epolito, who had obtained, on credit, plane tickets home through the Harrington Travel Agency of East Lansing. Although the tickets were paid for—players had canceled checks from their families' records to prove it—the NCAA again said purchasing the tickets on credit amounted to an advantage not available to other students.

Stolz viewed the NCAA investigation more as an annoyance than as a threat as he continued in 1975 to prepare for a football season that was sparking as much talk about town as the mysterious probe. Ohio State would be coming to East Lansing for the opener, the same Ohio State which had been upset 10 months earlier in East Lansing. The football talk, at least among MSU's players, focused on a probable Rose Bowl run by a team that had finished so strong in 1974.

Stolz wasn't disagreeing. Because he felt good about the effort to divorce himself from the Daugherty regime, and from a few of the boosters who seemed to be hanging too close, Stolz never envisioned serious trouble with the NCAA.

The things he knew about or was blind to—players borrowing Weyers' car, for example—Stolz was certain would be no serious problem. He and the players were aware of what was going on at so many places outside, and Michigan State certainly didn't subscribe to any of that ruthlessness. Or so they believed.

MSU players who had made any number of visits nationwide were definitely amused at supposed violations the NCAA and newspapers viewed with such alarm. The early '70s were a time when high school seniors could make as many weekend visits as they wanted to schools interested in paying their way and lavishing them from Friday through Sunday, and it was not uncommon for Pittsburgh-area players such as Tony Dorsett and Jim Epolito to make 18 recruiting visits their senior year.

The University of Georgia provided one of college recruiting's finer weekends. Upon arriving at Athens, one athlete who eventually signed at Michigan State checked in and was told he would be going that night to an elegant dinner and would need a suit jacket. When he explained he had not brought one, he was dropped off that morning at a local tailor's to be measured and fitted, and by afternoon was sporting an exquisite, double-knit ensemble complete with blue, patent-leather boots and pockets stuffed with $50 and $100 bills.

Clothes were common recruiting extras at certain places, and it was one of the reasons why several of Michigan State's suspended six players—the six who in September of 1976 sought a Federal Court injunction against their suspensions—were so nattily dressed as they appeared at Federal Court in Grand Rapids. A few realized as they looked at each other that their best attire came from recruiting trips.

Another feature at Georgia was the presentation of a portfolio containing pictures of some of the school's most breathtaking young women—"The Georgia Peaches" as they were known. Recruits needed only select the lady of their choice, who would happily become their weekend date. Dates, in fact, were regularly provided at a number of schools during the early '70s, including Michigan State and Ohio State. The difference was no portfolio. Dates were more conventionally arranged.

At the University of Kansas, a recruit would step off the stairs leading from plane to concourse and be greeted by a stunning blond who carried the title of Miss Kansas. Players would be routinely introduced at halftime of basketball games, and at later stops at student bars, they were fawned over by students buying them drinks and coeds anxious to give their full attention.

Woody Hayes played it clean, personally, at Ohio State. It was the way in which his recruiting pitches unfurled that humored—and sometimes antagonized—athletes who later compared their Woody stories.

Recruits entering the Jai Lai restaurant, where Hayes did his entertaining, encountered tuxedoed waiters, huge tropical fish tanks, and a piano player knocking off a crisp rendition of the Ohio State Fight Song. Woody sat at a table with his wife, Anne.

"We'd like you to help us celebrate our anniversary," he would explain, before getting to priorities.

"Do you like lobster?"

"Yes."

"Well, then you want two of them."

In the basement of the restaurant, Hayes had an "office" where after dinner—recruits chuckled over how many "anniversaries" Hayes seemed to have—he and the recruit could talk seriously about football at Ohio State University. If the recruit were Ohio State's kind of athlete, Hayes would tell him: "You're a Buckeye." And then, often, he would offer his hand in hopes that he and the recruit could make a "gentleman's agreement" on committing to OSU.

Hayes in the winter of 1973 was also telling recruits considering Michigan State that MSU would be on probation within two years. The recruiting of Cobb, Hunt and Hannon had convinced Hayes that Michigan State was buying Ohio talent and that it was only a matter of time until the NCAA lowered the boom.

Epolito, a Weyers recruit from McKeesport, Pennsylvania, was walking off the field after OSU's 1975 victory at East Lansing when Hayes stopped him.

"I told you," said Woody, "that you would be on probation."

It hadn't come down yet, but it was only months away.

Probation appeared more and more likely as the NCAA investigation stretched into autumn and word leaked that MSU would be defending itself against dozens of allegations. It added to the gloom of a season that had not gone as expected. Michigan State's long-awaited, long-trumpeted opener against the Buckeyes had created such a stir that radio station WVIC for two weeks ran audio replays of Jackson's 88-yard run that beat OSU in '74. Tickets became so hot that the largest crowd in MSU history—80,383—crammed into a stadium which, it developed, had been oversold to the point many customers who presumably had seats were forced to sit on concrete.

Ohio State thrashed MSU, 21-0, in one of Hayes' most satisfying Big Ten paybacks. Charlie Baggett had spoken cocksuredly in August about Michigan State's plans to knock off a Buckeyes team that in Baggett's estimation didn't return as much talent as Michigan State. Baggett threw three interceptions, a couple of which came as a result of bad routes run by a freshman starting his first game at Michigan State: Kirk Gibson. He and Gene Byrd of East St. Louis, Illinois, had been two of the better talents from a 1975 recruiting hunt in which MSU made a serious bid for quarterback Chuck Fusina, a Weyers recruit who eventually signed with Penn State.

Gibson was the surprise of the litter, everyone agreed. He had been a tailback and wide receiver for Waterford (Michigan) Kettering High whom MSU assistant Andy MacDonald spotted on film as he checked out another player from nearby West Bloomfield High.

Gibson was making an omelet at home when the phone rang on a Saturday morning in the winter of 1975. MacDonald was inviting him to visit Michigan State. Gibson, who had played in a league not known for cranking out major-college talent, had been looking at Central Michigan University as his best option, but he was acquainted with Michigan State. His mother had grown up in East Lansing, and Gibson had ridden his bicycle around campus. MSU may have been more appealing to him than Gibson was to Michigan State, but Stolz offered a scholarship.

Gibson knew he was up against prestige recruits such as Birmingham (Michigan) Brother Rice's Curt Griffin, and decided in the summer of '75 he would have to make an impression. Each morning at 9, he and a buddy would head for the track at Kettering or Waterford Mott High to run a series of laps and sprints: 880s, quarter-miles, 220s, 60s, 40s and 20s. Gibson's plan was to come to camp in August in such superb condition and with such speed that the coaches would be forced to notice.

They did.

During the first day's rotating, four-corner running and conditioning drills at Spartan Stadium, Gibson was staying well up on everybody.

"Hey, rookie," huffed Baggett, who was teaming up in the drills with gimpy-kneed Ted Bell, "you better slow up. You're gonna learn the hard way."

And then: "Hey, rookie, slow down. You're making us look bad."

Gibson later took an elbow in the gut from one of them, but kept sprinting.

The other trick, Gibson realized, was to show the coaches he could hit. He had heard that messing with the great strong safety, Tommy Graves, was asking for trouble. Graves was only a sophomore, but was king on defense.

While running a play during an early intra-squad scrimmage, Gibson cracked back on Graves and knocked him flat. The staff had seen all it needed: Gibson could run, and he could stick. He would start against Ohio State.

It wasn't only the Gibson-induced interceptions that ruined MSU's 1975 opener, and crushed the big plans to unseat Ohio State and march toward a Rose Bowl trip in 1975. Joe Hunt had made a terrible play just before the half that turned a 7-0 game into a 14-0 black hole—too many points to spot a team as mean as OSU, which led Hayes after the 21-0 rout had been wrapped up to say that it was all a matter of quality—some teams won the big games, and others talked about doing it.

Tenor had been set for a 7-4 season in which Michigan State never recovered from the Ohio State collapse nor its preoccupation with NCAA threats. MSU the following week snuck by Miami (Ohio), 14-13, but the locker-room mood was not sweet.

"You dogged our ass last week," Gibson fumed to the media, "and we're not talking."

Neither were Michigan State's executives as the NCAA investigation closed in. None of the NCAA allegations had been made public by October, and the university was likewise keeping quiet as it took a 13-member party to Denver for hearings before the NCAA Infractions Committee on October 13-14, 1975. Neither attorneys, nor any of the athletes from Ohio and Florida who accused MSU's coaching staff of illegalities, were allowed to appear.

It had become the great frustration in dealing with NCAA investigators: Legal representation was not welcomed by the probers. Due process was not part of the structure. It was guilty until proven innocent, and at Michigan State, evidence was turning up that football had been operating all too loosely.

As the NCAA continued questioning coaches and athletes, a third investigation of Michigan State was being run by the Big Ten. Weyers had spent a 2 1/2-hour session at Jenison being questioned by Berst and Big Ten Commissioner Wayne Duke. Weyers had not yet retained an attorney and was cursing his own stupidity as he walked from the room and said to Stolz: "I'll tell you, Denny, these guys have got us on a fast train out of town."

But it was not antagonism that had gotten Michigan State in trouble. The MSU Select Committee that had been meeting for hours each week, interviewing players and coaches, conducting out-of-town interviews where necessary—and getting stonewalled at Ohio State—was finding violations:

A $33.27 plane ticket to Cleveland bought on credit and repaid . . . a ride to Cleveland in a coach's car . . . loan of a coach's car . . . the Baggett bank-loan arrangement, which MSU argued it had discovered and corrected . . . the loan of football equipment . . . gifts of two football jerseys and a pair of football shoes . . . a booster paid for a recruit's dinner . . . Weyers' car had been used by a player to drive a prospect around campus for three hours.

Michigan State rejected a charge by Herman Jones, a wide receiver from Miami, Florida, that MSU Assistant Coach Charlie Butler had offered him a scholarship, spending money, a car, and transportation home during vacation. Jones said his girlfriend had also been promised financial assistance and an apartment.

Michigan State argued that polygraph tests indicated Butler was telling the truth but that the NCAA chose instead to believe the recruits. MSU's investigation determined that a booster who was accused of co-agreeing to Butler's promises definitely did suggest to Jones that he should request extra benefits for signing with Michigan State.

There were other violations that neither the NCAA, the Select Committee nor the Big Ten had apparently happened upon. A number of the gifts that Weyers believed were humanitarian assistance never surfaced. An overly active booster in Cleveland was never examined. Gibson, soon after he got to MSU, was told that long-distance phone calls would be picked up.

By January, another element of the Big Ten and MSU investigation centered around a "possible diversion of funds," the Select Committee reported—a slush fund. Newspaper reports indicated a fund-raiser at The Vineyards, a restaurant in Southfield, Michigan, had become a regular source of extra revenue for the football office's miscellaneous expenses. There had also been internal probes aimed at determining whether or not money was being skimmed from the MSU Football Bust and channeled improperly. The looseness with which some of the Bust's funds were handled had been considered a problem. And for some time.

Also working against Michigan State was its reputation as a repeat offender. The school had been on NCAA and Big Ten probation in 1953 for the Spartan Foundation's backing of an illegal fund, and in 1964, the NCAA hit Duffy Daugherty's program with three years' probation for unrelated funds misuse that had occurred in the late 1950s. The NCAA, however, suspended MSU's sentence when Daugherty showed that the problem had been corrected. The school's past history would nonetheless be no plus as Michigan State went on trial in 1976.

Nine months after it had announced its investigation of Michigan State, the NCAA was ready in January of 1976 to announce a verdict and sentence. On January 18, a five-person panel from Michigan State appeared in St. Louis to appeal sanctions that had not yet been made public. The MSU representatives steamed during a session in which Berst read from his notes all alleged wrongdoings, none of which MSU was allowed to address.

A week later, on January 25, 1976, the NCAA announced that MSU would be placed on three years' probation. The university's football team during that time would be barred from bowl games and national TV appearances. Its football scholarships would be reduced by 15.

Howard Weyers was being barred from recruiting on or off campus for three years. Charlie Butler would be barred from off-campus recruiting for one year, and the NCAA ordered that Jimmy Raye be reprimanded by MSU.

Wharton and Stolz the next day appeared at a press conference, flooded by hot TV lights in a conference room at the MSU Administration Building. Wharton was combative—saying that the NCAA had been unduly harsh on a school whose sins hardly warranted a penalty so severe. Stolz sat grimly in a chair as Wharton spoke. Neither his job, nor any of his staff's—except for Weyers—appeared to be in any danger.

Changes would begin to be made later that week.

On January 30, Jack Breslin stepped down as overseer of MSU athletics. Weyers, who believed Stolz had first discussed firing him during a November conversation with Acting Athletic Director Jack Shingleton, was finally fired at the February 20, 1976 meeting of the MSU Board of Trustees. At the same meeting, Joe Kearney was named MSU's new athletic director.

Three weeks later, on the night of March 13, 1976, Wharton called a closed meeting of the MSU Board of Trustees at Kellogg Center's Galaxy Room. Various matters were discussed, but nothing resolved, until one trustee, almost on impulse, suggested that Stolz should be fired. There was, surprisingly, little debate.

Another trustee said: "If we're going to fire Stolz, then we've

also got to fire Gus Ganakas." Ganakas was the MSU head basketball coach who had not pleased the Select Committee when questioned about a hypothetical recruiting matter.

Now on a house-cleaning frenzy that had begun almost sponta-
neously, the Board decided also to fire Burt Smith, the former athletic director who five months earlier had been reassigned.

Smith the next night was asked to resign, but did not, and soon
began litigation against MSU. Ganakas was called to Cowles House
during the weekend and informed by Wharton that he would be
reassigned.

Stolz would also learn by Monday that he was being fired, and
would, after consulting his attorney, agree to dismissal when the
announcements were made public on March 16, 1976.

Over in the MSU football office, Mary Kay Smith, the office
secretary, that day got a call from Stolz.

"You sitting down?" he asked.

"I just got fired."

Stolz went back to the office later that week, cleaned out his
desk, left and never returned. He would go on to successful head
coaching jobs at Bowling Green and San Diego State.

Howard Weyers was paid through August of 1976. He went into
the insurance business, later forming his own insurance brokerage
in Okemos, and to those who knew him, it was no surprise that
Howard Weyers would become a very wealthy man.

Three

"I'M HERE TO WIN FOOTBALL GAMES"

He knew from looking through a student brochure Joe Kearney sent him that Michigan State's campus was a cut above anything he had seen on the West Coast. But it was, Darryl Rogers admitted, a peculiar way to take a head coaching job: Never having set foot on the place. Looking at a pamphlet and student map of a university he had never seen, located in a town he had never been to, in a state he knew little about.

San Jose State's head football coach had agreed to take the MSU job even if it meant getting his first glimpse of the Big Ten school two days after he was announced as successor to Denny Stolz.

Now, on the morning of April 7, 1976, he could get acquainted with his new employers and home for the next four years. Rogers and his wife, Marsha, had arrived in East Lansing the previous night and would appear at an introductory breakfast the next morning. Long before breakfast, he left his room to wander about a campus that step by step intimidated as much as it awed him.

"Holy cats, honey, I don't like this place," he said after returning to the room. "Any place that has a stadium so high you can see it from any spot on campus is going to carry some pressure."

Rogers was serious. Michigan State had 40,000 students, hundreds of thousands of alumni, and that huge stadium towering above everything but the MSC smokestack as he gazed across the Red Cedar River. He had walked into the jaws of a monster and it was probably a good idea if he politely told Kearney and the MSU executives that he had made a mistake and should stick at San Jose State.

By the time they arrived at breakfast, Marsha had also taken in the sight of a campus bathing in the light of a spring sun.

"Boy," she said, "this is the greatest place I've ever been!"

Rogers felt better. His first impressions had been reinforced by a wife who was also facing heavy environmental adjustment in moving from California to Michigan. If his wife was turned on to Michigan State, it would be easier to concentrate on the pluses that first attracted him to the job. They remained enticing no matter if Spartan Stadium did make him tremble.

About all the Midwest knew about Darryl Dale Rogers was that he was a 40-year-old Californian whose affinity for the forward pass made his brand of football entertaining, win or lose. The win or lose qualifier was important to a Michigan State following prepared to take its licks as the first months of a three-year probationary sentence settled down on MSU. It remained the hardest thing to understand about Rogers: Why a coach who had been such a success on the West Coast would move 2,000 miles east to direct a football program jailed by the NCAA.

To Rogers, there was little mystery. Michigan State was Big Ten and one of the land's traditional powers through the '50s and '60s. Michigan State was Duffy Daugherty. Michigan State was probably a Top 20 team if you could get by probation, which Rogers wasn't viewing as negatively as MSU's fans. He had never been to bowls nor played on national TV at San Jose State, so another three seasons without either would to him be no serious setback. It was still a step up from San Jose State and the Pacific Coast Athletic Conference, and that four-year contract calling for starting salary of $34,500 was no trivial matter, especially when perks such as the coach's TV show promised to be a bonus. Buying a home, too, could be done in East Lansing for a fraction of what it required in the overpriced market outside San Francisco.

Rogers thought MSU fans naive to assume their school had lost its luster simply because the NCAA decided to play hardball. Besides, he said with trademark flippancy as he munched on his breakfast, the bacon and eggs at Michigan State were excellent.

The MSU job had been on his mind for almost six weeks, since late February when Kearney called him a few days after being named MSU's new athletic director.

"There may be a change at Michigan State," he told Rogers. "Would you be interested?"

Rogers liked it at San Jose State, particularly his working relationship with university President John H. Bunzel. But the answer was easy:

"Sure."

Kearney mailed him an introductory packet that Rogers, as well as 7,000 freshmen, would examine in the spring of 1976. When he opened it a few days later, Rogers was stunned.

This place is something else, he told himself. It's great. It's the way a major university should look.

A few days later, Denny Stolz was dismissed as head coach and Kearney was on the line to arrange an interview for April 3 in Chicago, where he and the MSU screening committee were convening. They would be interviewing not only candidates for the football job, but also for head basketball coach—interviews that were superfluous as far as Kearney was concerned. He already had decided Jud Heathcote would be his new basketball coach, and Darryl Rogers, whom he nearly hired for the Washington job that Don James ultimately won, this time was coming with him.

Rogers assumed when he took the job that a 1975 team that finished 7-4 would return enough personnel to give him and his new staff a decent base in '76. Closer inspection showed something quite different.

"Your football team is in the stands," Stolz told him when they chatted the week Rogers arrived in East Lansing. Stolz was referring to all the knee injuries that had robbed the '75 team of Kim Rowekamp, Tommy Graves, Ted Bell and others who were still recuperating.

Beyond the knees, defensive back Joe Hunt was suspended for the season, and five others were suspended for MSU's opening game at Ohio State. All the trees, flowers and sunshine MSU's campus could conjure weren't going to compensate for a lack of talented football players.

A look at MSU's 1975 films was even more sobering to a coach whose game was based on team speed and agility. Rogers couldn't believe that the Big Ten overall played with so many plodders at speed positions, and he noticed how many of those plodders seemed to be wearing green and white. He sighed and told himself that players you leave behind always look better than players you see for the first time. His first in-the-flesh glimpse would come the following week when spring drills began.

From the moment he greeted them at Jenison Field House, the players could see the difference in style, the way in which Rogers the Californian was so different from prim and proper Denny Stolz.

"How you guys play football directly impacts on my next house payment," he told them. "I'm here to win football games."

The players loved it—even such rules as, "If you're late, you don't practice," the Rogers dictum that was part of a system predicated on personal responsibility. Larger snippets of the Rogers style would come at MSU's first spring practice where the new coach intended to find out pronto who could run and who could throw the ball.

One player caught his eye as he romped up and down the grass field, clumps of long blond hair bouncing against his scalp.

"That's one linebacker who's going to play," Rogers mentioned to several assistants as they stood nearby.

"That's a receiver, Coach," one of them corrected.

Rogers squealed:

"A receiver!?"

It was a sophomore by the name of Kirk Gibson. Not even on the wild and wooly West Coast, where so many babies seemed to run before they could crawl, had Rogers seen anything like the lanky antelope with "23" stuck to his jersey.

Gibson was one more reason why quarterback was the project most critical to Rogers and an offense that absolutely required a major-college arm. The candidates, now that Charlie Baggett had run out of eligibility, were Marshall Lawson, Frank Angelo, Tyrone Willingham—who had some experience as Baggett's stand-in—and a sophomore redshirt from Pittsburgh named Eddie Smith. Rogers told the four of them at MSU's initial workout to line up and throw the football, which they did for about 30 minutes as he studied them for arm strength and form. A half-hour later the team had gathered together and Rogers announced:

"Eddie Smith will be my quarterback."

Smith was one of Howard Weyers' Pennsylvania recruits who had nearly quit the team a year earlier when Stolz asked him to sit out the season to preserve a year of eligibility. It had become apparent to Smith and everyone else that Smith would languish in the Stolz system that put a premium on the ground game. He was a shade under six-feet tall and weighed only 155 pounds—suicidal dimensions for a quarterback running a conventional Big Ten offense.

Rogers, though, was interested in one thing: A quarterback's arm. Smith impressed Rogers in how fast and how high over his head he released the ball. Smith was going nowhere with Stolz, and he might be going nowhere with Rogers if spring drills proved disastrous, but for now Eddie Smith was running the offense—skeptics be damned.

Spring practices were revealing to Michigan State's players something else about the new West Coast regime: There was a sophistication to workouts that they imagined came from pro training camps, or maybe from the way Californians supposedly lived. There was more freedom, less screaming, and definitely an appeal to a player's personal integrity. You hit plenty during drills, but if you wanted a drink of water, you got it. Rogers wasn't into a lot of rah-rah pep talk. He wasn't hanging posters or spewing slogans, but he had poise that carried with it an unspoken message that on his team phonies or non-performers would have a short life expectancy.

Hiring a coaching staff had been Rogers' first assignment back in April and had come down to a merging of three Stolz assistants with five from the outside. Bob Padilla, Marv Braden and Leon Burtnett were moving with him from San Jose State; C.T. Hewgley, an Army officer and coach who had most recently been running the program at Nebraska-Omaha, was coming in as offensive line coach; and Ray Greene, a former assistant with Jacksonville of the World Football League, was moving to MSU as receivers coach. The Stolz transplants would be determined during a selection sweepstakes that had everyone on edge.

On the eve of Rogers' decision, the assistants who had endured Stolz' final days and sweated out a preceding year filled with tension and discouragement, met at the staff watering hole, The Village Market (then the Starboard Tack), on Trowbridge Road. They would drink away the anguish of 1975-76 and toast to the camaraderie and friendship that usually outweighed the pettiness that crops up periodically on any coaching staff.

It developed into a memorable, uninhibited evening filled with as much humor as melancholy. Only three from among Stolz' old staff—Ed Youngs, Jimmy Raye, Andy MacDonald, Bill Davis, Ron Chismar, Charlie Butler, Dan Underwood and Sherm Lewis—were going to stick in East Lansing. The others would be looking for new jobs.

Rogers the next day hired Lewis, Underwood and Chismar. The staff was complete.

It was the way in which this loosey-goosey crew operated that was bringing to Michigan State's football office a flavor unlike anything seen during the Daugherty-Stolz days. It was, initially, the kind of attitude office longtimers resented as the Californians sauntered in, all but kicking sand off their sandals as they cooled out on a campus not quite as hip as colleges in their Pacific Coast homeland.

"Where do I go?" Rogers asked as he searched for a desk and chair.

There was a pleasant, low-key unpretentiousness about Rogers that seemed out of whack with the role of head coach, at odds with the personality his new assistant coaches and secretaries expected to confront. But Rogers over the ensuing weeks and months proved to be just what he had been the day he waltzed in snooping for his office: Easygoing and good-humored. There were other layers to him, including a certain mysteriousness he would carry in the public's eyes, but nothing troublesome.

Schedules were one major difference between him and Stolz. Minute-by-minute daily programs were part of Stolz' office management, but Rogers kept things flexible, expecting only that work assigned for a specific time would be completed on time. It was that ability to give-and-take that observers found so intriguing in a man who let nothing get past him. He was perceptive, had an amazing memory and sized up people well. But the hard edges were always blunted when someone such as Mary Kay Smith, the office secretary, might ask him a policy question about vacation schedules.

"You wanna put up a vacation schedule?" he would ask in the nasal, almost Muppet-like voice that marked his casual conversation and that acquaintances loved to mimic. Then would come the shrug.

"Sure, put up a vacation schedule. I don't care."

Rogers did care about his first season at Michigan State and a team that looked as if its on-field problems would be bad enough without all the NCAA courtroom hassles carrying over. The six players suspended by the NCAA as part of its sanctions against MSU—Joe Hunt for the season, Mike Cobb for five games, and the rest for one game—were in September of 1976 seeking a Federal Court injunction against the suspensions on grounds their rights to due process had been violated.

Bad enough, thought Rogers, that MSU had to prepare for an opening game at Ohio State—Woody Hayes had announced in Chicago in July that it was he who blew the whistle on MSU—but his team would be forced to do it without a starting quarterback, tight end, and defensive lineman, all of whom were among the penalized six. At noon on September 10, 1976, Federal Judge Noel Fox handed down a decision upholding the NCAA suspensions. Two hours later, the team charter took off from Capitol City Airport, heading for Columbus with Marshall Lawson at quarterback and freshmen starting on both sides of the ball.

Rogers' Michigan State debut went down as a 49-21 thrashing during which several things became obvious: (1) The team's overall speed was appalling, as evidenced during a 58-yard run by OSU's 265-pound fullback, Pete Johnson; (2) Gibson would be a plus, having caught several passes for big gains, the completions coming on simple routes against an OSU defensive backfield that had few clues about pass coverage; (3) To survive the '76 season, MSU would have to depend on freshmen like linebacker Danny Bass and tight end Mark Brammer.

It was the kind of day when a man might wonder how things were going back at San Jose State. A break would come the following week: Smith was coming back at quarterback and the schedule was lightening up, with Wyoming traveling to East Lansing. Just in time, Rogers concluded, as he analyzed game films that were about as uplifting as watching an autopsy.

Pounding into the offense some semblance of big-play terror was one thing Rogers thought MSU could accomplish in the early going. Smoothing Eddie Smith into a major-college quarterback would require time, of course, and getting him the respect of teammates would take just as long. He weighed only 158 pounds the week he debuted as a starter in MSU's 21-10 dispatch of Wyoming, and the coaching staff could see that players weren't convinced a flyweight QB was tough enough or good enough to be their offensive leader.

It bothered them the way he ducked away from contact and cringed when he was hit. This was Big Ten football, they reasoned, and if he couldn't take a hit he had no place on the field with guys who daily were being smashed and bloodied.

Smith began winning them over the third week of the season when he completed 18 of 29 passes for 324 yards—173 of those yards coming on passes to Gibson during a 31-31 tie at North Carolina State. MSU's offense was beginning to show the West Coast flavor billed when Rogers arrived. But big losses to Notre Dame and Michigan followed, and when MSU finished its season with back-to-back collapses at Northwestern (42-21) and at home to sickly Iowa (30-17), a coaching staff could at least deal with reality. Rogers touched on it in a closing-season message to his team:

"It's hard to win in the Big Ten," he said. "We haven't worked hard enough *to* win. We've got some work to do."

In came the aerobic torture season known as off-season conditioning, this segment customized to the specifications of a group that had the mobility of a herd of buffalo. In his first weeks at Michigan State, Rogers told his team, point-blank, that, "This is the weakest, slowest group of young men I've ever been around."

Now, in the winter of 1977, he intended to do something about it. Monday through Thursday at 8 a.m. the team would meet for a sadistic series of laps around the Jenison Field House track. They would stagger the distances, beginning with 220-yard dashes, followed by 100s, 60s, and then 40- and 20-yard sprints, every one of them run with Olympic Trials intensity.

Included in the workouts were agility and strengthening exercises that players regarded as human rights violations. They were known as "down-ups," 25 of them to a quarter, four quarters to a session. When the whistle blew, players hit the floor, stretched in full prone position, until two toots of the whistle signaled that they get back on their feet an instant before the whistle again blew and they once more crashed to the floor.

They were killers, and it was not uncommon for players such as Kenny Robinson of Ypsilanti to see their arms swell to double by the time the session ended and an interval of sit-ups began. The net result: Players like Gibson, who had come to Michigan State with natural running ability, discovered by the end of winter they were now blazing fast.

It would begin to make a difference in the autumn of 1977. Little, outwardly, had changed at Michigan State as Rogers headed into his second season. There had been a few staff changes—Burtnett, a bit edgy on a team where minus any title he was handling as much of the defense, if not more, than Padilla, had moved to Purdue with new coach Jim Young; and Marv Braden had gone off to the pros. In their places were two newcomers: Bob Baker, an old Rogers acquaintance who would work with the offensive backfield, and George Dyer, who had coached at colleges and in the Canadian

Football League, and who was coming to MSU as a defensive assistant.

Winter conditioning and a spring practice that had gone off with neither an off-field crisis nor threat from the NCAA had also been pluses as Michigan State began to realize that NCAA probation was passing the halfway mark. MSU's personnel situation was also improving, although there were areas—such as the offensive backfield—where the Spartans were still hurting, patching up with hustlers like Richie Baes, or junior college transfers such as Leroy McGee, whose idea of a rugged game was 12 carries.

It promised also to be a better season for the rapidly developing quarterback from Pittsburgh. Smith's freshman season had been an exercise in adjustments as the coaching staff kept things simple for a sophomore who was getting a crash course in major-college quarterbacking. Five to 10 passing plays, with few variations, comprised Smith's typical game-day menu.

By the start of MSU's 1977 season, he and his pass receivers—Gibson, Gene Byrd, Mark Brammer and the running backs—were becoming more daring, more sophisticated as Smith began to call more audibles at the line of scrimmage and in turn give the offense the potential for holding the ball. Rogers believed it was as smart to keep the ball by virtue of a sound passing game as it was to stick it in the arms of running backs whose big-play potential was limited.

It was a philosophy even a few of his assistant coaches had difficulty accepting. During one spring intra-squad game, Rogers stood on the sidelines as Smith passed the offense downfield, one completion after another.

"Don't you ever run on first down?" Sherm Lewis wondered. Rogers held out his hands, half-grinning.

"Is there a rule that says you have to?"

Michigan State opened the '77 season by beating Purdue, 19-14. But after falling, 23-21, to Washington State and its slick quarterback, Jack Thompson, MSU three weeks later had lost to Notre Dame and Michigan, and was sitting 2-3—State had also beaten Wyoming, 34-16—with Indiana next in line. It was 2-3-1 by the time the Spartans left Bloomington with a 13-13 tie set up when Padilla—trying to buy time for his defense—called time out just before the end of the first half. It allowed the Hoosiers to set up a field goal and ultimately led to a 13-13 deadlock that, by season's end, would help keep MSU from tying for the Big Ten championship.

But it would go more smoothly thereafter as Michigan State won its final five games to finish 7-3-1. It was a team that drew attention across the Midwest. Not only had Rogers earned a Big Ten Coach of the Year plaque, but Larry Bethea, the splendid defensive lineman from Newport News, Virginia, was the Big Ten's Most Valuable Player. Smith-to-Gibson had advanced, as well, to a point of petrifying some of the conference's less capable defensive backs.

Rogers continued to be surprised by how rigid Big Ten defenses remained. They all played slant defenses, angle defenses, that locked into position, offering little pass rush and zone pass coverage that was easy to pick apart. Even more flabbergasting was the absence of speed he continued to notice in a conference that wondered why it had such trouble at the Rose Bowl.

It wasn't as if Rogers had all the answers two years into his job at Michigan State. And he knew it. Although probation was heading into its final 12 months, the 20 scholarships MSU had been forced to forfeit were already beginning to hurt badly—hurt as much as the probationary stigma MSU knew was influencing home-state high school talent. Image had taken a pounding during the prolonged investigation of 1975-76 and there was little doubt the no-bowls, no-TV sanctions were keeping Michigan State in the dark and confining the school to second-choice status among loads of regional athletes.

MSU decided it would do better by recruiting more in the South and West, away from the probationary runoff that was making things so difficult in the Midwest. Rogers and his staff went to Washington, D.C., to get mammoth Angelo Fields . . . to Florida for James Burroughs, Bernard Hay and Johnny Lee Haynes . . . to South Carolina for brilliant runner Derek Hughes . . . to Montana for John Leister. The bulk of the crop would remain in-staters, but the team needed speed and athletes who could help immediately. And if that kind of support could be culled from the West Coast and from junior colleges, then Rogers wanted it, regardless of geography.

A few of his own assistants wondered whether probation seriously affected Rogers, the recruiter, who was no Barry Switzer nor prime-time Duffy Daugherty when it came to living-room salesmanship. Most irritating to them was his reluctance to seriously commit to an athlete. Rogers, they felt, had made it the hard way and resented 17-year-olds who had their hands out, and because of those feelings wanted the athlete to first pledge heart and soul to Michigan State before he got serious about reciprocating.

"Do we want this kid or don't we?" assistants would wonder before they spent the better part of a week chasing a running back through the sugar-cane fields of Pahokee, Florida. So often during those sessions when mom, dad and son were accommodating Rogers and an assistant, the staffer would practically scream to himself, wanting Rogers to come out and say to the recruit: "Hey, we want you at Michigan State. We need you." But too many times he would instead look at the television and never really come to the point.

Other staffers thought if he had stayed at Michigan State long enough to build real regional identity he might have been better able to walk into a home as the dynamic, imposing coach he really couldn't be during MSU's probationary period. Who, outside of East Lansing's tape-delayed TV audience, had even seen him standing along the sidelines? Those zoom-lens sideline closeups of a coach in control contributed to an aura Rogers lacked.

Recruiting was about the only complaint staffers had with their boss. His ability to get things done minus any formal office structure amazed those who had been around during the heel-clicking days under Stolz. If someone was a minute late for an 8 a.m. staff meeting, Stolz' entire day was ruined. Rogers merely expected that everyone would be punctual, and if someone wasn't— and had anything close to a good excuse—Rogers got on with business that he believed would always survive a five-minute delay. Staffers marveled at how the offensive staff might go home at 7 or 8 p.m., simply due to efficiency that eliminated extraneous meetings and debate.

Assistants liked Rogers also because he fought hard for their pay-raises, and helped them get dealer cars and golf club privileges. It was not an isolated observation. Secretaries remarked years later that he had an unmatched sense of fairness, a non-sexist way of running an office that did not preclude him from keeping wives out of the picture.

There would be no spouses meddling in office affairs or bickering over matters that Rogers considered within his domain. Business and households would remain as separate as church and state, except for Saturday nights after home victories, when Darryl and Marsha Rogers would take the staff and their wives to dinner at Walnut Hills Country Club.

Life had improved radically for Rogers since his days growing up in the sweaty industrial pocket southwest of Los Angeles known as Long Beach. There had been a broken home and tough times, none of which he was inclined to discuss, none of which seemed relevant when he had three daughters and a wife as delightful as the ones with whom he lived in a comfortable home in East Lansing's White Hills Estates. He had met Marsha through a friend at Fresno State, and had found in her the stability and warmth that perhaps had been lacking in earlier chapters of his life.

His family was the centerpiece of his life; football, particularly the way it was shaping up in 1978, was merely a bonus as his Michigan State experience became more and more satisfying. The team looked good as spring drills broke up in May of 1978. MSU had solid people on each side of the ball, a third-year quarterback, all those receivers, a couple of good-looking sophomore running backs in Steve Smith and Bruce Reeves, and a kicking game in Ray Stachowicz and Hans Nielsen that stood as strong as any in the Big Ten.

Rogers could look forward to a summer of golf—he would blow off an appointment if the day was nice and he had any chance of playing—and to an autumn far more promising than the previous two as the program externally and internally was becoming more rounded. There had been a few staff adjustments—Padilla and Greene had departed for head coaching jobs, Dyer was now defensive coordinator, and Walt Harris and Mo Forte were additions—but nothing that unsettled staff or players.

Helping matters was Gibson's decision to return for his senior year after an improbable spring in which he tried out for the baseball team, broke school and Big Ten records, made All-American, and signed with the Detroit Tigers as their first-round draft pick. Rogers had urged him the previous winter to try baseball on the belief it could help Danny Litwhiler, MSU's baseball coach, and perhaps improve Gibson's market value. No one, Rogers included, had anticipated that Gibson would send one home run ball after another sailing into the trees beyond Kobs Field and either into, or over, the Red Cedar.

Gibson had decided early that signing with the Tigers and playing a summer of minor league ball would not cancel his senior year of football. For that, everyone on the football team was grateful, no matter if it left his new employers squirming in the Tigers front office.

Gibson and Rogers had a mutual appreciation that partially explained Gibson's desire to come back. For all their differences in style and diplomacy, Rogers liked the fire that seemed always to burn within Gibson, the competitiveness that was set perpetually at full throttle. Gibson liked the way Rogers listened. He didn't subscribe to any caste system between coach and player, yet an athlete could respect him without feeling uncomfortable about dropping into his office to talk football.

It wasn't that way with so many of Rogers' players who found him aloof, or tough to get close to, but Gibson had discovered that talking football with Rogers had dual benefits. Gibson knew the coverages and reads as well as an assistant coach and could advance an idea that made sense to the offensive strategists. Rogers was into scoring points, and getting the ball to No. 23 was one of the quickest ways to collect them.

During a game in the '77 season, Gibson had run two consecutive bomb routes without getting the ball and was panting as he trotted back to the line. He motioned to Rogers to get him out and bring in a fresh receiver. Rogers held up his index finger, signaling one more try.

Smith the next play dropped back and hit Gibson on a bomb.

For all of his skills, it was the ease with which a 6-foot-3, 215-pound receiver tore across the green practice-field sod, almost nonchalantly outrunning everyone on the team, that most awed Rogers. He over the years had seen Tommy Smith and Lee Evans and the West Coast's best runners, and none of them ran with the raw power displayed by this athlete, who had never been coached as a runner. There had been notions a year earlier that moving Gibson to tailback might be the best way to juice up a backfield that was seriously undernourished. Rogers, though, studied Gibson's long strides and decided in this instance the best coaching would be the least coaching. Gibson would stick at receiver.

"He is as fine an athlete as you will ever encounter," Rogers told a Chicago media audience in July of 1978. The words were not original; the fact Rogers, who was not into pumping up players, would say it to a Midwest media gathering, in straight, matter-of-fact tones, indicated the degree to which he considered Gibson remarkable.

Michigan State's football tendency heading into its 1978 opener had been one of poor starts and fancy finishes, attributable mostly to scheduling. Notre Dame, Michigan and often another tough non-conference match always comprised MSU's first five games, which helped explain the many 2-3 starts that made it tough on fans aching to catch football fever in East Lansing. It might turn around, the staff told itself, if State would knock off Purdue in the opener at West Lafayette.

On a hot, sunny day at Ross-Ade Stadium, Michigan State went ahead, 14-0, in the second quarter and looked to be comfortably in control until it was discovered that Eddie Smith had broken his hand when he dived into the end zone on MSU's second touchdown. Bert Vaughn, whose Big Ten credentials amounted to one pass completion, replaced Smith, but Michigan State's offense was dead and Purdue came back to win, 21-14. Smith would be out for at least two weeks. Goodbye to that fast start Rogers had banked upon.

The Spartans a week later smashed Syracuse, 49-21, in a game distinguished when Gibson, on a post pattern, ran up the back of an official who never saw him coming. Both collapsed in a heap at the 15-yard line before Gibson, disgustedly, trotted back to the huddle.

"Watch out!" Rogers hollered to the back judge. "We might be coming that way again."

On the next play, on the identical pass route, Vaughn threw a TD bomb to Gibson.

Smith was back at quarterback a week later at Southern Cal, but could barely throw the ball as USC hammered State, 30-9. When Notre Dame came to East Lansing the following week, Smith's hand, although mended enough to permit him to play, was so sore that he asked Rogers, "Why don't I get it relieved?"—code language for having it shot with pain-killers. Rogers ruled against it. Tenderness from the needle insertion would only cost Smith another week of recovery.

Michigan State lost to the Irish, 29-25, but after Jim Browner had stolen the ball from MSU fullback Andy Schramm to score an early, back-breaking TD against State, Smith—whose hand finally felt normal in the second half—threw for 307 yards on a 27-for-41 spree that showed Rogers, belatedly, his football team had too much punch to be sitting 1-3.

"You can die here," Rogers told his team, "or you can yet make something of this season."

Whether the Notre Dame rally would make any difference against an unbeaten Michigan team at Ann Arbor was, at best, debatable. The Wolverines were their usual well-balanced, well-directed selves, anxious to keep the ball on the ground and out of MSU's mitts. But the script changed at Michigan Stadium.

With fullback Lonnie Middleton scoring twice, it was 17-0,

MSU, at the half as State hit Michigan hard with counters and draw plays that turned loose a ground game the Wolverines expected to be soft compared with MSU's scary pass attack. But neither was Michigan State's air show disappointing. The Spartans' first play from scrimmage was a play-action scheme called Three Base Pass in which Smith faked a handoff to Steve Smith, turned and lofted a bomb to Gibson, who had galloped past defenders biting on the fake handoff.

The ball was so close to being caught that Gibson years later would remember how he could feel breeze from the descending football brushing his fingertips. He knew on that opening play Michigan would have a horrible time defending.

Although Rick Leach, Michigan's quarterback, threw three interceptions on the day, he and the Wolverines were coming back hard in the second half. But the rally would fade on MSU's 70-yard, eight-play, third-quarter drive that featured Gene Byrd, on third-and-15, sprinting across the middle, leaping, catching Smith's bullet, and hanging on as he was torpedoed by Wolverine defender Mark DeSantis. Byrd was a superb talent who would finish his career with 114 receptions to Gibson's 112. In a 24-15 upset that spun around MSU's season, Byrd's third-down grab would go down as one of his best moments.

The toppling of Michigan would also suggest that a squad loaded with skill players and seniors might, after all, be the kind of football team anticipated coming into September. Michigan State had hit the Wolverines with 247 yards in the air and 247 yards on the ground. A passing game that was nearly unstoppable could now work even more boldly if secondaries had to play it warily against MSU's runners.

Back in East Lansing a week later, Michigan State scored two touchdowns on its first two plays against Indiana as Smith hit Gibson on an 86-yard TD and followed with a 55-yarder to Samson (Light Bulb) Howard. The pass to Gibson came on another of the crossing routes Rogers' offense deployed so niftily, Gibson sucking in the ball across the middle and sprinting through and past lunging defenders.

Bob Baker, MSU's offensive backfield coach, turned to Rogers, shaking his head as Gibson trotted from the end zone.

"He is not," Baker said, "your average bear."

The MSU pass offense choreographed by Rogers utilized three wide receivers and two running backs on almost every pass play. In his bread-and-butter crossing routes, Rogers brought to the Big Ten a technique by which intersecting receivers would run defenders against so much oncoming traffic—pick plays, really—that one receiver was bound to emerge free and clear.

Eddie Smith was the son of a retired Pittsburgh homicide detective and had become an exquisite reader of coverages who, with Gibson, developed a quarterback-receiver relationship based almost on telepathy. Gibson knew if he could pick out the slightest lane among the zone defenses secondaries played against Michigan State, the ball would be there by the time his feet hit clear turf. Gibson had also learned to keep his eyes down as he ran his route, tempting the defender to concentrate on Gibson's moves, rather than on Smith, which kept a defensive back from breaking on the ball until too late.

In most situations, Smith needed only to pick out a spot of single coverage and get rid of the ball, usually across the middle, which made it nearly impossible for defenses to blitz or to sack Smith. Or, he might go with an out pattern to the sidelines where Smith had a celebrated knack for getting the ball to a receiver a step in bounds. When State wanted to go for it all, there proved to be one pattern that was almost failsafe: One receiver running a post pattern, the other crossing over the middle. Whichever way the free safety broke, Smith would go opposite and often get six points.

Indiana finally perished, 49-14, in a game that pitted two head coaches not terribly fond of each other. Indiana's Lee Corso had agitated Rogers in August when he railed against wire-service polls that ranked teams on NCAA probation—a clear jab at Michigan State. Rogers believed a team on probation was paying a stiff enough price in its no-bowls, no-TV sanctions, particularly when the present coaching staff had nothing to do with previous sins.

As they met at midfield to shake hands after the game, Corso told Rogers that Michigan State had beaten the Hoosiers "fair and square." The insinuation that MSU's clean victory was somehow surprising, or noteworthy to Corso, burned Rogers. He was still fuming a few days later in the coach's locker room as he recalled the dig.

"I don't like that son of a bitch," Rogers wailed in a soft, sing-song voice. "I don't like that son of a bitch . . ."

Across the dressing room, standing under a hissing shower head, was Baker, who had an amazing ability to puff away on a well-stoked pipe even as he stood beneath cascading hot water. It was a sight typical of a good-humored staff that players considered as accomplished in fellowship as it was in its ability to coach football.

Although Michigan State was barred from going to the Rose Bowl, or any other bowl in its final season of probation, the '78 team began shooting seriously in mid-October for a Big Ten championship that would at least earn each player a handsome championship ring—the one tangible symbol of accomplishment allowed Michigan State by the NCAA. MSU followed its rout of Indiana with a 55-2 massacre of Wisconsin and a 59-19 pummeling of Illinois that would help establish Michigan State in 1978 as the Big Ten's greatest single-season scoring team in history.

But it was also developing by mid-season into a team that could play excellent defense—an element of the game in which Rogers had never been considered terribly accomplished. Mel Land was having an excellent season at tackle, as were the linebackers, Dan Bass, John McCormick, Mike Decker and Larry Savage. The secondary had Mike Marshall, Mark Anderson and strong safety Tommy Graves, one of the team's best comeback stories. He had come to Michigan State in 1974 from Norfolk, Virginia, a freshman who became a starter and looked as if he might crowd George Webster and Bubba Smith in MSU's circle of defensive legends.

But he tore up a knee during practice in 1975, and sat out the next two seasons following extensive surgery at Atlanta in which the knee was reconstructed. He no longer could move as fluidly as he had during his fabulous freshman year, but Graves, a thoughtful type who became one of the team's real leaders in '78, carried enough wallop and smarts to return as starting strong safety. He would eventually make the Pittsburgh Steelers—still less mobile than the athlete he had been before his knee shredded.

Michigan State wrapped up the 1978 season, and a co-championship with Michigan, by crushing Minnesota, 33-9, Northwestern, 52-3, and Iowa, 42-7. The games had become such blowouts that by the fourth quarter, even freshmen were getting in on the touchdown parties, none with any more style than tailback Derek Hughes, the South Carolina glider who averaged 10 yards per carry in his cameo stints.

With the big victories came a warmth that hung with players on the practice field and in the locker room. Probation had forced the players to stick together and adopt different forms of motivation—

such as the push for championship rings. Now they felt as though it was their own, personal triumph over hassles and bleakness that had smothered so much of their college careers.

Rogers had not been every player's favorite, but even those who found it difficult to get close to him gave him credit for plugging in a system that had made football enjoyable, and for shooting straight when players had questions.

"What do I have to do this summer to play," Jim Epolito, the tight end and long snapper, asked him after spring drills in 1977.

"You've got to get quicker," Rogers told him. "I need you to run a 4.7 (40-yard dash time). If you could come back at 6-6, 265 and do a 4.7, that's what I need."

Epolito was crushed. He was 6-2, 205 and was still recovering from knee surgery. But two weeks later he called Rogers and thanked him. It was the first time, he said, that any coach had leveled with him.

There was no trip to Pasadena as Michigan State met for its post-season banquet at Long's Convention Center in Lansing, but there was heavy celebration among a football community that was saying farewell to a final year of probation. Rogers was a hero at Michigan State. And feeling so good at the banquet that he could laugh as he repeated Dan Underwood's line after the Michigan victory that the Wolverines had "always been arrogant asses, and still were arrogant asses."

Rogers thought it a perfectly tame, light-hearted remark appropriate for an in-house gathering of MSU followers still savoring the upset of Michigan. But when he laughed and repeated the line a few nights later at MSU's Detroit Football Bust, media in the audience reported the remarks. Rogers had now started a full-scale war with a University of Michigan following and head coach with whom he had previously been at peace.

It was the very brand of diplomatic gaffe Rogers would have killed one of his staffers for making. There was some irony, insiders thought, to this pleasant man with a quiet but ironclad moral code—a coach who would have immediately booted an assistant caught fooling around on the side—tripping over his own careless tongue in a situation where he should have known better.

But that also was Rogers, they said. He was above reproach in so many ways, but vulnerable in matters he couldn't imagine others took seriously—like the banquet remarks—or in an area in which he personally placed little importance. Like money. Rogers simply didn't care that much about it.

"Do you realize you have $14,000 in a checking account and it's just sitting there?" Mary Kay Smith asked him as she handled some of his routine bookkeeping.

Rogers shrugged and said:

"What do you want me to do with it?"

His one material indulgence was housing, which he was constantly upgrading throughout his life. But dollars remained a low priority with him. Rogers didn't worry about salary levels or whether the waitress was getting a 20 or 25 percent tip. When the football office hosted official functions in which hospitality came from its budget, Rogers, a non-drinker, entrusted Mary Kay Smith with the bar bill and never asked questions.

There was such sensitivity to people, his observers noticed, but such a delightful lack of sensitivity toward himself. Newspaper stories, or TV and radio reports that might be critical of Rogers, never resulted in any outward anger from him.

"You can't control those things," he would explain, "so why worry about it?"

But he had amazing self-control, no moment more graphic than the afternoon in 1978 when he and his players walked off the sun-baked field at Purdue after losing to the Boilermakers, and began filing into the visitors' locker room at the far end of the west stands. A few Purdue fans stood in the bleachers and screamed at Rogers as he stood at the door, waiting for his players to gather. Jerome Stanton, a senior defensive back, had cramped up in the heat and was being carried inside as pain blanketed his face.

"Look at the coach!" one yelled, leaning over a concrete railing. "Doesn't even care about his players! Hey, Coach, don't you even care about that guy?"

It was vicious, demented squealing. But Rogers never looked up. He held the door until Stanton had been carried in, then gently closed it and addressed his team.

Rogers wanted the same poise from a staff that didn't always follow the Boy Scout code. George Dyer's free-spirited ways could be a particular irritant to Rogers, as on the afternoon at Highland Hills Golf Course when Dyer, having quaffed a few refreshments, fell, giggling, out of a golf cart. A few months later at a football rally at the popular student bar, Dooley's, Dyer had been persuaded to sing country and western music, a rousing performance that disc jockey Bob Berry mentioned the next morning on radio station WVIC. Rogers heard the report and was furious that a staffer had been hamming it up at a student watering hole.

Dyer, who always had a chaw of chewing tobacco planted under his lip, tended to be spontaneous. At one practice in 1979, he pulled the wet, black chaw from his mouth, stuck it in his hand and decided to have some fun at the expense of freshman lineman Howard McAdoo.

"Howard," he yelled, "come over here, son."

McAdoo wandered over and began staring warily at the moist clump of dark-colored slime in Dyer's hand. McAdoo could only guess what it was. He kept staring, disgusted, bewildered, a look of absolute revulsion on his face as other players cackled.

What Rogers, his staff and his team would encounter in 1979 would be far less amusing. A seven-game winning streak had polished off MSU's '78 season and, with a comfortable opening schedule in '79—Illinois, Oregon and Miami (Ohio)—Michigan State was heading toward a Top Ten national ranking as the '79 season began.

There had been big changes since 1978—Smith and Gibson were gone, and Bert Vaughn was now quarterback—but the heavy graduation losses seemed no serious handicap as the Spartans opened 3-0 to push their two-season winning streak to 10 games.

But the season, and MSU's team, would begin to crumble by the fourth week, when Vaughn fell on his elbow and punctured his spleen in a 27-3 loss at Notre Dame. Michigan the next week made MSU pay for its '78 upset by dumping the Spartans, 21-7. Vaughn was now out for the season, and three weeks later the MSU losing string had reached five. Internal problems also began cropping up, many of them pinned on a faction of players whose attitudes were bothersome.

It spilled over following one late-season practice when the team lined up for dinner in its private dining area at the International Center. Gene Byrd, one player who was known to cut in front of others in the dinner line, maneuvered into position ahead of some who had been waiting their turn. C.T. Hewgley, the career military man and offensive line coach, was the staff whipcracker. He saw Byrd make his move and thundered:

"No one bucks this chow line!"

Byrd responded with some sass, and Hewgley nearly attacked.

On a team known for its serenity during the previous two years, the dining-room clash was an incident of unprecedented ugliness.

But MSU's erosion of spirit and discipline had gone from an isolated incident to a common problem as the team took its five-game losing streak to Northwestern. On the night before the game, the team had settled into a meeting room at the Lincolnwood Hyatt to watch its traditional Friday night team movie. It was not an optional get-together, but many players were treating it as such, as Rogers soon noticed.

A few minutes into the movie, lights went on, the projector stopped and Rogers was on his feet, raging at the number of players absent. He blasted the team's attitude and went so far as to threaten forfeiting the next day's game.

Michigan State showed up at Dyche Stadium the next day, but Rogers was in no mood for delivering any pre-game inspiration. He had Jon Phillips, the MSU equipment manager, handle the pre-game speech.

"I want you tearing those hinges off the door on your way out," Phillips told players who found the idea of a non-coach speaking to them as unsettling as the previous night's outburst.

Michigan State beat Northwestern, 42-7, and the next week closed out its home season with a 31-17 victory over Minnesota, during which State didn't throw a single second-half pass. But in its finale at Iowa, in Hayden Fry's first season as head coach of the Hawkeyes, the Spartans sank, 33-23, to finish 5-6 and douse the football fires that had been rekindled a year earlier in East Lansing.

Unknown to any of the players, Rogers was definitely open to another job offer. Edgar Harden, the MSU interim president who had agreed to step in following Clifton Wharton's departure in 1977, had finally left the presidency. Harden was a man Rogers enjoyed immensely—precisely the kind of supportive, affable president Rogers was not encountering in Cecil Mackey.

His decision to leave MSU was made during a first meeting with Mackey when the MSU president asked Rogers, "Are you clean?" Insulted, and now bothered by rumored budget cuts, Rogers wanted out.

Seven weeks after the defeat at Iowa, Rogers accepted the head coaching job at Arizona State, where he would be joined by Joe Kearney, the MSU athletic director who was going to ASU as its AD in an explosive package deal.

Rogers gathered his team together in Jenison on the morning of January 15, 1980. He would be leaving Michigan State, he told them in a terse voice, and would be taking most of the staff. They would have a new head football coach.

Rogers dismissed them and later that week flew to his new job at Tempe, Arizona.

Four

SENTIMENT MISSES THE MARK

On January 17, 1980, two nights after Darryl Rogers and Joe Kearney announced their move to Arizona State, Michigan State's basketball team was playing Wisconsin at Jenison Field House. Midway through the game, fans applauded and cheered softly as two people carrying a 15-foot banner strolled around the outer perimeter of the basketball court. The banner said: "No More Carpetbagging—Loyalty to MSU Athletics."

The Rogers-Kearney exodus had shattered Michigan State. Staff, players, executives, fans, even lukewarm followers were taking the departures personally. To them there was something insulting, something conspiratorial about this simultaneous move of an athletic director and coach for the warmth and glamour of a Pac-10 Conference school tucked amid the buttes of suburban Phoenix. It was rejection. It was abandonment. It was opportunism, they reasoned, and they didn't like it.

The attitude in East Lansing was that MSU had been duped by West Coast natives who had used Michigan State as a stepping stone to greater comfort in a more familiar and inviting region. Seeing them flee to a Sun Belt campus in the dead of winter only added to their anger.

If new executives were in part the reason Kearney and Rogers were leaving, Michigan State's high-level officials were either defiant or pretended to ignore. They joined with the rank-and-file in concluding it was time to bring Michigan State people back to

69

Michigan State. That, they believed, would heal wounds and prop up morale that had sunk to rock-bottom.

The trauma was most acute at MSU's football office, which still was located inside Jenison. Players walked in and out, desperate to talk with Sherm Lewis or Mary Kay Smith or anyone else who represented security and stability. Two seniors, Rod Strata and Mike Densmore, helped get the team together for unity meetings and a continuation of the 7 a.m. winter conditioning sessions. Lewis and grad assistants Kurt Schottenheimer and Matt Means kept tabs on recruits and worked the phones, hoping to hold together a few recruiting threads until a new coach arrived.

Michigan State waited only a week before Doug Weaver was named athletic director, the first step toward returning old-line MSU people to East Lansing. The next step, the high-profile decision, would be in Weaver's hands.

Sentiment had been building to hire George Perles, the Pittsburgh Steelers defensive coordinator, who had played and coached at MSU before he went on to help Chuck Noll build a series of four Super Bowl champions. The Perles movement began on January 18, when Detroit News columnist Joe Falls wrote a major piece headlined: "Steeler Answer to MSU's Needs."

"Right now the people who care about Michigan State need something to give them a lift," Falls wrote. "They've been kicked in the teeth again. They need someone to rally around and give them hope for the future . . . (Perles) understands the situation at Michigan State. He knows what must be done to compete with Michigan and the rest of the Big Ten."

Perles, whose team was about to beat the Rams in Super Bowl XIV, spoke with Falls from Pittsburgh's Super Bowl camp. "I'll tell you, I'd give Bo something to think about," he said, a reference to Michigan's mighty head coach, Schembechler.

Perles that day became MSU's hot candidate. He had the essentials—he was a MSU man, born in Detroit, familiar with Detroit high schools, steeped in Biggie Munn-Duffy Daugherty tradition. And he had a reputation as a shrewd defensive-minded man who had helped conceive the NFL's most famous defense. His credentials seemed almost too good.

Weaver thought the same, and besides, Perles was no stranger. Weaver had been his freshman coach and had remained a friend. Only five years before, when Weaver was head football coach at

Southern Illinois, he had flown to Pittsburgh to visit Perles and spend a night watching football films. Now he was calling his old friend to have dinner and talk about Michigan State's head football job.

Conversation was pleasant as they dined at a restaurant in Pittsburgh. Perles was enthusiastic. He had ideas. He had confidence that rebuilding MSU could be done by playing clean and working the in-state high schools hard for talent Bo Schembechler had been dominating. Michigan State, he assured Weaver, was a gold mine that only needed direction and competence from someone who knew the turf.

Weaver flew back to East Lansing, telling himself Perles could handle the job. But something was lacking. Something Weaver couldn't pinpoint, whether it was concern about Perles' rough-and-tumble days as a player, or his potential for leaving the pros and making a smooth transition to a job that needed a man who could be as much statesman as football coach. There were only mild misgivings when he interviewed Sherm Lewis—the loyalist who now wanted a shot at head coach after serving as an assistant to Daugherty, Denny Stolz and Darryl Rogers. But Lewis could not approach Perles' credentials, nor his potential for inspiring a school and constituency angered and dispirited since the Rogers-Kearney announcement.

Other big-namers were interested in the job and Weaver intended to talk to at least one more candidate. Rollie Dotsch, another ex-Spartan who had been an assistant with the Green Bay Packers and head man at Northern Michigan, wanted badly to coach MSU, but Weaver was indifferent.

It was at a coaching convention at New Orleans that another old-line Spartan had ideas.

Frank (Muddy) Waters, who had built great teams at Hillsdale (Michigan) College and was now head coach at Saginaw Valley State (Michigan) College, knew of the turmoil in East Lansing and MSU's plan to bring peace by hiring a Michigan State man. Waters was sitting next to Northwood College coach Jack Finn at a coaches' meeting when Michigan State was mentioned.

"You know, Jack," Waters said, "I'm going to apply for that job."

"You're too old," Finn said.

Waters, who would turn 57 later that month, thought he had

little to lose. He had wanted the job since his playing days, and had gone after it in 1972 when Duffy Daugherty resigned, calling Burt Smith, then MSU's athletic director, to ask for an interview.

"Aw, not you, too," Smith had sighed. But Smith agreed to see him in Chicago, where Smith had meetings scheduled, and the two talked briefly. Smith said MSU was not interested in a MSU grad, and indicated Denny Stolz looked like the next coach. A few days later Michigan State named Stolz as its new coach and Waters returned to Hillsdale for the 1972 season, his final year as head coach at Hillsdale before leaving for Saginaw Valley.

Seven years later Waters understood the climate had changed in East Lansing. He flew home from New Orleans, left a message with Weaver's secretary, and hoped the phone would ring. An hour later, it did.

"Muddy, I'm returning your call, but I'm not returning your call, because I was going to call you, anyway," Weaver began. "Can you come down?"

"Hell, yeah," said Waters.

They met late on a Friday morning at Kellogg Center. An intended one-hour meeting stretched on into the afternoon. Weaver, hungry for a wholesome approach to MSU tradition, lapped up Waters' folksy way and his love for Michigan State. Weaver told him that first priority would be a clean program. Waters laughed and said it would be the least of his problems.

Weaver was surprised at the depth of Waters' MSU roots, and impressed that he still carried a practice-field pass from Biggie Munn's 1951 team. He wore his original MSU ring. He had a lifetime membership card to the MSU Varsity Club—a membership that had cost Waters $100 at a time he was making an annual salary of $3,000. Weaver was captivated. Waters had won big at the small-college stops and seemed to be respected by the academic circle. Now came a revelation that Waters was so thoroughly MSU as to be almost sappy.

Waters returned to Saginaw Valley feeling good about the interview, but doubtful he was a serious choice. Perles seemed to be the clear frontrunner. The fans wanted him, the media was following his every move and running daily stories about a man who seemed perfectly suited to a job and to the times. Waters got busy with his own recruiting at Saginaw Valley.

The following Tuesday, Waters took two high school players to lunch, gave them the SVSC pitch, and returned to his office shortly after 1 p.m. Doug Weaver had called, his secretary told him. Waters grabbed a phone. Seconds later, Weaver was on the line.

"Well, you got yourself a job," Weaver chirped. "Now get your ass down here."

Waters flew out of the office and drove, almost unconsciously, to East Lansing. After picking up Weaver, they drove to the home of Ken Thompson, right-hand man to MSU President Cecil Mackey, who was waiting along with various MSU officials and members of the Board of Trustees. It took all of 30 seconds for Waters to notice the chill. Several trustees were either cool or outright indignant. Others had come by to offer congratulations and size up a shocking choice for head coach who in one more day would turn 57 years of age—the same age as Duffy Daugherty when he resigned.

There was disbelief, and in some cases hostility, among the media and general public. Not once during the preceding two weeks had Waters' name been mentioned as a possibility, and the announcement that a 57-year-old man from Saginaw Valley State College was stepping in as successor to Daugherty, Denny Stolz and Darryl Rogers, shook the state.

Michigan State's football players were also flabbergasted. Rod Strata, a senior offensive guard who had been recruited by Denny Stolz, told reporters the only Muddy Waters he knew was a blues singer from the South. The standard statement from everyone—players to media to most of MSU's administration—was that Waters should be given a chance. The tendency to consider him a ridiculous choice seemed to diminish when the pleasant, white-haired man who had been a fullback for Biggie Munn, talked about himself and his football philosophy. But at a press conference the next afternoon in MSU's Administration Building, the most common remark was that Waters looked old.

It was recruiting, though, and not his age that was the question as Muddy Waters began work. The departure of Rogers and six assistants had gutted Michigan State's recruiting force, stripping it of manpower and chopping nearly three weeks from the heart of recruiting season. Sherm Lewis and MSU's grad assistant coaches had made as many phone contacts as possible, keeping MSU close to eventual signers such as Darryl Turner and Carl Banks, but with less than two weeks until letters of intent could be signed, MSU was in worse shape than it had been when probation came down four years earlier.

Waters, Lewis and the others put together a makeshift list of approachable recruits and hit the road. It was his reputed knowledge of in-state high schools, and his rapport with youngsters, that Weaver had considered among Waters' strengths. But with so few days to work, Waters decided to move cross-country. He went to Pittsburgh, St. Louis and Cincinnati, returned to East Lansing for a night, then flew to Hawaii the next day for a six-hour stay during which he signed three players.

He had been on the road three days and had not slept in a bed. Once back at East Lansing, he left for Lockport, Illinois, to sign lineman Ed Trubich, then flew to Escanaba in the Upper Peninsula to pursue tight end Jeff Nault. At midnight Friday, Waters sat in his car, surrounded by frigid air and 10 inches of snow, waiting for Nault to return from a high school basketball game. They eventually talked, but Nault signed with Wisconsin.

Back in East Lansing the following week, Waters got busy putting together a staff while he got acquainted with players. The new coach was still a mystery to athletes who were not entirely sure what to make of a man so different from the prototype football general. They had first met him during a morning workout at Jenison when he gathered them into the bleachers and introduced himself and his program. He was dressed mostly in green, including his socks, and immediately the players discovered in Waters a stunning affection for MSU and a flair for lacing sentences with Spartan sentimentality.

Some felt there was almost a high school flavor to it. Waters was speaking of "Spartan spirit," and Michigan State "tradition," evoking the names of Biggie Munn and Charley Bachman and his own days at MSU, all of which seemed ancient and unfamiliar to players too young to have remembered John F. Kennedy. The players were nervous. Bewildered. While there had been an almost amusing tone to Waters' corny address, there was a realization that the professional ways they had known under Darryl Rogers were now giving way to a malt-shop atmosphere. The prospects were scary.

The following week a group of seniors decided to call a private team meeting in an upstairs room at Jenison. Turnout was heavy as one of the seniors, prominent on offense, acted as spokesman. He suggested the team draft a petition requesting that Waters be released and a new head coach be appointed. Many agreed.

But another senior saw the futility of it.

"We're not professional football players," he argued. "We can't do that."

"Why can't we?" another player asked. "If enough players are behind it, we can get some kind of action. Why not try?"

The movement fizzled. Realizing players were powerless to hold a gun to MSU's administration, and knowing that they might as well hope for the best from a coach with a four-year contract, the players went ahead with morning conditioning and waited to see what would unfold at spring practice.

Waters, unaware of a near-mutiny a week into his regime, began searching for assistant coaches. It had been decided early that Lewis' loyalty and unsuccessful two-time candidacy for the head coaching job be rewarded with a raise and title of Assistant Head Football Coach. Waters also decided that grad assistant coaches Kurt Schottenheimer and Matt Means, who had helped Lewis hold things together in January, be made full-time staffers. He still had five spots to fill.

A first choice was his son, "Murky," who had been chief assistant at Saginaw Valley, and a MSU football letter-winner from 1966-68. But Michigan State's nepotism laws prevented a father-son tandem from working in the same department. Murky was a quick scratch.

Next he went for Buck Nystrom, an old MSU All-American who had coached briefly under Duffy Daugherty and now was at Colorado. But Nystrom was committed to Colorado and wouldn't budge. Waters called Al Fracassa, head coach at Birmingham Brother Rice, but Fracassa felt strongly toward his own players, had just seen his father enter a nearby rest home, and had perhaps the best high school job in the state. Fracassa, emotionally, told Waters no.

Waters was intent on getting good Michigan high school coaches whom he thought would give MSU an edge in steering top prep talent toward East Lansing. The Xs and Os, the teaching of technique, Waters believed inconsequential in building a staff. Football was football at any level. He subsequently hired three assistants with longtime state high school experience: Dave Driscoll, who had played for Waters at Hillsdale and who for 12 years had been head coach at Jackson Parkside High; Ted Guthard, an old Spartan lineman who had coached college ball briefly, and most recently was head coach at Bloomfield Hills Lahser; and Dick Comar, defensive line coach at Indiana State, who had built great teams at Southgate Aquinas High.

He finished by hiring Tyrone Willingham, an assistant at Cen-

tral Michigan who only four years earlier had played quarterback at
Michigan State; and Joe Pendry, a crackerjack offensive coach who
had played and coached at West Virginia under Bobby Bowden, before Bowden left for Florida State. Pendry had since worked as offensive coordinator at Kansas State, and as an offensive assistant at
Pitt, where he became friends with a Steelers coach named George
Perles. It was Perles, loser in the 1980 coaching sweepstakes, who
recommended Pendry to the Spartans' new head coach.

Waters was feeling more comfortable. With a staff intact, some
excellent players salvaged from the 10-day recruiting crush, and
resistance to his hiring fading by the day, he could relax and enjoy a
job so dreamy he had never bothered to ask Weaver about salary. At
a basketball game a few nights later, Waters was introduced at
halftime, and thought he might need a flak jacket as he walked to
center court. Instead, the student section rose and began chanting:

"Mud-dy, Mud-dy, Mud-dy."

It was like something from an old dream; like a fantasy that
began 37 years earlier, when a California native who had grown up
on the East Coast first became acquainted with a campus at East
Lansing. Waters had been in the Air Corps, stationed in Greensboro,
North Carolina, when his company boarded a train heading north
on a hot day in August. By the time it passed Cincinnati, a recruit
turned to Waters.

"I know now where we're going. Michigan State."

"Where's that?" Waters asked.

"East Lansing."

Waters had heard of Michigan and Ann Arbor, but never of this
place called Michigan State. The train arrived later that day, a beautiful afternoon, and backed into a coal yard from which Waters'
company marched across a sparkling green campus to quarters at
Mason Hall. They marched to the MSU Auditorium, where MSU
President John Hannah welcomed them and presented awards to a
group—Waters received one for scoring 98 percent on an Air Corps
physical fitness test—that would train at MSC until December.

From there, Waters continued as a physical fitness instructor
on bases in Texas, Colorado, California, Washington and Missouri
until he was discharged in 1946. He had played football, basketball
and track at prep schools, including Choate, and had been invited
by Michigan Coach Fritz Crisler to visit the University of Michigan
if he ever returned to the state, which Waters had been doing since
meeting a Michigan State coed named Mary Lou Ginther.

Crisler wasn't in his office the day Waters stopped at Ann Arbor. An assistant coach suggested he fill out an application, but Waters, put off, decided to see if an old martial arts instructor at Michigan State might have some influence there. The instructor was not in, but Football Coach Charley Bachman was.

"I don't have any scholarships," Bachman said, "but why don't you come by in the spring."

Waters arrived for spring drills in 1946, 23 years old, married to Mary Lou, and not sure if an old Air Corps cadet was cut out for football with kids four and five years younger. On his first day at practice, Waters carried three times for three 80-yard touchdowns. Bachman came up with a scholarship.

He spent the summer of '46 mowing baseball diamonds and hauling bags of cement on his back as Michigan State's construction boom began. Waters lettered as a fullback his freshman year and quickly became close with Bachman, who would be gently pushed out of his job at the end of the year as Hannah brought on the impressive Syracuse Head Coach Biggie Munn. Waters and Bachman would remain close until Bachman's death in 1985, but Waters would see in Munn the most magnetic of coaching traits.

It was Munn's ability to motivate, it was his knack for the dramatic and emotional, that helped bind Waters spiritually to Michigan State. And it was Munn who Waters would try to emulate when he became head coach. No moment had so affected Waters as the day in 1947 when Munn, in his MSU debut, marched his team into Ann Arbor and lost, 55-0, to Fritz Crisler's Wolverines. Munn had been Crisler's line coach at Michigan, and Crisler wanted badly to smash the traitor who had since moved to Syracuse, and on to East Lansing.

Part of the punishment was a locker room with drains that had been stopped up—intentionally, believed Munn and his team—forcing players and coaches to step through several inches of water and filth. Waters was a sophomore, but he remembered the scene almost 40 years later as Munn's greatest moment. Biggie stood on a bench, tears running down his face.

"I've been humiliated, we've been humiliated," Munn said. "But if you're the kind of guys I think you are, we'll come back and have our day." It was the kind of patriot's emotion Waters would try and evoke when he became Michigan State's head coach, an appeal that was more effective in a vile locker room in Ann Arbor than it would be 33 years later in East Lansing.

Waters was never far from MSU's influence or benefits as he began his coaching career at several Michigan high schools. After working at Walled Lake High and Albion High—at a Michigan State-Notre Dame game Waters ran into a coach from East Jordan High named Dan Devine, who sat in the end zone diagramming Notre Dame's defenses—Waters went to Hillsdale College when the school persuaded Bachman to relocate and build a football program. Bachman said he would come only if Waters became his assistant, which Waters agreed to do in addition to becoming athletic director. A year later, Bachman gave it up and handed the job to 31-year-old Franklin Dean Waters.

He would win 30 consecutive games, become NAIA Coach of the Year in 1957, and build Hillsdale into a small-college power, often signing, through Munn/Daugherty connections, players MSU felt were not quite good enough to make the Big Ten grade. About the time a change in school presidents convinced him life would not be the same at Hillsdale, Saginaw Valley approached him in 1974, where he would stay until January of 1980 when Michigan State called.

Although MSU's fans and staff began warming toward him, first signs of trouble came early in 1980 when Waters and his staff holed up at a Kellogg conference center in Battle Creek to put in place Michigan State's offense. It was evident immediately to Pendry and others that the new head coach was not acquainted with a major-college system as sophisticated as MSU's needed to be. The Xs and Os, which Waters believed to be simplistic and universal, were at a higher level here. Sets, blocking schemes, technique— even the language was different. Waters became more a participant than a director as Pendry gravitated toward control he would hold until leaving for the pros in 1982.

Another problem was Waters' tendency to nod off during meetings, or worse, during recruiting visits. It was thought by the staff to be a medical problem, since Waters was obviously getting to bed at night and was not always working man-killing hours. But it became particularly unsettling when Waters followed assistants into the homes of recruits. There, they discovered, it was necessary to keep him involved directly in conversation, otherwise the lids would close and a crucial visit could turn into an embarrassing disaster.

Waters had a brief bout with low blood-sugar that he believed caused some of the drowsiness. But, his assistants, he always said, never understood that he had learned a yoga-like technique during his days at prep school. It enabled him to steal a few minutes sleep while remaining in touch with his surroundings —whether it was a football meeting room or a recruit's home.

When he was alert and refreshed, Waters could be an excellent salesman. He had an easygoing, comfortable, fatherly way that reassured parents and athletes uncertain about life on a large, intimidating campus. Waters smiled and in his gentle voice made a student population of 40,000 sound like a church group.

He could also be unorthodox. When Waters was working on Lansing Everett High star Tim Cunningham, he visited Cunningham at school and learned that Cunningham was a fine saxophone player. "Play the Spartan Fight Song for me," he told Cunningham, who led him to the music room, played the tune, and then signed a MSU tender.

For Waters, such schmaltzy moments were the means by which he would establish a bond between coach and player. There was something old-fashioned, warm and enchanting about a head coach weaving a sort of father-son relationship, and this, he believed, was precisely what would heal wounds and return Michigan State to glory. There needed to be a feeling of kinship, the way he had felt it with Bachman and Munn. He needed only to generate a sense of family and spirit. If that could happen, he told himself, MSU was bound to win.

Players, though, were less convinced. It wasn't Waters as much as it was staff that unnerved them. A few of the assistants were relying more on slogans and rhetoric than they were on nuts-and-bolts football technique that developing college athletes knew was essential to beating polished Big Ten teams.

In one of the early meetings with Dave Driscoll, players were introduced to an excitable, impassioned assistant who came at them like a Dale Carnegie speaker. "Champions will do the things losers refuse to do," he told them, reciting a litany of Gipper-style bromides and football adages. Players looked at each other, some giggling. It was unlike anything they had experienced, or thought they would experience, on a college football team. One day at practice Ted Guthard attempted some inspiration by smashing his bare head against a helmeted player.

The athletes were more amused than inspired. But it wasn't nearly as comical during drills, or at times when players knew the light stuff should cease in favor of brass-tacks football. It had been obvious to all of them that Sherm Lewis was running the defense, and Pendry the offense, with Pendry functioning much of the time as head coach. It was Pendry who was stepping in constantly to correct the ways in which other offensive assistants were coaching.

"Goddammit, how did this happen?" he would bark, exasperated at something going on in the line, in the backfield, wherever. Players began looking to him for direction and counsel on and off the field. He not only had the football know-how lacking in other staffers, but players liked the way he listenened and understood, they liked the down-home wit and Appalachian twang that went so comically with his off-the-wall comments and expressions.

Film sessions with Pendry could be uproarious. He would explode at a player, berating him for a stupid mistake, then a second later floor everyone with a wailing indictment that could be as crude as it was nonsensical. "Tank," he said to tight end Terry Tanker, who was half-jokingly complaining about the size of MSU's playbook, "I'm gonna put so many plays in, your mind's gonna spin like the knob on an outhouse door."

Tanker was the perfect Pendry straight man, setting him up for one Appalachian zinger after another, as on the day Tanker bragged drolly about his blocking talent.

"Tank," Pendry shot back, "you couldn't knock a sick whore off a toilet."

Waters was frustrated by Pendry's influence, but almost powerless to stop a man so obviously in control. Pendry had the command he and some outclassed assistants were lacking, and if it meant the team would play better, then everyone could swallow some pride. Waters was content to climb upon a tower and observe practices with bullhorn in hand. If he didn't like the way a play was run, it was a chance to get involved, to reinforce his authority.

"Bring it back, everyone do it again," he would bellow through the horn. Or, if he didn't like the way the team broke from the huddle, Waters would infuriate players and Pendry as the bullhorn blared: "Aw, come on, you guys can do better." He had seen Munn twirl his whistle and shout the same command a thousand times during his own playing days. It bothered Waters that Pendry was becoming so much of a ruler, during practice and at the coaches' office, and he resented the "headphone games" and body English Pendry would employ if he didn't like one of Waters' orders or suggestions. Waters interpreted the grimaces and gestures as showing up the head coach. Whatever, it hardly affected players who were getting the message in a variety of ways that Pendry was calling the shots more often than Waters.

By the time MSU opened its 1980 season at Illinois, there was a sidelines taffy-pull going on between head coach and Pendry on play selection. Several times early in the Illini game, Waters had called for a hook-and-hitch pass, which would send the wide receiver on a simple curl pattern, then, after grabbing the quarterback's pass, he would pivot and flip the ball to a trailing running back sprinting by at full speed.

Waters had told Pendry repeatedly he wanted it sent in. Pendry, calling the plays, ignored it. In the second quarter, Waters was mad:

"Joe, I want that play!" Pendry finally sent it to the huddle. Bert Vaughn threw complete to Ted Jones, who whirled and tossed to Steve Smith as Smith rambled down the sideline, past the MSU bench and into the end zone 46 yards for a touchdown. Waters had won this one, but Pendry's control of MSU's offense and general football know-how had made him the team's indisputable nerve center.

For as much as he had taken charge of the offense and, in effect, the team, there was a limit to Pendry's involvement. He simply could not be everywhere at once. The defense ran steadily under Sherm Lewis and his staff, but complex offensive technique was another matter, especially in the line. Frustration had been mounting since some of the returning veterans discovered in spring they were now second string, either for motivational reasons or because they weren't playing up to par in a system some were rebelling against.

MSU's offense had changed considerably from the drop-back days of Darryl Rogers, with emphasis now shifted to sprint-out passes. There were changes in blocking technique that linemen rejected because, they felt, the instruction consisted more of screaming and yelling than actual teaching. Players like Strata decided after a couple of weeks to go back to their old styles and ignore the barking from Dick Comar and others.

Inspiration remained the theme with Waters and several new staffers. The head coach had a fanciful idea of what Spartan football should be about—how it should embody pride, affection and a good time—and how it should be scripted. Before each practice he would call the team together and tell the players a joke. Often, it was a corny joke that would leave them shaking their heads at a style most thought comically incompatible with major-college football.

Practices, similarly, were a mixed bag of work, frustration, exasperation and, in better moments, satisfaction. There was a perpetual appeal to the players' hearts and minds that sometimes substituted for nuts-and-bolts instruction. Howard McAdoo, an energetic if not terribly gifted defensive tackle, was getting slammed during one practice by a guard-tackle tandem. He picked himself out of the dirt and turned to Ted Guthard.

"Hey, Coach," McAdoo yelled, "how do I get out of this double-team?"

Guthard turned to him.

"Howard," he said, sincerely, collecting his thoughts.

"Desire."

The players may have laughed and wondered how this quasi-comedy show would ever be a serious factor in the Big Ten race, but their initial attitude was to make the best of it. There was enough talent returning to expect at least a middle-of-the-pack season that might exceed their 5-6 finish in '79. Pendry and Lewis were experienced, reassuring and valuable not only at practice but in quiet, no-holds-barred conversations where they acknowledged the disorder and often got as much spiritual boost as the players.

It helped that Waters was regarded by nearly everyone as a nice man. Players frustrated by his sleeping and by the jokes and bull-horn bleatings still considered him a pleasant fellow. A week after the Illinois opener, won by the Illini, 20-17, on a closing-seconds field goal, Michigan State traveled to Oregon where Waters hoped to get his first MSU victory. A day before the game, coaches and players took raft rides down the Deschutes River. Waters ate hot dogs with the team and was in his element. It was the intimate, father-son kind of atmosphere he had wanted to strike between head coach and the kids. But the next day Michigan State lost, 35-7, as Vaughn went out with an injury and Leister became MSU's quarterback for the remainder of 1980.

Although Waters' 1980 team lacked depth in the line, it was otherwise respectable: Steve Smith and Derek Hughes stacked up as two of the conference's better backs until Hughes went out early with a torn knee. Strata and Mike Densmore were fine guards, while the defense was creditable, with Steve Maidlow, George Cooper, Smiley Creswell, Bernard Hay and Mike Marshall among the best of the starters.

But back-up talent was thin. By the time Hughes, Densmore and others got hurt, MSU had neither the talent nor the drive to beat even middle-rung Big Ten teams. Waters got his first victory in MSU's third game, 33-7, over Western Michigan, but close losses to Notre Dame and Michigan followed, and the Spartans won only two more games—Northwestern and Minnesota—to finish 3-8. It was Michigan State's worst record in 13 years and, at least internally, suggested things might get worse before they got better.

Senior players eventually began to look at practice as simply a matter of putting in their time. Offensive meetings that once had been broken down by position, soon became overall meetings so that Pendry could consolidate instruction and avoid the risks of letting some of the staff go one-on-one with position players. Coaches' meetings were also fragmenting. Sessions that should have lasted 20 minutes were dragging on for an hour or more as Waters permitted everyone to have his say on what tactics or technique should be applied.

The dark comedy continued. There was uneasiness at MSU's football banquet as a team and university tried to focus on whatever honor had come from a 3-8 season. The highlight was linebacker Gregg Lauble's impersonation of a chainsaw, a mouth-and-arm harmonization that had become a staple in the Spartan locker room. It was outrageous, broke up an audience of 1,200, and helped lighten the evening. So, unintentionally, did defensive tackle Bernard Hay when he approached the microphone to accept an award.

Hay said that playing for a miserable Michigan State team had instilled in him character, that he had benefited from "being humiliated each week in front of 76,000 people." His impassioned tribute to misery was such an embarrassingly honest appraisal of the season that most of the crowd chuckled as it squirmed.

One person not at all humored by 1980's developments was Doug Weaver. Waters had been his first, and most important, decision as athletic director, the move by which his stewardship was being measured in its first year. And he suspected that it had been a mistake. Meetings between him and Waters had suggested the new head coach was not major-college timber. He was aware of player sentiment and of the convoluted way in which Waters' staff was functioning. Pendry, he understood, had become a kind of de facto head coach. Still, Weaver thought some of the troubles would correct themselves in time. Believing that Waters and the program would benefit from a vote of confidence by the AD, he extended Waters' four-year contract by a year.

Weaver did it even though he knew MSU's fans were becoming more and more unsettled. Early reservations had not been erased by a 3-8 year, although it wasn't only fans who had grievances. Waters was growing slightly impatient with a budget he believed was shrinking. There had been signals that the Cecil Mackey-Ken Thompson hierarchy was pressuring Weaver to watch his dollars. In fact, the athletic department's business office had projected a $500,000 deficit for fiscal 1980-81—a projection that vanished when a heavy sum of unanticipated Big Ten TV revenue appeared.

But Weaver was chopping at Waters where he could, partly out of spite for what he believed were unnecessary expenses. He didn't believe Waters needed to recruit Hawaii and distant ports where MSU was getting talent no better than could be found at home. It was a factor in Weaver's decision that MSU bus rather than fly charters to games at Ohio State and Purdue.

Weaver had made the decision, in part, to send a symbolic message to Waters that he watch budgets that technically had been increased since Darryl Rogers departed. But the decision to bus became an internal disaster and a public relations smudge. Although there was never any evidence it cost MSU recruits, other schools were aware of Michigan State's busing policy. The real problems occurred after a game. Players angry over a defeat climbed aboard a bus for a five- or six-hour drive home, broken up only by a stop at a restaurant that often brought more trouble. Schedules were difficult to meet, which meant restaurant staffs weren't always ready with the food. Irritable players became even more cranky.

Budgets weren't nearly the threat staff squabbling became following Waters' first season. Pendry had given up hope that Guthard and Comar could competently handle the offensive and defensive lines and went to Waters not long after the season ended.

"We're going to have to fire two coaches," he said. "Comar and Guthard."

"Ted Guthard?" Waters shot back. Guthard, an old Spartan lineman who was a key to MSU's high school recruiting in suburban Detroit, was pleasant and industrious and seemed perfectly acceptable to Waters.

Word spread through the office that Pendry had put together a hit list. Comar learned he was on it and came to Waters.

"Muddy," he said, angry and embarrassed, "I'll make him eat those words. I'll know that offense inside and out next season."

A couple of nights later, very late, Lewis and Guthard showed up at Waters' home in Okemos. They wanted to know if Pendry was going to win. Lewis was upset that Pendry wanted to get rid of Guthard—one of Lewis' defensive staffers.

Waters calmed them.

"I'm not getting rid of anybody," he said. "Ted, you're safe. And Sherm, you're still the defensive coordinator on this team."

Waters had been trying to tone down Pendry, but tough talk wasn't easy for the head coach. It might have been more comfortable had Pendry been slipping up or been having trouble with players whom Waters so fiercely protected. But Pendry had a sharp football mind and solid rapport with athletes, and along with Lewis, was the only coach on MSU's staff with extensive major-college experience. The flaws were a little easier to overlook when Pendry had so many pluses.

Waters' coaching introduction to Division I football had proved to be more of a transition than either he or Weaver foresaw. There were so many details that a coach never experienced at a small college. Like college all-star games. Although a 3-8 Michigan State team was short on distinguished talent, the Spartans had several seniors—Steve Smith, Ray Stachowicz and Strata—who might have gone to a Senior Bowl or Blue-Grey Game had the head coach promoted them. But Waters didn't know until it was too late that it was a coach's job to arrange spots. There was a scramble at the end—even Darryl Rogers, now at Arizona State, tried to help a few of his former players—but the teams were set.

Recruiting was the next project for Waters and a staff that had snagged Carl Banks and Daryl Turner during the previous winter's two-week frenzy. Now, with a full slate of assistants free to work from the start, Waters thought his knowledge of state high schools and his gentle way with young athletes would mark the start of regular talent raids by MSU. It was Waters' plan to establish national pipelines to Florida, Cincinnati, Cleveland, Pittsburgh, Chicago and Los Angeles. He would plant spotters—Florida was his first set-up—and use private pilots to keep MSU coaches in contact with recruits.

There was also a color-coded map of the United States spread across a wall in the Duffy Daugherty Building. Colored tacks, inserted in the player's respective hometown, indicated in descending order whether the recruit was a blue-chip, green-chip or red-chip recruit. The eventual problem was that MSU found itself in line for too many red-chips and not nearly enough blue-chip talents. Particularly in-state.

Waters worked steadily that winter on Jim Scarcelli, a fine athlete from Warren Woods (Michigan) High who ultimately told Waters he was going to Michigan.

"They've got the reputation," he said.

Things at least appeared to be going well with Rick Rogers, a Wayne Memorial High star who next to Detroit Catholic Central's Aaron Roberts was considered the state's best running back. Just before the February 13 signing day, Waters had taken Rogers to breakfast.

"I'm gonna come to Michigan State," Rogers said. Waters was elated. With Steve Smith gone and Derek Hughes recovering from knee surgery, the Spartans had to recruit a top-drawer freshman who could start immediately. The next day, Roberts, who had turned down an invitation to visit MSU or even meet with Waters, ran into Rogers. There had been a change of mind. Rogers now was going to Michigan.

Roberts was uneasy. He had intended to sign either at Michigan or Notre Dame. But he had grade problems that made Notre Dame a longshot, and with Rogers now heading to a Michigan team that had a good crop of running backs, Roberts was caught. MSU Recruiting Coordinator Steve Schottel got word that Roberts was wavering and might listen to MSU if Waters could get to the Livonia home of Cadillac dealer Ed Pobur, whose son, Ed, was a teammate of Roberts.

Waters was in Chicago and learned his flight home would be diverted to Cleveland because of fog in Detroit. It was finally arranged that he fly from Chicago to Benton Harbor, Michigan, on a Whirlpool Corporation jet, then ride by limousine from Benton Harbor to the Pobur home, where Roberts was sequestered in the family rec room.

Waters was met at Benton Harbor by the limo and a full picnic basket which he munched from as the car sped to Livonia. Late that night, he arrived at the Pobur home where in the rec room Roberts was waiting. He told Waters that Notre Dame was his first choice, Michigan his second, but that grades and the Rogers decision were weighing on him.

"I don't know what to do," Roberts kept saying.

Pobur piped up: "Aaron, you've got to sign."

The next morning, WJR morning man J.P. McCarthy was discussing recruiting with Michigan's Bo Schembechler. McCarthy asked about Roberts, the hottest name among state high school recruits.

"We expect to sign him today," Schembechler said.

Waters grinned as the car moved west along I-96 bound for East Lansing. He had on the seat next to him a national letter of intent with Roberts' autograph.

Roberts' prospects were MSU's biggest box-office plus coming into the '81 season. Season ticket sales were down, and in the Spartans' opener against Illinois, only 54,945 turned out as Illinois romped, 27-17. It would go down as MSU's worst single-season attendance—63,591 average—since the probation years of '76-77. Roberts would be equally disappointing. On his first carry at Michigan State, he was hit hard and high by an Illini defender and lost three teeth. It was an omen for a player who would never become the premier Big Ten back expected when he fell into MSU's lap the previous February.

MSU's other bright light on offense—quarterback John Leister—would also fade early. Four weeks into the season MSU had won only once, a 10-7 escape against Bowling Green, and Leister had lost his job to a greatly improved and savvy Bryan Clark. Leister was a hot recruit out of Great Falls, Montana during the Darryl Rogers reign, an athlete who had an excellent arm that would, years later, make him a high-level pitching prospect with the Boston Red Sox. Leister's problem was his field sense. He tended to be reckless. Impulsive. He could throw the ball a mile, and often did—straight into the arms of a defender.

Bad decisions and poor defensive reads were chopping down his status with Pendry and with Waters, and by the time Notre Dame had stuck the Spartans with a 1-3 record, State had a new quarterback, Clark, whose emergence was as surprising as Leister's fall from grace. The son of Detroit Lions Coach Monte Clark had been a low-priority recruit in 1978 who was given a scholarship almost as a favor by Rogers, who was a friend of Clark's. Bryan Clark had come on in 1979 when Bert Vaughn was injured, but then, because his arm was not as strong, lost his job to Leister. But by the fall of '81, weight-room work had transformed Clark into a 6-foot-2, 200-pound quarterback who not only was throwing better, but promised MSU the smarts and poise Leister was lacking in game situations.

Pendry particularly liked the way Clark handled "check with me" plays. Pendry would feed him a choice of two, three or four plays, and depending on the coverage, Clark would audible the choice. He rarely missed a call. Years of growing up in a football atmosphere—his dad had played pro ball, worked as an assistant to Don Shula and coached the San Francisco 49ers—had given him an Xs and Os edge that complemented an arm that now was major-college.

Clark had a pair of 300-yard games, and the Spartans won three straight to get them out of '81 alive at 5-6. But the winning streak had come against doormat teams Indiana, Northwestern and Minnesota. Reality returned during a 36-7 closeout loss to Iowa.

Little had changed inside the MSU football offices, which somedays resembled a bus terminal in terms of clientele. Waters, the softie, wasn't one to shoo away visitors whether they had business there or not. A regular crew of hangers-on that included at least one person who had been institutionalized dropped into the office to sit or chat and while away the hours.

Office Secretary Mary Kay Smith often took several hours of dictation in which Waters might send five-paragraph letters to 10-year-olds who had written to him. Waters also enjoyed long lunches with friends or football acquaintances whose numbers were kept on cards in his office Rolodex. Getting away from the office was a necessary break for him, and often, it was nearly 3 p.m. before he returned.

Budgets, likewise, weren't as tight as the charter bus trips implied. A $600 phone intercom system was purchased and never used. A $20,000 computer was brought in but not fully utilized. A general looseness had developed from office through the player ranks, where assistant coaches were frustrated by the way in which Waters protected and coddled his team.

Lewis and Pendry would chew on a player for slipping up, only to see him take refuge with Waters, who would soothe and comfort and discuss the situation in a grandfatherly way. Waters once dictated to the office staff a list of rules and regulations that would be handed to players. He was asked whether drugs and alcohol were to be included.

"That's not necessary," he said. "No Michigan State athlete would ever do that."

The obsession with MSU's past, with a romantic notion of

Spartan football, gripped Waters. In a pre-game address at an opposing stadium, he would point to the showers and tell his players how he and his teammates had showered in that very area 34 years before. Or he might vow that, "If we go down, we'll be carried off on our shields." Most players groaned at the melodrama but viewed it as genuine Muddy.

By the start of MSU's 1982 season, Waters needed to show clear progress—tough in a year that opened with a six-gun schedule: Illinois, Ohio State, Miami (Florida), Notre Dame, Michigan and another strong Wisconsin team. The salvation figured to be personnel good enough to eventually send nine players to the NFL and nine more to the USFL.

But almost instantly it became nightmarish. There were seven consecutive losses—five of them by a combined 22 points. Morale was disintegrating by the day and on the field there were moments that approached open rebellion. In a devastating 24-22 loss at Miami, MSU in the fourth quarter intercepted a Hurricanes pass at the Miami nine. The Spartans had been controlling the line of scrimmage and were moving neatly on the ground, when in came a play from the sidelines: a reverse. With the action going right, Waters wanted his split end, Otis Grant, taking the handoff and moving left.

The huddle erupted when it was relayed from the bench. "Change it! You've gotta change that play!" one lineman screamed at John Leister, who was quarterbacking. The play went. Grant was dropped for no gain, and MSU missed a 23-yard field goal.

A 24-21 loss to Purdue on Homecoming gave State its first 0-7 record in 65 years and convinced even Waters that his three-year stay at Michigan State was about to end.

"I still think we can get it turned around, but I don't know if I'll get the chance now," he said. "There is just too much against me right now . . . too much sentiment . . . Maybe there's somebody better than me."

Weaver already was preparing for a change in coaches. With a month to go in the season he asked Waters to resign, but Waters said he had never quit a job and wasn't about to quit at Michigan State. A few days later MSU won its first game of the season, 22-14, over Indiana, then came home for what most thought would be a breather against Northwestern. But a last-minute transcontinental pass by the Wildcats gave them a 28-24 victory and led to an on-field display that became a portrait of a team's football despair. Carl

Banks, the All-American linebacker, ripped off his helmet, threw it against the concrete end-zone wall, and collapsed on the field, crying after Northwestern had pulled off its razzle-dazzle TD.

The Spartans' last shred of dignity was gone. A 26-7 beating of a demolished Minnesota team the following week did little to help the team's spirit, and did nothing for Waters' chances. On the flight home from Minneapolis, Weaver stopped to congratulate Waters, then asked him to stop by his office the next morning.

Just before his 10 a.m. meeting with Weaver, Waters told his staffers—Pendry had left in late summer for a job in the USFL—that it looked as though it was over. He drove to Jenison, walked into Weaver's office, and was given a choice of accepting a letter of resignation, or a statement explaining that MSU was not where it had hoped to be, and "in the best interests of Michigan State" Waters was being dismissed.

"I won't quit," Waters repeated. "What am I gonna tell those kids?"

Waters would leave with two years remaining on his contract calling for annual salary of $50,000. The meeting with Weaver lasted an hour, after which Waters shuffled out of the office, got into his car, and drove to Cowles House, home of MSU President Cecil Mackey. It was worth one last shot, Waters told himself.

Mackey, obviously embarrassed, was brief: He would have to abide by Weaver's decision. Waters went back to the office to give word to his staff. They looked indifferently at films of Iowa, the team which they would close against, and then at 10 p.m. Waters went home to tell his wife their dream job was about to belong to someone else.

Five

TOUGH STREETS, STEEL CURTAINS

Saturday afternoon. Almost 1 p.m. A few hours to himself after a week of standing over four linemen who had become the NFL's best defensive front of the 1970s. Saturday breathers were even more pleasant since George Perles discovered that on the hill where his home stood in Upper St. Clair, Pennsylvania, his car radio could pull in Michigan State's football games.

It would require some choreography, of course. To keep neighbors from growing suspicious toward a man sitting alone in his driveway, Perles would wipe off the dashboard, sweep the carpeting, empty ashtrays, pretend that he was cleaning the car as he sifted MSU's play-by-play from the static and fade-outs that were the price a man paid for keeping up on his old school and team.

There was no sense kidding himself. Pro football was George Perles' business, but Michigan State was his passion. As great as it was to be an assistant coach on a NFL dynasty, Perles would trade all the Super Bowl rings and diamonds for a chance to go back to Michigan State as head coach.

There was something about college ball that to Perles was more enduring, more personal than the pros. At least when it came to Michigan State. It never failed that on Sunday mornings at the pregame meal, the big conversation between Steeler coaches and players was what had happened during Saturday's college games. The gang made sure Perles caught it good if Michigan State had gone down.

"Notice your boys had it rough against powerful Northwestern," offensive coordinator Tom Moore might say, making sure the harpoon hit Perles harder than it hit Moby Dick. Digs were part of the fun of Sunday mornings.

Although he had left Duffy Daugherty's staff in 1971 to join Chuck Noll at Pittsburgh, Perles had never separated himself from Michigan State. He brought Noll to East Lansing to scout players like Kirk Gibson and Mark Brammer, and he was always talking to his old colleague and high school coach, Ed Rutherford, who was working at a variety of jobs in MSU's athletic department.

Summers, too, were a chance to catch up with the gang when Perles and his family drove through East Lansing on their way to northern Michigan. They would stop at the University Inn for a day, sitting by the pool, sipping drinks and eating pizza with Rutherford and any old-time buddies who had been with him as a player in the '50s, or as a coach from 1968-71. Getting back to East Lansing was a powerfully emotional experience for a man who had played at MSU, graduated from there, met his wife on campus, and seen two of his children born in that same town.

To be head coach there was the dream. Not even the Steelers top job could compare to being in charge at Michigan State.

Noll understood the attachment. He wanted his assistants to have a crack at quality head-coaching jobs, and if it happened at their alma mater, then all the better. Noll wasn't sure how good a chance Perles stood in 1976, after Denny Stolz had been fired, but Perles at least had an interview the first week of April.

It proved to be little more than a courtesy. Joe Kearney, Michigan State's new athletic director, was from the West Coast and had his own people in mind. Moreover, old-line MSU people weren't especially appealing at a time when even MSU's executives thought it time to broom any trace of personnel from the Spartans' old Munn-Daugherty-Stolz era. Kearney, as expected, chose another West Coaster, San Jose State's Darryl Rogers. Perles returned to Pittsburgh and got busy on another Super Bowl season.

The head coaching itch would increase during Perles' next four years in Pittsburgh. Noll was doing his best to help, giving Perles the title of Assistant Head Coach as an added drawing card, but other than a shot at coaching the Baltimore Colts that never materialized, there had been few opportunities to leave for a job that was significantly better than his position with the Steelers. Until, of course, January of 1980.

Perles had heard rumors that Rogers was leaving Michigan State. The whispers got stronger as the Steelers set up in Los Angeles to play the Rams in Super Bowl XIV. Perles and Steelers assistant Dick Hoak were sitting in their hotel room early in the week when George Dyer, Rogers' defensive coordinator, stopped by to say hello during a trip in which he had been scouting California's junior-college talent.

"Just got called home," Dyer told Perles and Hoak. "I think Darryl's leaving."

It was announced later in the day that Rogers and Kearney were heading to Arizona State in a stunning package deal that had at least temporarily blown to pieces a football program that, in spite of a 5-6 finish in '79, had recovered from the probation sentence of 1976.

It might have been Super Bowl week for the Steelers, but Perles' mind was spinning. He knew that a Michigan State man who got barely a look four years earlier would seemingly have it better now that two outsiders had bolted for greener grass. What he didn't realize was the extent to which his name was popping up from Detroit to the West Coast.

Lansing-East Lansing support already was building among a group of sharp businessmen who had come to L.A. for the game. Bob Viney, a Spartan defensive end during the '60s and now an East Lansing restaurateur, was there, along with Joel Ferguson and Greg Eaton, two of Lansing's better-known movers and shakers. Perles knew them well and had helped them get tickets to the game and passes to a few of the ritzier Super Bowl functions.

It was a couple of days later that Joe Greene, the Steelers' great lineman, mentioned to Perles that Ferguson had been asking questions, wondering about Perles' interest in the MSU job, Perles' strengths, the basic profile of a man who seemed ideal for the Michigan State job. A day later, *Detroit News* columnist Joe Falls spoke with Perles and wrote that the Steelers assistant could give MSU the psychological boost and recruiting know-how Michigan State obviously needed.

Channel 4's Al Ackerman followed. During Super Bowl week Perles had helped Detroit's best-known television sports anchor set up interviews with several players from the state of Michigan. Ackerman, too, thought Michigan State would be wise to hire a coach whose NFL credentials and MSU background made him such an appealing candidate.

Following Pittsburgh's 31-19 victory over the Rams in one of the Super Bowl's classic games, Perles was cornered by broadcasters and writers anxious to sound him out on the MSU job. He hadn't been contacted, Perles explained, but he was interested. Absolutely.

He was now the clear front-runner, in the eyes of media and the public. Falls had essentially endorsed him. Jerry Green, also a *Detroit News* columnist, was pushing Perles. The *Detroit Free Press* was following him. Ackerman came back from L.A. convinced Perles was right for MSU, and said so on the air. Downtown Lansing, fueled by the Ferguson-Eaton initiative, joined in.

Perles went back to Pittsburgh and waited for a follow-up that came later in the week when Doug Weaver, hired as athletic director only a day earlier, called Perles to see if the man he once coached as a freshman might want to discuss coming home.

Perles met Weaver at the airport that night and the two went to dinner at a nearby Holiday Inn. The session was warm, Perles keeping the tone upbeat, saying this was a team that could be brought back to Top 20 status by hard work and the kind of effective recruiting that could be delivered by a man who had coached and grown up in Detroit.

Media focused on Perles as word came of the interview. There seemed to be no other serious candidates. Sherm Lewis, an assistant since the Daugherty days, had been interviewed, but Lewis did not excite a community that more and more was crying for Perles. Rollie Dotsch, another old Spartan who had been coaching in the pros, also wanted the job and was getting some attention. But Weaver never called.

By the end of the weekend, only a couple of weeks before high school recruits could sign national letters of intent, it appeared that George Perles would return to Michigan State as leader of a football program that needed a morale boost as much as it needed a proven coach and recruiter. On Monday, Perles was still the hot name, and by Tuesday morning, the day Weaver would announce his choice, it was clear to everyone—even to a husband and wife back in Pittsburgh—that Perles would be named.

Shortly after 1 p.m. on January 29, 1980, Weaver gave the go-ahead to Fred Stabley Sr. and Nick Vista, MSU's sports information team, to call wire services with the announcement. Minutes later it rolled across wire machines in every media agency in the state.

Curt Sylvester of the *Detroit Free Press* was first to phone Perles with the word that Muddy Waters of Saginaw Valley State College was Michigan State's new head football coach.

Inside the home on the hill in Upper St. Clair, it was as if a bomb had exploded. But amid the shock and crushing disappointment, Perles' voice was clear.

"Well," he told Sylvester, "I want to congratulate Muddy and wish him the very best. He's a good man and he'll get my full support."

Perles was stunned. Muddy Waters? He hadn't even been mentioned. What had happened? How could there have been such build-up, only to see a job he wanted so badly pulled away so cruelly?

Perles was handling it better than Sally. She was in tears—not so much because of any personal disappointment, but because she knew what the job meant to a husband whose composure impressed everyone, Weaver included.

He had intended to give Perles the news, personally, but couldn't get through phone lines tied up by so many media callers. When he did reach Perles, the man who had been turned down simply thanked Weaver for the consideration and promised his support and help. Perles had vowed from the instant he got the news that there would be no bitterness, no bad-mouthing, no burning of bridges. He would remain above it no matter how better-equipped or qualified he believed he had been for the job.

Besides, he told himself, the Steelers were coming off another NFL championship and there surely would be other opportunities— better, even, than Michigan State would have been. His name was now out there and would undoubtedly resurface whenever a coaching vacancy occurred and a candidates list was drawn up. He reminded himself of Chuck Noll's First Commandment: "If a person stays clean and keeps his mouth shut, good things will happen."

He told himself, too, that the Michigan State job in 1980 might not be the best position for a coach wanting long-term security. Perles felt better a few weeks later when he met Duffy Daugherty at the airport and drove his old boss to a coaching clinic in Pittsburgh.

"George, be glad you didn't get that job," Daugherty said. "You can't win there now. A composite of Bear Bryant and Amos Alonzo Stagg couldn't win there now—not this soon after probation. The squad's so depleted in talent. Muddy has no chance. Next time around it'll come your way, and then it'll be a much better situation."

There would be two more seasons at Pittsburgh, two more autumns of carrying a whisk broom out to the car on Saturday afternoons, two more years during which Perles would wonder if he ever would become a head coach, or simply carry on as a career assistant in the NFL.

In the spring of 1982, Perles and the Steelers were attending a benefit golf outing at Uniontown, Pennsylvania. When he called Sally that night to tell her he would miss dinner, she mentioned that John Ralston, the old NFL and college head coach, had left a message for George to call him back. Perles knew that Ralston was helping the new United States Football League secure and set up franchises. He guessed that the new Michigan Panthers entry was interested in talking with him.

He called Ralston that evening.

"George," Ralston said, "Myles Tanenbaum and the Philadelphia Stars are interested in talking with you about becoming head coach there."

Perles was surprised that it wasn't Al Taubman's Panthers franchise that had called, but he told Ralston he would be interested.

The new pro football league that was going to try and make it as a spring-summer novelty was a curious experiment that Perles realized might not make it. But he understood enough about the USFL to know that it was going to be well-financed, at least to the point of guaranteeing contracts. It was worth looking into.

Tanenbaum called soon afterward and arranged to meet Perles at an airport hotel in Pittsburgh. Already, a friend of Tanenbaum's had visited in South Bend with ex-Notre Dame Coach Ara Parseghian, inquiring of a man who knew coaches what he thought of George Perles. Parseghian endorsed him.

At the hotel in Pittsburgh, Tanenbaum and Perles talked for two hours about the league, the job, Perles' football philosophy, about the way in which the Stars would be structured. Tanenbaum said he would get back in a couple of weeks.

Ten days later, he called Perles and offered the job. Perles would receive a three-year contract with escalating salary totaling $400,000. He would receive a percentage of the gate, and there would be cars and additional fringes. His contract would be a personal contract with Tanenbaum that would protect Perles in case the league folded.

A 47-year-old man at a career crossroads had an easy decision. His $69,500 Steelers salary included a handsome Super Bowl bonus. There was considerably more money with the Stars, he had an ironclad contract, and best of all, he would now become a head coach after 17 years of working as a college and NFL assistant. It was time to try it at Philly.

Perles arrived in the Stars office on July 7, 1982, but not before he endorsed his old MSU friends and NFL assistant coaching colleagues—Rollie Dotsch and Hank Bullough—for other jobs in the USFL. Dotsch would go on to coach at Birmingham, while Bullough was being pursued by the Michigan Panthers until Paul Brown, owner of the Cincinnati Bengals, refused to free Bullough from his Cincinnati contract.

Perles was convinced that the day MSU turned him down in 1980 was the day he lost any chance, ever, for the head coaching job at Michigan State. It was one of the considerations made when he took the Stars job, and it was one reason why he didn't mind asking Joe Pendry, MSU's offensive coordinator whom he had recommended to Waters in 1980, if Pendry were interested in joining his staff at Philadelphia. Pendry did. Steve Furness, one of his old Steelers linemen, also came aboard, as did Larry Bielat, his MSU teammate and longtime friend.

The USFL season was still eight months away, but Perles enjoyed the building and shaping of a coaching staff. He liked having the freedom to put ideas and philosophy into effect minus the constraints that came with being an assistant. As for Michigan State, it belonged to an earlier chapter in his life. It was behind him. It was history.

Almost.

Perles could see that things were coming apart at East Lansing. You couldn't lose as many games as MSU was losing in 1982 (a 2-9 finish) and not have a shake-up at some level. But it didn't make any difference, professionally, since even if Muddy Waters were fired there would be no interest in a man who was once turned down and who now was head coach of a team that had yet to play its first game.

On November 14, 1982, Weaver fired Waters following a road trip at Minnesota. Perles began getting jittery but never publicly said a word to anyone. It was ridiculous, he thought, to even entertain an idea as crazy as George Perles returning to East Lansing.

He noticed, though, in the days that followed that no heavyweight candidates seemed to be emerging. There were no real favorites for the Michigan State job. Still convinced that Weaver would pick someone reputable from the outside, Perles minded his own business and got busy preparing for a training camp that would open in eight weeks.

He was all but crawling out of his skin as he returned home to Pittsburgh for Thanksgiving. Perles still had made no mention of his interest, had not called Weaver or anyone at MSU, but the longer the coaching search went on without the establishment of any clear front-runners, the more Perles began thinking that maybe 1980 hadn't been his last shot, after all.

On Sunday following Thanksgiving, Perles was still in Pittsburgh trying to relax and watch that afternoon's NFL games. He was also hoping the phone would ring. Unable to stand it any longer, he finally decided Sunday evening to call Weaver at his home in Okemos. Nancy Weaver explained that her husband was gone, but would get back to Perles the next morning.

The call came as promised on Monday, and Perles didn't waste any time. He would be interested in the job if Weaver were interested in talking. Weaver listened, somewhat surprised that a man once spurned and now employed as a head coach would still have MSU on his mind. He said he would call Perles in Philadelphia later in the week. The call came on Tuesday. Weaver would not do anything until after Wednesday night's Detroit banquet, although he could catch an early flight out of Detroit that would put him in Philadelphia at 11 a.m.

Perles was there to meet him. They got a suite under aliases that might help them dodge snooping reporters, then got busy, each anxious to get on with a deal that both knew should have been tied up three years earlier. Weaver's first concern was Tanenbaum, the Stars owner. Perles thought it an incidental matter because of a verbal agreement he believed he had with Tanenbaum concerning any future opportunities at Michigan State. Perles said he would handle it.

At 8 p.m., more than eight hours after they began negotiating, Weaver and Perles had agreed on a five-year contract that would make Perles the highest-paid coach in the Big Ten at base salary of $95,000. It was nearly $40,000 less than he was making with the Stars, but it would be worth a thinner paycheck to finally have the job he had wanted for so many years. Weaver said they had a deal if Tanenbaum approved.

They left the room and Perles called Tanenbaum at his home. Myles was gone, it was explained, to a fund-raiser at the University of Pennsylvania but would be home later. Perles, who had barely eaten all day, went to Charley's restaurant for some dinner and finally reached Tanenbaum at 10 p.m.

Perles explained that he had been offered the job at Michigan State and would take it. It was a cruel thing to leave the Stars at this point, he acknowledged, but as he had indicated before to Tanenbaum, the MSU job had been a career dream.

"You know, George, I'd never stand in your way," Tanenbaum said. "I want the best for you."

Perles, exhilarated, went to his apartment—Sally and the family were to have moved to Philadelphia from Pittsburgh as soon as a house deal was closed—which he was sharing with Bielat and Furness. Each had a two-year contract with the Stars, but Perles wanted both men at Michigan State if they were interested. They agreed on moving and celebrated into the early hours.

It was after 2 a.m. when Tanenbaum, minus any of the goodwill that marked their earlier conversation, phoned Perles. He was angry, upset and threatening legal action. A contract was a contract and Michigan State was making a mockery of an agreement he and Perles had made in good faith. Perles was chilled. Any contesting of his and Weaver's arrangement could cause the job, again, to explode in his face. Perles agreed to meet Tanenbaum and Stars General Manager Carl Peterson at lunch the next day.

Tanenbaum was a lawyer who had become wealthy in shopping-mall construction and was not accustomed to defeats nor serious setbacks. He knew his rights and he made it clear to Perles he could use the courts to hold Perles to his contract.

"Just stay for the first season," Tanenbaum said, "and then go to Michigan State in time for the fall."

Tanenbaum did not understand that getting started on recruiting was the critical priority for any new coach.

"George, what do you want?" Tanenbaum went on. "Money's no object."

"Myles, there's nothing monetarily that you could do that would keep me from taking that job," Perles said. "Any other job and it would be different. But I met my wife there. Two of my kids were born there. My mother's 90 minutes away, and my father-in-law's three hours away. I've got to have that job."

Pleadings and explanations had hit the boiling point. Perles could see the dream crumbling if Tanenbaum didn't understand how much Michigan State meant, if he threatened anything that might sabotage the delicate phone negotiations between Weaver and MSU executives. Tanenbaum, similarly, had invested heavily in a football franchise that did not need a coaching change a month before training camp opened. Furthermore, to him this was a matter of ethics and principle. Michigan State had raided his coaching office and never so much as asked permission to speak with him.

The debate carried on, into the parking lot, as the men left.

"Myles," Perles went on, becoming almost frantic, "I'm going to East Lansing if I have to walk there."

Tanenbaum understood Perles' affection for MSU. The two men had gotten along beautifully since their first meeting, and Tanenbaum would not crush a job opportunity that meant so much to Perles. They hugged, the bitterness giving way to genuine sentiment. Perles drove back to the apartment and Bielat then took him to the hotel where Weaver was carrying on contract discussions with Ken Thompson. Perles' huge salary would be a political risk, but palatable at a point MSU needed to show its rank-and-file it cared about football. Bringing Perles to town would be in everyone's long-term interests, financially and athletically, they said.

Perles assured Weaver he was free to go, and the contract was approved in East Lansing. Perles, though, would regret for years the assumption that he and Tanenbaum had a verbal agreement that would preclude any hard feelings on the part of the Stars owner. And later that day, when Tanenbaum announced he would seek compensation from MSU for taking his head coach, MSU would realize that salary might not be the only costs involved in bringing George Perles to MSU. Heavy legal bills and an eventual $175,000 settlement awarded Tanenbaum would push the complete Perles investment to nearly $1 million.

Money wasn't the immediate concern in East Lansing, nor in Philadelphia as word came that George Perles was MSU's new head football coach. After he and Weaver spoke, Perles called Sally at the home they were getting ready to move from.

"We're leaving Pittsburgh, but we're not going to Philly," he told her. "We're going to East Lansing."

Perles caught a plane for Detroit and was met at Metro Airport by his old friend, Ed Rutherford, who would become Perles' administrative assistant. Minutes after he walked from the plane Perles was at a pay phone calling Shane Bullough, a prep All-American at Cincinnati Moeller High who was the son of his old friend Hank Bullough; and Pat Shurmur, a fine All-Stater from Dearborn (Michigan)

Divine Child, who was the nephew of NFL assistant Fritz Shurmur. Recruiting could not wait even a day.

A press conference at Kellogg Center the following day showed Perles to be smoother and more polished than his reputation suggested. He also looked good. Dieting and regular jogging had pruned nearly 50 pounds from the man Pittsburgh fans had taken to calling "Georgie Porgie" during his more rotund days. But it was what he said that impressed and enthused the fans. Perles spoke of making the Rose Bowl his first priority. He saw no reason why Michigan State shouldn't be controlling in-state recruiting, and doing better in the rich preplands of Ohio and western Pennsylvania.

Above all, he said, making sure the message was heard loud and clear, Michigan State could do it not only legally, but by paying special attention to academics, family values, and even by instilling good manners in its players. He headed off the fears felt by some that he was a flashy NFL man who would quickly put MSU back on probation, saying that it was stipulated in his contract that cheating would get him and his staff fired. There would be no monkey business at a university that was just beginning to shake off the long-term consequences of probation.

Putting together a coaching staff was the next assignment. Bielat and Furness already were committed, while Buck Nystrom, the old Spartan All-American who was now at Colorado, had called the football office only hours after Perles was named head coach. Nystrom would come aboard, as would Nick Saban, a young defensive specialist Perles had gotten to know during Saban's years at Navy and Ohio State. Norm Parker, another old acquaintance with years of experience, would be hired, as would Charlie Baggett, MSU's quarterback during the mid-'70s, who was interested in coming home, and who was doing a solid job recruiting for the University of Minnesota. Ted Guthard would remain as the only holdover from Waters' staff, Steve Beckholt would stick as recruiting coordinator, and Billy Rademacher, the former coach at Northern Michigan, would also be added.

They now could begin gluing together a football program that was in ragged shape, physically and psychologically. It was apparent immediately as Perles watched films that Michigan State would have trouble in the offensive and defensive lines. There was neither size nor athletes good enough to handle the brutes populating America's better programs.

It was also clear to him, from feedback he had received, and from observation, that MSU's players needed to taste a bullwhip. There was a lackadaisical, do-it-if-we-want-to air that would have to be eliminated immediately.

From the moment Perles called his first team meeting, players knew it would be different. As opposed to Waters, who was inclined to wear sweaters and more casual clothing, Perles met the team dressed in sport coat and tie. There was silence in the Duffy Daugherty Building's main meeting room as Perles explained that winter conditioning would be rigorous and should be treated as high-priority time by anyone wanting to stay, not necessarily play, on Michigan State's football team.

It was deliberate strategy by a head coach who had learned as a schoolteacher that if you came in strong, you could later ease up and suffer no consequences. But to try and do it the other way— especially in a situation where nice-guy tactics had not worked— would be suicidal.

Perles ordered 7 a.m. running drills five days a week, with doubleheader agility workouts to be included on at least two after- noons weekly. Whether it could compensate for MSU's lack of per- sonnel was something even Perles doubted. The cupboard was look- ing awfully bare as he sized up MSU's offense and defense. Jim Rinella, a 5-foot-10 walk-on, would start at one defensive end. Mark Napolitan, another walk-on, would obviously be MSU's starting center.

The only running back was Aaron Roberts, who had been some- thing of a bust since arriving in 1980. Dave Yarema had started two games at quarterback as a freshman, but was lacking the kind of experience an offense needed. Daryl Turner was an exceptional wide receiver, there were a few defensive backs, and Carl Banks was as fine a linebacker as you could want. But beyond them, you were looking at a second-division football team.

All the more critical, Perles realized, that Michigan State get rolling with the recruiting. His experience as a Detroit high school coach and his personal pledge to re-establish MSU's in-state recruit- ing dominance were main planks in the Perles platform, and now, with only 60 days to duke it out with a University of Michigan team fresh from the Rose Bowl, Perles had to deliver.

It would help that Shurmur and Bullough were committing early. Shurmur was one of the true in-state prizes, while Bullough had the kind of regional and national clout to bring out-state credibility to a recruiting crop. Dave Houle and Mark Ingram were other in-state recruits who would sign with MSU, and that was good enough for a head coach who thought the best way to take on a dominant University of Michigan was with a punch in the nose.

"We knocked their socks off," Perles announced. "I think we're back in control in Michigan."

Perles had noticed when he arrived as head coach that there was a meek attitude in East Lansing regarding the rivalry with Michigan. True, the Wolverines had been cleaning up in the series, and in most years were Rose Bowl contenders and Top Ten material, but Perles thought Michigan State's inferiority complex was nonsense. MSU could and would compete, he told the world, and if getting the point across meant you had to fire up the congregation, then so be it. But it was questionable wisdom on a frosty February day when the University of Michigan was hinting that Perles could have all the players he wanted from an in-state talent crop that was on the thin side.

Perles' style within the university circle was more diplomatic and, consequently, more reassuring to those who remembered him during his early MSU days as a hard-boiled, shot-and-beer type from Detroit's tough, southwest-side neighborhood. Perles was exceedingly polite, was not above anyone, spoke with warmth and enthusiasm to groups on and off campus, and kept his bosses happy by constantly mentioning and crediting them for supporting a generously funded football program.

He was also adopting a personal credo toward MSU football that began to ring thin in later years. The priorities at Michigan State, he told one and all, repeatedly, would be (1) family, (2) academics and (3) football.

"You're all tired of hearing this," he would say, "but that's the way it's going to be here."

Winning, though, was another element that fans assumed Perles would address. It was a reasonable expectation, Perles thought, although it was a sure thing that fans weren't seeing the same things on film, and at spring practice, that told him MSU would need a lengthy reconstruction.

Beating the junior college bushes had at least provided MSU with a respectable running back, Carl Butler. But no matter how well his Stunt 4-3 defense worked, no matter how skillfully a sophomore quarterback might play, Perles had inherited an undersized, undernumbered team that he suspected was going to take its lumps.

Through the first two weeks of the season it seemed about everyone had underestimated what a new coach could do with personnel that was at least competitive. Colorado fell, 23-17, in the opener—neither Biggie Munn, Daugherty, Denny Stolz, Darryl Rogers nor Waters had won their debut games—and the following Saturday it was Notre Dame tumbling in a major upset at South Bend, as Phil Parker intercepted a batch of passes to help the Spartans win, 28-23. Daryl Turner had grabbed two touchdown passes from Yarema, tight end Butch Rolle had snared another, and if Carl Banks wasn't putting the Irish offense in a hole, Ralf Mojsiejenko was with several thundering punts.

East Lansing hadn't been so revved up over a football team since 1978. It hadn't been so universally pleased with a football coach in at least as long, and it had effectively shushed the critics who still complained about Perles' big salary. Back home the following week, MSU was leading Rose Bowl-bound Illinois until a shoulder separation knocked Yarema from the game, and from the '82 season. Illinois came back to win, and the Spartans were now looking at quarterback problems that would disable them for the season, transforming a promising 2-0 start into a 4-6-1 finish that at least suggested better things to come.

It wasn't so much stability on the field as it was stability in the office that convinced staffers Perles would be alright in East Lansing. If a meeting started at 8 a.m., it started not a tick later. Dealings with players and any form of team meetings were schedule priorities that could not be changed for anything short of personal funerals.

It amused a few of the office insiders to hear Perles continue with his "family first" spiels when anyone who had tried to book a family vacation discovered it depended heavily on what was, or was not, convenient to the staff calendar.

There were other elements to the Perles personality and lifestyle that didn't always add up. Legend had it that he had been known to patronize a few saloons during his days as player and coach, but rather than hightail it for Dagwood's following his work day, Perles as head coach was avoiding bar stops. It wasn't a matter of drinking—he liked to have a Scotch and water at home—but it was smart administrative policy.

"Loose lips sink ships," he would say.

It was also curious to see that a man who reveled in a man's world, who didn't care for women trainers invading team meetings or areas, could adapt so naturally to a role as household domestic. Perles often would clean the kitchen on Saturday mornings during the off-season, or wash several loads of clothes. It was only a matter of pitching in and helping Sally do things for which he had the same ability. Logical, thought Perles.

It was also consistent with a man whose home was indeed his castle. Inviting friends into the home was the ultimate gesture of respect and friendship, he believed. Serving a home-cooked Lithuanian dinner was another way in which guests were paid homage, and it was nothing Perles thought should be taken lightly by hosts nor visitors.

It was protecting his home and his family that made Perles so intent on taking care of their futures. Part of his contract at Michigan State included a substantial insurance policy for Sally and his kids. If he went suddenly—the death of Wisconsin Coach Dave McClain due to a heart attack in 1986 only reinforced Perles' feelings—he would at least make sure the family was safe from any financial worries.

How much of the Perles philosophy, the ethic, originated in that plain-Jane neighborhood near Tiger Stadium no one could measure. But he carried with him throughout his coaching career the reputation as a street-wise, block-tough veteran of an ethnic neighborhood whose values Perles proudly subscribed to. Friendship. Honor. Loyalty. Decency. You found it all, Perles thought, down on Vernor Highway, the place where moral or physical washouts were bound to be bloodied if they dared show their face.

Until 1951, when the family moved to a house in Allen Park, the Perleses lived at 7728 Pitt Street, Apartment 2, in one of Detroit's typical blue-collar neighborhoods. George's father, Julius, had come from Wilkes-Barre, Pennsylvania, and worked in the payroll department at Ford Motor Company. His mother, Nellie, was a housewife and superb cook who did her best to smooth and polish one of the neighborhoods most respected—even feared—tough guys. George Perles and Kevin McGuffigan. They were the two you did not want to challenge; two friends who could lick anyone around and, fortunately, never had to prove to the other who was toughest in this predominantly Irish neighborhood.

St. Peter's Church was the Lithuanian parish to which the Perles family belonged, but George was educated at public schools, at Harms Elementary, Wilson Intermediate, and at Western High. Sports interest and ability developed early. He was a catcher on the neighborhood Billy Rogell League team, and later a left-fielder on the gang's fast-pitch softball club, with a throwing arm more feared than his batting stroke. Football was another matter. No real weaknesses there, as he and Joe Carruthers at Western High became the best guard tandem in the state.

Sports were the main diversion in the old neighborhood, but not the only one. Perles and Jim Teets and the guys often, to make a few bucks, washed cars on Saturdays—scrubbing them up, then drying them off by taking the cars for a spin that might include a quick stop at Wesburn Golf Course. It was clean work that might be worth $10—big money in the early '50s when Friday nights were spent bowling at the old Beacon Lanes, where Julius often joined them for a game of pool. Or it might be a stop at Sammy's Pizzeria on Vernor where the crowds from Holy Redeemer, Western and Southwestern high schools congregated for entertainment, and often, for fisticuffs.

Fighting simply went with the turf. And as the gang looked back on it years later they would marvel at how clean and decent it had seemed back then. There was never any serious violence, never any guns or stabbings or ugly beatings. If you got whipped, fine. You'd get 'em next time. And you went home.

By his senior year at Western, Perles' reputation as a bull of an offensive lineman was earning him offers from Notre Dame, Michigan State, Michigan, Ohio State and Indiana. Perles and a Western teammate, Joe Selasky, decided to sign together at Tennessee. Their linemate, Joe Carruthers, was to join them there the following year, although circumstances later would persuade Carruthers to choose MSU.

Perles and Selasky decided not long after they arrived at Knoxville that neither Tennessee nor school was terribly appealing. Selasky left after only a few days, while Perles stayed the first quarter and completed 12 credits. He returned to Detroit and joined 14 others from the neighborhood for a mass Army enlistment.

While Perles was playing Special Services football in Hawaii, Daugherty and Alabama Coach Bear Bryant stopped in Honolulu for a football clinic on their way home from a trip to Japan. Daugherty, remembering Perles' reputation at Western, asked him to consider Michigan State when he was discharged, which Perles did when he came home in March of 1956.

Perles only hoped that a lean Army veteran who weighed 175

pounds might have an edge on the tenderfoot-freshmen who seemed more interested in Elvis than in smashing a few facemasks. It was looking good through a freshman season during which Perles played as a two-way tackle. Midway through his junior year he was a starter on Daugherty's varsity until the show closed on November 1, 1958, a 9-7 loss to Wisconsin at East Lansing. Perles was blocked during punt coverage and ripped ligaments in his knee. End of career.

If anything good came from the wrecked knee, it was Perles' sudden understanding and resolve that he needed to become career-minded. He had married Sally Bradford soon after arriving at MSU, on October 29, 1956, and children were now on the way. It made sense to someone captivated by the Daugherty aura and by MSU's campus charm that education and coaching be his focus, especially when it was Daugherty urging him to become a coach. He would get an undergrad degree in physical education in 1960, then work as a student assistant on the freshmen squad while earning his masters in 1961.

He was ready now in '61 to flee the MSU-Daugherty circle and to make it—or not make it—as a football coach. High schools were the natural starting point for a 27-year-old man anxious to find out for himself whether he had the ability and organizational touch that coaching demanded. An assistant's job at St. Rita High in Chicago—Chicago's Catholic League was considered the best high school football system anywhere—was the job Daugherty endorsed and helped him land, and after a year in Chicago, the MSU connection promoted Perles for a plum: The St. Ambrose High head coaching job, where over the next three seasons Perles teams twice would go undefeated and win a pair of Catholic League championships.

His apprenticeship completed, Perles was ready when John McVay, an assistant under Daugherty from 1962-64 who was now head coach at Dayton, offered him a spot on the Flyers staff. Perles borrowed a few chapters from the MSU defense now being run by his buddy, Hank Bullough, and helped a previously sour Flyers team win eight games in McVay's second season. Two years later, Daugherty was on the phone wondering if Perles might care to join his staff in East Lansing.

It was the easiest choice an assistant coach could make. Michigan State was home. Daugherty, in so many ways, remained his idol. MSU, too, was coming off the great '66 season and Daugherty continued to turn out head coaches by the load. To be back in East Lansing at age 33 was the best move, personally and professionally, Perles could imagine.

What he didn't envision was the collapse of Daugherty's mid-'60s dynasty. From the 3-7 tumble in '67, MSU would finish 5-5, 4-6, 4-6 and 6-5 during Perles' five seasons as an MSU assistant. It hadn't helped that Denny Stolz, the former head coach at Alma (Michigan) College, had been hired as a high-salaried defensive coordinator for a '71 season during which Perles remained in day-to-day control of MSU's defense. It meant that Perles could listen to a pro coaching offer that friends like Hank Bullough—who was now with the Baltimore Colts—thought would be a natural.

In the spring of 1971, Perles was showering following a workout during the final week of spring drills. The locker-room phone rang. Chuck Noll was calling from Pittsburgh wondering if Perles might be interested in applying for an assistant's job. Perles was enthused. Bullough—who had suggested Perles to Noll—had nothing but good things to say about the low-key man who appeared to be resurrecting one of the NFL's more pathetic franchises.

Perles flew to Pittsburgh and met Noll the following day for lunch and interviews at Three Rivers Stadium. They discussed family, money—Perles was making $13,900 as a MSU assistant—and football. It was looking good as Noll took him through an area where most of the Steelers assistants lived, explaining to Perles that he needed to speak with only one other candidate, Dan Radakovich from Penn State. Perles returned home in time for the Saturday Green and White intra-squad game.

On Monday, Noll called with word that he was going with Radakovich, who had more experience with linebackers. But hold on, Noll told Perles. By the end of the '71 season he expected to add another defensive coach.

"There are no criticisms," he assured Perles. "Stay the way you are."

Later that autumn, Noll called with an offer that included a $19,000 salary and use of a new Plymouth. Perles went over to Dagwood's for a beer with a few cohorts, then called Sally with the news they were going to Pittsburgh. As great as it had been coming back to East Lansing, a move to the NFL, for much more money and the chance to grow as a coach, was what he now needed.

Perles knew as quickly as he got to Pittsburgh that the NFL

would be his greatest adjustment as a coach. The football was more sophisticated there, and he was surrounded by excellent coaches, as well as by superior players, none of whom you were going to fool.

Noll knew the transition would not be simple. Figuring and coaching the Xs and Os would require some time, but he liked Perles' ability to relate to men, his work ethic, his enthusiasm. The rest would follow in time. So would appreciation for a man who enjoyed fellowship as much as Perles. "Social director," Noll called the man who organized get-togethers at his home, or at a restaurant, or wherever staffers could have a beer and shoot the breeze in one of those men-only settings Perles relished.

The on-field adjustment Perles would handle more gingerly. Joe Greene, Dwight White and L.C. Greenwood had been in Pittsburgh from one to three seasons, while Earnie Holmes was a rookie who could play. None of the Steelers front four was going to be overly impressed by a college coach who, they reasoned, had more to learn than any of them. No one had to tell Perles. He knew he would be studied closely at every practice, at each meeting. He would have to live with the pressure until dues were paid and respect could be gained.

He would also practice as much diplomacy as possible without being overly solicitous. He would invite feedback, listen closely, do his homework, but also stand his ground if challenged. Film breakdowns and scouting reports indicated what an opposing offense's tendencies were in certain down-and-distance situations. It was his familiarization with other offenses where Greene and others found Perles to be most helpful.

They also liked his what-you-see-is-what-you-get style and the fact that with Perles there were no secrets, no politicking. He could admit to them if he was wrong, and he was proving as seasons went on to be a good motivator. He especially worked well with players he thought he needed to push—Holmes, Pete Banaszak, Steve Furness. He was good at analyzing problems during a game and adjusting, and equally good at considering advice from players even if he chose not to use it.

The Steelers knew about Perles' reputation as an inner-city toughie, and they could see how he would use it as a way to identify with them, as a means particularly for Perles to pump electricity into Dwight White.

White had an "I'll-bite-your-head-off" approach that Perles

played on. There were moments when it appeared as though Perles was going to snap on a helmet and dash onto the field with them, and sometimes, it worked beautifully.

He wasn't always so prudent with the words. Following the '78 season, another Super Bowl year for the Steelers, Perles spouted off at a banquet. Benny Barnes of the Cowboys had been griping about officiating in the Steelers-Cowboys games.

Perles brushed aside Barnes and the Cowboys and their tendency to beat Pittsburgh in the preseason.

"We'll lose to Dallas in the exhibition season," he said, "and kick their ass in the regular season."

It was broadcast loud and clear both in Pittsburgh and in Dallas, which sure enough, beat the Steelers in a preseason game the following season. When their regular-season showdown rolled around, Perles was hounded for a week about the off-season promise. Pittsburgh won, 14-3, and Perles was off the hook.

Everyone in the Steelers camp realized as years wore on that Perles was getting anxious to become a head coach. Noll had helped out by knighting him with the Assistant Head Coach title, but it was also known in Pittsburgh that if Perles had his choice of jobs, it would be as head man at Michigan State. He talked about Duffy Daugherty all the time, and while he wasn't the quipster Daugherty was, Perles had an upbeat style that most figured would serve him well as a college head coach—at Michigan State or wherever.

Revival was the code word as his first three seasons as MSU head coach unfolded progressively, each better than the previous. From the 2-9 team he inherited came the 4-6-1 debut in '83, then a 6-5 finish in '84 that put Michigan State into the Cherry Bowl—its first bowl trip in 19 years. The big victory of '84: A 19-7 upset of Michigan at Ann Arbor—first time since 1978 MSU had beaten Schembechler's Wolverines.

It was set up when Bobby Morse—the kid from Muskegon, Michigan, whose grit and drive won him MSU's last scholarship in 1983—rambled down the sideline 87 yards for a touchdown that turned a Michigan punt into a game-breaking play for Michigan State. The only blemish was a third-quarter broken arm sustained by U-M's Jim Harbaugh, the young quarterback who dived on a fumble and collided with a pair of MSU defenders. It pulled the plug on Michigan's offense just as it appeared the Wolverines might be coming back. As sickening as it had been to see Harbaugh trudge off the field, his left arm obviously badly damaged, there was a limit to

MSU's sympathy on a day when it beat Schembechler and Michigan for only the third time in 16 seasons.

It also buoyed thoughts in East Lansing that life definitely was improving for a football team that had taken care of Notre Dame and the Wolverines in successive years. The talent bin obviously was improving as anyone who had gotten a glimpse of MSU's freshman tailback could tell. Lorenzo White was a 5-foot-11, 204-pound runner whom Charlie Baggett had pulled from the tough side of Ft. Lauderdale, Florida. He looked like a durable tailback who might be valuable by his sophomore season, but eight games into the 1984 season, White's freshman year at MSU, he had become a starter about to spin a web of 100-yard games, including a 170-yarder against Northwestern.

An offensive backfield that was in need of disaster aid a year earlier had suddenly grown bold with the arrival of the darting, fast-cutting freshman who got up snappily no matter how many linebackers had bulldozed him into the sideline on his last jaunt around left end.

The Spartans would finish 7-4 during an '85 season in which White became the NCAA's all-time best sophomore rusher with 1,908 yards, finished fourth in Heisman voting, and was a national attraction by the time MSU met Georgia Tech in the All-American Bowl, a game the Spartans would lose, 17-14, when linebacker Anthony Bell's game-clinching interception was called back on a roughing-the-quarterback call on defensive tackle Joe Curran.

Although Perles had shut down Yarema and the passing game in a bowl the Spartans threatened to smash open, he had in three years given MSU better back-to-back records than any Spartan team had managed since the '70s, and more down-the-line promise than any MSU team had shown since Daugherty's best days. Talent had been accumulated, recruiting was strong, and there appeared to be competence and coaching ability in Perles and his assistants. Perles was hot, not just in East Lansing, but statewide. Public service commercials for Blue Cross and Blue Shield featuring Perles warning against the consequences of stress and poor diet—a bit dubious, thought some familiar with Perles' zest for food—helped make him a household name and personality.

He was a frequent radio guest on J.P. McCarthy's WJR-AM morning show. He almost unfailingly returned phone calls from media, and most significantly, was staying clear of anything embarrassing or indelicate that might make his bosses uneasy. On the contrary, Perles was running a clean program and representing Michigan State in a fashion the school desired.

Internally, the operation was running smoothly. He was proving to be the most efficient administrator any of the office regulars had seen since Denny Stolz. And he was making sure his players stayed out of trouble, hit the books, and did their best to graduate.

If players liked his approachable, personal way of communicating with them, they found him to be no puppy dog on the practice field or in meetings. There was even an element of fear in the way they, as well as assistants, looked at him. You didn't anger Perles and not feel the thunder all the way to your toes. And he definitely ran the show. A player having a bad practice often would be upbraided by an assistant, complaining that, "I'm sick of getting my ass chewed because of the way you're practicing." Perles could get on an assistant as easily as he might rip a player.

They discovered, too, that he was a perfectionist who wanted no hairs out of place, particularly the night before a game. If the team arrived at its out-of-town hotel and Perles discovered that dinner was not ready on schedule, he could go nuts. Another pet peeve often cropped up on Fridays during Perles' roll-call on special-teams assignments. If a player didn't instantaneously acknowledge that he was left end or left guard, he was asking for a blast from the head coach. And nothing—absolutely nothing—infuriated him more than a player walking into a meeting late. The entire group would catch it for that indiscretion, although on the field it generally was Buck Nystrom, the raspy-voiced offensive line coach, or Nick Saban, MSU's young defensive coordinator, who did the serious yelling.

Perles was observant to the point of sometimes becoming suspicious. A player who looked funny, out-of-character, a player who might have been practicing poorly, could usually expect a drug test. The surprise to so many players, especially those who had been recruited by Perles and by Bo Schembechler at Michigan, was how the two coaches seemed so similar in philosophy and style. Those who encountered Schembechler at post-season all-star games drew the same conclusion. Each was tough, hard-nosed, disciplined and each man obviously cared a great deal for a kid's long-term success.

It was in the win-loss column that comparisons stopped. Perles was discovering that rebuilding MSU could not be accomplished by simple subscription to clean living. Getting talent comparable to the Michigans, Ohio States and Iowas of the Big Ten was not going to be easy, and neither would it be a cinch that MSU would win big even if the personnel improved measurably from talent crops harvested during the previous eight years.

Most bothersome to the players, even those on defense, was the snail's pace at which MSU was adopting a 1980s-style offense. Perles' devotion to basic running plays reminded some of them of how life must have been under Woody Hayes. The passing game consisted either of bombs to wide receivers like Mark Ingram, or dump-off passes to folks such as fullback Bobby Morse. Perles' decision following the 1985 season to hire Morris Watts as offensive coordinator was just the move players hoped might throw open the windows on an offense that too often had suffocated.

But jazzing up the offense wouldn't be an answer to a bewildering 1986 season that would see the Spartans lose four times in the final minutes—and not only to the heavyweights. Yarema, who had complained so about the offensive straitjacket in which MSU's offense had been working the previous three seasons, threw crushing interceptions that twice knocked out MSU as it neared last-minute victories over Iowa and Indiana.

The worst came against Iowa on October 4. Driving the length of the field, MSU had turned Spartan Stadium into a noise convention and given the CBS-TV audience a glorious finish as it moved to Iowa's 3-yard line with 1:30 to play. Yarema on first-and-goal rolled right, spotted tight end Mike Sargent, and threw squarely into the arms of Iowa defensive back Ken Sims.

The Spartans, who had driven the length of the field to the nine at Arizona State, only to lose on a blocked field goal, lost on another closing-moments Yarema interception against Indiana—one more sock in the stomach to a screaming home crowd—and then again the following week at Northwestern as tailback Craig Johnson's fumble at the Wildcat one led a parade of MSU miscues.

At the end of October, it appeared Perles and the Spartans— even after the early-season horrors against Iowa, and a following-week cave-in at Michigan—would finish 8-3 and march off to a third straight bowl game. MSU crushed Purdue, 37-3, and Minnesota, 52-20.

But a 6-5 finish would ruin all the plans, leave Michigan State home for the holidays minus any bowl invitation, and prove to Perles and fans that winning at Michigan State would never come easily.

Six

HIS IMAGE AND LIKENESS

In another hour or two it would be dark at northern Ontario's Lake Manitou. Now were the special moments during a summer when the sun would hang so high, so long over a shimmering Canadian lake, it was common to turn in during that almost-endless time of day known as dusk, when Biggie and Vera Munn would slip beneath the covers and listen to the wonders of a wilderness; especially to the comically eerie warbling of Manitou's loons.

Three or four dozen would gather in a bay outside the Munn cabin to squeal at each other in a spectacular symphony that never seemed to begin until Biggie pulled the quilt over himself and his wife, and with a faint chuckle, said: "All right, loons, start."

It was the Munns' private joke, at their most private haven, a place where Michigan State's athletic director could turn from the public world of big-time college athletics to a peaceful world filled with good fishing and glorious glimpses at Canada's wilds.

Clarence L. Munn, "Biggie" since his days as a six-foot, 200-pound All-American guard at Minnesota, was boss of a Michigan State athletic department that had grown in strength and fame in step with a school that President John A. Hannah was turning into one of the country's fastest-rising colleges. His life—from Minneapolis schoolboy, to state legend in football and track, to his years as football coach and AD—had been one of magnificent achievements.

Munn was considered the greatest high school trackman produced by the State of Minnesota. He held state records in javelin, shot put, relays, and in 1928 was undefeated in the 100-yard dash. He went on to the University of Minnesota to set Big Ten track records, while in football he was a two-time team Most Valuable Player, and Big Ten MVP in 1931, all leading to a spot in 1969 on the *Football News* first-team, 100-Year All-America football team.

It was probably natural that a man of Munn's style and personality, a man active throughout his life in the Boy Scouts, a man very much involved in community, would decide on a coaching career. He would spend 22 years as both an assistant and head coach, almost all of them successes, particularly his 10 seasons as head coach at Albright (Pennsylvania) College, Syracuse and Michigan State during which he rolled up a 75-16 record. He drove Michigan State to a 28-game winning streak from 1950-53, then a 28-20 Rose Bowl victory over UCLA in 1954, after which 45-year-old Biggie Munn decided coaching's challenges had been essentially exhausted. He was ready to become athletic director—even if it meant teaming with Hannah to nudge Ralph Young from the job—and turn his football masterpiece over to top assistant Duffy Daugherty.

As AD, Munn could handle matters well-suited to a hearty, gregarious man who was good with people. He saw in Michigan State the opportunity to mold an athletic department as dynamic as his football team and as exciting as a Midwest college—fresh with university status—that was now an established Big Ten member and national football power.

Hannah had known Munn when Munn was an assistant coach at Michigan under Fritz Crisler. He had noticed that Munn not only knew football well enough to serve as Crisler's top lieutenant, but that the burly line coach was so well-liked. Good indicators, thought Hannah, that Munn would soon be excellent head-coaching timber.

Sharing his opinion was Syracuse University. Munn had been an assistant there in 1937 under Ossie Solem, then left to join Crisler's staff for eight seasons until Syracuse brought him back as head coach in 1946.

Hannah became interested as he worked to build Michigan State into a post-war strength, and realized the school needed a football team that not only would be attractive to the Big Ten Conference, which had not yet invited Michigan State to be a member, but might also become a spark for campus pride and cohesion. Athletics were important to Hannah. To him, they helped balance and enhance an academic system that Michigan State was attempting to diversify and extend from its 90-year heritage as the Midwest's foremost agricultural school.

Hannah understood the boost Michigan State might realize from its football team. He realized also that a football program would need personality and leadership beyond anything that could be delivered by head coach Charley Bachman.

The eventual decision to reassign Bachman was not easy for Hannah. Bachman was a pleasant, conscientious man who had put together a 70-34 record through 13 seasons at Michigan State. Hannah, though, knew he needed a coach more dynamic, a coach who could wring more from his team than the 5-5 finish State recorded in 1946.

When Bachman had been hired in 1933, Hannah was Michigan State secretary serving President Robert Shaw, who was also Hannah's father-in-law. Shaw that year vetoed as "too young" Hannah's recommendation for head coach to replace Jim Crowley. Hannah's candidate: Frank Leahy, who would later become head coach of the Irish and earn a place alongside Knute Rockne as a coaching legend at South Bend.

This time, Hannah knew Michigan State needed a coach with youth and brilliance who would help a growing school maximize its athletic potential. Hannah wanted Biggie Munn. Two other candidates would be considered if Munn said no: Bud Wilkinson, who would later build Oklahoma into a national giant; and Wes Fesler, who was soon to become head coach at Ohio State.

For permission to speak with Munn, Hannah called Syracuse University President William P. Tolley, a personal friend of Hannah's who would permit his first-year head coach to talk with the folks from East Lansing. Hannah phoned Munn and an interview was arranged for the following week at Detroit's Statler Hotel.

A priority for Hannah and for Michigan State at the end of the 1946 season was to halt the University of Michigan's embarrassing football dominance. Michigan State had not won since 1937, and in their last three games, the Wolverines had won 20-0, 40-0, and 55-7. Hannah understood that if Michigan State could not play with authority against Michigan, national respect and Big Ten membership were longshots. Hannah got to the point during their Detroit interview.

"How long will it take you to beat Michigan?" he asked. Munn knew Michigan State's potential, knew that talent could be collected, coached, and in time, brought to Michigan's level. Three years was realistic. But Munn wasn't about to offer Hannah a risky timetable.

"Five years," he answered.

It sounded reasonable to the president, who wanted only that the rivalry become more competitive and less the mismatch it had become during the '40s.

Munn was not unhappy at Syracuse, but he saw in Michigan State the potential and resources to win big in an area familiar to him. It would also be a pleasure to take on his old boss, Crisler.

Hannah's offer was accepted. Munn would bring to Michigan State three assistants: Forest Evashevski, Kip Taylor, and Duffy Daugherty, Munn's line coach. Although neither Hannah nor Munn would project anything so dreamy, Munn and his staff began a spectacular chapter in MSU's football history: Opening with a 7-2 season in 1947, Michigan State over a seven-season span would go 53-9-2. Munn would finish with a 1953 conference championship and 1954 Rose Bowl victory in Michigan State's first season as a Big Ten member.

He would do it by recruiting All-American talent from Michigan, Ohio and Pennsylvania: Don Coleman, Frank Kush, LeRoy Bolden, Don McAuliffe, Dorne Dibble, Al Dorow, Bob Carey, Norm Masters, Don Dohoney, Earl Morrall, Buck Nystrom and Dick Tamburo.

He would do it by teaching. Munn—standing there twirling his whistle, grabbing at his pants, hollering, "Run it again," when someone malfunctioned—became a kind of caricature through the years. He would do it by inspiring and leading, and with the help of excellent staffers, many of whom (Evashevski, Daugherty, Bob Devaney, Dan Devine) would themselves have grand careers as head coaches. And with the success, Michigan State—no longer Michigan State College but now Michigan State University—was becoming the diverse, high-profile school Hannah envisioned.

Munn was only 45 when he stepped into the athletic director's office, but, emotionally, he was ready for the job. He had hit a peak with the '53 team that meant coaching could become little more than a pleasant repetition if he stuck with it. Munn wanted to stay in the limelight, but he wanted to move a notch higher, to steer an entire athletic department in the same manner that he had taken control of a football team and reached the top.

Had the broad man with the curly black hair been less dimensional, Munn no doubt would have preferred the stability and security of his football team. But Munn's energy and personality—his ego, also—made him a natural AD. People exhilarated him. So did community projects: scouting, Red Cross, Fellowship of Christian Athletes, anything socially constructive was for Munn great stimulus.

He was also a football coach who appreciated other sports. His own background in track and basketball gave him knowledge and insight into two high-caliber college programs (Munn years later would make an unsuccessful bid to bring to MSU a track coach at Michigan named Don Canham), while his interest in baseball and wrestling was strong. There was little in athletics, except for hockey, for which Munn had no real zeal. And during his first decade as AD, Michigan State often would stand as the Big Ten's winningest school in all-sports competition.

What Munn underestimated was the degree to which he would miss working intimately with young athletes. It was the one aspect of coaching from which he could never separate himself. The attention, too, was gratifying as head coach and not as easily reclaimed as athletic director. Munn liked being at center stage, and when Duffy Daugherty soon began enjoying life as MSU's leading sports celebrity, it ripped at the man who had brought him to Michigan State and made him head coach.

It was Daugherty's rapport with players that persuaded Munn to name him rather than Spartan assistant Earle Edwards as MSU's new head coach. Daugherty had personality and, like Munn, he had been a line coach whose years in the trenches Munn considered essential to a college head coach of the '50s. Munn, though, failed to perceive his own inability to let go of Michigan State's football team. He could not objectively foresee how a man with an ego in proportion to his girth would very soon resent a charmer such as Daugherty, whose Irish wit, speaking talent and charisma would make a winning coach such a national celebrity that Daugherty in 1956 would find himself on the cover of *TIME* magazine.

Munn would also note that Daugherty was making good money on the banquet tour and enjoying perks unavailable during Munn's era. It was only a matter of time until bitterness and bad feelings gripped them both, blanketing a raw working relationship that would endure, remarkably and by sheer necessity, for 17 years.

It began with Munn's outrage during the 1954 season, Daugherty's first, which saw MSU sink to 3-6 following the Rose Bowl year of 1953. Munn's meddling at a meeting of Daugherty and his staff led to an October showdown that set the tone for the rest of their years together. By the time Munn called a post-season meeting in Hannah's office—an attempt at coaxing the MSU president into sanctioning Daugherty as a first-season disaster—the relationship was beyond repair.

Daugherty's own Rose Bowl victory on January 1, 1957 would be the head coach's revenge and establish Duffy as a football man nearly as accomplished as Munn. But feelings between them never warmed for any length of time, and by 1958, as MSU turned over the ball repeatedly and lost, 39-12, at Minnesota en route to a 3-5-1 record, Munn could stand it no longer. Pete Waldmeir, then a *Detroit News* sports writer, was having dinner after the game in Minneapolis at Charlie's Cafe Exceptional, when Munn wandered in, all but begging for a reporter's ear.

"I've been in football since I was 14 years old, and I've never been dumb enough to think you can win 'em all," Munn began. "But when you throw the game away like we did today by losing the ball 10 times, it's terrible . . . just terrible.

"It was the most futile display I've ever seen. Utter futility. I've never taken losing so bad, but I cried after this one . . . When you have scratched and crawled a tenth of an inch at a time to build an empire, although it's a small empire, it takes a lot out of you to see it crash."

It was as subtle as a nuclear bomb, and made public one of college football's worst AD-head coach relationships. It also so embarrassed Michigan State that Hannah had no choice but to air out Munn and Daugherty on Monday at a closed-doors meeting in his office.

Despite Hannah's attempts to smooth over an internal nightmare, and despite orders that the two behave like something other than scrapping children, the acrimony continued throughout their years together. It merely became more private; a Cold War that thawed only for flickering moments when emotions of the moment rather than long-seated feelings took over.

One warm, but brief, episode came in 1965 as Michigan State rode the team train back to East Lansing from South Bend, a day on which MSU's 12-3 victory over Notre Dame clinched a national championship. Daugherty and Munn were standing on a platform at the end of the train, drinking in the glory of a 10-0 record and a Rose Bowl invitation. It was a marvelous moment for Michigan State, and Munn and Daugherty were ecstatic. Daugherty hugged his boss, tears in each man's eyes, and bellowed, "I owe this all to you."

The following Monday, *Flint Journal* Sports Editor Doug Mintline was in East Lansing to join Daugherty on a flight to Chicago, where Daugherty would speak to the Chicago football writers. Fog temporarily grounded the plane and left Mintline and Daugherty to kill time inside the Jenison offices. Munn happened by and invited Mintline to join him. He took him into his own office and had Mintline note all the fine MSU assistant coaches whose pictures hung on the wall, men who now were winners as head coaches at a variety of major-college stops: Bob Devaney at Nebraska; Frank Kush at Arizona State; Chuck Fairbanks at Oklahoma; Dan Devine at Missouri.

"They're all coaches I hired," Munn said, proudly. When the fog cleared, Daugherty and Mintline drove to meet their plane. Mintline along the way mentioned casually that Munn had given him a rundown on how he had brought to MSU so many excellent assistants who now were big winners as head coaches.

Daugherty nearly lost control of the car.

"That son of a bitch!" he roared. And then Daugherty explained how each of the MSU coaching alums had been hired, maintaining that it was he, not Munn, who had brought the talent to Michigan State.

In one sense, Munn did not disagree that Daugherty was good at building a staff and utilizing it. Following another of their in-office squabbles, this one an ugly battle over 100 comp tickets that Daugherty requested and Munn denied, Daugherty stormed out.

Munn turned and sneered: "Hell, he's not a football coach. He's a director of coaches."

It was at about the same time, a decade into their coexistence as AD and head coach, that Munn nearly dismissed Daugherty. Their relationship had hit rock bottom and Munn decided Daugherty could and should be replaced. His candidate was one of his old players, the enormously successful coach at Hillsdale College, Muddy Waters, who had stayed close to the scene at East Lansing. Munn built his case, presented it to Hannah, then called Waters.

"Hang on," Munn told the puzzled Waters. "Something's going to happen. Something big."

Hannah was not supportive of the move. When Daugherty later got wind of the plan and challenged Munn, the coup fizzled and Daugherty stayed put. Waters never learned until years later that he had been a phone call away from the MSU job nearly 20 years before finally getting it.

Much of the Munn-Daugherty bitterness was a product of their robust egos. Not until 1972, the year Burt Smith replaced the ailing Munn as AD, would Daugherty's picture be found on the cover of Michigan State's football media guide. Anytime the two were pictured on a MSU publication, Munn was always curious about the size of his photo versus Daugherty's. Such pettiness didn't anger Daugherty any more than Munn's cozy relationship with George Alderton, longtime sports editor of the *Lansing State Journal*. Using the pseudonym "Sam Spartan," Alderton wrote a weekly column in which he played the role of observer/insider. Daugherty was a frequent pin cushion, and in Daugherty's mind, Alderton was doing little more than parroting Munn's criticisms.

Other glimpses at the Munn-Daugherty friction abounded. On Michigan State's season-opening trip to Washington in 1970, Munn and Daugherty sat side by side in first-class seats on the team charter. During the entire four-hour flight they never spoke to each other. It was a minor, but obvious, portrait of a working relationship held together by each man's sufferance of the other.

Away from football, life was more peaceful and pleasurable for Munn. He enjoyed being Michigan State's athletic director and was popular with other MSU coaches, whose programs Munn generally treated very well. Munn had an eclectic view of college sports that he felt MSU must develop excellence in all sports, non-revenue as well as the money-making football program.

He got along well with coaches, made them feel important, and did his best to give them whatever they needed, which in most cases boiled down to a request by the non-revenue sports for more scholarships. Munn often obliged, even if it meant another splash of red ink on a budget that was constantly abused. Bad audits were almost an annual rite in an athletic department where good relations with his coaches—Daugherty aside—meant more to the AD than a balanced ledger.

Munn's strong public profile was consistent with a man who could speak the common man's language and do it with warmth. Coaches liked his straight talk and earthy sense of humor. Fans appreciated an AD who didn't always act like an AD.

In April of 1965, Munn and Gus Ganakas, then director of MSU's Ralph Young Scholarship Fund, drove to Marlette in Michigan's Thumb area for a high school spring sports banquet where MSU would receive a $100 check for the Young Fund. It was an unbearably hot and humid evening for a banquet that would typically run until half the school had been individually honored.

At the end of the evening, Ganakas, Munn, a school dignitary, and a son of the local MSU alumni group president, all piled into the car to make their way to the president's home for refreshments. The young boy introduced himself to Munn, who thrust out his hand, and in the same breath gleefully panted:

"Nice to meet you. Has your old man got any booze in the house?"

There was nothing flowery or formal about Munn when he was out mixing it up with an athletic constituency that leaned toward the hard-boiled. Near the end of his 17 years as working AD, Munn showed up at Grand Rapids for the annual Crying Towel get-together between Michigan and Michigan State fans, a pithy evening in which the two football followings trade verbal jabs a few days before the MSU-Michigan game.

On hand for Michigan was former assistant football coach and university celebrity Wally Weber, whose eloquence and ornate put-downs of MSU were classics. Weber finished his silk-wrapped oration chock full of literary references, million-dollar words, and magnificent chops at Michigan State, leaving everyone in stitches and anticipation as Munn strolled to the microphone in an ultimately impossible act to follow.

Munn took a breath. He leaned into the microphone and rumbled:

"Well, bullllllshit!"

In two words, Munn rocked the place and responded, crudely as it was, in Biggie Munn-fashion to Weber's comical wordstorm.

But the laughs away from Jenison merely masked a MSU athletic program that had become flat. By 1971, Michigan State was no longer the football force it had been during the '50s and '60s, and no longer an all-sports leader in the Big Ten. Daugherty was coming off four consecutive losing seasons. Basketball was fighting to make it as even a middle-of-the-pack contender. Only baseball, which had made it into the NCAA playoffs in May of '71, and wrestling were enjoying any noteworthiness.

Munn had turned 63 only a few weeks earlier, but in October of 1971 he was feeling strong and had been given an all-clear from his physical. There were no signs, no symptoms of illness, no indicators that Munn was in anything but fine health.

On October 7, Munn's secretary, Dorothy Miller, returned from lunch to find Munn sitting in his car in the parking lot outside Jenison. It was 1:30.

"I don't feel well," he told her. "Take me home."

She took him instead to Sparrow Hospital. There, Munn was able to place himself in a wheel chair. He was admitted, then moved to intensive care when it was determined he had suffered a stroke. He would remain for two weeks in intensive care, and be hospitalized for three months. He would not regain the power of speech lost at the time of his stroke.

Munn and Vera would spend the next two winters in Florida and live the remainder of the year at their home in East Lansing. But the stroke had devastated Munn, frustrating and humiliating a man who could understand all that was said to him, but who was now incapable of responding.

The Munns decided during the winter of 1974-75 that they would not go to Florida. Biggie was not doing well, although he was comfortable, especially when he could sit out on the back porch and drink in the fresh air, even on the coldest of days.

On March 10, 1975, Munn suffered a second stroke at home. Eight days later he died at Sparrow Hospital. He was only 66 years old.

In the weeks and months that followed Biggie Munn's 1971 stroke, Michigan State began adjusting to life minus a man who for 25 years had been at the heart of its athletic program. It wasn't that Munn, the administrator, would be missed. His talents were so thinly suited to business management that Hannah years earlier had made Jack Breslin, the MSU vice president, an overseer of athletics. Munn would function in all respects as AD, take care of the coaches and assume all duties attached to the role, but it was Breslin who would OK budgets and affect a great deal of policy.

Munn's leadership, however, would not be easy to duplicate inside the Jenison Field House offices. His personality and rapport with coaches were big pluses at a time when a burgeoning women's athletic program created even more strain on athletic department dollars.

Working alongside Munn were John Laetz, the department business manager; Bill Beardsley, ticket director; and Burt Smith, an assistant coach under Daugherty who in 1965 took over as Munn's assistant in charge of the athletic department's academic program.

Smith was a short, stout man with dark eyes and a University of Michigan pedigree. A Detroit native, he played hockey, baseball and freshman football at Michigan before moving on to Flint, Michigan, where he coached at Northern High School. Daugherty had brought him to MSU in 1954, and for 17 years Smith had been moving slowly and steadily through the athletic department, as coach, administrative assistant to Daugherty, assistant to Munn, and in Munn's absence, as acting athletic director.

Smith knew how the network worked in college athletics. He understood diplomacy, understood egos, and knew how to stay in the good graces of admissions officers who determined ultimately whether an athlete would or would not be admitted. He knew a few things about people, as well. He was fairly good with names and a good bet to return phone calls. He was also a competent speaker who could come across favorably with an audience. In essence, Smith, while not dynamic or overwhelming, was safe. So safe that he could be entrusted with Munn's duties on an interim, and finally, fulltime basis when in May of 1972 MSU chose him over Temple University's Ernie Casales, a candidate backed by MSU President Clifton Wharton Jr., who became president in 1971.

There began on a spring day at MSU a 41-month reign that would accompany some of Michigan State's greatest athletic turbulence: The resignation of Duffy Daugherty; racial demonstrations on Jenison Field House's basketball court; a "secret" vote later made public that helped send Ohio State rather than Michigan to the 1974 Rose Bowl; a walk-out by MSU's basketball players; and most damagingly, the arrival of NCAA football investigators in the spring of 1975.

The investigation would overshadow the construction of a new ice arena, an astonishing football upset of Ohio State, and a revival of MSU's hockey program. It would be a time when boosters and zealous assistant coaches helped put a football program on probation, and the resulting commotion would, in October of 1975, be interpreted as a contributor to Burt Smith's dismissal as athletic director.

Nothing quite so ominous was imagined as Smith settled in as MSU's new athletic director. He was a known quantity who most thought would shift smoothly from his position as academic advisor to an AD's job which more and more involved dealing with academics and policy complexities.

Smith had maintained a comfortable relationship with athletes during his six years as Munn's assistant and saw no reason to change style when he became AD. What had worked on the practice field during his days as an assistant coach, had also worked as academic supervisor.

Still, others thought it crass and beneath the dignity of an athletic director to speak so roughly when players appeared at his door.

"Get your goddamn ass in here," he would shout to them. It was the kind of verbal rough-housing so many of the athletes found comfortable, while it was also a way in which MSU's new athletic director—not nearly as colorful or accomplished as Munn—could establish himself as a capable, likeable successor to a MSU legend.

Only five months into his tenure as fulltime athletic director, Smith ran into an administrative roadblock that would frustrate his bid for autonomy and characterize his remaining years as AD. Duffy Daugherty had rocked East Lansing with his October resignation. It would now be up to a new athletic director to make the single most important personnel decision that would affect Michigan State's sports program. Smith was determined to name his own man, and also, to cement himself as boss. He would avoid the old Munn-Daugherty wrangling by naming a man who would not operate independent of the athletic director.

Smith assumed his recommendation would be rubber-stamped by MSU's administrative panel that included Wharton, Breslin, Faculty Representative John Fuzak, and Clarence Underwood, who had succeeded Smith as athletic department academic advisor.

Smith's man was Barry Switzer. Oklahoma's offensive coordinator and top assistant to Sooners Coach Chuck Fairbanks had just the sizzle and the youth Smith wanted for MSU, and following a flight to Norman, Oklahoma, and interview, Smith made it clear to Switzer he would be Michigan State's new head coach. There was no doubt in the mind of MSU's athletic director. He understood before moving into the job that he would have the authority to name head coaches. Certainly, Michigan State's executives would OK this bright, energetic young coach from one of America's great football programs.

The Switzer candidacy disintegrated during formal interviews. Smith's hand-picked head coach, the man with whom he would work to carve a hot new era for MSU football, tumbled from contention during a disastrous interview that featured a windy opening statement, and bold requests for private jets and credit cards.

Smith's endorsement was pushed to the side as the committee instead chose a safer candidate, Denny Stolz, whose knowledge of MSU's program, absence of strong negatives, and background as head coach of Fuzak's son at Alma (Michigan) College, combined to make him the winner. But Smith would not forget, or recover from, a personal defeat at such a critical time.

Administration of the athletic department also settled into a split of responsibilities that did not reinforce Smith's position nor his power. Breslin initiated a series of monthly staff meetings in which he maintained essential control and management authority. He divided up tasks among Smith, Underwood, and Beardsley, the business manager who had thirsted for the AD position and was assuming as much control as possible.

Smith might have staved off the intervention had he been more forceful or more dominating. But among coaches and associates, his reputation grew as a procrastinator who would not make the quick decisions that would have given him status in an athletic department Breslin ran only because he believed he had no choice.

Particularly bothersome to the Jenison Field House gang were Smith's frequent conversations with his wife, Margaret. They were perceived as policy-making discussions the AD required having with his closest advisor. Coaches or staffers checking on a matter with Smith often got the same response: "Wait until tomorrow."

They all knew what it meant: Smith needed to confer with his wife. But Margaret was not his only confidant. There was a small network of friends upon which Smith relied heavily for advice and counsel. Harold Shnider, a local optometrist, was, along with his wife, among the Smiths' closest associates; A. Dean Watkins, businessman from Lansing, was also part of Smith's unofficial cabinet; and Ken Ericson, Smith's son-in-law from Brighton, was another in the trusted circle.

Whatever internal dissatisfaction existed toward Biggie Munn's successor was muted by the relative success of MSU's athletic program and, particularly, by a rebounding football team. Stolz' first year as head coach had been a modest breakthrough: a 5-6 season that had seen him, with a good deal less talent, win as many games as Daugherty had in '72. Most encouraging had been Michigan

State's recruiting during the winter of '73-74, a bonanza harvest that included a number of high school All-Americans and premier talents from the Ohio-Pennsylvania area.

MSU's basketball team was competitive and, for a while, appeared to be a Big Ten contender behind Lindsay Hairston, Mike Robinson and flashy sophomore Terry Furlow. Hockey, too, was becoming one of the school's hottest tickets. Amo Bessone's team was stocked with super scorers that only packed students and fans all the tighter in a concrete barn known as Dem Hall that the next season would give way to glamorous new Munn Arena.

There was an appearance of health and vigor in MSU's athletic department, as much as had been seen in the seven years that marked Michigan State's slide from national football giant to run-of-the-mill Big Ten resident. By November of 1974, the Red Cedar was nearly shaken from its bed when MSU upset Ohio State, 16-13, and in the season finale, when the Spartans destroyed Iowa, 60-21, to finish 7-3-1, it appeared the football program had returned to Top 20 status and re-energized an entire university.

It was a public perception more than it was an internal appraisal of Smith's leadership. Breslin was not happy with budgeting, direction, management, nor with the way he believed Smith was casting him as villain when coaches complained about too little money or too few scholarships. Coaches thought Smith to be tight-fisted and prone to give lip service more than direct assistance. Smith argued that his hands were tied by Breslin. The relationship, based on mutual tolerance in the early going, was deteriorating even before a pair of 1975 incidents rattled the athletic department offices and set in motion a series of high-level dismissals.

A first disaster was the January walkout of MSU's black varsity basketball players in a dispute over Gus Ganakas' decision to start freshman forward Jeff Tropf, a white player from nearby Holt. Fall-out from the boycott—which was resolved a day later when the players were reinstated—gouged the university and so weakened Ganakas that he would be reassigned 14 months later.

It would also reflect on an athletic director who was not visibly involved in handling a major controversy or dealing with the players. The walkout was a prelude to April's bomb blast, MSU's announcement that NCAA investigators had arrived to interview players and coaches regarding charges of illegal football recruiting.

It would signal nine months of anxiety, confusion and fear within the Michigan State athletic circle. Press reports of illegal activity or questionable arrangements, such as the car loan provided quarterback Charlie Baggett, chipped away at MSU's insistence the school had done nothing seriously wrong. Beneath the cloud that had spread across MSU's campus, Smith presided over an athletic department gone from revival to turbulence. And Breslin, himself a few months away from athletic department exile, was becoming more impatient with the athletic director.

On September 30, Breslin called Smith into his fourth-floor office at MSU's Administration Building. For a variety of reasons, he told Smith, Michigan State, with the approval of Clifton Wharton, was reassigning him and naming a new athletic director. Smith would be brought into Breslin's office as an assistant to intercollegiate athletics. There would be an orderly transition and Smith could maintain an office in Jenison if he wished. Smith left the office and returned to Jenison.

Within hours he was on the phone with WJR Sports Director Bob Reynolds, a friend and media contact who three years earlier had endorsed him for the fulltime AD position. On that night's 6:15 sports show, Reynolds delivered news of the reassignment with almost a verbatim account of the Smith-Breslin conversation. Reynolds then lashed into Breslin and the MSU hierarchy for dismissing Smith and holding him at least partly responsible for an investigation that, as nearly as could be determined, centered on a football program that as of October had not been penalized for anything.

Breslin was enraged that Smith had obviously gone to Reynolds with a story Breslin considered incomplete and one-sided. The next morning there was a call for Smith, whose reassignment had not been announced by anyone but Reynolds.

"Have your ass out of there by noon," Breslin snapped. "Jack Shingleton is moving into that office immediately."

Smith wanted no part of the Jenison scene and asked for an office in the year-old Munn Arena, where he could stay clear of athletic department doings and involve himself with hockey-related matters. At a time when Munn was still in touch-up stages, Smith's office was truly spartan: a cement block niche with a desk, chair, phone and little else.

The man who would replace him was Jack Shingleton, 53, MSU's nationally respected placement director who had become an unofficial administrative trouble-shooter at Michigan State. His athletic background was sparse—Shingleton played varsity tennis at Michigan State—but Shingleton had business command and leadership abilities Breslin thought ideal, especially at a time the athletic department was reeling from the NCAA investigation.

Breslin wanted an end to in-house bickering and finger-pointing. He wanted from Shingleton accountability and the toughness for which Shingleton was known across campus. Conversations concerning the AD job had occurred between Shingleton and Breslin, but never in specific fashion until Shingleton's phone rang on the morning of October 1.

"Jack, I want you to take over as athletic director," Breslin began. "I'd like you to get over there as soon as possible."

Shingleton was stunned.

"How soon?"

"This morning, if possible."

Shingleton said he would take the job—Breslin emphasized it would be as acting AD, and not necessarily as a permanent assignment—on the condition he have authority to run the department according to his own instincts and feelings. He was not privy to all matters relating to the investigation, but Shingleton wanted authority to deal with coaches. Breslin had no disagreement.

Although Shingleton did not want to embarrass Smith, he believed his only hope at realigning the department was to establish himself as boss immediately. He phoned Smith and wondered when he could begin moving into the office. Smith had retained a lawyer with thoughts of starting suit against MSU (he eventually filed a $3.5-million suit against MSU; it was settled out of court). Smith was not firm on a timetable.

"Burt," Shingleton said, "if things aren't moved out by tomorrow, I'll have to move them out myself."

Shingleton arrived at the athletic director's office the next day to find many of Smith's articles and belongings still there. As promised, he moved them out and began work as MSU's acting athletic director. But Shingleton was also watching out for Smith. He made sure that for the remainder of the football season, Smith continued to represent MSU and host friends in the AD's booth in the Spartan Stadium press box.

Shingleton's bold, almost callous, act of phoning Smith and inquiring when he might take over was characteristic of a man whose geniality was subordinate to business principles. He was regarded not only as the country's top placement director, but at Michigan State, Shingleton had become a refuge for executives hunting a fix-it man.

Shortly after Clifton Wharton left MSU to become chancellor of State University of New York, university execs were staring at a Performing Arts Center drive initiated by Wharton that had raised only $3 million. Deadline for going ahead with the project was only six months away and MSU needed $12 million. Edgar Harden, who had been brought in as interim president when Wharton left in 1977, approached former president John Hannah for assistance. Hannah then turned to Shingleton to help ramrod the fund drive. Six months later MSU had secured $12 million and The Wharton Center for Performing Arts was launched.

Several years later, when new President Cecil Mackey was embroiled in battle with the Alumni Association, it was Shingleton whom he pulled from a meeting with General Electric in New York to help smooth over an ugly civil war. Shingleton had also been called in as mediator in the mid-'70s when MSU's Intramural Sports Department clashed with Mike Marshall, a major league pitcher and doctoral candidate in kinesiology who had sparred regularly with IM officials over use of facilities.

Shingleton believed that authority, discipline, organization and fair-minded business practices were the key to departmental integrity. He concluded that too many coaches were acting autonomously and with no real regard for chain-of-command. It was the kind of situation, he believed, that would fragment an athletic department or at the very least lead to inefficiency.

One of his first orders was that all coaches no longer would call the Big Ten on a policy matter. They would first check with Shingleton's office. Several days later, Shingleton got wind of a call made to the Big Ten office in Chicago from MSU's basketball office, which was only a couple of doors away in the Jenison nerve center.

Shingleton stepped through the doorway to find assistant coach Vern Payne taking care of some paperwork. Shingleton quizzed him about the call, assuming it was made by Gus Ganakas, the head coach.

"I made the call," Payne said.

"You?" Shingleton thundered.

Shingleton ripped him, loudly, for several minutes, accusing Payne of disrespecting authority and flaunting a command that had been made only a couple of days earlier. When Ganakas returned later, word was left to report to Shingleton and he, too, was blistered by the new AD.

It was later in the day when Sylvia Thompson, secretary to the AD, reported that Payne was typing out his resignation. Shingleton was not moved.

"I want it here, and I want it signed!" he roared. Payne never delivered it, and in fact, months later presented a gift to Shingleton when Shingleton left the athletic department, telling his old boss how much he "respected" him.

Never during the Munn or Smith years had coaches seen an AD operate in such a heavy-handed fashion as Shingleton. And it wasn't only coaches feeling the lash. Shingleton noticed quickly that Beardsley, the business manager who all along had craved the AD's job, was growing huffy toward his job and Shingleton's presence.

"Jack, I know more athletics than you," Beardsley said. "I should be in there. Not you."

Shingleton half-smiled and said, calmly: "Bill, I would like your help in running this department. But if you think I can't run it without your help, try me."

The two men never had another problem.

Establishing authority and streamlining department structure were Shingleton's first priorities when he arrived for a job that would require immense study. Athletic policy was becoming a complex network of rules, regulations, bylaws and issues in which Shingleton had little experience.

It helped that Fuzak and Wharton (Breslin had stepped down in January as supervisor over athletics) were handling the university's response to NCAA investigators. Shingleton could administrate and bone up on the workings of the Big Ten Conference, as well as how it and Michigan State fit into the whole of a galaxy known as the NCAA.

Before long, Shingleton began feeling more comfortable as AD, although he was not warming toward the glad-handing which obviously was part of the job. Shingleton was a business man, an author, a World War II pilot and veteran of the corporate-academic world who did not cotton to fanaticism or boosterism. Accommodating a certain amount of that went with the AD territory, at least at Michigan State.

But it was never easy for Shingleton to give in to a segment of rooters who thought MSU's athletic director should be hybrid Spartan. The Green and White zealots made him uncomfortable. Nervous. Unsettled. There was almost a demeaning air to fans who were enveloped by their passion for a university's sports teams.

Shingleton never even owned that AD's wardrobe staple, the green sport jacket. It wasn't him. Wasn't the kind of thing a placement director-turned-athletic director could wear convincingly. Or comfortably.

It was also one shortcoming the 1975 football team was going to address. At the end of the season, Denny Stolz' players wanted to show their new boss how much they appreciated his help and interest during the two months he had been working as AD. They presented to him an elegant green sport coat, finely trimmed in rich material and colors, with every accessory but epaulets on the shoulders.

Shingleton was deeply touched by the gesture and by their sincerity. He wasn't about to tell them there was as much chance of him wearing the jacket as there was one of his wife's dresses.

The job went on. For better and for worse. Administratively, it was its usual mixed bag of headaches and pleasures. The biggest problem was Shingleton's inexperience in dealing with the workings of college athletics at conference and national levels. But he was a quick study, a man who usually was reading two or three books at a time, and he had a definite philosophy on how athletics and academics should inter-relate.

One move was the reduction of non-predictors—athletes who did not meet minimum academic requirements but who could be admitted as exceptions. Shingleton believed the vast majority of eligibility and disciplinary problems at MSU existed because of athletes admitted as exceptions. Their numbers were trimmed.

He also continued on his mission to turn coaches and players into snappier, more efficient types who would toe the line and straighten out a university image that in one year had taken a serious tumble. One irritant was the practice by some black basketball players of turning their back on the American flag during the National Anthem.

Shingleton discussed the matter with Ganakas.

"They will face the flag," Shingleton said, "and if they don't, I will remove you from the floor."

At the next game, all players stood facing the stars and stripes. Even Shingleton was surprised at how deftly Ganakas had dealt with players who only 12 months earlier had walked out of Jenison in a pregame dispute over Ganakas' starting lineup.

It was, at many times, a satisfying job Shingleton thought he might want permanently. He stood in the Jenison Field House press box at one Big Ten basketball game and looked down at the crowd below, the band blaring, the way the lights shimmered off the players' warm-ups, and thought about how far he had come from his student days when he swept out the football stadium, and helped freeze the ice rink behind Jenison for 60 cents an hour.

Shingleton told the *Lansing State Journal* in January that he would consider the job under the right circumstances. But he wasn't a fan of the travel or the long hours. Neither did he think a man so orientated toward business, where structure and efficiency were easier to design and results were easier to achieve, could avoid frustration fighting a three-headed monster known as college athletics.

Ultimately, it would not matter what Shingleton felt toward his job. The NCAA announced on January 25, 1976, that Michigan State was being slapped with three years' probation and other sanctions for violations in its football program. A new athletic director and new head football coach were only weeks from being named.

Seven

CHANGES IN STYLE

The low point had come on a cold, gray Sunday in January when NCAA officials hit MSU's football program with three years probation. There would be no bowl opportunities, no national television, a significant reduction in football scholarships, and the reputation as cheater that MSU now would bear. It had seemed that nothing could match the NCAA sentence for shock or disruption to a university athletic department. But six weeks later, after a lingering debate over who was responsible for what part of the football scandal, the Board of Trustees would decide at a hushed-up Friday night meeting to fire both Denny Stolz, MSU's head football coach, and Gus Ganakas, the basketball coach who had come off a respectable 1975-76 season, and a coach whose problems had nothing to do with football investigations. Board members also decided that Burt Smith, who had been reassigned in October, would also be dismissed.

It was trauma enough for one university to ax one of its high-profile head coaches. Michigan State had gotten rid of two in one fell swoop, and it had come not even two months after probation had transformed a proud, vibrant university into a campus community disgraced and humiliated by wrongdoings and upheaval.

Adding to the turmoil was the presence of an athletic director whose title remained "acting" AD. Michigan State would find it difficult to rally around a man whose position and authority had yet to be clarified or made permanent.

It was going to be agreeable either way to Jack Shingleton. He would stay if the job were structured correctly; if he had full authority and support from an administration that had not yet asked him to stay on. But he would just as happily return to the Placement Office if MSU decided to bring in new blood.

It had been decided in Clifton Wharton's office, with support if not pressure from the Big Ten, that Michigan State go outside its own family in search of a permanent AD.

One name was particularly attractive: Joe Kearney, director of sports programs at the University of Washington, who was leaving Washington because of friction with vice-president Al Ulbrickson. Kearney was not a new name to MSU's execs. When the school four years earlier had looked at replacements for Biggie Munn, Kearney was invited to apply. But he was happy at Washington and never followed up.

Now was a different situation for Kearney, and for MSU. Kearney wanted work at a high-profile university and knew the Big Ten well from years of Rose Bowl inter-mingling. Three schools in the Far West had asked him about heading their programs, as had two in the South. But none had Michigan State's stature, its high-level conference connections, its resources or, perhaps, its potential. An athletic director arriving on the heels of probation could wait out the storm and help resurrect a program that was bound to bounce back. And look very good doing it.

Kearney arrived in East Lansing in February 1976 for a day of interviews and campus tours. Kearney, the executives noted, not only had plenty of personal polish, but his credentials were appealing to a university looking for a proven major-college leader mindful of the rules.

At Washington, he and the Huskies had been considered among the Pac-10's true squeaky-cleans. Kearney also had a reputation as an AD who hired good coaches. A sharp judge of character and talent, said those who knew him in Seattle. A good salesman, as well. It would be no small plus at MSU, which had a good deal of name-repair to do within the state and across the nation because of its NCAA misdeeds.

Stout and almost moon-faced, Kearney had reddish hair and a flair for speaking in upbeat, energized sentences that had great institutional appeal. Avoiding negatives and sticking to the high road was the Kearney credo. Not until his final days at East Lansing would Kearney confront the kind of controversy he would essentially avoid during a four-year stay at Michigan State.

It all combined to make Kearney a candidate ideal in the eyes of Wharton, and an easy sell to a Board of Trustees that was anxious to escape political heat and community gloom over the football disaster.

Kearney was appointed AD at a board meeting on February 20, 1976. Four days later he was brought to East Lansing for an introductory press conference at Kellogg Center that would color him as a man with an endless supply of right answers. It was a sunny, warm, spring-like day on campus, and Kearney took advantage—even including an overdone put-down of his golfing talents.

"You know how people are given golf clubs, shirts and slacks at golf outings?" he began. "Well, I've been given an old German helmet with Afrika Corps painted on it because I spend so much time in the sand. I've been given a book on fauna and flora because I spend so much time in the rough. And I was even given a small chainsaw because I spend so much time in the trees."

On coming to a school that was only four weeks into a three-year probationary penance, Kearney became almost senatorial:

"You recognize the known negatives," he said, "and you accentuate the pluses of the overall program. You get innovative and use imagination, and articulate to the public what you're doing."

He made doubly sure to appeal to a Michigan State camp that wondered if it could repair its reputation, let alone gain parity with the rival in Ann Arbor. "Michigan State represents the people of Michigan, just as the University of Michigan does," Kearney insisted, "and there's no reason why both can't be successful."

Kearney's only slip-up at his unveiling was a bad analogy in which he confessed to knowing little about hockey. It didn't matter, he said, since he had come to Washington knowing nothing about crew, but had eventually developed interest and expertise in an important sport at the seaside campus. The remarks did little to soothe hockey fans at Michigan State, who were enjoying a fabulous season that saw the Spartans come within a sudden-death goal of reaching the national semifinals at Denver. Kearney immediately was in trouble with a semi-provincial crowd that customarily viewed itself as the athletic department's step-child.

Kearney worried instead about media and fan response in East Lansing as he boarded a plane back to Seattle. He would head to

Hawaii for vacation before returning to Michigan State to begin work on April 1, and he wanted badly to start off right at this complex place known as Michigan State.

Media people were stunned by a man so anxious to please, particularly after so much venom had been traded by both sides during the past year. They got a quick lesson in Kearney's public relations talents when, without exception, post cards from Hawaii arrived in their offices a week later. Kearney was passing on hellos to a group that had been spattered with "no comments" since NCAA snoops arrived a year earlier.

Kearney's vacation along Hawaii's sands would be anything but idle time. He had two immense assignments that had to be tackled as quickly as he returned to Michigan State. A head football coach and head basketball coach needed to be hired. Immediately. Working on a candidate's list and sending out feelers would keep him busy between munches on his macadamia nuts.

The search had already turned more difficult than Kearney intended. He wanted for Michigan State his two head coaches at Washington: Don James, whom he had brought to the football team from Miami (Ohio); and Marv Harshman, the Huskies' respected basketball coach. Two coaches of this caliber would give MSU an instant break, Kearney concluded. But neither James nor Harshman was anxious to leave success at Seattle for uncertainty and difficulty at East Lansing.

Kearney would need to look elsewhere.

He was back on campus on April 1, pleased at the reception and anxious to hire head coaches whom Kearney hoped would excite and enthuse a MSU camp that needed any kind of brightener. Interviews would be held that weekend in Chicago, a convenient stop for candidates who would be coming in from across the country. It would also ensure the panel some privacy at a time when the media were all but bugging walls attempting to learn who was destined to take over the Spartan football and basketball programs.

The interview schedule was full: Dick Crum from Miami (Ohio); Jim Mora, defensive coordinator at Washington; Darryl Rogers from San Jose State, Roy Kramer from Central Michigan, Ed Youngs from Denny Stolz' MSU staff (interviewed in East Lansing), and former MSU players George Perles and Rollie Dotsch were all hoping to land a MSU football job that was considered a pearl even if the school were facing three bleak years of probation.

Among the basketball coaches to be questioned were Don DeVoe of Virginia Tech, Lee Rose of University North Carolina-Charlotte, Darrel Hedric of Miami (Ohio), Bill Hess from Ohio University, and Montana's Jud Heathcote.

In Kearney's mind, there was little doubt who would emerge No. 1. His candidates were Rogers and Heathcote. He knew them well from his West Coast dealings and in the case of Rogers, had passed him up, with regrets, when James won the job at Washington. Only if his two favorites wilted during interviews, or only if the screening committee overruled him—a suicidal maneuver for a school that had committed so much to an AD it needed to please—would Kearney's preferences toward Rogers and Heathcote lose out.

On April 5, there was a slam-bang, same-day announcement that Rogers and Heathcote were coming to East Lansing. They were unknowns to Michigan State's audience, but the selections certified that MSU had separated itself from any of the inbreeding that Wharton, the Big Ten office and a good segment of the public believed was responsible for Michigan State's NCAA crimes.

Kearney had brought to Michigan State new faces that appealed directly to football's needs, and the perceptions that haunted MSU basketball. Rogers, a young Californian with a religious belief in the forward pass, could maximize the entertainment value and success of a team gearing up for three years in the NCAA clink. Heathcote, a witty, foot-stomping disciplinarian, would instill boot-camp character in a team that fans still held in contempt because of the 1975 walkout.

Kearney returned to East Lansing feeling very good. In less than a month, MSU's hang-dog air had given way to enthusiasm and excitement. Some crackle had returned to campus. And inside Jenison, Kearney was establishing tempo and presence.

There were differences, for sure, in style and comportment. One noticeable distinction: Kearney, who held a doctorate in higher education, was keen on his title. Calls to his office were answered by secretary Sylvia Thompson and the greeting: "Dr. Kearney's office." Kearney's preference for the inclusion of "Dr." was strong, although not obsessive. He was "Joe Kearney" when he returned his own phone calls, but he clearly liked the "Dr. Joe" moniker that became popular around campus.

Helping Kearney tremendously as he settled into his new job were obvious diplomatic strengths. He had a politician's ability to say the things a crowd needed to hear—no small plus as he met with alumni and supporters who were like shell-shocked soldiers following the previous winter's ordeal.

Names were going to be a problem for a while. But he had a technique that helped at those moments when someone he had met a couple of times, but whose name escaped him, came by to shake hands.

"How ya doin', podner?" Kearney would say gleefully. It was the same technique favored by Jack Kinney, the omnipresent alumni director, whose dealings with national alums created an even tougher name challenge.

"How's the old pro?" Kinney would ask, pumping hands and slapping the "old pro" on the back, whoever he was. Trying to keep names straight among thousands of MSU grads, staffers and followers would have overwhelmed even Dale Carnegie. In any event, during the next four years Kearney would greet his share of "podners."

He had no 100-day scheme to turn around Michigan State or heal wounds that had been years in the making. It was not possible to do so, and most certainly, it was not politically smart for a politically shrewd man to make any such promises. Kearney instead took a modest approach. He would study and evaluate MSU for six months before making any serious policy changes.

He would also drop discreet nuggets where appropriate. Building and expansion projects were a favorite subject when the crowd was small. A new basketball arena, Kearney said, almost dreamily in a casual conversation, might work on the tennis courts south of Spartan Stadium. It could be part of a multi-story structure, with restaurant and . . . Kearney liked to fantasize about things far away from the drawing board.

Double-tiering both ends of Spartan Stadium was another pie-in-the-sky idea. It could happen, he said, if football caught fire and the Spartans became a hot ticket. Then, Kearney said, eyes flashing, Michigan State would play before a potential crowd of 105,000. It would certainly be something, thought Kearney, although he suspected it would not happen within his time. Michigan State was not going to be his last stop before retirement. He had told himself that when he took the job.

By summer, Kearney had been at Michigan State three months and his influence was being felt, if not radically, at least in ways that showed his would be a mildly but not wildly progressive administration. Full-page color ads promoting MSU's new passing game began appearing in regional editions of magazines such as Sports Illustrated. Promotion was a hallmark of Don Canham's athletic department at Michigan, and it was a philosophy shared by Kearney.

He was also taking care of his coaches. Or, if he wasn't shoveling more money in their direction—the quickest way to a coach's heart—he was at least saying the right things.

Strolling back from Kobs Field one spring day, Kearney and Danny Litwhiler, the MSU baseball coach, commiserated over another rough day for a team that had not been tearing up the Big Ten through the '70s.

"We've got to get you some help," Kearney said to Litwhiler.

It was the kind of commitment that made a night-and-day difference in a coach's morale. Kearney's remedy wasn't overwhelming—the promise of an extra tender or two over a three-year period—but it was the kind of acknowledgement coaches, especially non-revenue coaches, had been hungering for.

Rogers and Heathcote were faring much better. Generally speaking, both were getting the help a head coach desired from an athletic director who wanted his 1-2 men contented.

Rogers' office worked almost autonomously, the way so many major-college football programs operate, while Heathcote's challenge was to re-ignite basketball interest at a campus where hoops no longer were fashionable. Kearney would help there, accompanying Heathcote on his expeditions to campus dorms where MSU was hoping to establish a student following that would at least give MSU some grassroots energy.

It was going to take heavy salesmanship in Kearney's first year at Michigan State. The teams would be little help. Rogers' pass offense was bright, and Eddie Smith and Kirk Gibson were two fabulous sophomores, but the Spartans finished 4-6-1. Heathcote's basketball team had respectable talent in Greg Kelser, Bob Chapman, Edgar Wilson and freshman Terry Donnelly, and there was a snap to Heathcote's coaching style, but the Spartans rolled home with a 12-15 record (10-17 until Minnesota was later ordered by the NCAA to forfeit two games).

About all Michigan State had managed in Kearney's first year was to survive the brutal arrival of probation. During a reasonably upbeat first 12 months that featured Rogers' pass offense and Heathcote's solidity, fans and the multitudes on campus began to realize probation was no death sentence. In two more years Michigan State would be among the free and untainted. And what no one could be sure of on that first anniversary of the NCAA sentence, was that in April, a couple of weeks after Kearney's first anniversary as MSU athletic director, the fun would begin at Michigan State.

Kearney was in Colorado Springs for the Western Collegiate Hockey Association meetings when word came that Lansing Everett's Earvin (Magic) Johnson had lit up the town by announcing he would play basketball at Michigan State. Phones at the Jenison ticket office nearly suffered meltdown.

"We've got an incredible run," Dee Strong, the MSU ticket manager, told Kearney. "We could sell out right now."

A remedy was concocted by which student tickets would be split into packages. No one could get a ticket for the entire season, but a majority of fans would get a peek at the young man from Everett who was being counted on to do more than people like Heathcote or Gus Ganakas thought possible in the Big Ten.

By autumn, MSU was a new school. The football team was on its way to a 7-3-1 record and Rogers would be named Big Ten Coach of the Year. The basketball team turned Jenison into a winter carnival as Johnson and crosstown prep rival Jay Vincent took MSU to the Big Ten title and nearly to the NCAA Final Four before Kentucky, the eventual NCAA champion, nipped State, 52-49, in the finals of the Mideast Regional.

Spirits were up and so were contributions at a university where the donors had been backing off since bad news became the norm during '75-76. The athletic department's reserve was climbing from bare-bone numbers to an eventual $1.5-million nest egg by the end of Kearney's stay. Brighter times were bringing more money and, most gratifyingly, a new attitude to a school where, for years, extreme ups and downs had been dance partners.

Kearney was having a ball as MSU bounced back, and a big break was the lack of interference from above. Ed Harden, a gracious man who had taken over on an interim basis when Wharton moved on, knew the university, liked athletics, and was neither meddlesome nor dictatorial. Harden gave Kearney the freedom to run his department minus conflicts that for Kearney always meant a move elsewhere.

Kearney above all liked the jolt he got from being a man with visibility, a man who had a flair for the public relations aspects of his job. It was that element—not the policy-making responsibilities, not the budgets—that he most enjoyed. And it was that affinity for making appearances that led Kearney to seek hiring an assistant AD who could take care of the paperwork and free him up for even more commissioner-style duty.

Cecil Coleman, a former AD at Illinois, was one candidate Kearney wanted to bring to MSU in just such an administrative slot. Shingleton was also asked by Kearney if he might want to come aboard, although a position never was cleared.

All the while, coaches found Kearney pleasant and agreeable, but a snail when it came to decisions. Staffers might write Kearney a memo or letter about a matter, hoping for a firm response, but often the correspondence would come back with the notation: "See me." It was particularly frustrating when getting a session with Kearney could be rough.

Rogers and Heathcote were talking about their boss one day in the Jenison offices, speaking well of an AD with whom neither had a serious problem. "Yeah," Rogers sighed, "Joe's a good man."

"Good man," answered Heathcote, "except for one problem."

Heathcote dragged one foot behind him as he shuffled a few steps.

Much to the frustration of a few colleagues, the two high-profile coaches generally got what they needed. Rogers had a stubborn streak as wide as Grand River Avenue and was rarely, if ever, shot down, although one duel came in the summer of '79 when MSU was attempting to re-admit defensive back James Burroughs, who had left school following his sophomore year. Burroughs, an excellent athlete, decided at mid-summer he wanted to return to MSU. It was five weeks into summer session and Kearney explained that to get Burroughs the proper courses at that point would be nearly impossible.

"It can be done . . . it can be done," Rogers insisted.

It required some administrative arm-twisting, but Rogers won. Burroughs got his classes and was eligible for his junior season.

In the fall of '78, Michigan State began rolling toward a Big Ten trifecta that would see the Spartans tie for the title in football (probation would knock MSU from the Rose Bowl), win the conference and NCAA championships in basketball; and, with help through rainouts, take the Big Ten baseball crown. Even the cheerleaders were NCAA champs.

Probation ended in January of '79, which was one more example of the school's enormous ability to hit absolute highs and lows within short periods of time. Three years earlier the school—

ravaged by probation and firings—was a mass of devastation. By the spring of '79, it was amid glory. A NCAA basketball championship had transformed MSU from probationary disgrace into a glamourous school which once again had national prominence and respect.

The party would last all of nine months.

Magic Johnson left MSU for the National Basketball Association in May, returning the basketball program to ordinary status. The football team disintegrated at mid-season and finished 5-6 after a 3-0 start. And Kearney was getting nervous.

Cecil Mackey had been appointed MSU's new president in July. By the time he and right-hand man Ken Thompson settled in, Kearney and Rogers were both of a mind to get out of East Lansing as soon as possible.

Rogers had his first trouble with Mackey in their first meeting.

"Are you clean?" Mackey asked.

Rogers was insulted, while Kearney had already gotten indications that Mackey and Thompson would be hands-on execs who would clamp down on budgets and end the breezy era of athletic department autonomy.

By January, both were ready to leave for the kind of pitch Arizona State would make. Arizona State asked Kearney just after the Rose Bowl if it could speak with Rogers, and not long afterward, the same officials wondered if Kearney might also consider an AD job. Kearney initially said no. When he was contacted a week later at the 1980 NCAA meetings, Kearney said he would speak to ASU only if he were being offered a specific job. He would not risk the politically dangerous position of being a candidate, which could make life at MSU difficult if word leaked.

Within a week, Arizona State had decided a Rogers-Kearney package would be its best option. The deal was powerfully attractive to two men whose affection for the West had never wavered during four years of Michigan winters. Now, with a threatening president taking over, Phoenix and ASU looked like an oasis. Particularly if an AD and head coach, both sticklers on working with agreeable people, could move their partnership to ASU.

The announcement was made on January 15, 1980. That quickly, East Lansing was hit with another hurricane—this one named Controversy.

While Michigan State burned over the Kearney-Rogers exodus—a move that because of its behind-the-scenes arrangement particularly infuriated fans and followers—Georgia Tech's athletic director was scanning the *Atlanta Constitution* sports page. The story said Michigan State Coach Darryl Rogers was considering leaving for Arizona State.

While driving home, Doug Weaver heard that not only had Rogers resigned to take the ASU job, Joe Kearney, MSU's athletic director, was going with him. Weaver pulled his car into the garage and stepped inside the home outside Atlanta. His wife, Nancy, stood looking at him.

"If they want you," she began, "and you want to go, let's go."

Weaver grinned. Michigan State hadn't called and the best guess was MSU would not. Even if the new executives were interested, Weaver wasn't sure Tech was the place to leave. It was one of the South's best schools and Weaver had just hired a new head football coach, Bill Curry, who expected his AD to hang on.

But the thought overwhelmed him. Michigan State was his school. Michigan State had set his life in motion. Michigan State was home.

Within a week, Ken Thompson, assistant to new president Cecil Mackey, had called to arrange an interview. Thompson, faculty representative Gwen Norrell, and Jim Pickering, a member of MSU's Athletic Council, flew to Atlanta to interview Weaver at an airport hotel. Several days later, Doug Weaver was on his way to East Lansing as MSU's fifth athletic director in eight years.

As with Kearney four years earlier, Weaver's first assignment was to hire a new football coach. No new task here. Weaver had just finished shopping for a new coach at Tech, hop-scotching across the land to interview Jerry Glanville (Atlanta Falcons), George Welsh (Navy), Jerry Claiborne (Maryland), Jackie Sherrill (Pitt), Bobby Collins (Southern Mississippi), and Curry with the Packers—interviewing each at his own workplace.

By the time his plane touched down at Capitol City Airport, Michigan State's new athletic director could hear the wailing clear across town: No more interlopers at MSU. The fans wanted loyalty and commitment, preferably from someone with MSU breeding. From an objective standpoint it seemed almost juvenile—this collective hurt a university was feeling over the departure of two men who simply left for better jobs. But it overwhelmed Weaver and established obvious criteria as he began a coaching safari.

George Perles was the hot name. Pittsburgh's defensive line coach was a MSU man raised in Detroit who had the credentials MSU's camp thought necessary to avoid any more West Coast escapes.

Henry Bullough and Rollie Dotsch, two more from the Spartans' glory days, were also popular. Wayne Fontes, an assistant at Tampa Bay of the National Football League who played at Michigan State, was mentioned. So was Bill McCartney, defensive coordinator at the University of Michigan. State fans were so angry with Rogers and Kearney that even an assistant from the enemy camp was acceptable as long as he had the savvy and loyalty which seemed to mark McCartney. It didn't hurt that Weaver had helped recruit and coach McCartney when both were at Missouri.

Sherm Lewis, the only assistant coach who had not followed Rogers to Arizona State, was also a contender at a time when Weaver was getting advice, phone calls and telegrams from everyone.

His name was not once mentioned in the press, nor did there seem to be the slightest cry for him anywhere in the state. But one man kept rolling through Weaver's mind: Muddy Waters, a legend at Hillsdale College who now was coaching at Saginaw Valley State College.

It would come down to a decision between him and Perles. An interview in Pittsburgh had not turned Weaver off to Perles, a player he once coached at MSU. He would do, Weaver thought. There was just something that didn't seem quite right. Maybe it was Perles' reputation as a bit of a rough-houser during his MSU days. Maybe it was the wheeler-dealer aura of the NFL.

Whatever, Weaver was ripe to be bowled over during an overtime interview session with Waters. Loyalty? Love for school? Dedication? Green and White?

Weaver couldn't believe that the white-haired man speaking of Biggie Munn, of Charley Bachman, of Duffy Daugherty, could be so genuine and carry such bold credentials from his small-college coaching career. Weaver knew Waters had been respected at Hillsdale. He knew also that Waters had recruited without frills or funny business. If Michigan State needed help from the family, no one seemed better suited than Franklin Dean Waters.

Weaver learned quickly that the man counted on to heal wounds and restore pride was not an instant hit with fans expecting a higher-profile selection. Weaver had underestimated the campus

MSU Photo

Ellis Duckett's blocked punt helped win the '54 Rose Bowl for State — Biggie Munn's (inset) last game as coach.

MSU Photo

A 41-yard field goal by Dave Kaiser gave MSU and Duffy Daugherty a 17-14 Rose Bowl win over UCLA in 1956 — the Spartans' last Rose Bowl victory.

The Daugherty pipeline ran nationally during the glory years. A few of the talents are shown here (from the left): Bob Apisa, Clint Jones, Bubba Smith, Gene Washington and George Webster —five members of the great mid-1960s teams.

George Perles (just behind Daugherty and to his right) returned as an MSU assistant in 1967 — just in time for Duffy's final, disappointing seasons.

Word of Daugherty's retirement leaked a month early, so he waved to the crowd before dumping Purdue in '72.

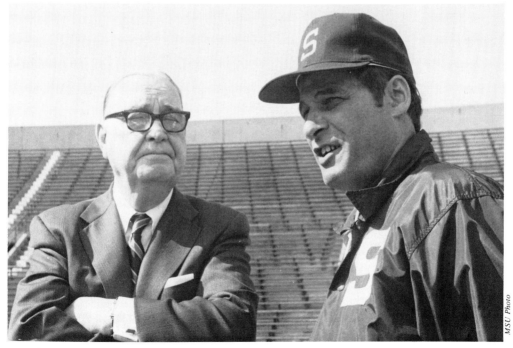

All-hairs-in-place Denny Stolz (right) replaced Daugherty. His staff's recruiting got him some big wins...and big trouble. Former MSU coach, Jim Crowley — one of Notre Dame's Four Horseman — is pictured with Stolz.

One of college football's most dramatic runs was this 88-yarder by Levi Jackson that pushed MSU past Ohio State in '74 — and helped convince OSU Coach Woody Hayes that something was rotten in East Lansing.

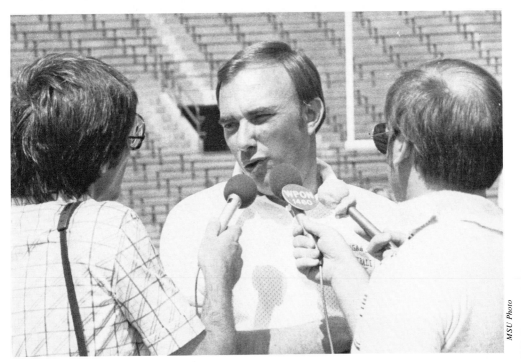

MSU Photo

Some Spartan followers agreed that Darryl Rogers talked out the side of his mouth. But he brought the forward pass to the Big Ten, and may have left MSU at the right time.

MSU Photo

MSU Photo

Flanker Kirk Gibson (left) and quarterback Eddie Smith (right) formed one of football's most exciting pass combos from 1976-78.

Muddy Waters encountered more than his share of problems during three years as Spartan football coach from 1980-82.

George Perles and quarterback Dave Yarema led MSU to a pair of bowl appearances — and three straight winning seasons — during Perles' first four years as coach.

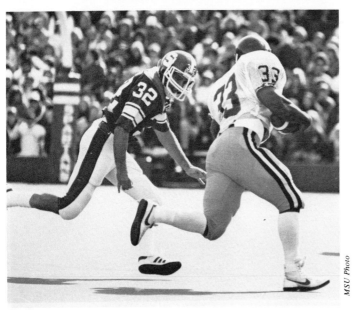

Phil Parker (32) had a nose for the ball during his career, especially under Perles.

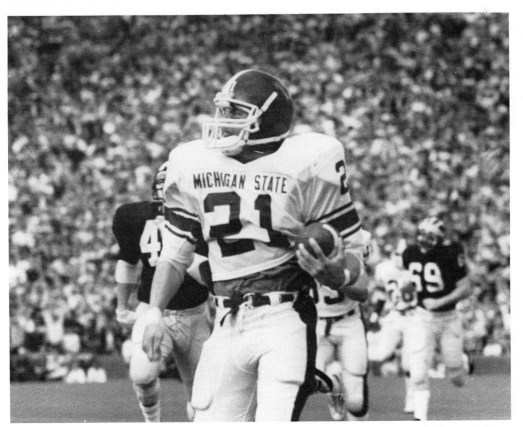

Bobby Morse's 87-yard punt return just before halftime helped MSU upset Michigan, 19-7, in 1984.

Perles' biggest breakthrough may have been the recruiting of star tailback Lorenzo White.

Basketball Coach John Benington (left) is shown here as assistant to Pete Newell (right). Benington was passed over when Newell left, then returned to the top MSU job in 1965.

Forddy Anderson had the most dramatic loser in Final Four history — and, it was said, a taste for the fast lane.

Johnny Green was discovered by Spartan coaches while playing pick-up basketball in the upstairs gym at Jenison Field House.

Gus Ganakas saw his solid 1974-75 team walk out over Jeff Tropf's presence in the starting lineup. Here, his JV players are introduced before losing to No. 1-ranked Indiana.

Ralph Simpson played only one year of varsity ball before turning pro.

Silky-smooth Mike Robinson's soft shooting touch was a highlight of the Ganakas era.

MSU Photo

The best orchestra Jud Heathcote conducted was the 1979 national championship team with Magic Johnson playing First Chair.

MSU Photo

A flying Greg Kelser was a familiar sight during the late '70s, — often stuffing Magic's alley-oop passes through the hoop.

MSU Photo

The rivalry of the No. 33's — Johnson and Larry Bird — began during Michigan State's 75-64 victory over Indiana State in the 1979 national title game.

Magic's jersey was ultimately retired.

Photo by David Kryszak. Reprinted by permission of The Detroit News, Inc., a Gannett Newspaper. Copyright 1979.

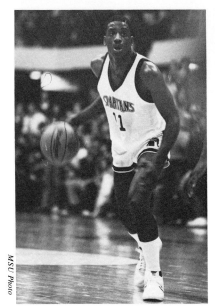

The brothers Vincent — Sam (left) and Jay (right) — both liked offense the best.

Scott Skiles (foreground) survived problems off the court; Larry Polec (background) survived Students Against Polec. Together, they led surprising MSU to college basketball's Sweet 16 in 1986.

John Kobs (left) served as Spartan baseball coach long enough to have the field named after him. Part of his success was putting the ball into the capable hands of pitcher Dick Radatz (right), who went on to become one of baseball's all-time great relievers.

Tom Smith (left) took over for Danny Litwhiler (right) in 1983. Neither coach ever got the budget required to hit baseball's big time, but produced competitive teams.

Steve Garvey went on to become a household name.

Kirk Gibson's (seated) year of Spartan baseball resulted in a lucrative contract with the Detroit Tigers. Witnessing the 1978 signing are (from the left): Gibson's parents, Robert and Barbara; Tigers General Manager Jim Campbell and then-scout Bill Lajoie.

Photo by Edwin C. Lombardo. Reprinted by permission of The Detroit News, Inc., a Gannett Newspaper. Copyright 1978.

MSU Photo

MSU Photo

Bob Boyd left shortly before hockey games were switched from old Demonstration Hall to newly built Munn Arena.

Even playing in Dem Hall beat getting up at 2 in the morning to water Michigan Tech's outdoor rink for Amo Bessone, shown here coaching during a game at Munn Arena.

With Norm Foster (above) alternating with Bob Essensa from 1983-87, MSU continued its long tradition of great netminding.

Don McSween spent four years as a standout defenseman from 1983-87.

Coach Ron Mason (left) had more going for him on the recruiting trails than just a manila folder, reaching the Final Four three times from 1984-87. One of those recruits was Kelly Miller (right), another in a long line of hockey-playing Millers from Lansing.

Duffy Daugherty (seated) and Biggie Munn (standing) were never nearly as close as their nameplates were in this photo.

Happy times ended in dismissal for Athletic Director Burt Smith.

AD Joe Kearney eventually replaced Burt Smith, but bolted to Arizona State just four years later along with Football Coach Darryl Rogers.

Under AD Doug Weaver, the Spartan sports complex has added a football practice building and indoor tennis facility, and is finishing a new arena that will seat close to 16,000 fans for basketball and other events.

and community mood when he took the job, and he now understood that naming Waters was not the most politically brilliant move he had made in college athletics. Faced with disbelief or even hostility from fans, there would be even more pressure on Waters, and the man who hired him.

Weaver shook it off. He had an effervescence about him that tended, at least on the surface, to neutralize these things. It was the trademark of a humorist—the style of an extrovert who would laugh and please an audience, just as he had during his wisecracking days on the Spartan football field. Three consecutive years he had won the Oil Can Award as team humorist. Now, he was out to prove that not only was Doug Weaver still the nice guy, still the friendly man with a sense of humor, but that he was also a good athletic director.

Weaver was born and raised in the farmland of Goshen, Indiana, and had originally come to Michigan State by a strange route—from Yale, where he had studied as a freshman. He was a good student and athlete at Goshen, but at 5-feet-9, 160 pounds, neither Indiana, Purdue nor Notre Dame—schools he wanted to attend—was interested in a pint-sized farm boy, even if he was good with a quip. Family friends convinced him to try an Ivy League school, Yale, where an under-sized man could play football and still experience the heights of American academic excellence.

Weaver thought it a smart idea. For a year. Going from Goshen to New Haven, Connecticut, was a staggering cultural adjustment that could be handled, but Ivy League football left Weaver cold. It wasn't the game he knew was played at Midwest schools. The decision was to try it at a place called Michigan State where Biggie Munn's teams were becoming national terrors, and where a smaller player just might fit in on a team not known for its size but for the ability of its head coach to pump the most from his players.

Once in East Lansing, Weaver felt as if he were at home. Michigan State had the fresh-air atmosphere missing at Yale, and the kind of football team that not only played top-drawer athletics, but made room for a shrimp of a lineman. Weaver lettered three years—1950-51-52—and all at center.

It had not been as blissful as the Oil Can Winner let on. When he was 21, still a year to go before getting his degree and Air Force ROTC commission, Weaver had personal problems that he thought would be best handled if he left school. The trouble wasn't anything that would be discussed with anyone except, perhaps, a Jack Breslin, who had played for MSU a few years earlier and now was working as an assistant director for alumni relations. Breslin persuaded Weaver to stay. A year later, Weaver had his degree, his commission, and a steady girlfriend named Nancy Doty, who would become his wife.

The friendship with Breslin continued as years and experiences showed Weaver how dangerously close he had come to bankrupting his life. In 1972, Breslin invited Weaver—then at UCLA as an assistant coach—to lunch at a restaurant north of Malibu. Breslin was interested in discussing the athletic director's job at Michigan State with an old friend who had picked up a law degree in between coaching stops in the '60s.

It had been an eventful two decades since Weaver had been at Michigan State. He had gone off to the Air Force for two years, returned to MSU to work as freshman coach and as varsity assistant, then had gone to Missouri as an assistant before taking the head coaching job at Kansas State in 1960. Six years later he was fired and decided that at age 36 he needed to do something radical with his life. Coaching was obviously a gamble. But sports administration, another interest, was more secure, except that it would require more academic or business experience than he had collected in 10 years of walking the nomadic path of a coach.

Practicing law was one option. Weaver, an English major as an undergrad, had a decade earlier been set to try law school when Duffy Daugherty spotted him at the MSU Placement Center and sold him on the idea of joining his coaching staff. Now, in 1966, Weaver's first shot as a head coach had collapsed and law looked particularly attractive to a coach whose career had hit a definite ceiling.

An obvious problem was handling law school with a wife and three children. Weaver decided if it was going to happen, it would be at the University of Kansas. He had a name that would help him get accepted at Lawrence, and by paying in-state tuition, it would be just enough break to make the whole impossible idea feasible.

Getting fired hadn't been Weaver's only trauma during the previous year. Nancy, who was having a difficult time with a congenital condition, underwent her second spinal fusion in the summer of 1966. Weaver was on his way from Manhattan to the Topeka hospital where Nancy was recovering when he was greeted at the door by a nurse.

"Don't worry, Mr. Weaver," she said, breathlessly, "your children are all right."

Weaver turned white.

The nurse explained that a tornado had just hit Manhattan. Weaver's home was destroyed. But the kids had been taken to the basement by Nancy's parents, who had flown up from Florida to help out during the recuperation. No one had been harmed.

The scare only made Weaver more determined to put some direction into a life running high on frustration and disorder. The house in Manhattan—rebuilt after the tornado, while the Weavers lived in a home vacated by the athletic director—was sold, the equity tossed into the bank for living expenses, and Weaver and his family headed to Lawrence for the start of law school in February of 1967. A pension fund he had accumulated was also cashed in, and there were major adjustments in lifestyle. Dust Bowl austerity was back in vogue—at least in the Weaver household.

It would help that Pepper Rodgers was head coach at Kansas and a Weaver friend. Weaver was invited to join the staff as a graduate assistant coach. It was nice work for an ex-coach who did not want to leave football entirely, and who needed badly the $250 or $300 a month Rodgers paid him. Best of all, Weaver wouldn't have to do any recruiting.

But it was no party trying to fit law school, football and family duties into a 24-hour day. Weaver would finish working with the defensive ends at practice, then hunker down for an evening of meetings that would go until 10 p.m. After meetings, he could look forward to cracking the law books until 2, 3 or 4 a.m. In a few hours the schedule would begin all over again. For three years the law school rigors would last. And by the time he passed his bar exam in 1970 and became a law partner in the firm of Jack Brand, Weaver would wonder after a few months whether law had been his smartest move.

It didn't have the spark or energy he had known in football. Its real benefit—if ever realized—Weaver knew would be its ability to push him above the chalkboards and film projectors and into the administration of college athletics.

The chance to get back into football would come in 1971 when Rodgers took the head coaching job at UCLA. Weaver was asked to come along as an assistant and accepted. It was just the opportunity a lawyer itching to get back into football wanted. And it would be a bit easier on him, going home from a 10 p.m. meeting knowing that a man could climb in bed and sleep rather than burn midnight oil over a law book.

Weaver's conversation with Breslin the following year never led to the interview Weaver had hoped to get just before MSU named Burt Smith its new athletic director. Already, he had turned down one job waiting for something on the level of MSU athletic director: Dan Devine's request that he come to Green Bay to become the Packers' personnel director.

College athletics were still Weaver's goal. Still the inspiration for having endured those three years as a sleep-starved law student.

Another job crisis was on the horizon. Kansas was looking for a new head football coach, and Weaver seemed headed back to Lawrence until his bid was shot down in its final stage by the Kansas Board of Trustees. Next came an invitation from Southern Illinois, which in 1973 was looking for an athletic director. Weaver thought it was the place to start, until, after moving in at SIU, the school chopped budgets and fired its head football coach, which left the new AD to work also as head coach.

Three years later, Georgia Tech invited Weaver to move to Atlanta to become AD and AD only. It was nearly 10 years since Weaver had committed to law school as a career boost, and now, finally, it was about to pay off.

There would be grand moments at Georgia Tech—getting the school into the Atlantic Coast Conference—and bad ones, none much worse than when Weaver was ordered by the president and board to fire his old coach and friend, Pepper Rodgers, following a 4-6-1 season.

Through the next four years Georgia Tech's real benefit to Weaver would be its reputation. He was athletic director at one of the South's best schools, an institution with great academic heritage whose prestige would help mightily when Michigan State began shopping for Kearney's replacement in January of 1980.

On the day he arrived in East Lansing as Michigan State's newest athletic director, it was clear some of the old Weaver traits had not changed during 24 years of travels as coach, lawyer and AD. He obviously liked people, and he certainly had a thing for Michigan State: "It was at Berkey Hall where I met my wife . . . it was right there that we practiced . . . it was the day Biggie took us . . ."

Weaver's obsession with Spartan nostalgia was overwhelming. It also contributed to his feeling that Muddy Waters, a man who wallowed in memories of Michigan State's good old days, would be the answer to a football program that needed to rediscover Munn-style values.

It was returning an entire athletic program to the simple sweetness of the '40s and '50s that Weaver soon realized would be difficult at a school as bruised and as vulnerable as Michigan State. Probation, a year after it expired, was still being felt on a football team gouged by earlier recruiting limitations. Basketball fortunes had plummeted with the departure of Earvin Johnson. Hockey was on the way back, but still struggling as Ron Mason worked to reconstruct a program that had fallen apart during the late '70s.

It didn't help that money was tight. The new bosses, Cecil Mackey and Ken Thompson, were watching the pennies of a program that was not generating oceans of revenue. It would help Waters that MSU's Duffy Daugherty Football Building was ready to open in the winter of 1980. The football operation needed not only to show vitality and growth, but there was also a need for new facilities. Locker rooms, coaching offices, weight-training areas—everything was suffering by comparison to some of the country's brighter and steadier football programs.

The pepped-up facilities proved to be no more boost during the 1980 season than Waters' strategy for reviving a droopy football team. The Spartans finished 3-8, and it wasn't only the record that made Weaver wonder if he had made the right choice back in January. Meetings with the new head coach weren't as reassuring or as inspiring as that interview session had been back at Kellogg Center. Weaver knew, too, that Joe Pendry, the offensive coordinator whom he didn't particularly adore, had been taking charge either by default or by design.

It was one of the reasons the reality of directing Michigan State's athletic department was far removed from the Shangri-La atmosphere Weaver had known during Munn's days. The job was now so complex. And, in a way, it could be intimidating. Coaches seemed always to be griping or complaining or begging for money. Fans were impatient and often irrational. It didn't help that MSU was always being compared to the smooth, efficient, nationally prominent program down the road in Ann Arbor. Don Canham's shadow easily stretched 80 miles, far enough to fall upon Weaver and Michigan State.

Weaver's style was to work quietly and avoid any atttempt at duplicating the oratorical command Canham held. It was difficult, though, not to develop an inferiority complex when an issue arose and the AD at Michigan—best in the country, consensus had it—was always the one contacted, always the one quoted. Weaver was seldom sounded out, and if he were, the responses were carefully constructed and offered almost apologetically.

"I'm not a hot ticket," he would say.

Emerging within Jenison's offices was the profile of an athletic director comprised of conflicting styles: Sensitive yet sometimes ruthless, open and witty yet stand-offish. He could float along on such a high that the job's exhilaration would nearly overwhelm him. His car might be left with its engine running in the parking lot. He would pull into a self-serve station and absent-mindedly try to put regular gas into a diesel car. Weaver could step back and laugh at himself, but he wanted also to be taken seriously. Hence the occasional frustration.

His sensitivity came through in the way he sometimes dressed down an underling. Weaver had the knack for doing it in a way that might leave the offender doubting that he or she had been disciplined as much as consulted. Tough letters, too, were often feathered. Weaver's legal background—his ability to shape thoughts and sentences delicately—obviously helped. It was clear to most associates that Weaver, intellectually, was as heavy a hitter as had worked in the AD's office at Michigan State. It was his method of administrating that could drive a staffer nuts.

The coaches' frustration would come when the seemingly personable, outgoing, full-of-fun, Oil Can monopolist became so elusive and distant when they wanted a meeting. He was there, but he wasn't. Appointments were difficult to arrange. See me before 7 a.m., or after 7 p.m., he might say. Or, see so-and-so instead.

Was he threatened by employees? Was he uncomfortable dealing with tough matters in the softening atmosphere of one-on-one meetings? No one knew. But it bothered coaches and staffers, particularly those who believed that the Holy Trinity of revenue-producing head coaches—Waters or George Perles, Jud Heathcote and Ron Mason—got everything they wanted at the expense of the non-revenue sports. It was a charge that angered Weaver. It bothered him all the more at a point in the mid-'80s when football, basketball and hockey were doing well, and now it was followers of a depressed baseball program who were yelling about budget neglect.

"There weren't that many complaints about baseball until recently," he would say, slyly, half-smiling, suggesting that baseball became a focal point only after the big-gun programs began thriving. An unspoken thought Weaver wanted to toss at the critics: How many national hockey championships had Michigan won, or threatened to win, since he became athletic director? But Weaver would have his tongue cut out before letting loose with that one. Especially when MSU's brilliant coach, Ron Mason, had been a Joe Kearney hire.

Weaver was having a tougher time with his own hires. Although the football team perked up in 1981—a 5-6 finish—the 1982 season would disintegrate into Michigan State's worst football effort in 65 years. He would fire Muddy Waters in November, then hear a nearly statewide call for his own scalp. Weaver had been architect of the Waters era and as such, it was argued, he should also go if Waters were axed.

Pressure was on as he started a coaching search the day after Thanksgiving, 1982. Weaver understood that to save his own job and compensate for the mistake he had made with Waters, he needed to pull off a double play: He must hire a crackerjack coach who could put the football program into immediate order, and he must select someone universally popular with the MSU audience. George Perles was probably the man, but Perles was head coach of the United States Football League's Philadelphia Stars and was making a bundle. Even if he wanted to come to East Lansing, Michigan State could hardly expect that Perles would take a 50 percent paycut.

Another possibility: Don Nehlen, head coach at West Virginia. Nehlen had coached at Bowling Green and on Bo Schembechler's staff at Michigan, and might leave for a shot at a job that had more resources than West Virginia. Weaver called Fred Schaus, athletic director at West Virginia, and got permission to speak with Nehlen. If neither Perles nor Nehlen worked out, another candidate would be Wayne Fontes, an ex-Spartan who was an assistant coach with the Tampa Bay Bucaneers.

Weaver was pleased—excited, really—when Perles called him three days after Thanksgiving, saying he would be interested. Becoming a head coach in the pros obviously wasn't Perles' ultimate dream. And he was aware enough of college football's realities to know that MSU wasn't about to meet the $150,000-per-year in salary the Stars were paying. Weaver realized there was a chance it could work out.

A meeting was arranged for the following Thursday at the Stadium Hilton hotel in Philadelphia. To avoid reporters, Weaver had checked the two of them into a suite under aliases, Harry Schwartz and George Good. Neither of them needed a replay of the 1980 episode that had seen Perles lose to Waters just as the world expected Perles to be named.

It was only minutes before each realized George Perles was going to become Michigan State's next head football coach. It was still the only job Perles ever had wanted, and Weaver, as contrasted with their dinner at Pittsburgh in 1980, felt good about Perles. Perhaps it was the difference in situations—Weaver needed Perles as much as Perles wanted MSU—but the athletic director saw a different man than he had seen at dinner in Pittsburgh in 1980. He couldn't pinpoint it, but there seemed to be more maturity, more polish, more of the kind of aura a Big Ten head coach should carry.

They ordered a pot of coffee and began hammering out details, not all of which was salary and fringe benefits. Because Perles had a three-year contract with the Stars, Weaver had earlier suggested that he call the Stars owner, Myles Tanenbaum, for permission to speak with Perles.

"I'll handle it," Perles assured him. "It'll be no problem. Myles is a great guy, and I explained to him when I took the job that my goal has always been to be head coach at Michigan State."

Weaver didn't feel like arguing. He and Michigan State were about to get their man and he didn't want any complications. If Tanenbaum had a problem with Perles' departure, it would come after Perles agreed to take the job at Michigan State. To approach Tanenbaum now was to invite a hangup that could ruin Perles' shot at a job he, and now Weaver, wanted desperately to happen. Even Weaver's legal background persuaded him it was the way to handle a matter that showed no signs of becoming a problem. But he did ask Perles to confirm with Tanenbaum that there would be no interference.

The meeting lasted until almost 8 p.m.—nearly nine hours after they had holed up at the hotel. Perles would receive a five-year contract with annual salary of $95,000, and would become the highest-paid head coach in the Big Ten. It was salary unheard of in a conference that paid coaches competitively, but back in East Lansing, where Cecil Mackey and Ken Thompson were feeling as much heat as Weaver for the football program's plight, it was decided in the president's office that whatever the investment, Michigan State was not in a position to quibble about paychecks. It was time—politically and athletically—to commit to a football team that was considered a university resource.

During a Board of Trustees meeting the next day, details of Perles' contract were relayed from Weaver in Philadelphia over the phone to Thompson, who carried them to Mackey and the Board. The contract was approved and now, almost three years after Perles had been snubbed by Michigan State, he was being brought back to the kind of reception never given for Denny Stolz, Darryl Rogers, nor most certainly, for Waters.

But amid all the celebrating there were those either angered by the Perles appointment or by the money he was making. Peter Fletcher, a member of the Board of Trustees, thought the salary was exorbitant. The Board, in fact, had considered the idea of firing Weaver.

But the most serious commotion was taking place in Philadelphia, where Tanenbaum was seething over the loss of a head coach he expected to be there for the start of the USFL's first season, which was only 90 days away. Tanenbaum felt Michigan State had stolen his coach, and he wanted compensation. Heavy compensation.

Weaver, Perles and Michigan State went on about their business. Lawyers would take care of the Tanenbaum matter and his $1-million suit against MSU. Tanenbaum later settled out-of-court for $175,000 and the knowledge MSU had spent several hundred thousand dollars in compensation and lawyer fees for its successful courtship of Perles.

Within a year, Perles had taken MSU from its 2-9 disaster in 1982 to a 4-6-1 finish, and a big upset of Notre Dame, in his debut season. A year later MSU came in at 6-5 and played in the Cherry Bowl—its first bowl visit in 19 years. And a year later, after Perles' team climbed to 7-4 and made another bowl apperance, after the basketball team made a stunning run during the NCAA tournament, and after Ron Mason's hockey team won the NCAA championship, Weaver began to relax and enjoy a job that he, like Perles, had spent most of his life wanting.

He was given a six-year contract extension in 1986. His critics weren't pleased, but Weaver could finally say law school had been worth it.

Eight

WALKOUTS AND WALK-ONS

The bus pulled into Jenison Field House's parking lot sometime after 3 a.m. on another of Michigan's bitterly cold first Fridays in January. It wouldn't have seemed as forbidding as 15 sleepy players and coaches stepped off the bus and into the chill had Michigan State opened its Big Ten basketball season with more aplomb than it had shown in a 93-86 tumble at Purdue, a game on January 2, 1975 that featured 56 points by Boilermaker forwards Wayne Walls and Walter Jordan.

Worse, MSU would get no breather the next day when Indiana, No. 1 in the country, rolled into Jenison for an afternoon game that promised to show a 6-2 MSU team whether or not it had a shot at shaking up the Big Ten's upper division. Gus Ganakas knew something had to be done with the front line or Kent Benson, Scott May and Steve Green would treat themselves to the same smorgasbord from which Walls and Jordan had dined the previous night.

Keeping its composure was MSU's challenge at this, the most delicate time on State's schedule.

"Let's not panic 'cause we lost this game," Ganakas told the players. "We played pretty well tonight. It's a tough place to win at."

Ganakas and his assistants, Vern Payne and Dick Versace, would work on revamping the front line during a Friday that promised to be no picnic for the players. It was registration week for students who needed to secure winter-term housing and endure the hassles of class registration in an area of the Men's Intramural Building known as "The Pit." Surviving that session would help prepare any athlete for the rigors of the Big Ten season.

At their staff meeting the next morning, Ganakas, Payne and Versace pondered the prospect of stopping an Indiana team that chewed up any sign of defensive weakness. What to do with MSU's Swiss-cheese forwards, freshman Jeff Tropf and junior Terry Furlow, was the question as they considered who would start.

"I think what I'll do is go with Pete Davis at guard," Ganakas began. "Let's start him. He'll give us 10 minutes of good basketball. Give us a little lift at the outset. And then let's go with Tom McGill at one of the forwards. We need one, stabilizing defensive player."

Payne and Versace liked the idea, initially. But the longer they thought about it, the more it seemed unwise when Ganakas had made such a point Thursday night of telling his players not to panic. Tropf obviously was the forward who would be replaced— Furlow was experienced and usually a superb offensive player—but he had played well in a big victory over the University of Detroit and had scrapped and helped out nicely for a 6-foot-8 freshman who needed experience.

Sound point, said Ganakas. Tropf would stick at forward, but Pete Davis would start at guard as MSU hoped to get the jump on a Hoosiers team that had just flown in, exhausted, from the Rainbow Classic in Honolulu.

Although it was common for Ganakas to discuss strategy and personnel decisions at practice with Lindsay Hairston, MSU's starting center and team captain, Ganakas never told Hairston at Friday's short workout that he was considering any lineup changes. Ganakas went off later that night to scout a high school game, unaware that most of his team was unhappy that the white freshman from nearby Holt was starting ahead of more experienced black players such as McGill. It was one of the specific gripes among a list of general grievances the players were feeling toward a basketball program they believed was being held to second-rate status by an athletic department much more lavish in its support of football.

Their general distress over the way MSU seemed to view basketball—budgets, food on the road, the way doors were left open during practice as MSU continued its state-ordered reduction in seating at Jenison—provoked the players to call a team meeting that night at the apartment of guard Bill Glover. While it wasn't offically a blacks-only meeting, neither Tropf nor Jim Dudley—who was dressing but not playing because of a bad ankle—had been invited to discuss whatever business was on the agenda.

It wasn't long into the session before MSU's administrative abuse of basketball became a dead issue versus the more pressing matter of why Tropf continued to start in place of McGill. It was, in the minds of a majority there, a clear matter of racial preference. Crowds were overwhelmingly white and Tropf obviously was someone with whom they could identify. He was also a neighborhood hero to the Lansing-East Lansing fans and symbolic of MSU's immediate basketball future—a young big man who seemed poised to become the team's dominant player once Hairston and Furlow moved on.

The team would have to do something about this, one of the 10 players gathered at Glover's concluded. A walk-out might work. Yes, agreed another, but let's work on it.

Edgar Wilson, a freshman from Dowagiac, was nervous, even scared as the discussion went on. He suggested that the team write out a list of grievances and present it to Ganakas, a man whom most of the team liked very much. Several players agreed with him. But the walk-out seemed to many of them the only way in which Michigan State would address real problems and knock off this foolishness of starting a freshman who in their eyes had no business starting.

Bob Chapman and Davis, who unknowingly was scheduled to start the next day, joined Wilson in arguing that a walk-out might be a serious mistake. But the prime spokesmen—Hairston and Glover—were saying the only way complaints could be acknowledged and stands could be taken was if 10 of them stood unified on all matters. A walk-out, included.

They would wait and see what happened at the next morning's pre-game meeting.

Ganakas and his assistants were in a second-floor conference room Saturday morning at the MSU Union as players began filing in, grabbing Cokes, apples and oranges and sitting down at a long conference table. At 10 a.m., Ganakas moved to a chalkboard to begin going over assignments that, he hoped, might keep MSU in it against a tired team that would face the compound problem of dealing with a very loud and excited Jenison Field House crowd.

"Okay, May . . . Furlow will be taking him," Ganakas began as he scrawled the Hoosier-Spartan matchups on a board. "Jeff, you'll be on Steve Green."

Ganakas turned around to see Hairston holding up a hand at the end of the table.

"Lindsay?"

"Coach, Jeff can't guard Green."

Tropf sat at the table, stunned. Ganakas was floored, but thought to remind Hairston that the previous season Green had scored 35 points against him. He recovered and said to Hairston:

"That's my decision to make."

The 10 black players got up from the table, turned and walked out the door.

Neither Ganakas, Payne, nor Versace knew quite how to react to a scene so baffling. Was it a bizarre practical joke? A collegiate prank that would end in a few minutes when the players came strolling back to the conference room—equipped with some form of explanation?

For the next few minutes the coaches tried to sort it out until, finally, it became apparent the walk-out was premeditated and obviously serious.

"We'll play without 'em," Ganakas said. "Beaumont Tower's bigger than they are."

There were almost three hours remaining until tipoff and the only thing Versace and Payne could do was get on the phone and round up as many junior varsity players as possible. Since classes would not start until Monday, many of the JVs were back at their homes finishing vacation and had not planned a return to campus until the next day.

Telephone messages from Payne, Versace and Pat Miller, the JV coach, that they would be playing Indiana in place of the varsity players staggered each of the fill-ins, some of whom were coming in from as far away as Bay City. Ganakas had decided not to suppress word of the walk-out but to play the game and advise executives what had happened.

He was sunken, sickened and embarrassed as he drove home to clear his head and begin making phone calls. One realization already had hit him: If this thing lasted until game time it would be professional suicide. He could say goodbye to a coaching career that had been looking bright as he headed into the thick of a Big Ten season in this, his sixth year as head coach at Michigan State.

One of his first calls was to Jack Breslin, MSU's athletics over-seer, who told Ganakas to do what the coach believed should be done. MSU's administration would back him all the way in a situation as rebellious as this.

A while later, Miller called Ganakas with a bulletin:

"They're here," Miller said. "The team's here."

"Tell Dick not to give them any equipment," Ganakas answered.

"Well," said Miller, "they've already got it."

By the time Ganakas arrived at Jenison and met Payne and Versace outside the players' locker room, he had no idea what to say or do. He still had no idea as he opened the door and saw the 10 players sitting with heads down in front of their lockers.

"Anybody got anything to say?" Ganakas asked.

Hairston looked up.

"Coach," he began, "it's nothing against you, or nothing against Jeff. All we want to do is win."

Ganakas could see that if there wasn't universal remorse among the players, there surely was an acute case of embarrassment. What he wasn't getting was anything remotely close to an apology or a request for forgiveness.

Hairston spoke up:

"So, Coach, we're just waiting to hear what you're gonna do."

Ganakas answered:

"You're suspended."

It was not what they had hoped to hear. The players began walking from the dressing room when Ganakas approached Davis. "Pete," he said, "you were gonna start." Davis was in tears as the 10 players walked out the door, through a tunnel that meanders its way to Jenison's north end, on a path that would march them defiantly along courtside, in front of the east bleachers where fans aware of the trouble booed them heavily.

Word had been spreading through Jenison that some type of mutiny had taken place among the black players. The prospect of a dozen clumsy scrubs taking on the No. 1-ranked team in the nation was such sheer comedy that the crowd became almost frenzied during warmups as the players nervously took their jump shots and shuffled through the lay-in drills.

Indiana Coach Bob Knight knew about the walk-out and hardly desired to kick off the Hoosiers' Big Ten season against a pick-up team. He also sympathized with Ganakas, whom he liked.

"Gus," he said, "you want Buckner (Quinn Buckner, the Hoosiers' fine guard) to talk with them? What can I do?"

There was nothing Indiana could do but accept apologies from a school that had turned its Big Ten home-opener into a basketball tragicomedy. MSU's only consolation was a sellout crowd that looked with such curious delight at the outmatched players flopping about on the court as MSU's pep band pounded and blared away. From an early, scared-stiff phase, the Spartan stand-ins had graduated to an almost dream-like stage brought on by pure adrenaline.

Moments before game introductions, Dudley bounded to the MSU bench where Miller had taken a seat alongside Ganakas, Versace and Payne. Ganakas, feeling a bit weary, had told Miller to handle the coaching duties—what few there would be.

"Coach," Dudley shouted to Miller as the crowd roared, "if we hustle we can beat 'em!"

Ganakas and Versace looked at each other, their jaws nearly scraping the hardwood.

When a MSU golfer and part-time basketball player named Brian Mullaney hit the game's opening basket, Jenison exploded. But entertainment value from a basketball farce would being to diminish rapidly, long before Indiana took its 107-55 victory back to Bloomington. Knight was forced to apologize to Ganakas at halftime for the massacre, but explained that with tough games coming up the following week, his team needed work.

The remainder of Michigan State's missing varsity had retreated from Jenison to an apartment shared by teammates Cedric Milton and Benny White. There they discussed the revolt, speculated about futures, and with the possible exception of Davis and Wilson, agreed that the rebellion had been warranted and would, in time, be constructive.

Within two hours they also realized the walk-out was national news as the White-Milton phone began ringing. Aware that the press was about to corner them, the players decided to return to their own rooms and apartments and wait until Sunday to decide on second-day strategy.

Ganakas returned home Saturday night to find a crowd of visitors waiting, many of them spitting out racial remarks at a nauseating pace. University and public sentiment was heavily in Ganakas' favor as the walk-out became portrayed as black insolence versus the authority of a Big Ten coach who never had been regarded as oppressive or heavy-handed. At a more distressing extreme, racists were unaccustomed to incidents so tailor-made to white prejudice and righteousness.

Ganakas still had no idea how a crisis this explosive, this damaging, could possibly be resolved without costing him his job or the players their MSU careers. There was limited administrative assistance since Burt Smith, MSU's athletic director, was at hockey meetings in Denver. It was still something Ganakas and his staff would have to work out on Sunday, when a coach's nightmare might somehow appear less hideous than it seemed on a cold January night.

By the next morning, Ganakas and his assistants were feeling much better. They had Tropf and Dudley—one potentially good player, one respectable—and a competent JV player in Mark Talaga of Bay City. There was the feeling that MSU might win a game or two with this gang of basketball ragamuffins, and that a head coach who survived such trauma—and earned a couple of victories, to boot—would be considered fairly the hero in East Lansing.

Just before he left for church, Ganakas got a phone call from Payne. The players, Payne said, had met and were now asking to be allowed back. Ganakas said he would discuss it after church, but when he returned home, the players were sitting in a circle in his living room, ready to talk peace.

Glover had now emerged as group spokesman and began repeating lines that Ganakas decided was simple reiteration of everything that had been said the day before.

"Look," Ganakas said, "go get something to eat and we'll meet at 3 p.m. at Jenison."

When Ganakas pulled into the Jenison parking lot later in the day, it looked as if MSU was hosting another matinee game. There were cars parked everywhere, most of them carrying media anxious to learn what the second day of a college sports drama might bring. Ganakas wondered, as well.

In Smith's absence, MSU President Clifton Wharton had appointed Clarence Underwood, MSU's assistant athletic director and athletic academic advisor, to act as mediator in discussions between players and the coaching staff. MSU had a home game scheduled the following night against Ohio State and needed to determine immediately whether the players would be reinstated, suspended permanently, or even if the season might be canceled.

The players huddled upstairs. Underwood met with them, then returned to Ganakas' office.

"They want to play Monday," Underwood reported. "They wonder what you can do to reinstate them."

Ganakas discussed it with Payne, a black assistant who had joined the MSU staff a year earlier.

"I'm still planning on going with the JVs," Ganakas said, "but I like those other kids. I recruited them and I want to keep them."

"Suspend them for the Ohio State game," Payne suggested, "and then meet with them one-on-one and decide what to do, individually."

Underwood relayed the message, and quickly returned.

"They want to play Monday, and then have a consultation with you."

Ganakas refused. Several minutes later the players walked into Ganakas' office. Hairston spoke first.

"Coach, we'll do whatever you want us to do," he began, getting eventually to the words that Ganakas had wanted to hear since 1 p.m. Saturday:

"We're sorry."

Ganakas threw up his hands.

"That's it. Let's play ball."

To the media jammed together outside, Ganakas would smile and explain that it was a "lover's quarrel" and meant nothing against the long-term relationship a coach enjoys with players who remain, in so many ways, kids. He and the players could forget about this stunning incident, Ganakas explained. He only hoped the public would.

From the tone of telegrams sent to his office on Monday, he quickly realized a predominantly white world outside was not about to welcome back 10 rebellious black basketball players. Racism was on display in a manner he had never experienced—not even three years earlier when Jenison's floor had twice been occupied by black protesters.

Ohio State Coach Fred Taylor would offer little help. Before Monday night's game, Taylor—who was being criticized in Columbus for failure to recruit talented black players—said he disagreed with Ganakas' decision to reinstate. It typified the sentiment against players whose primary objection to MSU's basketball program lay in the presence of a white teammate. Any of the players seeking sympathy for MSU's alleged basketball abuses found it disintegrating against perceptions that the players' own prejudice inspired an unforgivable, treasonous act.

Ganakas and the players—who were greeted cooly by fans who turned out for the Ohio State game—realized they had a major public-relations project ahead of them, even after an 88-84 victory over the Buckeyes in which Tropf, as usual, had started. An initial step would be taken during the pregame playing of the National Anthem. In contrast to their past indifference or head-hanging contempt toward a sacred United States custom, the players would pay heel-clicking respect to the American flag.

For the rest of the season, players generally cooperated with whatever Ganakas wanted, just as courtesy and diplomacy were practiced more rigidly than previously had been the case on MSU's basketball team. It was also becoming a snappier on-court squad. State came back from the Indiana debacle to go 10-7 in its final 17 games, good for a 17-9 finish and a 10-8 record and fifth-place spot in the Big Ten—Michigan State's best overall record since Ganakas had become head coach.

But the scar now blemishing Ganakas and the MSU basketball program would stick. Tropf and Dudley still believed teammates resented them as the team's only white players. Tropf knew the day of the walk-out that he was finished at MSU, telling himself that it wasn't entirely a matter of racism. It was that politics had taken precedence over winning. All anyone had to do was look at game films to see the white kid was purposely being denied the ball—it was a four-man team wearing a five-man disguise.

While Tropf had never encountered any blatant racist hostility from his teammates—he roomed at various times with several of them, and for years believed most of the 10 got caught up in something they never imagined would grow so ugly—he could not go on at Michigan State. The walkout, he realized, would hang over his head and mar MSU's basketball program for as long as he remained on campus. He asked Burt Smith in March to release him from his letter of intent, and later that year transferred to Central Michigan University. Dudley moved on to Marquette University. Ganakas understood he was powerless to argue otherwise following a winter so traumatic.

Ganakas also knew the team's image—as well as his own—needed extensive repair, even if a 17-9 season had gone down as his and MSU's best in years. Nothing, he realized, would restore a community's basketball interest and affection more quickly than a winning team. He had survived the January walkout and in doing so saved the careers and enhanced the futures of 10 college students.

Not until March of 1976 would Ganakas realize that fallout from the January 1975 incident was only one of the reasons why he was being dumped as head basketball coach.

In an upstairs gym at Jenison Field House, the usual early-autumn pick-up games were in full swing in 1955 as Bob Stevens, Michigan State's freshman basketball coach, wandered by to take a look at the material. Seldom would he see anyone talented whose name or reputation he did not know, but the man gliding across the court, leaping high above the basket, was not only a mystery but a marvel.

Stevens raced downstairs to the office of Forddy Anderson, MSU's head basketball coach.

"Hey, Forddy!," Stevens yelled. "Come here!"

What they watched for the next few minutes astounded them. How had an athlete so gifted gotten into Michigan State without anyone tipping off the basketball office? Furthermore, who was this one-man aerial act who could do things human beings simply were not designed to do on a basketball court?

He was Johnny Green, Marine Corps veteran and native of Dayton, Ohio, who had never played basketball at Dunbar High. A Marine Corps captain and MSU alum had told Green before his discharge that Michigan State was an attractive school for servicemen anxious to take a crack at college.

Eighteen months after Stevens spotted a diamond among the roughcut set-shooters in Jenison's loft, Green—now known nationwide as "Jumping" Johnny Green—and Michigan State were playing in the school's first NCAA Final Four. MSU never survived the semifinals, although everyone agreed that a 74-70, triple-overtime loss to North Carolina made Forddy Anderson's team the most dramatic loser in Final Four history.

It also suggested to MSU's hardcore basketball following that the sport had finally arrived on a campus where Munn-Daugherty football tradition ruled. It wasn't that Michigan State nor its fans had ignored basketball. Jenison drew its crowds—as high as 14,000 in pre-fire marshall days—although it was long after football season had ended and the holidays were gone before a ticket became hot. Biggie Munn was not the greatest hardcourt fan in the world, but as athletic director at least made sure that MSU's basketball program was in the hands of a solid coach. A man like Pete Newell.

Newell, a future NCAA championship winner at Cal-Berkeley, a future general manager in the National Basketball Association, and a man who would influence such coaches as Bobby Knight, had come to Michigan State in 1950 from the University of San Francisco. In the game of basketball, Newell's Five Steps were akin to Moses and the Ten Commandments: 1. Simplicity 2. Continuity 3. Opportunity 4. Adaptability 5. Flexibility.

Newell ran a patterned, futuristic system built around a reverse-action offense that featured double screens, and a "help-out" defense that combined the best principles of man-to-man and zone defenses. He was considered by many to be a genius, and when MSU would host a pre-Christmas doubleheader with UCLA, Kansas and Notre Dame, Newell arranged clinics that were masterpiece instruction for coaches fortunate enough to hear himself, John Wooden, Johnny Dee and Jack Gardner kick around the game's intricacies.

During his four years at East Lansing, Newell coached a number of quality players—among them Al Ferrari, Bob Carey, Keith Stackhouse and Julius McCoy—and it was Ferrari and McCoy whom Forrest (Forddy) Anderson would inherit in 1954 as Newell moved on to California.

Anderson had taken Bradley to the finals of the NCAA and National Invitation Tournament, and it was precisely that brand of national clout Munn wanted at Michigan State. He was also looking for a snazzier version of the game that might less resemble Newell's defensive-minded system and more approximate the fast-breaking, high-geared offenses favored by Big Ten teams such as Indiana, Illinois and Iowa.

Anderson definitely liked it fast—his basketball, and his life. He was a great speaker who could charm and humor an audience on a par with Duffy Daugherty, who normally preceded Anderson's final act when both were seated on the same speaking dais. He also had a passion for social life that included a deep appreciation for cocktails and women.

"It's not the game that counts," Anderson would say, smiling. "It's after the game!"

He might not have been the most diligent coach at pre-game preparation, but Anderson was a motivator whose personality was naturally tuned to inspiring players. There was a merry string of big seasons beginning with the NCAA tournament team of '57, followed by a 16-6 effort in '58, and climaxed by the '59 team's 20-4 finish that saw Green, Bob Anderegg and Horace Walker take Michigan State two games into the Mideast Regional at Raleigh, North Carolina, before losing, 88-81, to Louisville.

It would begin heading downhill the next year as Anderson's recruiting started to nosedive. Over the next six years there would be only one more winning season—a 14-10 finish in 1964—before Anderson exited in 1965 following a 5-18 disaster that would bring St. Louis Coach John Benington back to East Lansing as MSU's new head coach.

Benington, an Ohio native who had played for Newell at San Francisco, had come to Michigan State as Newell's assistant and seemed the natural successor until Munn made it clear he wanted an established coach with a sharp track record. Benington stayed at MSU as Anderson's assistant, then left for Drake, and eventually for St. Louis University until Jack Breslin spearheaded a move in 1965 to bring him back—a move that quashed applications made by assistants Gus Ganakas, Bruce Fossum, and Stan Albeck, a graduate assistant coach who would go on to coach in the NBA.

During his four years as Spartan coach, Benington would probably draw as much affection from campus and community as any prominent head coach had managed at Michigan State. The kicker was he never had to try very hard. Father of nine children, he was regarded as a nice man, but no goody-goody. In contrast to the yarn-spinners who worked an audience almost manipulatively, Benington's was a Will Rogers-style humor that branched off into practical jokes, particularly if he could get an appropriate person to swallow a put-on telephone call.

He was so considerate that sometimes Benington's charity was almost humorous.

When Michigan State in 1968 was mounting the recruiting equivalent of D-Day in an effort to sign Detroit Pershing's Ralph Simpson, Benington and Ganakas were on their way to Detroit when Benington spotted a disabled car on the shoulder of west-bound I-96. They had a heavy appointment scheduled with Simpson's coach, Will Robinson, and time was critical. But Benington wasn't about to leave two couples freezing as they stood outside their dilapidated car.

"John, what are you doing?" Ganakas asked, nervously, as Benington slowed down and prepared to turn the car around. "We don't have time."

Benington held up his hand.

"You've always got time for people."

He and Ganakas pulled up behind the disabled car, changed a tire on the wreck, then bid the four goodbye. About the time the fifth lugnut was tightened, Benington and Ganakas discovered that the two couples were themselves running behind on an important date: In 30 minutes it would be post time at Jackson Harness Raceway.

Benington's basketball style was a version of the defensive-oriented game he had grown to appreciate under Newell. Gone were the full-throttle offenses popular under Anderson, replaced by the more disciplined, more patterned approaches that Newell had been implementing more than a decade earlier.

Gone, also, were the losing records. Benington's first season, 1965-66, was a 17-7 comeback that saw MSU finish second in the Big Ten thanks to some splendid basketball by Stan Washington, Bill Curtis and Matthew Aitch. It was Aitch, Lee Lafayette and Steve Rymal helping Michigan State the following year to a 16-7 finish and a tie for first in the Big Ten with Indiana. But there was no NCAA tournament berth for MSU in 1967, when a 27-team tournament settled tie-breakers by taking the school that had gone longest without a NCAA invitation—in this instance, Indiana.

Benington soon was running out of talent in the same way Anderson's well had gone dry through the early '60s. The next two seasons were mediocre 12-12, 11-12 finishes that would be trivial discomfort in comparison with what lay ahead for the John Benington family.

Benington away from basketball enjoyed a laugh, a beer, and the satisfaction a man gets from taking care of himself. Racquetball was big among the coaches and athletic department personnel— Benington, Ganakas, Amo Bessone, Grady Peninger, Bruce Fossum, Hank Bullough, George Perles, and others—and men from the Alumni Office such as Jack Kinney and Frank Palamara, all of whom would play a game or two during noon hour then repair to the commissary for some soup.

Ganakas-Benington vs. Kinney-Palamara was a frequent doubles combination that permitted each man to handle a specific role geared to physical limitations. Benington and Palamara were excellent at keeping the ball in play and acting as set-up men for heavier hitters such as Ganakas and Kinney. In April of 1969, Ganakas returned to his hometown of Mt. Morris, New York, to be honored at an all-sports banquet. It meant that Bob Nordmann, the freshman basketball coach and racquetball newcomer, would team with

Benington as Ganakas' fill-in for the daily combat with Kinney-Palamara. They went three full games, after which Benington began having difficulty breathing in the locker room. He lay down on a bench and, by the end of the day, it was determined that John Benington had suffered a heart attack.

While a cardiac could be catastrophic to a 47-year-old man whose livelihood was the high-stress coaching profession, Benington's prospects for recovery were considered excellent—as they were for a basketball team that in October would welcome Ralph Simpson. By summer, Benington was jogging and playing an occasional round of par golf on days when his celebrated short game compensated for the greens he missed.

On September 9, 1969—five months after his heart attack—Benington had just played in the Ingham County Golf Outing at Walnut Hills Country Club and with Ganakas had an invitation the next day to play golf at the Country Club of Lansing. Benington planned to work a half day at the office and drop by the elegant old club on Lansing's west side, but decided the next morning to cancel and instead get some work done at Jenison before he took the car in for a tune-up.

At 6 p.m. on September 10, Benington's daughter called Ganakas at home to ask if he had seen her father.

No, Ganakas explained. Their theory was that John had dropped off the car and probably ran into a delay.

After another of the Benington children phoned Ganakas a while later to say her father still wasn't home, Ganakas called Bob Nordmann and they agreed to head immediately to Jenison. Barb Benington, John's wife, would meet them.

When Ganakas arrived, Nordmann and Barb Benington already were in the coaches' locker room. They had found John dead in the shower. Another heart attack had struck while he showered, about 5:30 p.m., apparently after jogging.

Benington's death slammed a campus and community aware of the kind of person he was, as well as the caliber of husband and father he had been to his wife and nine children. There had been something special about a man whose goodness and intelligence had been on such effortless display.

There was also, in ensuing days, a business decision to be made in Biggie Munn's office. Basketball practice was five weeks away, and Michigan State needed to appoint a head coach quickly. It was obvious to Munn that for continuity's sake, Gus Ganakas should move from assistant to the top job. There would be nothing "interim" about the status of a capable coach who had always gotten along well with Munn and who had applied for the job four years before.

Ganakas' evolution at Michigan State had begun 23 years earlier when a New York native and Marine veteran who had just gotten off Okinawa began shopping around for a college. His mother had just moved to Scottville, Michigan, and his brothers, aware of Michigan State's reputation as a school that welcomed servicemen, thought a man interested in coaching would be smart to try it at East Lansing.

He played junior varsity baseball and football at Michigan State, graduated in 1949, became a graduate assistant basketball coach while earning his masters in 1950, then took a job in October of that year teaching math at Olivet (Michigan) High School. A year later, he was at East Lansing High School as assistant football, basketball and baseball coach under Pat Peppler, who would go on to become general manager and then head coach of the Atlanta Falcons. By 1952, Ganakas was head basketball coach at East Lansing High and a follower of MSU Coach Pete Newell, and a close friend of Newell's assistant, John Benington.

As high school coaching jobs went, there weren't many better than East Lansing High, where quality athletics were part of the community's advantaged social fabric. Vince Carillot, who would later join Duffy Daugherty's staff at Michigan State, succeeded Peppler as head coach when Peppler joined Earle Edwards at North Carolina State, and after Carillot left for MSU, Roy Kramer, later to become head coach at Central Michigan University, headed football. Ganakas concentrated on basketball, along the way turning down head coaching jobs at Albion College and Ferris State, both small Michigan schools.

In late spring of 1964, Carillot invited Ganakas to lunch at Kellogg Center after it had been announced that Bob Shackleton, who had been directing the Ralph Young Scholarship Fund, was leaving to become alumni director. Would Ganakas, then 38 years old, be interested in taking on a fund-raiser targeted to Michigan State's athletic boosters?

It was about as tough a decision as Ganakas had ever faced. On the plus side, the job had a sports flavor, he lived only three blocks from campus on Elizabeth Street, and he now had six children, which even at East Lansing High meant tight budgeting. The case against it was that Ganakas loved coaching and wanted eventually to get a premium college job.

He decided to take it—and almost immediately began second-guessing himself even as all the summer golf outings he was obliged—and loved—to attend filled a good part of the early schedule. It had become something of a family joke after his daughter, Marcy, innocently explained to friends that her daddy no longer was a high school coach.

"What's your father doing now?" someone would ask.

"Oh," Marcy answered, "he plays golf for Michigan State."

By autumn, Ganakas realized East Lansing High actually opened without him, and his queasiness over leaving coaching was bordering on anguish. It had nothing to do with a job as pleasant as the Ralph Young Fund. Daugherty and Munn treated him warmly; there was a Rose Bowl trip in December 1965, and a football national championship that made Ganakas' fund-raising safaris less arduous; and Forddy Anderson was communicating with him not only as a friend, but in coaching dialogue that made Ganakas feel as though he were still part of the fraternity.

Anderson was dismissed following the '64-65 season and Benington brought back as head coach. One of Benington's eventual questions to Munn was whether Ganakas might be interested in becoming freshman coach as well as Ralph Young director. But John Hannah, the university president, doubted anyone could effectively serve two masters, and discouraged the idea.

A year later, Benington assistant Sonny Means took the head coaching job at Western Michigan. Benington got on the phone:

"Gus, you interested in the assistant's job?"

Ganakas rubbed out his cigar.

"Yeah, give me two seconds."

Recruiting was the real adjustment to becoming a college coach, but he had been on the road years earlier with Benington and knew the ropes as well as the rigors. No recruiting trips were as unique as the pilgrimages Ganakas and Benington would make to see the Moberly (Missouri) Junior College team coached by Cotton Fitzsimmons. In a town that to the MSU staff resembled Durand, Michigan, basketball was such a community staple that Moberly's old gym swelled each game night with an array of townsfolk, among them elderly fans tapping their canes at courtside.

It would also produce its share of talent for Michigan State in

Matthew Aitch, Bernie Copeland and Harrison Stepter. Junior college recruiting was helpful at a time when marginal academic qualifiers could get their grades up and benefit nearly as much from good JC coaching as they would playing on a freshman team. It was all the more convenient in an era when the NCAA prohibited freshmen from playing varsity football or basketball.

Ganakas was back to being Ganakas, the graying Greek and classic extrovert who enjoyed good jokes as much as he liked people and basketball. It made him want all the more a head-coaching job at a school big enough to make leaving MSU worthwhile. In 1966, Munn was the first to alert him that Eastern Michigan was interested in speaking with him about its opening.

Ganakas talked it over with Benington, who had no reason to shoot down EMU.

"A head coaching job is a head coaching job," Benington told him. Ganakas, though, wasn't sure that leaving MSU and the Big Ten was the smartest move for an assistant so new to major-college coaching. Recruiting at MSU was tough, and it would be even tougher at Ypsilanti. When he turned it down, Eastern Michigan hired Alpena (Michigan) Community College Coach Jim Dutcher, who would go on to become an assistant at Michigan and later head coach at Minnesota.

Ganakas got busy with recruiting that for most of 1967 and '68 centered on a Pershing High star named Ralph Simpson. Simpson had become a statewide celebrity the previous year when he and Spencer Haywood led Will Robinson's Pershing team to the state Class A championship, and to a mythical summit as perhaps the state's best-ever high school team.

The courting of Ralph Simpson began during 1968 when former MSU player Ricky Ayala, a Detroit hospital administrator, hired Simpson's father, Ralph Sr., on the hospital staff. The job required that Ralph Sr. take an eight-week course at Michigan State, a time when Ganakas entertained him at barbecues, showed him around, and even repaired the huge divots Simpson was gouging—and ignoring—during an introductory round of golf at Forest Akers Golf Course.

Ralph Sr. had played some basketball with the Harlem Globetrotters and knew the game as well as he knew a phony. Benington, he liked. In the framework of Benington's system, his son, he believed, would get the coaching that would enhance him and prepare him for a pro career that might financially benefit the entire Simpson family. As for Will Robinson, the tough taskmaster whose forte at Pershing was the use of a game-long, full-court press, he was remaining impartial. Benington and Ganakas knew if they didn't get Simpson after a couple of dud recruiting years, they could fold the tent and see if Pete Newell knew of any job openings.

Simpson signed.

His freshman year only certified what everyone had known: Simpson was spectacular, and only getting better as he matured and in 1969 prepared for his sophomore year and his first season on Michigan State's varsity. Benington's death in September jolted Simpson, but obviously was having no effect on his scoring skills as he and Ganakas each debuted in new roles with the varsity. Simpson, a 6-foot-5 guard, averaged 29 points per game, but couldn't best Purdue's Rick Mount for the Big Ten scoring title. Ganakas' only complaint was that Ralph Sr. was having a tough time letting go of his son.

Visits and advice had been coming all too frequently from Ralph Sr. until matters finally got out of hand in MSU's Big Ten opener at Indiana.

As the teams were walking off the court at halftime, Ralph Sr. slipped up behind Ganakas.

"Gus, Gus, lemme talk to Ralph at the half."

Ganakas was in no mood for parental meddling.

"Ralph," he said, "you've gotta get out of here."

Father, though, succeeded in catching up to a son who didn't care to be bothered or counseled on what he had been doing wrong during his first 20 minutes as a Big Ten player.

Michigan State won the game, 85-84, when on an in-bounds play in the closing seconds, MSU got the ball to Simpson at midcourt and let him ballhandle his way to the buzzer.

The next day Ganakas called Ralph Sr. at home and asked if they could meet at Brighton. A conference was in order.

"Ralph," Ganakas said when they met later, "you've done a lot for him. You're a good father. He needs your love. But now he needs only one coach."

"Well," Simpson acknowledged, "maybe I've been wrong."

Not as wrong as Ganakas would prove to be in the spring of 1970, when rumors floated that MSU's sophomore prize might be thinking of taking a big-dollar offer from the budding American Basketball Association.

Simpson hadn't been talking pro, nor giving Ganakas any indication that he would be anywhere but MSU for at least another year. He was a courteous, even conservative player whose only basketball liability was the occasional feeling that he needed to score 40 points. Ganakas knew the only way Simpson would leave is if there was pressure exerted on him to take the big money. And that pressure was coming from those who feared the ABA might collapse, or at least trim back, its megabuck offers.

In early spring, Horace Walker, the ex-Michigan State star, called Ganakas to tell him he heard Simpson was going pro. There was more of the same chatter at the NCAA tournament.

Ganakas needed to know either way, since recruiting priorities hinged on whether Simpson was staying. A guard at Moberly Junior College named Charles Dudley—he would go on to play in the NBA—wanted to play at Michigan State, but with Rudy Benjamin playing alongside Simpson, Ganakas didn't need another guard unless Simpson was departing. He finally called Simpson into his office.

"I've got to know what's going on," Ganakas said, "because if you go, I can at least take Dudley and pair him up with Benjamin."

Simpson was blunt.

"I'm staying."

In early June, Ganakas was running drills at the John Benington Basketball Camp when word came crashing down that Ralph Simpson had signed a $1-million deal with the ABA's Denver Rockets. Coaches from across the country were phoning Ganakas' office asking him to denounce the signing of a player who had become the first athlete signed and admitted as a freshman to a four-year school who had declared that family financial need—"hardship" in sports parlance—mandated that he turn pro.

The superstar was now gone. Dudley had signed with Washington. Ganakas was looking at a team in 1970 built around Benjamin, River Rouge (Michigan) star Bill Kilgore, and swingman Pat Miller from tiny Menominee, Michigan. There wasn't the sizzle in 1970 there had been with Simpson on hand, but for all his shoot-em-up skills, Michigan State finished only 9-15 the previous season when Simpson was lighting up Jenison. Michigan State would actually improve to 10-14 in 1970 when yet another recruiting battle was blazing away in Detroit and in Pontiac.

The high school prizes during the winter of 1970-71 were Detroit Kettering's Lindsay Hairston and Pontiac Central's Campy Russell. In the same way Simpson had been wooed as a junior, the hunt for Russell and Hairston had been going on for some time—

since the previous year when Russell was given a then-allowable summer job at a MSU alum's Cadillac dealership. After he became a part-time salesman at the dealership during his senior year, Russell could legally be given a car to drive that everyone connected hoped might double as an enticement to attend MSU.

There was little doubt in Ganakas' mind that Russell and Hairston were going to different schools to avoid conflict and on-court comparisons. And if one player had the edge over the other, it appeared Russell, a spectacular forward, had more raw talent than Hairston. Michigan State was considered in the lead most of the way—even in Michigan's eyes—but Wolverine Coach Johnny Orr and his assistant, Fred Snowden, won Russell's signature. Michigan State was left to chase and eventually sign Hairston from Kettering.

Recruiting was picking up as Ganakas settled in for the '71 season, his third as MSU head coach. It would seem so ironic as it all unfolded that a non-recruited player was causing so much squawking across town and campus. The problem was Ganakas' son, Gary. He was a 5-foot-5 guard who had played on East Lansing High's great 1968-69 team of Blake Ashdown, Brian Breslin and T.C. Blair that made it to the Class A state quarterfinals before losing to Ypsilanti.

Although Tates Locke at Miami (Ohio) had said he would take Gary as a non-scholarship player, Gary Ganakas wanted to try it at Michigan State. It didn't bother his father, who in the spring of 1969 was still an assistant to Benington and figured to have a head coaching job elsewhere by the time Gary was a sophomore.

A year later, Gus was getting ready for his second season as MSU head coach and sophomore Gary was reporting with the varsity in what would become one of the more uncomfortable and controversial personnel matters a head coach could face. Ganakas at first suppressed Gary in favor of established talents such as Benjamin, Miller, Paul Dean, Brad Van Pelt and Mike Robinson, the super-shooting sophomore from Detroit Northeastern.

As the season moved on it was Nordmann, now a varsity assistant, and Aitch, MSU's freshman coach, who kept telling Ganakas that the team played better when its pint-sized ballhandler was setting up an offense and dishing off to Kilgore, Miller, Benjamin and the sharpshooting Robinson. Gary began seeing more and more court time and hearing more and more boos from a crowd convinced that this situation was hardcourt nepotism.

Ganakas & Ganakas remained a sticky partnership during the

'71-72 and '72-73 seasons when MSU finished with identical 13-11 seasons and twice produced the Big Ten's leading scorer in Robinson, whose soft, one-handed jumpers were devastating. But there arrived in the autumn of 1972 two new varsity players: Hairston, who had finished his apprenticeship with the freshman team; and Terry Furlow from Flint (Michigan) Northern High, who in the first few weeks of practice showed stunning potential in this first year the NCAA was allowing freshmen to play varsity basketball.

Wayman Britt had been the heavy recruit on a Flint Northern team that had won its second straight state Class A title under Head Coach Bill Frieder. Michigan State had been recruiting Britt hard as a replacement for Gary Ganakas, but as with Campy Russell, lost to Orr and Michigan. Furlow was considered a long-shot prospect whose grade problems made him even less appealing to those college coaches who even knew about him.

In June of 1972 Ganakas got a call from Frieder.

"You guys have any interest in Terry Furlow?" he wondered.

A small forward—Furlow was 6-foot-4—wasn't one of MSU's priorities.

"I'd take him," Ganakas answered, "but I don't want to go through a lot of red tape on grades. I hear they're bad."

When Furlow took his Scholastic Aptitude Test and scored big, Ganakas mailed a tender to a player whom he knew only by reputation, and would not formally meet until Furlow walked up and introduced himself in September. Furlow had even come to Michigan State and gone through orientation and room registration as a regular student, unaware that class and room packages were arranged for incoming recruits.

Ganakas learned something else on the day he first met Furlow in Jenison's upstairs gym. Furlow had obviously made incredible progress during the summer. He could jump and shoot about as well as anyone Ganakas was welcoming back. And there was another plus: Furlow's personality. He was intelligent, extroverted, and he had a sense of humor.

When Furlow came out for formal practice a month later it was all the more apparent to Ganakas that he was looking at a unique basketball character whose personality was a perfect match for the vibrant game he played. Furlow had no fear. And unusual for a freshman, he had no qualms about agitating team elders. It wasn't long before Hairston and others began resenting the smooth cut-up with the deadly jumper.

Although his freshman season was a steady, seldom spectacular winter in which he averaged 10 points a game, Furlow's penchant for the colorful and controversial hit high gear during his sophomore season when No. 2-ranked Notre Dame arrived at Jenison on February 4, 1974. Michigan State was 11-6 as the Irish arrived and two days earlier had beaten Purdue on a last-second shot by Robinson. It gave MSU a four-game winning streak that by Monday night turned Jenison into a thundering barn jammed with fans shrieking for an upset of Digger Phelps' gang.

Michigan State started hot and was keeping it tight into the closing minutes. It was 89-89 when the Spartans took a timeout and set up for a final shot that figured to go to Robinson, or perhaps to Furlow, who already was 12 of 13 from the field. Michigan State got it in-bounds, whipped it around the perimeter, and then to Furlow, who was at the top of the circle when he sprang and lifted a shot that with nearly 10 seconds showing seemed utterly astonishing to a crowd and a team banking on no worse than overtime.

Furlow knew before he released the ball that he was shooting too soon. The ball fluttered and fell before it even reached the rim, settling meekly into Notre Dame's hands as the MSU crowd melted into the bleachers. Notre Dame made a quick trip down the floor and won it, 91-89, on freshman Bill Paterno's long jumper. The big upset never happened, unless one counted the team's and community's attitude toward Furlow.

In the locker room afterward, Ganakas was confronted by a basketball team that at the very least wanted Furlow's head on a platter.

"He is one of ours," Ganakas reminded teammates who weren't in the mood for brotherly love.

It wouldn't be Furlow's last brush with controversy. Nor during the next two years would it typify his remaining evenings at Jenison.

Furlow the following year would sucker-punch Illinois' Rick Schmidt and be placed on Big Ten probation, then smack Don Kaverman, an assistant MSU trainer. Including his involvement in the January 1975 walkout, Furlow had done his level-best to avoid any MSU medals for citizenship.

It was his scoring skill that on so many nights was breathtaking. During one five-day period in January of 1976, Furlow scored 50, 48 and 42 points on the way to a 29.4 points-per-game scoring average that made him a first-round NBA draft choice and, indirectly, set the stage for a final tragedy. Furlow was killed on May 23, 1980, when his Mercedes collided with a telephone pole outside Cleveland. Medical examiners later found in his system traces of cocaine.

Through the years of incidents and episodes, Ganakas never lost appreciation for the player whose mischief was overwhelmed by the sparkle in his personality. Furlow had not enjoyed the most stable of home lives, and Ganakas often wondered what a person so naturally bright and inherently decent might have been like had he grown up with a father at his side. You didn't overcome those imbalances overnight.

Furlow's final game at MSU—an 86-82 loss to Wisconsin on March 6, 1976—was also the final game for Ganakas as MSU head coach. Ganakas couldn't believe a 14-13 record would get him reassigned, but he was aware that conversations with MSU's Select Committee investigating abuses by the football program had not gone smoothly.

Ganakas was asked by the committee what he knew of a third-party offer of $5,000 that supposedly had been made toward the recruitment of Campy Russell. Ganakas said he never heard of any such offer.

He also was aware of the heat on MSU Football Coach Denny Stolz and wanted to put Stolz in the best light possible. When MSU President Clifton Wharton—in whose office the questioning was taking place—asked Ganakas how he would respond to a $5,000 enticement, Ganakas decided to forgo the righteousness.

"Look," he said, "I know what you're getting at. In this day and age, it depends. I don't know what I'm supposed to say . . . a coach needs a fund of money."

As he left Wharton's office and stepped toward the elevator, Leland Carr, MSU's attorney, said to Ganakas:

"Gus, you're telling it the way it is, but it wasn't what they wanted to hear."

On March 16, 1976, Ganakas was removed as basketball coach and reassigned within the Michigan State athletic department.

Nine

Magic

Joe Kearney thought the easy answer to two coaching vacancies at Michigan State was to bring in the two men he had hired at Washington: Don James and Marv Harshman. Both men were excellent coaches. Both had integrity and the ability to put together winners, James as Washington's head football coach, and Harshman as the Huskies' head basketball coach.

The problem as MSU's new athletic director returned from Hawaii in late March of 1976 was that neither James nor Harshman was interested in leaving Seattle for East Lansing. His next choice to lead MSU's football team was easy: Darryl Rogers would be offered the job. He had turned down Rogers in favor of Harshman when he hired James as football coach, and he remembered how telling Rogers he had lost was his toughest conversation as an AD.

Basketball was less clear as he thumbed through his notebook, examining names and conferring with men like Harshman whom he knew could give him solid references. One name was attractive: Jud Heathcote of Montana. He had been an assistant to Harshman at Washington State and Harshman regarded him as one of the better basketball minds in the West. He was 48 years old, tough, disciplined and knew basketball intimately. Kearney liked his credentials.

During the final week of March 1976, Gwen Norrell, a member of MSU's Athletic Council, who in three years would become

MSU's Big Ten Faculty Representative, was on the phone lining up appointments for the heavy slate of football-basketball interviews that were scheduled for Saturday, April 3, in Chicago.

Norrell reached Heathcote at the Montana basketball office in Missoula.

Would he be interested in the job? Could he interview Saturday at 1 p.m.?

"I cannot interview Saturday at 1 o'clock," Heathcote explained. "I have three players coming in for a recruiting weekend and I couldn't make it to Chicago."

Norrell saw no options. It was sad that neither the committee, nor the coach, could be more flexible. But he had his own business concerns.

"Well," Heathcote said, "I guess I cannot interview. Thanks, anyway."

Later in the day came another call. Norrell wondered if Heathcote could make it to Chicago for a 3 p.m. interview on Sunday.

"Well, yeah," Heathcote said, running Sunday's schedule through his mind. "The kids will be gone by then. I could get a flight . . . Sure."

Michigan State had interviewed Darrel Hedric of Miami (Ohio), Bill Hess of Ohio University, Don DeVoe of Virginia Tech, and Lee Rose, then of University of North Carolina-Charlotte. Good candidates, all of them, thought the interviewers. But Heathcote would not disappoint Kearney nor fail to impress the committee.

The key question: What would he do if his team walked out? Poison from the January 1975 MSU player walkout had killed so much basketball interest on campus and in town.

Heathcote never hesitated.

"I'd resign," he said.

The committee was as impressed as it was stunned.

"If my players walked out," Heathcote explained, "it would mean that I would have lost control and that I no longer had any hope of regaining any coaching direction. I would have to step down."

Heathcote mentioned something else.

"I'm a screamer," he said. "You need to know that."

If Heathcote had said he was bringing an entire All-American team to Michigan State, the committee would not have been more pleased. Michigan State wanted a lawman as much as it needed a basketball coach. If Heathcote got a bit throaty, fine. It was time to put some crunch into a basketball program that had lost respect from the community.

A three-hour plane delay put him on his doorstep at 3 a.m. Monday. His wife, Beverly, told him Joe Kearney had called and wanted him to phone back. Heathcote was exhausted and wanted only to go to bed. If the job were his, he told Bev, then it would still be his in the morning. Heathcote collapsed into a deep slumber. Bev tossed and turned the rest of the night, wondering if by the next day Missoula or East Lansing would be home.

Kearney phoned the next morning with word that Heathcote was Michigan State's choice. Starting salary would be $25,000 and length of contract four years. Welcome to the Big Ten.

Heathcote, like new football coach Darryl Rogers, had never seen Michigan State nor East Lansing. He viewed MSU the way coaches viewed any potential job move: What could it do for him, professionally? You didn't need to see a campus, nor watch the players work out, nor set foot in the arena, to know whether or not a Big Ten job was superior to his place in the Big Sky Conference.

When he got to East Lansing and took his first look at Jenison, he wondered about taking the job sight unseen. Kearney led him into the arena, jingling keys and turning on the lights.

"Gee, Joe," Heathcote said, "we had a better arena at Montana."

"I would hope so," Kearney deadpanned.

Heathcote was a man of the West—born at Harvey, North Dakota, educated at Washington State—but moving to Michigan was no real concern as he and Bev discussed the opportunity. Coaching at the Big Ten level was to coach in a conference where a man whose talents were considered high-caliber could exercise them among the coaching elite. You could be better-recognized here. You stood a greater chance of getting better talent from major metropolitan areas more accessible than they had been at Missoula. In all respects, the MSU job was a step up. It was all that mattered.

There was, in addition to this barn of an arena they called Jenison Field House, another surprise in store for Heathcote: The team. As he was getting acquainted at MSU, Heathcote happened across one of those regular pick-up games varsity players and upper-crust outsiders often organized in Jenison's upper gym. He was feeling very good as he watched Lindsay Hairston, Terry Furlow, Bill Glover, Tom McGill and Pete Davis rip up the floor.

"Hey, we might have a helluva squad here," he was saying.

Heathcote introduced himself and asked the players who they were, what class they were in.

Hairston was a second-year pro. Furlow was on his way to the National Basketball Association. Glover, McGill and Davis had no elegibility remaining. Heathcote was left to figure out what he would do with a team built around Edgar Wilson, Greg Kelser and Bob Chapman.

Recruiting, he could see, offered little promise. By mid-April only one of Gus Ganakas' top 10 high school recruits had not committed, Bill Madey, from Park Ridge, Illinois. But when Heathcote knocked at the Madeys' door, only Madey's mother was home.

"Didn't he tell you?" she asked. "He signed last night with Purdue."

Heathcote was getting desperate. He understood enough about the Big Ten to know MSU lacked sufficient front-liners to take into a major-college season, let alone enough depth. He decided to bring in two junior-college transfers he had rejected at Montana: Nate Phillips and Les DeYoung.

He discovered that a 6-foot-2 guard from Parkland North High in St. Louis had not yet committed—Terry Donnelly. He was no franchise player, but Heathcote thought he would help a backcourt that at the moment consisted only of Chapman. Donnelly signed and would soon into his freshman year be starting. Another player he liked was a slender, 17-year-old athlete from the Virgin Islands, Ron Charles, whom Heathcote had seen play while he was coaching the Pan American team. Charles would try it at MSU.

Heathcote was facing another challenge as he settled into a job that made him wonder increasingly whether he should have held out for something a bit better-stocked. The racial fallout from 1975's walkout had left doubts among some whites and blacks that anyone could erase community division. If Michigan State brought in a white whip-cracker, what would that portend for black players whose main complaint had been administrative insensitivity to basketball?

Several black businessmen took Heathcote to lunch soon after he arrived and wondered how he would handle it at Michigan State. A session that Heathcote thought would be a friendly, get-acquainted hour among some of the program's stauncher boosters, turned abruptly serious. What made Heathcote think he could coach black athletes? What did a man from the lily-white West know about black culture? About the sociology of black kids?

"Well," Heathcote said, "I've got a black kid right now at Montana who's twice as good as anyone here. That same team would beat this one by about 20 points."

Micheal Ray Richardson was the player, and had in fact developed a player-coach relationship with Heathcote that Richardson would cite 10 years later as the closest of his often-spectacular, ultimately troubled, college and pro career. Whether it would be representative of his coach-player relations at Michigan State, not even Heathcote knew. But he wasn't nearly as worried about race as he was about talent, or about rebuilding basketball interest at a school where it had become fashionable to badmouth hoops.

Heathcote thought it would be a temporary problem. Most heartening, of all the complaints he was hearing about basketball, he heard no tearing down of Ganakas. If they stuck with you as a coach, Heathcote said, then it was only a matter of rekindling interest and putting some quality players on the floor. It was purely a case of apathy, he thought, as he and Kearney in the fall of '76 began appearing at student dorms, attempting to stir up grassroots interest in a sport and a team that was temporarily not in vogue.

He was also doing his best to make sure that a high school senior from Lansing Everett named Earvin Johnson kept Michigan State in mind. The best strategy there, he thought, was to stay out of the way and let his coaching and MSU's direction reassure Johnson that MSU was attractive.

Heathcote still didn't know that much about the 6-foot-8 talent who supposedly did everything from bring the ball upcourt to play pivot. He had seen Johnson's name on a list of best juniors from the '75-76 season, and Fred Stabley Jr. of the *Lansing State Journal* had told him in an introductory call that Heathcote would drool over the kid at Everett. But he wanted to make up his own mind, just as Johnson, a Gus Ganakas fan, would have to decide for himself if Heathcote and MSU still appealed.

Heathcote's MSU debut, an 81-76 loss to Central Michigan University, unveiled a team deeply deficient in heavyweight talent. MSU's most impressive moment of the evening had come on a soaring Greg Kelser dunk that blew away screaming students at Dan Rose Arena who were not yet reacquainted with a shot the NCAA had that season reinstated.

Heathcote's early fears about the hometown audience were both right and wrong. True, there were only 4,000-5,000 customers showing up on most nights, but he noticed in December, during a

99-94 loss to a good University of Detroit team, that those who were showing up were interested and supportive.

They congratulated him on the way MSU played in a close loss to a talented team. They liked the way the new kid, Donnelly, seemed to be fitting in. Alfred Brown, a transfer from Lansing Community College, had some curious appeal and so, generally, did this entire makeshift team of talents and non-talents who at least played competitively, and with a certain blue-collar ethic. Watching these guys go at it beat staying home on a Saturday night.

The tension, though, was building as Lansing's high school basketball stars, Johnson and Lansing Eastern's Jay Vincent, overshadowed anything happening at Jenison—except, of course, on the nights when Everett-Eastern games were such statewide attractions that the games were moved to Jenison.

It was during a game midway through MSU's Big Ten season that a group of students carried through Jenison a long banner that drew applause and cheers as they moved about the crowd: "We Want Earvin and Jay—Bad," it said, which was the understatement of the year at a school whose basketball future lay in the recruitment of two 17-year-olds.

Michigan State had a diplomatic interest in making sure that Johnson and Vincent were treated as equals during the delicate winter months when decisions were being formed. In truth, Vincent, a 6-foot-7, 225-pounder, was not regarded by most talent scouts to be in Johnson's immediate galaxy. Michigan did not care for the excess lard which Vincent obviously carried but concealed so well during his command performances. Johnson was the target at Ann Arbor. Vincent was just another prepster that one of the Big Ten's annual contenders could afford to treat lukewarmly, or concede to Michigan State. Johnson demanded the Wolverine staff's full attention.

Michigan State's hard assessment of Vincent was that he would perhaps, in time, become a good front-line player. He was a desirable talent, for sure. But one who would require some work, and some discipline at meal time. The other necessity for getting Vincent would be in his possible effect on convincing Johnson to join the Michigan State basketball bandwagon. The two players were as friendly as a city's prep rivals/superstars could be, and had talked all along—probably because it so pleased the public—about playing together in college. When Vincent announced at a Lansing Eastern press conference in March that he was signing at MSU, a city and a coaching staff knew they had come a step closer to winning the Johnson-Vincent grand prize.

It was helping Michigan State that Heathcote's first season as head coach revealed him to be such a stickler for discipline and court intelligence. A 17-year-old who knew the game as well as Johnson could see that the new coach was a sharp basketball man whose foot-stomping and arm-pumping could be endured. It was helping, too, that Michigan State was winning a game here and there—including a big one early over defending NCAA champion Indiana—and staying within a bucket or two of a half-dozen others. MSU's 10-17 record (later adjusted to 12-15 because of forfeits that were part of NCAA sanctions against Minnesota) was no prize, but even Johnson could see the coach may have helped steal a game or two along the way.

What the coach was not doing was bothering Johnson. Plotting a recruiting strategy on Johnson was easy: Michigan State would leave him alone. Heathcote and Assistant Coach Vern Payne knew fully that Earvin Johnson would have been sewn up early had Gus Ganakas remained as head coach at Michigan State. To pressure Johnson or try overly hard to convince him that Heathcote was as good a coach, or as fine a man, as Ganakas would be suicidal against a person as sharp and as aware as Johnson.

Heathcote hoped that MSU's on-court performance during the 1976-77 season would illustrate to Johnson that Michigan State would be to his advantage, athletically and personally. Payne, who would take care of the more delicate contact work, would have an even trickier assignment. He needed to keep Michigan State in Johnson's mind, showing him in tactful, timely ways, that there were still good people at Michigan State—including Ganakas—who would make MSU beneficial.

Payne attended all of Johnson's games, but never went further than to make sure Johnson knew he was there. Payne wanted to be seen. Nothing more. He would sit back and allow the rest of the coaches to scramble for their "bumps"—quick hellos and exchanges—and not get involved in crowding a superstar who already was growing weary of the attention and pressure.

The University of Michigan was at a disadvantage in dealing with a player tucked within the MSU den. But Johnny Orr's assistants—Bill Frieder, Mike Boyd and Dan Fife—were playing it very smoothly. They maintained an almost-daily routine of chats and correspondence and school visits that Johnson found attractive.

Following practice one afternoon, Frieder and Fife were in the gym, displaying a poster on which Johnson's class schedule and daily U-M agenda was neatly lettered. He stared at it, intrigued by the clarity and simplicity with which the supposedly awesome college experience was being presented.

Michigan knew how to work. MSU's shadows were nothing Orr and his staff thought overwhelming in persuading Earvin Johnson to move away from the pressure of Lansing for a more comfortable environment, a 70-minute drive from his home.

Johnson wondered about the advantages of moving a step from the Lansing-East Lansing swirl. Pressure to stay home, pressure to choose Michigan, pressure to make a decision, had been growing so heavy that Johnson complained he could not even go to the rest room during a college game without fans blanketing him, all of them wondering where he was headed.

Payne understood. So did Charles Tucker, the clinical psychologist and consultant to Lansing's school district, who was also a friend and guiding light to Earvin Johnson and his family. Tucker had his hand on the pulse. He was a man who passionately enjoyed playing basketball, who had been involved in pick-up games with Johnson and Lansing's elite players, and a man, contrary to suspicions, who had been befriended by Johnson and his family and not vice versa.

Tucker played the role of casual man, but he was razor sharp—an intuitive sort who knew basketball players from around the country, yet was careful about sharing himself with just anybody. The Johnsons he liked. His trust, basketball savvy, and knowledge of manipulators were what Earvin Johnson Sr. most valued during a year that had become a blur for him, his wife and his son.

Tucker clearly wanted Earvin Johnson at Michigan State but was soft-pedaling it. Maintaining integrity with the family and with Earvin necessarily meant that a friend not join the tug-of-war going on for Johnson's body and soul. It was a time for those closest to Johnson to understand his tension and ease it in whatever way, which was what Payne—a Tucker friend—understood as he gingerly kept in touch with Johnson.

Payne made sure that game tickets MSU could legally provide a recruit were to be picked up at the Payne home. It enabled him to see Johnson in a comfortable setting where Earvin could meet his family and take refuge from the community's howling wolves. Johnson, as the season and his visits spun on, was also developing a friendship with MSU players whom he often visited in the Michigan State locker room following games. He was becoming comfortable, but then again, so was he getting acquainted with Tommy Staton and Joel Thompson and the gang at Michigan that, likewise, had welcomed him inside to talk about Michigan basketball and the game he had just seen.

Johnson would leave Crisler Arena, the sounds of Michigan's Fight Song and catchy melody of the "Let's-Go-Blue!" refrain, all banging around in a mind that said "Michigan" as he cruised home. It would be the next day, when his mind cleared enough to let Michigan State creep inside, that the tussle began all over again.

Nothing was resolved by the time Everett won the 1977 state Class A title in an overtime victory over Birmingham Brother Rice. Johnson, though, was looking forward to a tour of West Germany as part of his spot on a United States high school all-star team. It would be a chance to escape recruiting agitation and perhaps think more objectively about this colossal career decision.

He arrived home in April, determined to make a decision during the week of April 18. His thoughts increasingly were to go with the prestige program: Michigan. There was such allure to a team that already was established, that required no rebuilding program.

Orr and Frieder were feeling good. Johnson was attentive, enthused as they sensed he might ignore the hometown pleadings and opt for Ann Arbor. His head was telling him Michigan, but a heart that had been set on MSU until Ganakas was reassigned, still beat for MSU. Faintly.

His announcement would come on Friday, April 22, at a press conference at Everett High. By mid-week, even Michigan State's staff began thinking that the local prize was heading east. The longer he held out against a community's collective prayer, the more chance there was of him signing hurriedly at Michigan.

It had not helped that MSU's main contact, Payne, had just been named head basketball coach at Wayne State University. Payne immediately called Johnson's parents. His decision to leave, he told them, was purely a career move. They should not confuse his desire to become a head coach with any dissatisfaction at Michigan State.

On Wednesday morning, 48 hours before Johnson would announce, Payne stopped for coffee at the Big Boy restaurant on Trowbridge Road. He walked in and saw Frieder and Boyd sitting at a table eating breakfast.

"Hi, Vern," said Frieder. "Congratulations on the job."

The men were loose, smiling, obviously feeling very good. No one had to tell Payne that Michigan was in the lead. Payne left and drove immediately to Heathcote's office.

"Jud," he said, "I've got to see Earvin right now."

Heathcote, too, had grown alarmed. On Monday he had been stood up at an appointment scheduled with Earvin, his father and Tucker. Heathcote's intelligence reports also indicated that Michigan was about ready to score. The word was Michigan had suggested Johnson, as MSU's tallest player, would be forced to play center. It was time to make a few things clear.

Payne drove to Everett and called Tucker.

"Tucker," he said, "I want you to get that kid out of class. I've got to see him in the library."

Payne and Johnson talked, late in the day, Payne attempting a final argument for why Johnson should choose Michigan State. He appealed to Johnson's personal history. Hadn't Earvin arrived at Dwight Rich Junior High as a gangly kid who put a middle school on the map? Hadn't he done the same thing at a high school which was previously short on basketball tradition?

He had always cast his lot with the underdog and emerged a champion. Now he had a chance to do it at a major university. Moreover, thought Payne, whereas Johnson would go to another school as a superstar athlete, his potential at Michigan State transcended athletics. It was a matter of his roots. His heritage. An entire city and community would be elevated to the same heights as the university for which he played.

The other matter was more tender: Ganakas versus Heathcote. Johnson still had doubts because he did not know Heathcote the way he had known Ganakas.

The university was bigger than Gus Ganakas, Payne told him. Gus had tremendous charm and was one of the truly fine human beings Payne had come to know, but, he told Johnson, the support group was still there: Ganakas, players such as Greg Kelser and Bob Chapman, and all those hometowners to whom he remained close. What Heathcote would give him was excellent coaching. And that, said Payne, was what he needed most.

"Earvin," Payne went on, "if you want to come to Michigan State, if it's important to you, then you've got to sign right away."

Payne couldn't give Michigan 48 hours to dissuade Johnson. He needed the signature immediately.

Johnson nodded and said: "I'll sign, Coach."

He told his parents that night, and the next day at Everett High, with Heathcote, Payne, Tucker, Everett Coach George Fox and his parents on hand, Johnson signed the letter of intent. It would remain their secret until Johnson had the chance to announce at Friday morning's press conference.

It was a moment Johnson and much of the state had been building toward as the week progressed, his decision seemingly reduced to a coin flip. The Friday morning press conference was attended by such crowds, and by so many TV crews, that it was as if royalty had arrived at Everett.

Johnson was seated at a table at 9 a.m., staring at the throng ahead, when the room quieted and he prepared to end the suspense. He leaned into the microphone.

"Are there any questions?" he asked, straight-faced. The crowd chuckled. He had to be kidding.

Johnson again leaned into the microphone.

"Next fall," he said, "I will be attending Michigan State University."

There was a roar among the students and locals who had burrowed into the room, and before noon, most of Lansing-East Lansing was celebrating the simple signature from a 17-year-old athlete whose skills and personality might, in time, crush the gloom that descended during football's troubled days of 1975-76. Basketball had become the city of Lansing's energy and personality during the Johnson-Vincent high school era, and the thought of two prep superstars taking their collective show to Michigan State was overwhelming.

Getting a MSU basketball season ticket soon became the new material priority among age groups that previously worried about a car, a home, or a condo in Florida. Having access on a regular basis to the voltage Johnson and Vincent had brought Lansing the previous winter was to own a piece of the rock.

It was in East Lansing that Heathcote, no sooner than the ink had dried, began telling the mobs to cool it, to not expect miracles from two teenagers who could not possibly dominate a league as quick and strong and talented as the Big Ten.

Heathcote in the summer of 1977 was feeling like a Lotto winner, but still not sure whether he had inherited championship-caliber talent or ulcer-inducing pressure. If anything, he thought the arrival of two imports, Mike Brkovich of Windsor, Ontario, and

Swedish 7-footer Sten Feldreich, had at least given Michigan State some backcourt support and front-line depth to go with the two super preps on whom so much rested.

Earvin Johnson, some thought, would have a tough time making that gliding move to the basket on which he feasted so in high school. Better zones and sharper defensive players would cut him off, forcing a player who did not have a classic jump shot to make it or break it from outside. He could score in his own inimitable ways, but Johnson would find the going much rougher among the Big Ten's bullies.

Jay Vincent would have an even tougher transition, they believed. He was too heavy. Too lethargic. In a fast-tempo game he would drag down an offense that could not afford the luxury of a thick-trunked forward whose strength was a soft shooting touch.

It was why, during the early weeks of practice in 1977, that Heathcote and his assistants, Don Monson and Bill Berry, were torn between going with Vincent and his offense at starting center, or opting for mobility State would get from the human pipe-cleaner, Feldreich. Heathcote and his staff would shake their heads during practice when Feldreich went on 10-minute sprees in which he could be sensational, once blocking three consecutive shots by Kelser.

"Geez, Greg," Heathcote said, wryly, "why not go up again with that?"

Kelser stood, defeated, at the sidecourt.

"Hell's sakes," he panted, "it's embarrassing enough to have three blocked. I'm not gonna give him another."

Johnson's development was another matter entirely. It required no basketball genius to see that the same talents with which Johnson had overwhelmed high school teams were going to be very difficult to check on a college court. Heathcote was seeing not only a 6-foot-8 player with rare ballhandling and finesse skills, but equally impressive, an 18-year-old who had such excellent basketball instincts that he could project what a coach wanted done on a court.

It would signal the evolution of a 6-8 backcourt general whose personality would become an asset equal to his ability. Johnson was no freshman, the team elders acknowledged. He was a collegiate pro who on his worst days could do things with a basketball—and, consequently, to the flow of a game—they could do only in dreams.

Heathcote's answer to a player so multi-dimensional was to let him play—in whatever role MSU needed during a 40-minute game. In his and Vincent's MSU unveiling, a 68-61 victory over Central Michigan University on November 28, 1977, Johnson posted up, he led the fast break, he made his share of turnovers but showed how he would change the scope of a college basketball's offense.

"They're screwing him up," said Johnny Orr, the Michigan coach, who had watched the game. "They're having him do too many things."

Heathcote argued that he probably had not entrusted enough to Johnson, which he wanted to prove the next week as Michigan State traveled to Syracuse to play in the Carrier Classic at the Syracuse University's Carrier Dome. Johnson, in a 92-64 victory over Rhode Island and a 75-67 loss to a very good Syracuse team, so floored observers with his passing, ballhandling and scoring that he was named tournament MVP.

He was, finally, beginning to be universally recognized as "Magic" Johnson, the moniker tacked to him by sports writer Fred Stabley Jr. of the *Lansing State Journal.* To an outside world getting its first real glimpse at Johnson's on-court hocus-pocus act, it seemed an appropriate nickname. And most gratifying to Heathcote, Johnson's act was making the other players—Kelser, Bob Chapman, Terry Donnelly, Ron Charles, etc.—so much better.

MSU was 6-1 three weeks after the Carrier Classic, but had not beaten anything approximating a Top 20 team when it marched into Calihan Hall on December 21 to play highly ranked University of Detroit. U-D Coach Smokey Gaines—Dick Vitale had become athletic director—had splendid talents in Terry Duerod, John Long, Terry Tyler and Earl Cureton and by most estimates had U-D's best team since the Dave DeBusschere era. He also had at Calihan a packed house, simmering as it waited to see whether the new kid at Michigan State had the stuff against a Titans team that, as usual, bounded onto the court in an elaborate, spotlighted pre-game introduction in which players exploded through hoops.

Michigan State went on to dismantle U-D at both ends of the court in a 103-74 slaughter that indicated some serious underestimation had taken place. Neither Heathcote nor his Michigan State players thought they would be playing with such fury a couple of weeks before the Big Ten season opened.

Johnson still wondered what would happen when the Iowas and Minnesotas lined up opposite them with their brawny front lines and backcourt speedsters. It would be a different game, surely.

Third or fourth place was the best guess on where MSU might finish when you looked at that small front line of Kelser (6-7), Vincent (6-8) and Johnson, who was playing as much guard as forward.

Heathcote wasn't sure, but he liked the way Kelser was blossoming in his junior season and the way Vincent seemed to be settling in at center. Kelser, particularly, was getting a lift from Johnson. Heathcote had discovered upon coming to MSU that Kelser was a magnificent athlete who could run and jump—and not play basketball especially well. He was good around the basket, and had led the Big Ten in rebounding as a freshman, but his reputed jump shot was very bad and he lacked the kind of court savvy that came naturally to Johnson.

Kelser, though, was a worker. A relentless worker whose intensity at practice was matched only by Johnson. Quite a contrast to Ron Charles—"No Sweat" as he was called by Don Monson—or to Vincent, whose trips downcourt so often resembled a home-run trot.

"You know, Jay," Heathcote would tell him, "if you run down that court a little harder you're gonna pick up a couple of points because Earvin's going to get that ball to you."

Vincent discovered in time that the easy baskets were coming in proportion to the pace at which he and his 225 pounds migrated downcourt. Opposing defenses were in turn learning something about Vincent: You had to watch him away from the basket. He shot with grace for such a thick brute, and after he had hit three or four 14-footers, front-liners moved out on him, freeing up the baseline for some Kelser-Johnson acrobatics.

The schedule figured to be one break for Michigan State as Heathcote's team got ready for the 1978 Big Ten season. Taking a team so young on the road, especially at some of the nastier stops, would be the risky way to begin an 18-game schedule that annually stands as a race against minds as well as bodies. Michigan State would begin by hosting Minnesota and Wisconsin.

Minnesota stood at the onset of 1978 as tough as any of the Big Ten's best—tall, smooth, talented, but in the closing minutes of Johnson's Big Ten debut, Jim Dutcher, the Gophers coach whose team had a nine-point lead and the game in its mitts, pulled the Gophers out of their zone defense and Johnson and MSU gobbled it up to win, 87-83.

The Spartans opened so fast and so powerfully through January that Heathcote's team was radically changing the complexion of a school previously known as a football college. Michigan State basketball was now drawing Jenison sellouts and blockbuster local TV audiences. Johnson was the hottest freshman in college ball, averaging about 17 points per game, and grabbing control of the offense as he begged teams late in the game to send him to the free throw line.

There was no sign so far that MSU's new kids, who were supposed to endure such nightmarish transitions, were wilting against the Big Ten's best. Kelser was playing extremely well, feeding on Johnson's bullet passes underneath, and Bob Chapman, after a terrible January, began warming up.

It had been anything but warm in the Midwest the final week of January 1978, as MSU barely escaped from two feet of snow that smothered Michigan and Ohio en route to its date with Ohio State, a 70-60 victory that pushed State to 7-0 in the Big Ten and 15-1 overall.

The snowstorm subsequently knocked out gymnasium heat, kept the team from practicing, and forced the squad into eating from food reserves of debatable origin, all of which provided Michigan State with a comfortable excuse as it snow-shoed into Indiana to meet Bobby Knight's Hoosiers.

About the only MSU highlight in a 71-66 loss to IU was Kelser's low-orbit slam-dunk, which he started just past the time line, coming in on an angle from the right side, hanging all the way to the basket. Three nights later, back at Jenison, there were more dramatics—this time supplied by the University of Michigan's Mark Lozier, whose 18-footer at the buzzer beat MSU, 65-63, and hinted that freshman whizzes and Big Ten championship plans might yet encounter some snags.

Anyone closely analyzing game films or watching MSU practices suspected differently. The team had too much talent—most of it in the person of No. 33, who was directing offensive traffic while continually developing a unique form of diplomacy with his teammates. It would have been difficult for cohorts to have resented any athlete playing as well as Johnson on a team that had become such a regular winner and Big Ten power.

But Johnson was careful. He had a coach's sense for what teammates should be doing, but an ambassador's tact.

"Hey, big guy, hey Jay," he'd say at practice, "just move a little, and I'll get that ball to you."

Or, "Hey, Ron, you just turn a little, and I'll get it to you."

Players benefiting personally and collectively were finding in Johnson the ideal teammate. The fact he could take a joke and treat people nicely was not hurting him among the Greg Kelsers of the world, who for all their intelligence and model work habits, could get a bit self-centered when it came to getting the basketball.

What Johnson did not appreciate were the second-line players beating him to a pulp during some of MSU's more energetic workouts. Reserves such as Dan Riewald and Jaimie Huffman played all-out, which translated into bumps and knocks Magic thought unnecessary.

"Coach," Johnson would wail, "I'm supposed to take this in a game, not practice."

Michigan State's mid-season mini-crisis blew over quickly as MSU came off the Michigan fall to win 10 of its next 11 games, sewing up the Big Ten title at Wisconsin with an 89-75 victory in which MSU hit the offensive boards so hard it nearly pushed the Badgers' noses through the glass. Its next step would be a new world known as the NCAA tournament, beginning at Indianapolis against Dave Gavitt's team from Providence College.

The NCAA opener went as much of the Big Ten season had gone—an easy 77-63 victory over Providence that would send MSU to the Mideast Regional at Dayton, Ohio. First up: Western Kentucky, coached by Gene Keady, who would soon be moving to Purdue. The Hilltoppers perished quickly, 90-69, and now it was Kentucky, Southeast Conference legend, bringing Mike Phillips and Rick Robey into the Mideast Finals against a brash Big Ten team that was beginning to grab coast-to-coast attention as it lay one game away from the NCAA Final Four.

For such a greenhorn when it came to tournament basketball, Michigan State was handling the NCAA pressure well as its Dayton stay progressed. Players were relaxed and so, for the most part, was Heathcote, whose chief complaint lay in various *Lansing State Journal* articles. Criticism or observations from the hometown press, however warranted or mild they seemed to media and the public, were perhaps Heathcote's No. 1 irritant through the years.

Although Kentucky was big and physical, Michigan State thought it would have the edge in maneuverability as it got ready for Joe B. Hall's gang. And MSU did. State led by five at the half, then by seven as Chapman scored on a break off the second-half tip.

What followed would leave Heathcote second-guessing himself for years.

Michigan State attempted to play cozy with its second-half lead, quieting down, holding onto the ball, taking no chances, as its offense geared low. MSU had strung out the court when it had its running shoes pumping in the first half, forcing Robey and Phillips to plod up and down the hardwood. But when State let up, the lead began evaporating. Kentucky hunkered into a 1-3-1 zone that worked beautifully as Johnson, whom they wanted to shoot from the outside, did. He missed several from way out and now the momentum had hopped to Kentucky. The Wildcats ran a pick-and-roll, high-screen offense that ultimately sent Kyle Macy, the former Purdue guard, to the free throw line where he would make a string of one-and-one shots that sank MSU, 52-49, and helped carry Kentucky to the NCAA title.

It was a measure of how Johnson, Vincent and Company had changed basketball at East Lansing: Michigan State came off its best basketball season in 19 years, but had come so close to winning it all that the thought of what State had missed, versus what it had gained, was haunting as MSU watched Kentucky beat Duke for the NCAA title.

It was the community, though, that would not let loose of Johnson or the MSU basketball team. Magic was hero to the schoolkids, to the students, and most certainly to so many adults whose basketball interest up to that point barely exceeded their intrigue in MSU's lacrosse team. Magic Johnson could do no wrong, as was clear at the MSU basketball banquet, packed to the rafters at Long's Convention Center.

Johnson stepped across the dais to a standing ovation as his turn to speak finally came. He positioned himself at the podium deliberately, the way he set up for a free throw. When he touched the microphone it fell from its bracket and sent the sound of clatter ringing through the dining room.

"We win the Big Ten championship and all they give us is a cheap old microphone," he said, as the crowd roared.

"And," he went on, warming up, "I thought we'd do better than having to eat chicken again. Figured they'd at least give us those nice shish-kebobs."

It wasn't Bob Hope, but after the season Johnson had delivered, he could have recited the alphabet and brought down the house.

As the spring and summer of 1978 slid by, Heathcote realized what everyone in the world of MSU basketball also understood: Nothing less than a NCAA championship could satisfy during the

'78-79 season. He had everyone returning except for Bob Chapman and Sten Feldreich—Chapman had been a senior; Feldreich had returned, homesick, to Sweden—and with a year's seasoning, Johnson, Vincent, Kelser, Donnelly, everyone, stood to play even better than they had during the Cinderella debut of '77-78.

Heathcote figured a September exhibition series in Brazil would be just the tune-up Michigan State could stand as he plotted what would be his and MSU's best shot—and, perhaps, its last if Johnson went pro—at the grand prize. Brazil was an experience that could not be explained, only comprehended by those who were playing in front of the massive crowds approaching 60,000. The games were physical, the refs were appallingly in favor of Brazil, and the crowds were inclined to shout anything and throw anything—including *centavos*—on the court that might disrupt these green and white-clad visitors from some place called Michigan State.

It was a series that seemed at the time exactly what MSU needed: Toughening against good teams in difficult circumstances, especially when MSU beat Brazil in the finals with a fouled-out Kelser on the bench. It was time to get cracking as the Spartans headed back to Michigan, feeling now as if the road would take this team all the way to Salt Lake City and the NCAA championships.

Practices were snappy, streamlined as Heathcote convened them for the official start of drills in October. Ron Charles, the lanky, 6-foot-7 Virgin Islands front-liner, was working his way into the lineup, and Brkovich, a fantastic outside shooter—"The Golden Arm," they called him—could be used as a zone-busting perimeter player now that his self-confidence was creeping, by the inch, upward. It had been such a problem as to be almost humorous. Brkovich, ultimate nice guy, wasn't always sure that a humble Canadian such as himself belonged on the court with these stars.

He was only the best outside shooter Heathcote had ever seen. But if he missed two shots in a row, it was depression time.

"I'm off, I'm off, I don't what it is," he would say, despair in his voice. "Coach, you've got to help me with my shot."

So they would stay after practice, the both of them, working for 45 minutes on a shot that needed as much help as Ted Williams needed with his baseball swing.

Heathcote knew that percentages applied even to a shooter of Brkovich's caliber.

"You know, Brk," Heathcote would say, "you missed a couple, but if you'll only take that third shot it'll go in."

Brkovich's dark, Yugoslavian eyes would light up.

"Yeah?"

"Yeah."

And he would promptly bury an 18-footer.

Kelser was the man with whom Heathcote had worked longest in an effort to make his once-atrocious jump shot presentable. Even at 51 years of age, Heathcote could still shoot it out with about anyone on the team, and more critically, he could teach the jumper as well as he taught other facets of the game. Players respected his instruction because in one lesson Heathcote had the ability to make them a discernibly better player.

There wasn't a whole lot he could do with Johnson. The kid could play. In all regards. True, that jumper of his wasn't to be confused with the form exhibited by Ohio State's Kelvin Ransey, but Johnson got the ball in the hole. Whatever it took—drive, dunk, hook, bank, pull-up, push-shot—he got it in there, making sure it was high-percentage, whatever his choice.

He was also pulling the most amazing on-court heist in player-coach history and getting away with it cleanly, and, to the benefit of all concerned.

Johnson somehow could tell the coach to fly a kite when Heathcote intervened in a way that Johnson perceived as threatening his, and the offense's, court independence. He never showed up the boss, he never thwarted Heathcote's position as head coach. But because of his unique talent and understanding of the game, Johnson, as time passed, could run the show and reject Heathcote's interference when he thought there was encroachment.

"Ease up," he would say, dribbling from his point-guard spot as Heathcote yelled instructions Johnson thought confining.

"Back off," he would bark, giving Heathcote the trademark gesture, a quick wave of Johnson's right hand, delivered at belt level.

Incredibly, it was never viewed by players or assistants as a power play. Nor by Heathcote, who could respect Johnson's constant campaign to loosen up Michigan State's often-deliberate, always-disciplined offense. Any other player challenging the coach would have been drop-kicked by Heathcote out the doors. But Johnson was not any other player. He was a talent and a basketball student whom teammates and even the head coach could respect.

Michigan State opened as expected, crushing the weaklings, taking care of the likes of Indiana and Oregon State as it won the Far

West Classic, and losing only once in the Big Ten pre-season, to North Carolina, 70-69, when Vincent's pet shot, the short jumper, spun off the rim at the buzzer.

MSU was 7-1 and ranked No. 1 in the country as it opened the Big Ten season at home, cleaning up on Wisconsin and Minnesota to move to 9-1 before taking its Magic show on the road against good teams from Illinois and Purdue.

For the suspenseful among MSU's audience, a basketball mystery plot would begin to develop on January 11, 1979, at Illinois' Assembly Hall, where the Spartans were meeting Lou Henson's Illini. MSU was having trouble against the Illini's packed-in zone and finally went down, 57-55, on Eddie Johnson's buzzer-beating baseline jumper that chopped down the country's top-ranked college team.

Two days later at Purdue—the Big Ten's meanest place to play basketball was Mackey Arena—Arnette Hallman threw in a 25-footer as the clock died to give Purdue a 52-50 victory and make it two consecutive spills at the hands of last-second snipers. It was such a spectacular moment at Purdue, that new Coach Lee Rose led his team in a galloping parade around the court's perimeter that looked like something copied from a bad TV game show.

Heathcote's squad was staggering as it returned to East Lansing. Twice, Big Ten teams had huddled in their zones and built a fortress in front of MSU's half-court offense. Twice, MSU had been held to fewer than 60 points. Johnson and a few of his colleagues thought MSU was playing into too many hands, sitting back and complying with defenses in the same way Michigan State had done the previous March against Kentucky.

Heathcote was arguing that patience, defense, discipline and shot selection would bring MSU out of it.

Michigan State ripped Indiana, 82-58, at Jenison to pull out of its slide, and two nights later, on a tense, one-and-one situation in which you could hear hearts beating in the Field House, State got a pair of last-second free throws from Brkovich to send the game into overtime against Iowa. The Spartans then exploded to win, 83-72, as Brkovich, the man whose confidence needle so often pointed toward empty, had contributed to one of the most dramatic—and most critical—victories of the Johnson era.

The home-floor comeback was only a reprieve. At Michigan the following week, State's offense was back in the quicksand, allowing Keith Smith's free throw with no time remaining to help

Michigan to a 49-48 upset. MSU, former No. 1 team, former Big Ten favorite, was now 4-3 in the Big Ten and soon to be 4-4 by the time Northwestern partied against a team that got into foul trouble and watched the Wildcats blow them out of McGaw Hall to the tune of 83-65.

It was January 27.

Five weeks remained in a Big Ten season that was, for MSU, all but dead. The team called for a meeting in Heathcote's hotel room following the game. Subject: What had happened to a team formerly regarded as the best in the land, but now losing by 18 points to Northwestern?

The players gathered in Heathcote's room later that day, mostly to offer weak analyses and remedies for what might restore Michigan State's old basketball personality. They had gone from being the Big Ten's free-wheelingest, most swashbuckling team to a status of collegiate wimp—a timid squad waiting to be punched out by bullies as well as by 98-pound weaklings. Michigan State had lost its identity.

Johnson finally spoke up. His teammates had been waiting for this.

"Jud," he said, "in order for us to win the Big Ten and national championship, you have to sit down and shut up and let us win."

Support was slow to come, but other players, gently, made it clear they agreed. Follow-up conversation was brief. Peacefully, the players left.

Once again, the same act by any other player would have either crumbled because of his personal vulnerability, or have been regarded by the coach as so mutinous as to lead to suspensions and other acts of retaliation.

But the players respected Johnson and, while they also respected Heathcote, all felt as if the windows should be thrown open and vigor restored to MSU's offense. Johnson knew the pace at which they could play and still maintain on-court integrity. Heathcote, privately, had to agree it was worth a try. State was 4-4.

Five nights later, on February 1, 1979, MSU's baffled fans jammed Jenison to see if anything could yet be salvaged from a season that had opened so brilliantly and faltered so rapidly. Ohio State would be a test—a good, but not great, team that MSU had been chewing up for the past six years.

MSU started smartly, controlling the tempo, moving to a steady lead until Johnson, with 6:19 to go in the first half, drove to the basket and came down on his ankle. Jenison was a tomb as he hobbled off the floor and limped to the training room.

Michigan's State's on-floor confidence had marched away in step with Johnson. The Spartans were struggling, fighting to stay even with the Buckeyes as the second half ticked away, OSU moment by moment gaining command.

Inside the training room, MSU Trainer Clint Thompson worked on Johnson as they listened to the game on radio. Johnson was crying. MSU had been up and now was behind. No way could the team go 4-5 and survive.

"Clint, I gotta go out," Johnson said. "I gotta go out."

Thompson kept working on the ankle.

"You can't go out."

"Clint," Johnson said, now committed. "Wrap me up."

Thompson nearly mummified Johnson as he wrapped tape around the foot and leg, bowing to a player you did not easily dissuade.

Johnson walked out of the training room, into the tunnel that leads deep into the Jenison locker-room area. He pushed through metal doors at the northeast end of the Field House and slowly walked into the arena. Fans at that end picked up on it first, the sight of No. 33 walking determinedly toward the MSU bench. They came to their feet, yelling, screaming, roaring, the sound amplifying through Jenison as fans caught a glimpse of the player who would rescue Michigan State. It was as if John Wayne and the cavalry had ridden in, bugles blaring.

It was the most emotional moment 40-year veterans of Jenison Field House could remember.

On the court, Greg Kelser sat in front of the scorer's table, waiting to go in. When the crowd exploded, Kelser was overwhelmed. Thrilled. He assumed MSU fans were responding to his arrival. He was not disappointed to see that Johnson was returning.

Michigan State quickly regained control as Johnson, despite the pain, played with his old bravado. Kelvin Ransey's jumper tied the game at the end of regulation, but Michigan State won, 84-79, in overtime. It would be the start of 10 consecutive victories that would wrap up a Big Ten tri-championship with Purdue and Iowa, an outright title turned into a shared title when Wisconsin's Wes Matthews sank a half-court shot to beat State, 83-81, in the Big Ten finale at Madison.

It mattered little to a team that had its wheels heading into the

NCAA tournament against the winner of the Lamar vs. University of Detroit contest. A U-D victory—the Titans were favored—would set up a beauty of a matchup between MSU and U-D. The team gathered at Kelser's apartment to watch the game, and were surprised to see Lamar stomp on the Titans. They were also pleased to hear Lamar players talking during a post-game interview about their plans to chomp on MSU.

"We went through one team from Michigan," one player squawked, "and now we're going to cap it off."

Heathcote was fearful that he and assistants Edgar Wilson and Dave Harshman had a major motivational project ahead. They had been talking up U-D, but now, with Lamar next, they had to build another team into a giant. The Lamar game would be remembered as one of only two tournament games in which Michigan State was truly fired up.

During warmups, the MSU players had heard Lamar's squad yelling and hollering, cussing at Heathcote and in general behaving like a cocky crew of loudmouths.

"Let's go," Johnson said as they walked to center court for the opening tip. "Let's work on 'em."

Michigan State waltzed, 95-64, then moved to Indianapolis for the Mideast Regional featuring State, Notre Dame, Toledo and Louisiana State. MSU and LSU would meet on Friday, March 16, immediately following the Toledo-Notre Dame match that would go to the Irish.

Again, no contest, as the Spartans cruised, 87-71, setting up a Mideast championship game on Sunday between Michigan State and a Notre Dame team loaded with future NBA talent: Kelly Tripucka, Bill Laimbeer, Tracy Jackson and Bill Hanzlik, as well as a good-shooting guard in Rich Branning.

Notre Dame would go down as the other game in which MSU's emotional level was at a peak as the game began. Heathcote had worked hard on his team, reminding the players that Notre Dame had turned down a chance to meet MSU on national TV in a regular-season game when ND refused to play in East Lansing, insisting instead that MSU come to South Bend. He and the team had sat in the bus, mesmerized, as they rode to Market Square and saw the herds of fans decked out in green and white, their blood boiling with excitement. We can't let down these fans, Heathcote and the players agreed.

It was obvious to the head coach that his team was as emotionally fine-tuned as it had been all season. He could spare the pre-game speech. He wrote instead a simple note on the blackboard: "Let's go kick some ass."

Heathcote also wanted MSU to break to a quick lead that might keep Notre Dame out of its zone, and with that in mind, he cooked up a special greeting for the Irish: Kelser, should he get the tip as expected, would knock the ball to Johnson. Johnson in one motion would flip the ball into the forecourt as Brkovich swooped in for a fast-break bucket.

It worked perfectly. Brkovich—who had discovered in a February wipeout of Kansas that he could dunk the ball in a game—grabbed Johnson's tip and rocketed in for the slam. A stunner off the start. But the customers at Market Square Arena, as well as the millions watching on NBC television, were only getting a preview.

Johnson and Kelser put together their most dazzling 40 minutes of basketball in Michigan State uniforms. Johnson fed Kelser with one deadly pass after another, Kelser crashing the ball through the hoop on a parade of seven slam-dunks, none more awesome than when Johnson, looking to his right, flipped a blind, cross-the-body pass to the left and into the hands of an oncoming Kelser for the dunk. MSU won, 80-68, and now was headed to Salt Lake City for the NCAA Final Four. State would meet Pennsylvania—surprise winner in the East Regional—with the winner facing either DePaul and Mark Aguirre, or unbeaten Indiana State and Larry Bird in the championship game.

Having been 4-4 in January, and having chopped its way through 10 consecutive Big Ten games, Michigan State was looking at the Final Four not as a high and mighty setting in which, win or lose, it had already succeeded, but as a chance to move workman-like through the two steps that remained toward a national title.

The Notre Dame aerial show had certified MSU as the most explosive team at Salt Lake City. DePaul and Aguirre were power-ful, and Indiana State and Bird had been outlasting everyone, but no team appeared to have eight cylinders moving as smoothly as Michigan State.

Penn would get the first lesson. The Ivy Leaguers missed bunches of shots, and Michigan State's speed game was so fluid that the Spartans ran to an astonishing 50-17 halftime lead on the way to an eventual 101-67 massacre. Indiana State slipped by DePaul, 76-74, when Aguirre missed a last-chance shot, sending MSU and Indiana State into the finals, Magic Johnson versus Larry Bird.

The next day, DePaul Coach Ray Meyer was asked to pick a winner. Not easy to do when his team had just been beaten by an undefeated Indiana State.

Meyer smiled and said: "I don't think any team is playing better than Michigan State."

To keep Bird from single-handedly destroying his team, Heathcote altered State's vicious match-up zone to put either two defenders or, at the very least, a man-and-a-half on Bird at all times. If he could be contained, MSU should have it easy. The Spartans had too many guns, even if Vincent had been sitting out almost the entire tournament with a stress fracture of his foot.

State played it cool in the first half, taking good shots, keeping its poise, and biting into Bird as it grabbed a 37-28 lead at the half. Kelser got into foul trouble in the second half, at a point MSU looked to be on the verge of a runaway, but Donnelly hit four bombs from the outside to loosen up the Indiana State zone. Bird, although playing with a sore hand, finished with 19 points on 7-for-21 shooting as Michigan State calmly rolled to a 75-64 victory.

Brkovich's two free throws against Iowa . . . Johnson's dramatic return in the Ohio State game . . . a big, three-point victory at Iowa in February . . . so many escapes. They all combined to make possible an overpowering tournament sweep—five victories by 104 points, a NCAA record—and send MSU home to airport welcomes, downtown parades, and to a community feeling very fortunate to share in a celebration so unique.

The NCAA title would, however, loom as a double-edged sword. Johnson had now won a state championship at Everett and a national championship at Michigan State. He was ready for the pros, who very much wanted a shot at this 19-year-old marvel who played with such style and grace.

Had MSU fallen short, there was nothing to be decided, Johnson said to himself. He would be back. There was no hurry to turn pro when college ball had offered this very unique brand of thrills.

But he would be invited to Los Angeles the following month to get acquainted with the Los Angeles Lakers, the NBA's elite West Coast franchise, who by virtue of trade had the No. 1 pick in the NBA draft. They wanted Johnson. And he—by the time Tinseltown's glamour had been absorbed, by the time Kareem Abdul-Jabbar had spoken with him, by the time Lakers owner Jerry Buss had given him a grand and glorious tour—wanted to play with a pro franchise where he would not need be a messiah. Magic Johnson could go to L.A. and be a star among stars, in a town unlike anything a Lansing native could imagine.

On May 11, 1979, Johnson called a press conference at the MSU Faculty Club. The day before, as everyone wondered what his decision would be, Johnson had tried to grab Heathcote.

"Coach, got to talk with you," Johnson said.

Heathcote just waved him off.

"No you don't," he said, not wanting to put Johnson through any anguish. "I'll find out tomorrow."

Until 4 a.m. Johnson tossed the matter back and forth, arguing against a decision he had already made. There was no way around it.

That morning, 25 months after his Everett High press conference, Johnson stood in a plush room at the club and explained in a soft voice that he would be turning pro.

Across all of Lansing and East Lansing, it was as if everyone had anticipated the news. No one seemed overly upset.

No one was about to begrudge an extraordinary young man doing something, at last, for himself.

Ten

FALLING STARS

Withdrawal from the Magic Johnson basketball habit Lansing and East Lansing had gotten hooked on during the past few years would be tough, everyone realized, as Johnson made his decision to turn professional in May of 1979. Michigan State a month earlier had been forced to turn down half the 3,000 applicants who cared not what it cost to buy a seat at the annual MSU basketball banquet at Long's Convention Center, an event so hot that WJIM-TV televised the entire dinner and discovered later its ratings approached that of the Super Bowl.

Winters without Magic could hardly be the same. Gregory Kelser, too, was gone, destined for the pros following a season and career in which Johnson and Kelser's capacity for hard work had made Kelser look much better, perhaps, than he was. It was one of the reasons why Charles Tucker, Kelser's as well as Johnson's advisor, recommended that Kelser avoid any post-season all-star games that might diminish the luster he had gained through MSU's NCAA tournament sweep.

Jud Heathcote, in the summer of 1979, would have to mold something from Michigan State's returnees:

Jay Vincent: To players who enjoyed kidding a popular teammate about his considerable girth, he was known as "Fat Daddy." Vincent's sore foot was recovering and he would be expected to give MSU a substantial scoring lift the following season. That MSU had been able to blow apart five NCAA tournament teams without him said tons about the fury with which Heathcote's team had played.

Terry Donnelly: He, quietly, had given MSU three seasons of stable backcourt play. Not until Indiana State begged him to shoot in the second half of the championship game—Donnelly responding with four perfect jumpers—had he made any indelible impression on the outside basketball world. But his teammates liked him. Donnelly, beneath the on-court dispassion, played with fire. He was perpetually psyched, and knew enough to let Michigan State's superstars have the limelight during the big seasons of '78 and '79. He would bring poise and experience to the next team.

Ron Charles: "No Sweat" had filled in brilliantly during Vincent's absence, spreading those long arms within Heathcote's match-up zone defense to give MSU a front-line wingspan as wide as a Boeing 747. He was an excellent offensive player underneath—it explained his 65-percent shooting mark—and was quick and nimble. Charles would be invaluable in MSU's transition to life minus Johnson and Kelser.

What the public did not understand was why Charles' teammates called him "Bobo." Ron "Bobo" Charles. Even Heathcote had been heard calling him that.

The players were keeping all explanations to themselves, but it had everything to do with Charles' magical attraction to MSU's women. Spring quarter at MSU had been dubbed "sperm term" by a basketball team aware of how male-female chemistry seemed to explode once flowers bloomed, trees budded, grass greened and swimsuits emerged at the MSU outdoor pool.

It was the charm Charles held over women—teammates noted how campus lovelies considered him "cute," and how they found his Virgin Islands accent captivating—that led them to anoint Charles as "King Bobo," shortened in time to "Bobo." Basketball teams, like fraternities, had their own language and culture.

Also figuring heavily in MSU's 1979 rebuilding project would be Mike Brkovich. He still had his confidence problem—anyone watching him dogpaddle through the NCAA championship game could see that—but he was a delightful person who had that awesomely accurate jumper, and a player who needed to score bushels as Heathcote revised his on-court blueprint.

There had been other additions and subtractions since MSU left Salt Lake City: Jaimie "Shoes" Huffman, Johnson's old Everett teammate who followed Johnson to MSU, had been invited to transfer a few months after getting his nickname from NBC's Al McGuire. Heathcote wasn't wild about hearing the crowd yell "Shoooooooes," imploring that Huffman be sent into the game when Huffman's talents were not judged as Big Ten-caliber.

Recruiting had been so-so following a season in which Michigan State figured its national title should put it in position to land the country's top talent. Ralph Sampson and Terry Cummings were rumored to have decided against MSU when Johnson's pro intentions became known, and Sidney Green and Marty Embry definitely ruled out State when Johnson departed, which left MSU with an incoming crop of Herb Bostic, Derek Perry, Bill Cawood, and transfers Kurt James and Kevin Smith, the former U-D guard who was being counted on to provide scoring and some of the pizzazz that departed with Johnson and Kelser.

Heathcote was looking at a team considered to be more talented than his '76-77 squad, but well beneath the elevation at which State had played with Johnson. His celebrated coaching talents would now be on the line three years after he first arrived in East Lansing.

It had been a remarkable, exhilarating, and yet turbulent stay in East Lansing for the man whose foot-stomping, arm-pumping, head-jerking, on-court tirades were his trademark. Heathcote, to those who observed him, was one of coaching's true fascinations, and in many ways, one of its real contradictions.

He was a basketball student and analyst of national acclaim if one went by the appraisals of such lofty coaches as North Carolina's Dean Smith. MSU insiders did not dispute it. Heathcote had an uncanny ability to break down basketball film and take in its most intricate structure. He could absorb what 10 men were doing simultaneously, zeroing in on weaknesses, strengths, adjustments, methods and motivations. He was, above all, his players and staffers thought, the best basketball teacher they had ever encountered; so schooled in technique, so precise in his instruction.

If there was a fault, it was that Heathcote's ability to analyze and comprehend basketball films and systems did not automatically translate into clear relaying of that data to players not on Heathcote's basketball plane. He spoke in simple language, but he had a complex knowledge of the game that simpler basketball minds did not always grasp. It could lead to impatience on both sides.

It had also become obvious that the astute on-court coach was not the world's best recruiter. Heathcote became sensitive over the years toward his great coach/poor recruiter tag, but he did not always dispute it. Recruiting he did not care for. Period. The groveling so many coaches seemed to go through as they begged and pleaded a high school player to come to their school was not Heathcote's cup of tea.

He was repulsed by the payoffs he knew were selling so many of the country's best talents on various schools. And in murky, dingy Jenison Field House, Heathcote was finding a perfect scapegoat for the many in-state talents that annually seemed to go to Michigan, Iowa, Iowa State, Syracuse—at so many places that were winning out over Michigan State.

Heathcote enjoyed telling the story of Granville Waiters, a big center who ultimately signed with Ohio State after visiting MSU.

"You play heeeeere?" Waiters asked, astonished, as he and Heathcote stepped into an empty Jenison during Waiters' campus tour.

Jenison was indeed a problem when out-of-state recruits saw it during practice, or as joggers circled it during mid-day hours. It became a different facility altogether during games, when crowds packed in around the floor, beneath the bright lights, and MSU's pep band pumped electricity through the mobs settling into their bleacher-style seats. It was an arena of such intimacy that some recruits could find Jenison irresistible.

Many times, out-of-staters never had that experience. However, consensus had it that arenas were not for most recruits the deciding factors. Campus, tradition, a head coach's personality— other elements seemed to make a greater difference. Heathcote was considered excellent once you got him into a high school talent's home—a comfortable, sincere humorist who knew how to defuse a parent's eventual question, "Will we see you ranting and raving on the sidelines?"

It was getting him into the home that could be rough. He was not one to become instantly sold on a recruit, and until he was, home visits were not easily arranged by assistants who knew they needed to sell a kid on Heathcote.

Away from the basketball court, Heathcote also seemed to be a contradiction in personalities: He appeared most often as the friendly, easygoing, intelligent quipster whose dry, lightning-quick wit made him the funniest coach in the Big Ten. But he could also reveal himself to be an ultra-sensitive man quick to temper, particularly when the media pricked his grape-thin skin.

It became axiomatic among local press that the better Heathcote's team played, the more intolerant he became toward MSU's coverage. One story that he did not like—the word "negativism" was central to his vocabulary—one paragraph, sentence or word with which he took exception, could send him on the warpath for days or weeks.

His obsession with media questions and story angles became so consuming that in 1979 it nearly ruined his week at the NCAA Final Four. Heathcote wore a sour expression from the moment he and the team arrived in Salt Lake City to the day he and his NCAA championship entourage departed. He had wanted to dispense with many of the pre-game interviews in which the NCAA required all schools to participate. He complained about the media "pressure" which he believed hounded his team.

He resented all the questions and comparisons media people were directing toward the Magic Johnson-Larry Bird showdown. He was fighting almost daily with the *Lansing State Journal.* And worse, far worse, a coach with a sense of humor as unique and as delightful as Heathcote's was suppressing that wit at a time when his national image was being shaped. His absorption with the media as adversary was subverting his personality. Jud Heathcote, warm and witty back home, was coming across as a cold sourpuss in front of the national press.

People better acquainted with Heathcote saw it as a departure from form. He had a talent for humor uncommon in the prim and proper world of coaching, where so many men worked like politicians on image and charm. Heathcote could get by very nicely by being himself, a man equally good with the barb, the joke, the dinner-speech anecdote, or more impressively, with the impromptu, situational comment that fractured those around him.

Media around the Big Ten annually looked forward to his act at the conference's basketball press conference in Chicago, a tedious, day-long session in which coaches make consecutive presentations on how their teams stack up heading into the new season. Heathcote would invariably start his spiel with a spin-off or dig aimed at the coach he was following, or with one of the jokes he seemed always to be hearing ahead of anyone else.

He also had learned one of humor's basic lessons: Nothing so genuinely pleases an audience as a speaker who can poke fun at himself. Heathcote—again in contrast to a man so sensitive to outside criticism—often picnicked at his own expense.

"You need talent to get a program, and a program to get talent," he told one East Lansing group. "I'd say if things continue as they are, I can take this program from mediocrity all the way to oblivion."

Introduced at a post-season MSU basketball banquet, Heathcote strode to the microphone as 1,500 guests stood, applauding.

"The last time I got a standing ovation was at Montana when I announced I was going to Michigan State," he began. "It was in a bar. Two guys applauded, the third fell off his stool, and the bartender cried because he needed the business."

But if Heathcote could harpoon himself, he was equally good at jabbing others. His players, included.

"I was at a party Saturday night and a guy came up to me and said he knew just how we could get that new field house we've been wanting," Heathcote was saying in the winter of 1982. "Yeah, just use all those bricks Kevin Willis has been throwing at the basket and you'll have a palace.' "

It was because he put it to himself so regularly that Heathcote could get away with roasting a colleague like Football Coach George Perles, or Reggie Myles, the retiring pro at Walnut Hills Country Club, where Heathcote played golf regularly. Myles, on the night of his retirement dinner, was seated at the head table with his wife, Phyllis, when it came Heathcote's turn to speak.

"Part of the reason Reggie and Phyllis have gotten along so beautifully over the years is that they've had a 50-50 marriage," Heathcote began. "Phyllis ran the house and Reggie ran the streets."

Coaching colleagues were a Heathcote favorite, usually because he got along with them so well. Perles was zinged at the Walnut Hills Spring Stag, when he gave another of his stock speeches about laying "foundations" and building a good "foundation" at Michigan State, and how strong administrators were the "foundation" of any program.

Heathcote followed, Perles squarely in his sights.

"Our basketball team next season," he told the audience in a slow, bone-dry delivery, "will try and build a good foundation . . ."

Banquets were a specialty, but Heathcote never needed a large or particularly receptive audience to be sharp, nor did he insist on speaker's fees. Almost a year after he came to Michigan State, he was asked to speak at a builder's dinner at the Lansing Hilton Hotel, waving his hand when asked what the stipend might be.

He was reminded a month later about the date.

"Oh . . . I was going to see the Catholic League playoffs in Detroit," he said, upset that he had booked something on a night when recruiting responsibilities were the heavier priority. "But I told you I'd be there and I will."

Heathcote arrived on time at the Hilton. The group he anticipated would be 100 or more consisted of about 15 men, tucked into a small, windowless meeting room. Heathcote gave a 30-minute talk, opening with a stream of jokes and one-liners that had the group in tears. Afterward, well past the point he owed any responsibility, on a night he had other things to do, he joined the men for a few beers back at the suite.

The humor would come harder during MSU's 1979-80 follow-up act, during which it became clear that great basketball had exited with Johnson and Kelser. Michigan State had lost its first-team thoroughbreds, and through weak recruiting was now hurting as much on the bench. State finished the '79-80 season 12-15 overall, and was ninth in the Big Ten with a 6-12 record. Vincent's 21.6 points-per-game average and Big Ten scoring title were all that had been salvaged.

Two seventh-place Big Ten finishes would follow in the 1980-81 and '81-82 seasons as MSU's recruiting sabattical left either Vincent, Kevin Smith, Brkovich, Derek Perry, Ben Tower or Vincent's younger brother, Sam, as MSU's talent base in a conference that did not treat kindly teams shy on top-drawer personnel. MSU had been gluing itself together since 1979, a survivor rather than a contender.

There had been moments when it looked as though Michigan State had patched up, such as during the 1981-82 season when Heathcote had Smith, Sam Vincent, Kurt James, Evaristo Perez and Cleveland Bibbens alongside Tower and a 7-foot junior-college transfer from Detroit named Kevin Willis. But injuries and a general lack of cohesion—Kevin Smith could score but never functioned in the manner Heathcote wanted—combined to make it three consecutive dismal winters in East Lansing following the back-to-back glory years.

A boost had been expected in 1981 when Michigan State signed Sam Vincent, third superstar from the Lansing prep circuit in five years to choose MSU. The surprise—and an indication of MSU's recruiting trials—came as Michigan finished as close to landing Vincent as it had come with Johnson in 1977.

Sam Vincent had developed at Lansing Eastern High into one of the more remarkable high school talents Paul Cook had turned out in his decades as a Lansing prep basketball coach—better, at the same stage, than his older brother had been. Sam was a prototype guard who could shoot, run and jump with a style rare among high school athletes. MSU had to have a neighborhood player of Vincent's stature, particularly one whose brother was just wrapping up his four-year career at State.

Michigan Coach Bill Frieder was treating Vincent as he had treated Earvin Johnson: As a player whose hometown meant nothing to Michigan's recruiting strategy. Vincent liked Frieder, whose basketball camp he had attended the previous year. There were weekly visits and regular chatter, a system of communication that Heathcote was not matching as he sat back, playing it cool with the backyard prize.

Vincent was leaning toward Michigan when he called his brother for advice. Be careful, Jay had told him. Eric Turner was completing an excellent freshman season at Michigan and would return at point guard, where Sam expected to play. Frieder and Michigan would be an excellent choice, but he should go where he had the freedom to play his own game.

The next evening, Sam Vincent was in the stands for Michigan State's home victory against Northwestern. He went upstairs afterward, to Heathcote's office, to visit, not intending to sign. Heathcote had a pen ready. Vincent signed a Big Ten letter of intent.

Vincent started as a freshman and averaged 11.7 points per game, and Heathcote sensed in the winter of '81-82 that Michigan State had enough talent to contend. But the season developed into another winter setback in which State limped home with a 7-11 Big Ten record. Players wanted a looser, more up-tempo offense. Heathcote wanted defense and a more structured offense. Smith and Vincent were offensive-minded guards who enjoyed scoring more than playing defense, while the front line stumbled in step with the backcourt. A bad combination good for another seventh-place finish.

With Smith gone in 1982, Heathcote needed, among other things, a new guard he could pair with Vincent. MSU had recruited the player considered Michigan's best high school senior, swingman Patrick Ford from Detroit Cass Tech. And a new kid coming in from a small town in Indiana might at least give State the bench clout it had been searching for the past three years. But if Ford or any of the key regulars failed to work out, Michigan State was looking at another lost winter.

Heathcote had few illusions about the recruit from Indiana, Scott Skiles, a six-foot guard from the small town of Plymouth who had talent, but probably not the speed or raw athletic tools quality Big Ten players possessed. Michigan State's service reports mentioned him as a brilliant scorer, and a letter from a fan in that area had suggested MSU take a look at him. But he was not high on the lists of Purdue or Indiana, nor even Notre Dame, which was only a half-hour drive from Plymouth.

Heathcote had asked Skiles' high school coach to send game films that might at least answer a few basic questions. The film came—an 8-millimeter reel on which you could barely see the players, or gain any detail on this kid Scott Skiles who was scoring 56 points in the game film his coach had sent Heathcote.

Michigan State would at least take a look at him. Bill Norton, then an assistant at MSU, saw one game at Plymouth and got back to Heathcote.

"Jud," Norton said, "he's not very big, but he's your kind of guard. I think you ought to see him."

Heathcote decided the best glimpse would come at the Indiana state tournament semifinals at Indianapolis, where Plymouth and its hot-shooting senior would be playing against better-caliber talent in a high-pressure setting.

Heathcote watched the first half. No, he told himself, the kid isn't a Big Ten player, and Heathcote walked outside to grab a sandwich and coffee, convinced there was nothing more to see.

He thought some more. He had only seen him play two quarters; it would be smart to at least watch him during second-half warmups. The Plymouth players were all white kids who stood from 5-foot-10 to 6-foot-1. From a distance, they all looked the same. Heathcote noted that Skiles' form was not good—the way he held the ball over his head when he shot—until he realized at introductions that the player he had been watching was not Skiles.

Scott Skiles came onto the floor in a flat-footed gait that impressed Heathcote even less, and when he scored 19 points, Heathcote was firm: Skiles would be a player, but not at Division I.

Heathcote took a bus to the airport shuttle area and walked across the street to a hotel. He phoned Norton, who that night planned to take a look at Ypsilanti High prospect Keith Armstrong.

"You watch Armstrong," he told Norton. "I want to watch Skiles once more."

"He played good, huh?" Norton asked.

"No," said Heathcote. "He played crappy."

Skiles in that night's championship game was superb—a scorer, a ballhandler, a sharp court player who Heathcote thought compensated very well for his lack of speed and height. He was worth bringing to East Lansing if Michigan State could get him.

Skiles wasn't sure what his options would be as spring, 1982, arrived and schools where he had always dreamed of playing, like Purdue, showed no interest. Cincinnati, Fresno State, Arizona State, New Mexico and Maryland were showing interest, but Skiles knew of only one assistant who had been watching him: A man hanging around whom Skiles' coach identified as Bill Norton, a staffer from Michigan State.

Skiles wanted to play in the Big Ten and was interested in MSU even if he knew nothing about Michigan State or Heathcote. He asked others about the Spartans coach and discovered that Heathcote had a reputation similar to Indiana's Bob Knight: Either people loved him or hated him, and everyone had his own story about Jud Heathcote.

A visit to the Skiles home, a pretty yellow house with black trim just south of town, went well. Skiles liked Heathcote and appreciated the no-nonsense style, the way in which Heathcote said Scott was neither a great shooter nor defensive player, but that if he came to Michigan State he would have a chance to play. Skiles already had looked at a map. Michigan State, he was surprised to see, was not that far away. He was enthused. He would sign.

He would also come to MSU intending to play, and play regularly. He had seen MSU against Indiana and Purdue and had concluded that the sharp freshman, Sam Vincent, was a better off-guard than point guard. Patrick Ford, the big-name recruit from Detroit, he knew was 6-foot-5 and no threat to become an offense's playmaker. With Kevin Smith gone, Skiles thought at the very least he would be first guard off the bench.

He told his father, Rick, that he was going to MSU with one idea in mind: He would start at guard.

Heathcote was beginning to think the same as his team got

together on October 15 for the start of drills. Skiles had talent and, clearly, he knew the game of basketball. He was doing strategic things that Heathcote had not seen in a freshman since Magic Johnson had arrived.

But he needed work in every category, beginning with his shot. It was a push shot that Skiles could hit regularly because he had a very good hand through the ball, but Skiles needed to hit it more quickly off the dribble. Heathcote, the shooting professor, would revamp that immediately.

Skiles also needed an attitude readjustment. That much was clear to Heathcote as well as to the players. For an 18-year-old kid fresh from the Indiana hinterland, he was a cocky devil who thought the motion offense that Bobby Knight preached and practiced, and that was subsequently copied by every high school coach in the state, was the only way to play basketball. Heathcote had other ideas—and made sure they were understood—but he appreciated Skiles' spunk and his basketball intelligence.

Skiles became a starter midway through December, and by the time MSU's Big Ten season got going, the freshman with a bulldog's court temperament was the hottest new player in the conference. He scored 35 in a triple-overtime victory over Ohio State that headed MSU to a 17-13 finish that would include a two-game stay in the National Invitation Tournament, and a 9-9 Big Ten record worth a sixth-place tie.

Vincent had played steadily and, at times, superbly, in a sophomore year in which he averaged 16.6 points per game. But it was Skiles' arrival—he was named Big Ten Freshman of the Year—that meant Heathcote had finally returned to Jenison a team built around several high-power talents.

The problem with Skiles remained not one of ability, but of attitude. Even Skiles would wonder long after he left MSU how teammates had kept from punching him out at practices. He had been so bossy, such a know-it-all in directing players and telling them where they should be and what they should do. It had been at its worst during Skiles' first weeks at practice, when, struggling, Skiles decided to quit playing the meek freshman role and revert to being the court general he had been at Plymouth.

It was not, initially, the best strategy. There were days at practice when Skiles could feel the tension building as players reacted not only to Heathcote's barking, but to the impudence of this slow white kid who thought he was some kind of player-coach.

"Get over here, get over there," Skiles would bark, pumping his arm. Teammates thought he could have avoided aggravation and bad will if he only had learned to say, "Hey, the play's supposed to go this way."

Not always did the problems stem from ego battles between Skiles and Vincent. Their relationship smoothed out as the year went on and as both realized they could get the ball enough to meet their scoring needs. Vincent was acknowledged generally as a warm, personable athlete whose interest in theater and the arts was consistent with a certain sophistication—a level of operation that guarded against extreme pettiness.

But he liked having the basketball. He liked being free to dance downcourt, weaving and gliding to the basket. He hated playing defense. And in that respect, he had a soulmate in Skiles.

During a rookie season in which he was twice named Big Ten Player of the Week, Skiles was finding that adjusting to life at Michigan State was a more manageable task on the basketball court than it was away from Jenison. It was dormitory life that made him miserable. There were more students in Wonders Hall than there had been at his entire hometown high school. He had roommates, and people pounding on his door, and it only got worse as he started scoring all the points.

It was so exhausting, so relentless, that Skiles by the end of his freshman year had made a private decision to leave Michigan State. He already had his parents and other intimates putting out feelers on a possible transfer when he packed up in June to return home for a summer of blessed peace, far away from the stereos and noise that too often made life at Wonders unbearable.

It was about three weeks later that Skiles began getting restless. He missed his friends, he missed the campus, the coaches, the pick-up basketball games. He missed everything but the dorm. He knew now that he would return to Michigan State and, as a sophomore, could abandon the dorm for a more comfortable life at Twyckingham Apartments, a short distance from East Campus on Hagadorn Road.

It would make the whole difference. Skiles had freedom to roam and visit friends, but he could also return home and shut the door. Athletes who found it difficult to escape their lives in a fishbowl valued time on their own—even if all you did was crack a book.

Skiles had another reason to become enthused toward his

sophomore season: MSU's 1983 basketball team. It looked as solid as any squad in the Midwest as he and Vincent, who was now a junior, would team with the rapidly improving 7-footer, Willis, and with a slew of front-liners: Ben Tower, Derek Perry, Richard Mudd, Larry Polec, Ralph Walker, Patrick Ford—whose freshman season had become a bust—as well as powerful, 6-foot-8 transfer Ken Johnson, and freshman guard Darryl Johnson.

Ken Johnson, it was envisioned, would be the muscular power forward MSU had for so long been missing. With two future pros in Vincent and Willis returning—both at the top of their game—and with Johnson coming in from Southern Cal, Skiles could swing into his sophomore season and help make State a Big Ten favorite and perhaps a power in the NCAA tournament. Heathcote could not argue. When a reporter from *Sports Illustrated* magazine arrived at East Lansing to get the MSU scouting report, Heathcote was told that no team in the country looked as good to the reporter as Michigan State. *Sports Illustrated* in its preseason edition ultimately picked MSU to finish eighth in the nation.

Having an athletic and potentially dominating big man in Willis was the distinction to Heathcote's '83-84 team. He had coached more talented teams since he came to Michigan State—Earvin Johnson's presence assured that—but never had MSU played with a legitimate pivot man of All-America potential. Willis, for all his rough edges, for his humble basketball background, for the inexperience and poor grades that forced him to play originally at Jackson Community College, had by his senior year become a solid Big Ten center.

His personality was another subject altogether. Willis was different. He was extroverted in some ways—as at training table and at airports, where he could be heard for great distances—and plainly wild at other times. Skiles never got over his introduction to Willis, when both worked as security guards at the University Inn during September of 1982. Willis, thought Skiles, was the most off-the-wall, out-of-control person he had ever met. It was ironic, thought Skiles, that he and Willis would be called to knock on hotel rooms when neighbors complained of noise in an adjacent room.

Skiles became just as bewildered during his first two seasons when Heathcote continually ragged on him to get the ball to Willis in the right spot at the right time.

"Well," Skiles would say, not always to himself, "there is no right time."

But Willis, through unusual athletic skill and enormous capacity for hard work, had made himself a basketball threat by his senior season. There was such diversity to his talent that Willis' 4-minute, 54-second mile remained in 1987 the Michigan State basketball record. When he ran the first quarter in 60 seconds, Heathcote and assistant Mike Deane had to tell Willis to slow down to save himself for the finish.

He went just as hard in the weight room after arriving at MSU as a 205-pound stringbean who could barely bench-press his weight. By his senior season, Willis was bench-pressing 300 pounds and so impressing the pro scouts that Atlanta would make him its first-round draft pick.

His attitude, too, made him a rare player in the minds of MSU coaches and players. It was not his own statistics or performance, but rather, what the team had done that dictated Willis' demeanor. If he had played poorly and MSU had won—as was known to happen—Willis was on a high that transcended any of the numbers next to his name.

Willis, though, would be the first casualty of an '83-84 season that would seem nothing short of cruel to Heathcote and players who thought it was their turn to fill Jenison and spark a turnaway audience at the MSU basketball banquet.

Willis sprained his ankle in an opening victory over Central Michigan, played sparingly during the next month, and for the remainder of the season could not make a power move to the basket. The inside force which a 7-foot senior was expected to lend never became an element to MSU's offense.

Another mini-disaster developed when Ken Johnson was ruled ineligible until the start of MSU's Big Ten season in January. Transfer hold-ups prevented him from playing in any of the pre-conference games—contests in which a player who had missed most of the previous season absolutely required game experience.

The third strike would came in January, in the Big Ten opener against Iowa at Jenison Field House, when Vincent sprained his ankle midway through a 73-72 victory over the Hawkeyes. Vincent would miss three weeks during which State lost seven consecutive games (one victory was later awarded MSU because of forfeits made by Wisconsin as part of NCAA penalties).

Skiles, too, would have a bad sophomore season as he attempted to become a one-man band during the Willis-Vincent rehabilitation. Michigan State's forwards often were made to disappear,

Darryl Johnson, the good-looking freshman had a complicated debut, and MSU was on its way from Top Ten status in the preseason to a 16-12 finish (15-13 before the forfeit) and fifth-place tie in the Big Ten. Not even the NIT would take a tournament chance on the Spartans.

It would also spell the end for Patrick Ford, the Detroit Cass Tech star, whose mysterious inability to crack Heathcote's system— or Heathcote's inability to crack Ford—resulted in a transfer to Western Michigan University.

Vincent's setback was less severe than his team's, but he had hoped his junior season would set up a senior spectacular that could make him one of the National Basketball Association's early draft picks in 1984.

Heathcote thought Vincent handled team needs and his pro ambitions reasonably well, but Sam, like his older brother, could frustrate. Sam had never made defense a personal mission, although he always thought Heathcote exaggerated the issue. If you missed your first shot in front of Heathcote, Sam liked to say, and made your next one million, Jud tended to brand you as a bad shooter. It had been that way with Richard Mudd, he thought. Mudd had been told so many times over the years that he had bad hands that there was never any chance of him developing a knack for catching the ball. His confidence level had early on transferred to another school.

Passing was another point of contention between Heathcote and Sam Vincent. Heathcote repeated after Vincent's sophomore year that he had to become a better passer—that he had to catch the ball on his fingertips—but he never believed Vincent listened until Magic Johnson that summer offered the same advice.

Heathcote's grievance against Jay had been strictly a matter of work habits. His hustle, his weight, his practice pace were not on the same plane as a Magic or a Kelser or a Kevin Willis. It was never a matter of personality problems since Jay, like Sam, was a splendid fellow whom you liked even when you were ready to hang him from a backboard. But Heathcote had advised Jay's agent to forsake big rookie money for a longer-term, no-cut contract when the Dallas Mavericks made him the first pick of the second round of the 1981 NBA draft.

By the start of rookie camp, it appeared smart strategy. The Mavericks had wanted Vincent to report at 235 pounds. He came in at 242. By mid-season he was at 244, and Dick Motta, the Mavericks coach, was ready to pink-slip him even if it meant eating the multi-year contract. But Heathcote had told Motta the previous summer to be prepared: Jay would be unimpressive initially. His weight would add to a coach's frustration. But if a coach were patient, Jay was a multi-dimensional player whose all-around talents would make him eventually a valuable player.

Later in the season, Motta had changed his tune. Jay Vincent was helping out. He could do a variety of things. Smart second-round pick we made here, Motta was saying.

It was never easy to say that Heathcote was mellowing or changing his coaching technique as the years wore on, but he grew to appreciate assistant coaches who told him if he had been too hard on a particular player. Those close to him believed that it was perhaps his own sensitivity toward people that explained why Heathcote was so sensitive to things said or printed about him or his team. If someone were in trouble or had a difficult personal problem, Heathcote made sure a phone call or a note followed, if it were appropriate. It was to him a matter of belief more than style.

As for his habits, everyone close to him knew they weren't changing. He would give a pre-game talk to his team 45 minutes before tipoff, but Heathcote, always uptight, would invariably arrive an hour before the speech. He would pull up his socks at the same time, fasten his tie nervously, and in accordance with his many superstitions, if Michigan State were winning he would put MSU's defense on the left side of the chalkboard and its offense on the right. If State lost, the order was reversed at the next game.

His incredible memory—it helped explain how he was able to catalog so many jokes—enabled him at halftime to point out specific mistakes made at specific times by individual players. His post-game mood was always dictated by the game's outcome. If State had won, he was Coach Mellow. If not, he could be an unbearable grouch.

He was as intense a coach as anyone had seen at Michigan State, and while he was NCAA champion in courtside fury during games, Heathcote had seemed to balance his life effectively. He liked to laugh and he enjoyed a beer, and he most definitely enjoyed a round of golf at Walnut Hills—or any other course to which he could get an invitation—as long as members of his foursome observed a cardinal rule: Stay out of his line of sight during the golf swing. If during his backswing he heard anyone breathe, if his eye caught so much as an alligator on an Izod shirt, Heathcote would react the way he might against a MSU charging foul in the final seconds of a one-point game.

It was because he could get away from basketball that no one overly worried about a 57-year-old man's health in 1984. He was carrying too many pounds on those battered knees, but that put him in step with most men of Heathcote's vintage. His diet was typically American in that he ate too much fat and way too much salt—he would salt his draft beers before drinking them, and before each meal automatically salt his food—but nothing seemed terribly out of whack. He had a nice life. Not enough basketball victories, but a nice life.

On September 26, 1984, Heathcote was home mowing his lawn on a Thursday afternoon when he felt a catch in his chest. Driving home from Flint that night, he felt the same thing. He returned to the basketball office on Friday and toward noon began feeling cold, clammy and nauseated. He sat in a chair in his office, complaining to Doug Weaver, MSU's athletic director, about the queasiness.

"Maybe," Weaver said matter-of-factly, "you're having a heart attack."

"Yeah," Heathcote answered, calmly, "maybe I am." By the time Heathcote arrived at Sparrow Hospital, doctors were confirming that Heathcote had indeed been hit with a heart attack. He would remain in the hospital for two weeks and convalesce at home until November—Indiana Coach Bobby Knight would pay a surprise visit to his home—by which time the strength was back, the diet was under strict control, the schedule was cut back, and the courtside eruptions were only temporarily toned down.

Mike Deane had filled in during Heathcote's recuperation at no perceptible loss to the team. Deane was an Easterner, a psychology major whose basketball concepts and philosophy patterned the head coach's. He knew how a young man's mind worked, and he knew discipline and structure. He also had absorbed a giant dose of Heathcote by the time he departed for the head coaching job at Siena College in 1986. Speaking with Deane was like speaking with Heathcote: Same rhythm and cadence, same emphasis on the key word of a phrase, same ability to dig deep within the language to coin a descriptive title or catchy tag that might best explain a technical or analytical aspect of basketball.

"We like to say that freshmen not only want to *start*, they want to *star*," Heathcote would explain in typical fashion.

"Larry Polec is perhaps our best basketball *athlete,*" Deane said early in Polec's carrer, the voice and phrasing a carbon copy of Heathcote's, "but perhaps our worst basketball *player.*"

Heathcote and Deane would combine during the 1984-85 season to help bring MSU its first NCAA tournament invitation in six years as State finished 19-10, including a 10-8 Big Ten record. Sam Vincent, who could be periodically breathtaking on shooting and basket-driving sprees, averaged 23 points per game and Skiles 17.7, while Ken Johnson—back at center after a miserable junior season at forward—averaged 10.8 points and enjoyed a more relaxed winter.

The coaching staff could also relax. Keeping Johnson underneath the rim was preferable to having him roam more than 10 feet from a basket to which he and the ball were often strangers. The RBP—Rim By Pass—had been a notorious Johnson statistic during his junior year, but at center, he was getting the dunks and follow-up baskets that diminished the number of outside shots Johnson unwisely continued to take.

Johnson's work underneath, Vincent's senior-year dramatics and Skiles' shooting all would combine to earn MSU a first-round NCAA tournament assignment at Houston against the University of Alabama-Birmingham—a game the Spartans would lose, 70-68, on some late turnovers that MSU felt sabotaged a Michigan State team clearly stronger than UAB. It was one of the perils of being unfamiliar with tournament pressure, the players admitted privately. Big Ten basketball was more rugged, but NCAA tournament basketball could do things to your body and mind you never felt during the regular season.

Except, perhaps, in the case of Skiles.

He had been learning about spotlight pressure since the previous summer's legal scrapes in Plymouth and back at East Lansing. He had been arrested in Plymouth and charged with possession of cocaine and marijuana after being stopped by a local policeman, who allegedly found marijuana residue in a passenger-side ashtray, and cocaine in Skiles' gym bag. He awaited a spring trial in Plymouth.

In September of 1984, a month after his arrest in Plymouth, Skiles was charged with drunk driving after East Lansing police arrested him on his way home from an off-campus party.

Skiles' image as a hard-nosed, tough guy had always been balanced by his off-the-court politeness and the stubborn way in which he handled jeering road fans anxious to taunt Michigan State's cocky backcourt gunner. Now, Skiles had a full-scale problem. His image had tumbled at home, and with the arrests, enemy fans had even more reason to curse and harass the agitator from MSU.

Skiles and his attorney—arguing they did not care to go through a protracted trial—agreed in the spring of 1985 to plead guilty to a misdemeanor charge of marijuana possession. Skiles was sentenced to a one-year suspended jail term, one year of probation, 120 hours of community work and a $100 fine. Three days later, he pled guilty to a misdemeanor charge of impaired driving stemming from the September drunk-driving arrest. He was sentenced to one night in jail, fined $300 and had his driver's license suspended for 90 days.

The legal hassles were now history, as far as Skiles and the MSU coaching staff were concerned. They would now get busy with the 1985-86 season, Skiles' senior year at MSU that would place even more importance on State's backcourt now that big-man Ken Johnson and guard Sam Vincent were gone.

"You've had a good year," Heathcote told Skiles, "but you don't do things that will make you a pro player. Let's concentrate on you getting your degree and laying a good foundation for the future."

It was essential in the NBA to have quickness and speed beyond Skiles' capabilities. You could overcome slow-footedness by being an extraordinary shooter, but as good as Skiles was, Heathcote could not see him shooting his way onto a NBA team. There, good shooters were cut by the bunch.

Skiles had raised his talents an entire level the previous season when he spent his summer at Plymouth shooting and playing almost non-stop basketball. Instead of hitting six of 10 shots, he began hitting eight of 10. Instead of being dominated in the occasional Magic Johnson pick-up games he would enter during visits to East Lansing, he was holding his own.

He would spend the summer of '85 at summer school in East Lansing and play basketball every day, including weekends when he would drive back to Plymouth to play in Saturday-Sunday summer leagues. At MSU, Johnson and his pro friends—Isiah Thomas, Jay Vincent, Mark Aguirre, etc.—were always playing at Jenison, and Skiles during the week was always welcome. Very welcome, as the summer rolled on.

"Hey," Johnson told Heathcote later that summer, "that Skiles can play." Skiles was shooting with so much more range. He could always shoot almost equally well with either hand, but now he was hitting routinely from 20 feet. Heathcote could see that Skiles' game had climbed another level. The pro potential was emerging.

MSU's official practices began on October 15. Three weeks later, on November 6, 1985, Skiles had wrapped up practice and was looking forward to a leisurely evening. No practice scheduled the next day meant a player had time to study and relax, and maybe, for the first time in nine months, stop by a student hangout and have a beer. He had been avoiding any such place since his arrests from the previous year, and was obliged to stay away under terms of his Indiana probation. But he was thirsty and restless and his friends were pestering him to join them. A beer wouldn't hurt.

He parked his car behind the popular student bar Dooley's— Tom, the manager, had told him he could park there in a pinch— and wandered with his friends to an intimate place called B'zar. He drank four, probably five, beers and they had tasted so good to a person dehydrated from practice. He also had not eaten anything since mid-day.

Skiles stayed even after his friends left, and now it was getting late as he walked from B'zar, across Albert Street, and considered what to do. His friends lived only four blocks away and he could stay there rather than risk getting pulled over on his way home. He felt strong and in control, but there was no sense taking a risk.

A cab pulled up at the stoplight as Skiles crossed the street. A thought flashed: "I should take this cab to my place." But he thought again. If he did that, then his car would be towed from behind Dooley's. He got inside his red Fiero, the car with Indiana license plates and a Michigan State decal across the rear window, and headed down Albert. A police car pulled up on him with its flashers spinning. Skiles got out, had his car searched, and was told to recite his ABC's, which Skiles would forever contend were recited clearly. The arresting officer claimed they were slurred.

A breathalyzer test showed Skiles' blood alcohol level at .11— .10 is regarded as legally drunk in Michigan—and Skiles was on his way to jail and to a 2:30 a.m. call to his parents in Plymouth, who were reliving the nightmare of a son telling them once again he had been arrested.

He was released from jail the next morning and now, accompanied by his mother and Deane, drove straight to Heathcote's office for a decision on how MSU would handle an incident as embarrassing, foolish and as threatening as Skiles' third arrest in 14 months.

Heathcote could see no option. "I don't think there's any choice," he said, "but to suspend you until things are sorted out."

Skiles went home to the apartment he lived in by himself to think about a life and a career that had very likely been permanently altered by a stupid stop at a bar. He had told Heathcote he would do whatever was necessary—transfer, sit out the year, anything—to lessen the pressure on MSU and make amends for something this damaging. And it was Heathcote he worried about as he sat at home and listened to the phone ring.

There had been some speculation that Skiles' troubles in the summer of 1984 helped induce Heathcote's September heart attack. He was concerned now that this latest crisis might lead to more health problems.

Skiles next tuned into the media debate about his situation, and within a couple of days, the mail began arriving: Angry mail. Hate mail. He had never paid close attention to the drunk-driving issue because he had never felt it affected him. Now he was feeling the emotion of it, the trauma and suffering of those who had lost loved ones, the condemnation of those who did not drink and drive, or those who did not drink, period.

Skiles began to understand the powerful emotions of drunk driving. He was confronted by parents who had lost children to drunk drivers, and it was because of such anguish that he decided to save all the letters he received—even the ones from alumni who said Skiles was a disgrace, that he should be stripped of his scholarship and of his academic credits.

Some of the letters were demented, but most of them Skiles thought were honest reactions to an inexcusable mistake. He forced himself to read them. They had a point, he said. If he had put himself through college, absorbing the heavy expenses and working a couple of jobs to pay it all off, he would also have resented an athlete on scholarship abusing his privilege to the degree he had. He would have written a letter himself.

Skiles had no expectations of playing as his suspension lingered through the weekend. He had sat at home watching MSU's exhibition game against Czechoslovakia and taking notes on things he might be able to pass on to Darryl Johnson and Vernon Carr, the guards on whom everything would fall if he failed to return.

Heathcote debated what to do. The community, the state, the entire Midwest seemed to be frothing over the Skiles incident. He understood the circumstances and they simply did not support any charge that Skiles was a drunk or a criminal. He had erred in an utterly stupid and incomprehensible fashion for someone with two strikes against him, but Heathcote had Skiles' future to worry about, first and foremost. And Heathcote was still haunted by his expulsion of a high school player years before whose life had been blemished by a rules structure that needed, on occasion, to be flexible. Skiles had a career and a life ahead of him. Booting him off permanently would be of little benefit to anyone, including teammates who had a right to play on a team that looked as if it could go places.

Heathcote also knew that any move to reinstate Skiles would be construed as a self-serving move. He understood, as well, that he would suffer within his own fraternity—and maintaining respect from his coaching colleagues meant everything to Jud Heathcote.

He would put it to a team vote.

Skiles was brought to Jenison and apologized to his teammates, after which he was asked to leave while players voted on whether to bring him back. It was unanimous for reinstatement—a vote, Skiles knew, that likely would have gone the other way two years earlier. He was especially gratified because players such as Darryl Johnson, Carr and Mark Brown would have played heavier roles without Skiles on the team.

He was reinstated as public opinion and media flak exploded around Skiles and Heathcote.

Back on the court, he came prepared for chilly or ugly crowd receptions that would haunt him all winter. He also brought with him his new, long-range jump shot, and the resolve to make his senior season a run for the NCAA championship. It had been his goal for the past year.

On January 16, 1986, Michigan State was 11-2 overall and 2-2 in the Big Ten as it got ready to meet Iowa in a game at Iowa City. Ivan Maisel from *Sports Illustrated*, who was there for the game, called Skiles in his room to ask for an interview. Skiles had not been talking about his legal problems with the media, but called Heathcote to get his opinion.

"It might be a good time," he told his coach, "to get my opinions expressed."

He and Maisel talked. That night, Skiles had a poor game in an

82-71 defeat that the next day was bothering him. With *Sports Illustrated* on hand, with a big game at Iowa begging Skiles to star, he had played shabbily. He told himself it would be his last poor game of the season.

The following night at Minnesota, Skiles had 45 points in a staggering shooting show that coaches later estimated would have been a 62-point night had the Big Ten been playing a three-point shot. He followed with a 41-point game, with a 43-pointer against Ohio State, and with a pair of victories over Michigan that helped MSU win 10 of its next 11 games and 11 of its final 13 for a 23-8 record, and 12-6, third-place Big Ten finish.

He, Johnson and Carr became the essence of a three-guard, no-center offense that used its speed and superb shooting skill to blow away the Big Ten in the season's final six weeks. And, to the amazement of those who had watched Skiles win the Big Ten scoring title with a 29.1 average, he had done it while playing before opponent crowds that verbally assaulted him from introduction until final buzzer.

Handling vicious crowds was the one element of his senior season in which Skiles took the most pride. He had learned a lesson five years earlier about dealing with that—back when he was at Plymouth High, when he nearly led the state in scoring, when every time he touched the ball, the crowd would wail: "Scot-tee . . . Scot-tee." He certainly had a knack for bringing people together, Skiles told himself. He even took a stream of abuse and profanity from Purdue Coach Gene Keady, who did not appreciate Skiles' milder taunts of Boilermaker guard Mack Gadis as Skiles guarded him.

Skiles would take his experience in dealing with pressure with him to the NCAA tournament, which he and the Spartans were initiating with a date against Washington—a game State would win, 72-70, when Skiles sank a pair of free throws with two seconds to play. Georgetown and its 24-9 record would be next, but MSU killed the Hoyas, 80-68, in a nationally televised contest in which Skiles would slip a behind-the-back pass to Larry Polec—MSU's most memorable NCAA assist since Johnson-to-Kelser had been in vogue seven years earlier.

MSU was headed to the Midwest Regional at Kansas City for a semifinal game against the very talented Kansas Jayhawks. MSU was in high gear with its running game going, its free-throw shooting the best in the country, its front-line entourage of Polec, Carlton Valentine and Barry Fordham filling in smoothly.

Michigan State was down at the half, 46-37, but blazed its way back to take a 62-61 lead with 10:21 to play. State was still leading when Jayhawk star Danny Manning fouled out with 2:21 to play—an infamous moment in NCAA clock history as the official time-piece at Kemper Arena froze on 2:21 for some 15 seconds after the ball had been in-bounded. Heathcote raged down the sidecourt, pounding his fist on the scorer's table, but the only compensation was a technical foul called on Kansas Coach Larry Brown, which sent Skiles to the line for two technical shots and a one-and-one opportunity that could wrap up the game for MSU and send State into Sunday's Midwest finals against a slower North Carolina State.

Skiles made his two technicals, but missed the front half of his one-and-one. Polec, likewise, missed a one-on-one, as did Mark Brown, the freshman. Kansas made up six points in the final minute to tie the game, 80-80, and set up an overtime that Kansas would dominate on the way to winning, 96-86.

The clock would be remembered as one of those quirks that supposedly never happened in the regal NCAA tournament. But Michigan State understood that it had been the missed one-and-ones—almost automatic during the regular season which saw State lead the nation in free throw percentage—and not the clock that had wrecked a chance to take its three-guard carnival act to the Final Four in Dallas.

In the locker room afterward, Skiles sat silently next to Polec. There were no tears, but he could see the pain on each teammate's face. Heathcote came by.

"Scott and Larry," he said, speaking to the team's two starting seniors, "if you want to speak at the press conference, let's go. If not, that's fine."

Polec had represented a special, personal victory for the MSU basketball team. He had come to East Lansing as a project—a great athlete whose basketball skills were so underdeveloped he would need several years of refinement. He had also been an insecure teenager in need of attention when he got to Michigan State.

Now, long after he had endured the Students Against Polec movement that one student two years earlier had formed in protest of Polec's alleged talents, Polec had developed into a solid player and, more significantly, had blossomed into a person coaches and teammates appreciated.

"Hey, Larry, you got 11 rebounds tonight!" Heathcote would say after a big win.

"Yeah," Polec would answer, smiling sheepishly, "that's more than most nights." And he would laugh and congratulate Heathcote on the victory.

The team returned to its hotel in Kansas City following the overtime anguish, Heathcote sitting sullenly in his room, agonizing over what he believed had been a missed trip to the Final Four. He would have bet his salary that MSU would whip N.C. State in the Midwest finals. And he wanted badly to take that team to Dallas— to college basketball's big stage, where a coach's talents are on display before his cohorts every bit as much as his team's.

It would not happen, nor would the rebuilding process go at all smoothly in 1986-87, as MSU adjusted to life without Skiles in much the way it had adapted seven years earlier to basketball without Magic Johnson. An 11-17 record followed, as across the street from Jenison, work continued on a $30-million arena that would be the basketball team's new home.

Midway through the winter of '86-87, Skiles returned to Jenison to be presented with the Big Ten's Most Valuable Player Award for 1986. He stepped to midcourt, lights burning hot, the crowd on its feet, and Skiles at that moment knew it:

The new place could never match Jenison Field House.

Eleven

FLORIDA ON
$4 A NIGHT

Before his next fishing trip to Ontario could begin peacefully, Biggie Munn faced a personnel decision in the spring of 1963. John Kobs, 39 years at Michigan State, was retiring as baseball coach and Munn wanted an established, respected baseball teacher to take control of a team that was not an athletic department showpiece, but a team that was essential to a balanced Big Ten program.

Baseball had a climatic problem in the North that kept it from becoming a high-profile sport that could do for MSU what it did for programs at Miami and Arizona State and Southern Cal. It was an annual predicament at Old College Field. High waters from the Red Cedar River often converted the baseball field into a delta that would not dry out until, it seemed, about an hour before Michigan State was to begin its April home schedule. Crowds sometimes barely exceeded a gang of chilled regulars seated in a trailer that doubled as MSU's baseball press box: WKAR radio's play-by-play man, Jim Adams; Bob Gross of the *Lansing State Journal*; and sports publicists Fred Stabley Sr. and Nick Vista.

Rain, snow, bitter winds and 50-degree temperatures would remain a risk until May, at which time, around the 15th, MSU would generally complete its home schedule on a weekend so sunny, so glorious, that the 1,000 or so people who had strolled out to eat a hot dog and catch some baseball, bemoaned the end of a season that never had time to catch on.

It was baseball's perpetual Catch-22. Munn knew it, but he supported the game and wanted a coach who could give it some status, some impact at the Big Ten level. He wanted the man he had met through Kobs a few years earlier, Danny Litwhiler, head baseball coach at Florida State and former major leaguer.

Litwhiler had gotten his start in college coaching from Kobs and had invited Kobs and Michigan State during the Ron Perranoski-Dick Radatz years of the late '50s to play some spring games at the Tallahassee campus. Litwhiler and Munn had hit it off immediately. Munn was a hearty, full-of-life type who Litwhiler could see gave an athletic department presence, and probably, good direction. Litwhiler was a more soft-spoken, gentlemanly coach whose glove rested in a showcase at the Baseball Hall of Fame because of a string of 187 errorless games during the 1941-42 seasons.

Litwhiler had credentials and integrity, Munn concluded, and in 1963 Litwhiler would be his first phone call.

"Biggie, I really don't want to move," Litwhiler told him. "I like it here."

"That," said Munn, "is why I want you."

Litwhiler agreed finally to talk with an athletic director who was not easy to shake. He flew to East Lansing, stayed at the Munn home, and became even more impressed with the Michigan State AD and his wife, Vera. Litwhiler knew he could work with Munn and shoot for a major-college program that might make a dent in the NCAA tournament. It was also a chance to move to a Big Ten conference that in 1963 stood as the top intercollegiate sports conference in the country. He loved the folks at Florida State, but the MSU job seemed too good.

Litwhiler was making $8,500 at Florida State and would come to Michigan State at a whopping $13,500. An added plus: His $4,000-per-year budget at Florida State would be increased 50 percent to $6,000 at Michigan State.

Litwhiler returned to Tallahassee and told FSU executives he had no choice but to leave for a better offer at Michigan State. His bosses came back, raising Litwhiler's salary to $11,000, explaining that FSU could pay more if Litwhiler had a doctorate. They would, however, throw in a four-year scholarship for his son, Danny.

The scholarship weighed heavily, as did a $2,500 raise. Litwhiler and his wife, Dot, had five children, and clothes alone were ripping at the family budget. When friends as good as he had at FSU were making every effort to keep you, Litwhiler thought a scholarship and raise sufficient reason to stay. He called Munn's office to explain there had been a change of mind, and learned that Munn had already departed for Canada, where he and Vera annually fished, and where MSU President John Hannah often joined them. The cabin was deep within Ontario's wilderness, but Munn had left word with his secretary, Dorothy Miller, that emergency radio communications could be made each night at 7 p.m.

He had just gotten off the water with a stringer-full of lake trout when Miller sent word that Munn should call back. He left camp, got to a phone, and listened as Litwhiler explained the FSU counter-offer.

"Dammit," wailed Munn, "is that all the trouble is?

"I'll give you $15,000."

Litwhiler had parlayed a 1950s invitation to Kobs into a job that nearly doubled his income, offered a better budget, and would not need stem-to-stern rehabilitation as he sized up the program John Kobs had directed since 1925.

There was a fine-hitting first baseman, Jerry Sutton, who swung the big bat any coach needed for the middle of his lineup. And although there were never enough arms on any college team, Litwhiler thought he could shape a staff as he began work on September 1, 1963.

What he thought MSU needed as much as talent was an improved baseball complex. It would start with a new, metal fence to replace the snow fence that stood in a semi-circle around the outfield. Litwhiler could see it would be a matter of time before an outfielder impaled himself on one of those sharp-edged stakes that jutted out. He also needed a rest room for players and fans who were on their own during the course of a game.

Michigan State needed some legitimate stands, as well, to replace those dangerous bleachers through which a woman would fall the following spring. And Litwhiler had another idea as he inspected a ball field that sat so peacefully against the banks of the Red Cedar. Center and right field backed up almost against the river, but beyond left field were several acres of open land between the outfield and the Red Cedar. Litwhiler thought it would add to the field's intimacy and charm if trees could be planted behind left field, creating background scenery that would give the field even more distinction.

Litwhiler struck a deal a couple of years later with Bruce Look, a Michigan State catcher, who had signed a big-league contract and who would go on to play for the Minnesota Twins. Look would donate money to pay for the trees, a plan that Hannah later vetoed on the grounds that tree-plantings would be too permanent for a baseball facility that Michigan State had considered moving. Litwhiler got Look to instead buy a new scoreboard clock.

Baseball at Michigan State had never been the kind of high-profile sport that challenged football, or even basketball, when it came to drawing fans or generating interest. But Kobs, a 6-foot-2, 240-pound man who had also worked as a MSU assistant football coach and as its first head hockey coach, regularly built winning baseball teams that spawned their share of big-leaguers: Robin Roberts, Hobie Landrith, Al Luplow, Jack Kralick, and the great pitching pair who would become big-league bullpen giants: Radatz and Perranoski.

Michigan State had never won a NCAA championship, nor was it a team that manhandled the Big Ten, but Litwhiler knew there was ample in-state talent if you could keep the guys from signing major-league contracts. Litwhiler had been one of the smart ones back in his Pennsylvania youth. He had gone on to Bloomsburg (Pennsylvania) State College and gotten his degree before arriving in the majors in 1939 to begin a 12-year career.

But baseball players all had the same dream that too often overpowered better judgment. They all wanted to make the big leagues. All wanted to get on with a career that for most had been an obsession since they were young boys. Even if Litwhiler and the wiser observers knew that, at best, three percent of those who signed ever played an inning of big-league ball, it was difficult to convince a person caught up in a dream that college would be a sound first stop. Especially when a scout was dangling a $3,000 bonus in front of your face.

He was unacquainted with Michigan and the Midwest when he came to Michigan State, but Litwhiler's 30 years in baseball had introduced him to a network of established baseball men who could help a head coach whom most of them liked. He knew scouts like Ed Katalinas and Lou D'Annunzio of the Detroit Tigers who could give him a strong reading on whether a player not mature or talented enough for pro ball might be major-college material.

D'Annunzio was working Florida for the Tigers when Litwhiler in 1966 got a letter from one of his old Florida State players, Don Murray, who was now teaching at Chamberlain High in Tampa.

Litwhiler, said Murray, needed to see a Chamberlain athlete named Steve Garvey. He's your kind of player, said Murray.

Litwhiler got on the phone with D'Annunzio.

"Good power, Danny," D'Annunzio explained. "Good hitter."

Litwhiler wanted more.

"He doesn't have an arm. I don't think he'll make it professionally. Not with that arm."

"Is he a college possibility?" Litwhiler asked.

"Yeah . . . oh yeah."

"All right," Litwhiler said, "then here's the $100 question: Would you give him a scholarship?"

"Yeah," D'Annunzio said. "I think I would."

Litwhiler followed through and discovered that Garvey had wanted to play in the Big Ten, but was 0-for-9 on scholarship offers. Garvey's only question during a recruiting visit to East Lansing was whether it would be permissible to play football.

"Sure," Litwhiler said, "if it's okay with your parents."

Garvey signed with MSU and that autumn joined the Spartan freshman football team for workouts that would run smoothly until Garvey jammed his shoulder. The following spring, Garvey, whose throwing arm ranked as no prize to begin with, now could not throw a baseball across the infield. From third base he would bounce throws to first.

His bat, though, was fast and powerful. Litwhiler played him. By his sophomore season, Garvey's arm had improved—he had also lettered as a defensive back on Daugherty's football team and escaped injury—and his bat and glove continued to get better. Garvey batted .376 and hit nine homers in 1968, which was all the Los Angeles Dodgers needed to see. Garvey, with two years of eligibility remaining at MSU, signed a rich contract with the Dodgers and would during the 1970s and '80s become one of the game's best-known players and personalities, an athlete whose clubhouse problems at L.A. and subsequent divorce from MSU sweetheart, Cyndy, would make him as much a headliner as his hitting.

Garvey's football-induced injury was only one reason why Litwhiler and Football Coach Duffy Daugherty through the years would have one of the athletic department's more tense relationships. Litwhiler never bickered or griped about the situation, but Daugherty had no reservations about asking Litwhiler if a football player who was purportedly a baseball talent might be brought in on a baseball scholarship. It would prevent Daugherty from going over his own scholarship limit and theoretically help Litwhiler and the entire MSU athletic department. Litwhiler usually cooperated.

The problem was some of the alleged baseball talents appeared to have peaked in Little League. It was suspected in some instances that the football coach may have been doing a friend a favor. There were also times when a player that Daugherty decreed absolutely essential to spring football drills—like Steve Kirkpatrick—looked as if he might be better off helping the baseball team.

The fall baseball class Litwhiler taught appeared also to be a convenient repository for various football players of questionable scholastic commitment. Some of the gridders chose not to show up, while others clearly were sleeping through class. Tests were often abysmal.

If academic reports were so bad as to affect eligibility, Daugherty was not disinclined to call up Litwhiler, woe in his voice.

"Why, Danny, this young man has to pass," Daugherty would say. "Why, if we don't have (name) and (name) on Saturday . . ."

Litwhiler would do the best he could under such circumstances— giving a likely flunk-out a chance at extra credit for a book report or for a paper. It was one more subtle bit of pressure within an athletic department where pressure was so often the norm, and where feelings among coaches could run raw as budgets and politics combined to make athletics a subordinate issue.

Daugherty had an ego and had power, and as his clashes with Munn had illustrated, the football coach did not care for interference or second-class treatment. When the MSU Athletic Council petitioned to fill one of its places with a varsity coach, Litwhiler was voted by the coaches to serve. Daugherty exploded at the appointment, believing his team was most directly affected by conference and university policy. It did nothing to improve football-baseball relations.

Although Garvey would sign a major-league contract in 1968, as would pitcher Mel Behney and, in 1969, outfielder Rick Miller, Michigan State by the late '60s was building the core of what loomed as a championship club. Shaun Howitt, a power-hitting centerfielder, was developing rapidly, as was catcher-outfielder Ron Pruitt, third baseman Rob Ellis, outfielder Gary Boyce, catcher Bailey Oliver, and several excellent pitchers in Larry Ike, Rob Clancy, Brad Van Pelt and Lansing's Dave Leisman.

The talent would combine in 1971 to give Litwhiler his best

club—a Big Ten champion that would finish the year 36-10 and make it into the NCAA tournament before losing out to Southern Illinois.

Clancy that season would roll up nine consecutive victories for a 10-1 record, while Ike would go 8-1. Ellis would hit a record 14 home runs, while Pruitt would collect seven triples—a MSU record that stood 16 years later. Boyce would hit almost .400. It was a club that would win more games than any in MSU history, and a club that had prospered in an era when baseball scholarships to Michigan State totaled perhaps nine versus the 20 to 25 dispensed by powers such as Southern Cal and Arizona State.

Talent began to weaken quickly at Michigan State as Munn suffered his stroke in October of 1971, and MSU's athletic department hunkered in for tighter budgets under new Athletic Director Burt Smith. Salaries, budgets and scholarships were in for tougher days and, in time, so was Michigan State's baseball team.

Litwhiler had been including as an essential part of his program an annual spring trip to Florida, where the team could get a week or 10 days of concentrated competition against good baseball schools. It would be valuable not only as preparation for the regular season, but as a recruiting enticement to players who could look forward to escaping indoor training for March sunshine and the chance to play on a real diamond against a team such as the University of Miami.

Burt Smith, in one cost-cutting proposition, had suggested that the baseball spring trip be chopped. Jack Breslin, a former MSU baseball player, and the university vice-president who was then watching over the athletic department, quickly shot down the idea. A spring trip was vital.

Paying for a Florida trip on an annual baseball budget of $20,000 was another trick altogether. From that outlay came travel expenses, uniforms, bats, balls, and whatever meager recruiting, if any, that could be worked from it. It was soon clear that if MSU's spring trip was to survive, Litwhiler would need other revenue.

The baseball team's Florida trip—even by the normal, dehumanizing, bargain-basement standards college students practiced during spring migration—was an exercise in austerity. Rooms normally were booked at the Miramar Hotel on Biscayne Bay, an unusual hostelry that featured one elevator operated by a maintenance man, fuzzy black-and-white TV, small bathrooms, and an unbeatable rate: $16 a night in the early '70s, or $4 per man if players were assigned two to a bed, four to a room. Players were then given $4 a day for meal money—supplemented by occasional cafeteria meals, or smorgasbords—which made for a daily per-player budget of $8. Lansing auto dealer Max Curtis would help arrange on-site cars for the travelers.

It was cutting corners, but it was the difference between going home for the break, or playing baseball in Florida. Litwhiler in the early '70s devised another plan that would cut costs and allow the team to fly to Florida, rather than drive, as was the case for most schools. He set up charter trips available to Michigan State baseball fans who could, at low rates, accompany the team to Florida and enjoy a spring baseball vacation alongside the team.

But even $4-a-day rooms and fast-food diets were not enough to balance MSU's baseball budget. Litwhiler annually had to scrape up thousands of dollars extra.

His first project was a style show held in conjunction with Jacobson's department store of East Lansing at the MSU Kellogg Center's Big Ten Room. Among those modeling in the MSU baseball team's first and last venture in contemporary apparel was Brad Van Pelt, the all-around sports great who pitched for Litwhiler's team, and his fiancee, Mary Scott.

It proved to be too much work for too little return. Litwhiler, though, would get another money-making lead in the spring of 1973 when he helped direct a NCAA regional baseball tournament at the University of Minnesota. Paul Giel, Minnesota's athletic director, mentioned to Litwhiler that he had raised money by holding wine and cheese parties. You could, in most cases, get the wine and cheese donated, and with no overhead, money could be made.

Litwhiler began talking with people back home. Jim Hough, *Lansing State Journal* columnist and a close friend of Litwhiler's, would help arrange a wine donation through the Werner Brothers winery of Paw Paw, Michigan.

Dr. Malcolm Trout, a university professor, would speak with his friend, Earland Kondrup, of the Arthur Cheese Company of Arthur, Illinois, about possible help on the cheese. Kondrup and Arthur came through, as did Michigan State's food connections.

Party-goers would pay $10 per couple and enjoy as many wines and cheeses as they cared. Litwhiler would clear about $2,000, and in one pleasurable evening not only assist his budget, but realize strong public-relations benefits for the baseball program.

It had never been easy during the regular season to devise ways for a team of hungry baseball players to eat nutritionally sound meals that would keep a program from bankruptcy. The usual in-season format for in-state road games was to encourage everyone to eat a good breakfast at home. Sandwich essentials—bread, beef, ham and cheese, mustard, mayonnaise, etc.—and fruit were then carried aboard the bus so that by 11:30 a.m. or noon, the team could stop for a quick pre-game lunch.

After the game, a stop at a Kentucky Fried Chicken outlet would serve as an early dinner, or as stop-gap nutrition until the players made their own dinner arrangements.

Out-of-town road trips were more generously funded. About 4 p.m., after the last class on the day before a game, the team would board a bus for one of the Big Ten stops—Ohio State, Indiana, Illinois, Purdue, etc.—that could be reached by a reasonable drive. Litwhiler had been trying for years to provide dinners that were digestible and affordable. There came a perfect solution: MSU's food services could prepare airlines-style hot plates loaded with huge servings of beef, chicken, vegetables, etc. that could be carried aboard the bus in insulated, portable ovens and served hot when the team stopped at picnic grounds along the way.

With the Coca-Cola Company donating beverages for team meals, major cost-savers had arrived. The team would stay at comfortable overnight accommodations—the student unions if opponent schools maintained them, or at hotels where reasonable rates could be obtained, such as The Leamington in Minneapolis, owned by former Texas Rangers owner Bob Short.

Money was no more a concern through the mid-'70s than was talent on a Michigan State team that had, following the big year in '71 and through 1977, finished second, sixth and four times in fourth. Litwhiler was becoming more involved in international baseball programs as part of his activity in the American Baseball Coaches Association. He was traveling to Japan and Korea, enjoying amateur baseball on a broader stage, minus any of the financial or political hassles that went with college coaching.

It also meant that more and more of the in-office tasks were falling on Assistant Coach Frank Pellerin, a Michigan State baseball letter-winner from 1941-43, who had been an assistant under Kobs and Litwhiler since 1952. Pellerin had been passed over for the head coaching job when Litwhiler was hired in 1963, but stayed on as assistant when Litwhiler arrived. A situation far from ideal for either party had worked for more than a decade, and would continue to work in its sometimes-frazzled way until Litwhiler retired in 1982 and Pellerin in 1985.

To players, Pellerin had one name: The Eagle. Players who had watched him oversee the indoor batting-cage games that were a winter baseball staple, could understand how anyone so observant, so eagle-eyed had picked up a tag that stuck with Pellerin for years. He was, in addition to batting-cage maestro, a man of incredible statistical ability.

"Do you know," he would say to one of the pitchers, "that on a 3-1 pitch, a batter will hit your fastball for a single 83.6 percent of the time?"

Pellerin had personal statistics on every pitcher's success ratio with various pitches on various counts. He figured numbers on hitters, on catchers, on base-running situations, on every facet of the game. But it was in the indoor batting cage at the Men's Intramural Building—MSU's winter baseball training area—that The Eagle reigned supreme.

The cage was a net configuration in which batters could take full cuts against pitchers who were protected by screens. The net prevented any ball from escaping the enclosure, no matter how it was hit. It was Pellerin's assignment to observe the net games and determine whether a batted ball was a base hit or an out. On such scoring decisions would occasionally rest a prospect's fate in the spring, when 24 to 27 players were selected to make the Florida trip.

Baseball at Michigan State began with fall workouts, when as many as 100 or more walk-ons might turn out with the established starters and scholarship players, all hoping to stick with the team through winter and into the spring.

It had been essentially a three-man coaching operation through the '60s and '70s: Litwhiler, Pellerin, and Tom Smith, a former major-league catching prospect from Coldwater, Michigan, whose days in the Milwaukee Braves organization ended in 1962 in a plate collision with a youngster from the Cincinnati farm system: A pepper-pot infielder by the name of Pete Rose. Smith had worked as a baseball staffer, and then as a volunteer coach during the budget-crunching '70s, when he was employed as a MSU physical education instructor. It had become one of the longest-running intact coaching staffs anywhere at Michigan State.

It had also withstood the death in 1971 of Litwhiler's wife, Dot, who had been ill for almost a year, and the staff had celebrated a couple of years later when Danny married Pat James, a widow with five children. Theirs would become one of the athletic department's happiest marriages.

Litwhiler's team had managed to play competitively through the mid-'70s, thanks mostly to players like Al Weston, Brian Wolcott, Larry Pashnick, Jerry Weller, Rodger Bastien and Ken Robinson, but franchise talent had not been arriving in the clusters. Franchise players, period, had been scarce at Michigan State, although several players from the Pontiac area had told Litwhiler in the fall of 1977 that Kirk Gibson, MSU's big football receiver, could help.

Litwhiler was curious.

"Can he play?" he asked them.

"Yeah. He's pretty good. He's not a good fielder, but he can run."

"Can he hit?"

"Yeah, he hits it to the shortstop and he beats it out."

"Does he have any power?"

"Oh yeah, when he gets a hold of one."

A few weeks later, Litwhiler was sitting across from Gibson at Michigan State's Grand Rapids Football Bust. It was time to try some salesmanship.

"Gibby, why don't you come out for baseball?"

Gibson nodded slowly.

"Yeah," he said, "I've been thinking about it."

"Well, don't think about it. Come out."

Litwhiler later approached Darryl Rogers, the MSU football coach. He would need Rogers' blessing.

"Can he play baseball?" wondered Rogers, not sure his wide receiver had baseball skills.

"I don't know," Litwhiler said, "but I'd like to have him try it."

Rogers was enthused. He had always—even at San Jose State—encouraged football players with multiple talents to apply them to other sports. And Gibson certainly did not need spring football practice.

"Well," Rogers said, "I'd like to have him try it, too. I'd rather he be out there helping you, than here getting hurt. I want him back in the fall."

Two months later, Gibson was taking his first swings in the indoor arena.

Litwhiler was floored.

Hanging from a swivel was a tire that gave hitters a durable, consistent target by which they could groove their batting strokes. Gibson, in his first turn, was so pulverizing the tire that steel bands and wires were flying around the gym.

Litwhiler thought that if Gibson could make reasonable contact, the team had just added Superman. More evidence turned up when Mike Marshall, the major-league reliever who was working toward a doctorate at MSU, stopped by practice to throw to the hitters.

Gibson took his turn and sent one of Marshall's pitches tearing into the netting. Everyone in the gym knew that if he had hit it at Kobs Field, it would still have been going.

"Oh," said Pellerin, nonchalantly scoring the cage game, "that's an out. Fly ball."

Gibson roared: "THAT'S AN OUT?"

Marshall, not one for flattery, afterward walked off the floor with Litwhiler.

"Boy," Marshall said, "he has a good swing."

Gibson would go on to hit .450 during MSU's spring trip to Texas, along the way launching a home run to left-center that was the longest ball anyone at Pan American University had ever seen hit. Litwhiler was more impressed by a Gibson line-drive that went between the second baseman's legs. It never touched ground until it got to the outfield, skidding on two hops against the fence.

The football-to-baseball experiment was working out, although breaking in back home, with different pressures working on him, would be tough. After three games, Gibson was 0-for-12. He walked back from the plate following his last at-bat and told Litwhiler he was quitting.

Litwhiler thought he was kidding. But Gibson wandered over to the auxiliary dugout and sat down, staring glumly at the ground. Litwhiler thought it was time for a chat.

"What's the problem?"

"I'm sick of this," Gibson said. "It's no fun. I'm making a fool of myself in front of all my friends."

"Hey," Litwhiler said, "that's going to change. Tomorrow. Maybe the next day. You're too good a hitter. Look at spring training: Was that fun?"

"That," said Gibson, "was down there."

"You were hitting good people. The pitching there was as good as it is up here."

"I don't know . . . In football if this happens, I can go out and hit somebody. I can't do anything here."

Litwhiler wasn't sure Gibson would be back. His new outfielder was plainly distraught.

But the next day, Gibson showed up, got dressed, and hit a home run.

He was beaming as he crossed home plate and waltzed to the dugout.

"Is it fun now?" Litwhiler asked him.

There would be another near-disaster when Gibson, while washing dishes at his apartment, reached into the disposal and gashed his hand. Litwhiler thought he was finished for the spring, but Jim Madaleno, the excellent team trainer, worked on the hand, keeping it clean, and in a week Gibson was back in the lineup and about to ignite.

One home run after another followed, most of them tape-measure shots hit over the trees behind the right-field fence, and beyond the Red Cedar River. He hit one during batting practice at the University of Michigan that sailed over the roof of the tennis building. Drives that even reached the tennis building were considered boomers, and anything that landed on the roof was monstrous. Gibson had cleared the entire structure.

During one three-game spree, Gibson hit eight home runs—he also stole a record-tying 21 bases on the season—and now the pro scouts were storming East Lansing. Gibson's phone rang continually.

The Tigers had an early first-round draft choice in 1978, and were curious about the new slugger at MSU, even if he were certain to go in the first round of the 1979 National Football League draft. The Tigers contacted Tom Smith to see if Gibson might be interested in taking batting practice at Tiger Stadium. Gibson went to Detroit on the first Saturday of June. And put on a show.

Gibson had not swung a wood bat in years—colleges all used aluminum—and at random grabbed the bat used by Tiger catcher Lance Parrish. Dick Tracewski, a Tiger coach, was throwing batting practice.

"Throw him a change-up," Parrish yelled.

Gibson sent a stream of pitches sailing into the upper deck, one hitting the facing of the second deck and rolling all the way back to the infield. He hit line-drives with such topspin that they were tearing divots from the outfield turf.

Gibson was drafted in the first round by Detroit, signed, and spent his summer at the Tigers' Class A club in Lakeland, before reporting back to East Lansing in August for the start of football drills at Michigan State.

MSU had finished second in the 1978 Big Ten baseball race with an 11-5 record (32-21) and would, in 1979, win its first Big Ten title in eight years with a team that was so undistinguished it had an overall record of 28-27. But it snuck through the Big Ten season at 11-4, and with the help of rainouts, took a Big Ten championship. Jim Cotter, Brian Wolcott, Jay Strother and Mark Pomorski got enough people out at the right times to carry a team that was getting the bulk of its hitting from Ken Robinson, Rodger Bastien, Chris Dorr, Mark Russ, Ken Mehall and Joe Lopez.

It was the brightest a Michigan State baseball program had been in almost a decade. Brighter, too, internally than it had been since the days of Munn as Joe Kearney, MSU's athletic director, was paying attention even if he did not radically increase the budget.

"We've got to get you some help," he told Litwhiler following a game in 1976, the season MSU would finish 15-23.

Kearney had a way of acknowledging a coach's frustration that helped smooth a tight-money situation. It removed the adversarial tone from AD-coach dealings and made cash-flow problems seem as more of a collective crisis than an individual penance. But it was no fun asking players to put on uniforms so old they were yellow.

The numbers were real: Before Litwhiler departed in 1982, MSU baseball's annual budget was still under $25,000 per year, while a program such as Michigan was approaching $75,000 and Iowa almost $40,000. A number of MSU non-revenue sports, such as women's softball and women's volleyball, were getting from $5,000 to $10,000 more than baseball. Litwhiler, during the mid-'70s, had attempted to generate more money by starting a baseball chapter of the summer MSU Sports School. But a decree soon followed that all Sports School proceeds were to be forwarded to a general athletic department fund.

It became all the more refreshing for Litwhiler to get out of town, or out of the office, on international baseball projects or community fund-raisers. It also frequently left Pellerin to smolder in the baseball office as phones rang and paperwork piled up.

It did not help that Litwhiler's allergies and Pellerin's cigar clashed. Litwhiler often would start coughing, and Pellerin, disgusted, would step to the window, throw his cigar onto the lawn, put on his coat and walk out the door. Office visitors joked that outside the office window there had to be a mound of half-smoked cigars as big as the Sleeping Bear Dunes.

"Frank, as soon as you get rid of that cigar, I've got an idea," Litwhiler said one morning. "You know, when we're running the cage game today, on the first pitch, when the pitcher comes set, we can work a sacrifice or a hit-and-run."

Pellerin was burning like the ashes on his stogie.

"That'll screw up the cage game," he huffed. "I've got to count pitches."

"No," Litwhiler assured, "just subtract the pitches. It'll be all right."

"Well, maybe. If you're interested, set it up."

That afternoon at practice, players were lined up against the wall, standing idle. Pellerin was still fuming.

"Well, Danny wants to change things," he explained to the players. "I don't know. He's got to explain it."

Litwhiler arrived a half-hour into practice, as often was the case if he had fund-raising business. He was aghast.

"Well," Pellerin explained, "you want to change the game. Explain it to 'em."

"There's no reason," Litwhiler said, "to just stop everything."

Pellerin, in a soft aside, acknowledged that maybe there wasn't.

Ten days later he still was not speaking to Litwhiler.

The rift was so serious that Tom Smith decided to act as mediator. He explained to Litwhiler that an assistant coach making a good deal less than the head coach, but handling a good deal more of the dirty work, had become a bit resentful.

"I can understand that," Litwhiler said. "I want to make it up to him."

Smith went to Pellerin.

"Look, Frank, he's out of the office a lot, sure," Smith explained, "but if Danny's not out there making money, we're all out of business."

Smith arranged a bury-the-hatchet dinner between the two coaches, picking them up in his Volkswagen van. When the coaches got in, Litwhiler rode shotgun and Pellerin, still miffed, retreated to the very back of the bus.

At dinner, Smith pulled out a list of grievances and ticked them off one by one.

On every point, on every suggestion from Smith, Litwhiler and Pellerin were in agreement.

"Why, that's no problem," each would say before Pellerin eased into a couple of jokes he had heard while bowling the previous night. An hour later, they jumped aboard Smith's van.

Both Litwhiler and Pellerin sat in the rear seat.

Smith had been involved through the years as a meagerly paid assistant, then volunteer coach, before succeeding Litwhiler following the '82 season. He was a considered by MSU players as a humorous, knowledgeable baseball teacher whose big-league career may or may not have been heading anywhere when Pete Rose crunched him during a plate collision in the Florida Instructional League in 1962. Rose was trying to score from second base on a single to right and, as Smith took the throw, plowed into him, spinning Smith around and driving his right shoulder into the ground. The shoulder was fractured. Smith later received condolences from a few of Rose's teammates, like Mel Queen, who had little use for the cocky switch-hitter.

Smith and Rose would meet again, in 1981, again in Florida, during Smith's three-month sabbatical spent with the Detroit Tigers and Manager Sparky Anderson. Smith was set on becoming a head baseball coach at a major university—there had been no commitment on the MSU job—and decided the best preparation would come via a return to the big leagues. Anderson welcomed him, and later re-introduced him to Pete Rose when the Tigers met Philadelphia in a Grapefruit League game on a cold night at Lakeland.

"Peter," Anderson yelled, "come on over here . . . You know Tommy Smith."

There was a flicker of recognition as he and Smith shook hands.

"You and Tommy played in the Instructional League in the old days," Anderson explained. "You ran over him. You remember him."

Rose wasn't sure. Or didn't care to be sure.

"How ya doin'?" Rose asked.

Smith congratulated him, said he had followed his career, wished him the best.

"Yeah, well, hey, I gotta get back," Rose said, stepping away. "Nice running into you again."

Rose's word choice was coincidental, but ironic. Smith, though, had never held any grudge, nor any real regrets over an injury that persuaded him to get on with college and get his degree—and end the dream of playing big-league baseball that Smith, if he were brutally honest with himself, knew would be a longshot.

Smith would endure the years as a $10,000 assistant, then resign in the mid-'70s to take a full-time job teaching physical education at MSU, which at least provided better salary. He would also work as a volunteer baseball assistant until 1982, when he won out over Dick Radatz to become only MSU's third head baseball coach since 1925.

The job had changed. Litwhiler's salary at retirement was $42,000, but Smith was initially offered $18,000—$3,000 more than Munn had offered Litwhiler 19 years earlier. Salary was eventually increased a few thousand, but to bring in the two assistants Smith felt essential—Rob Ellis and Jeff Kawaski eventually were added—would have to be done on combined salary less than Pellerin was making at retirement. And, as of 1987, MSU's baseball budget was still sitting at $27,000, forcing the baseball office to raise $35,000 annually. Spring trip expenses, alone, ran $20,000.

Doug Weaver had been cast, as had Burt Smith a decade earlier, as prime villain in the annual athletic-department soap opera known as Spartan baseball. Bad budgets. Underpaid staff. A potential revenue sport struggling to stay afloat. Weaver heard the complaints. Regularly.

He could not dispute that budgets at Michigan and Iowa were often double or greater what they were at Michigan State. He could ask what the University of Michigan's hockey budget was versus MSU's, or whether Iowa's men's athletic funds also financed a women's program. He could ask whether other Big Ten schools supported as many sports as the 25 sustained at Michigan State. With the exception of Ohio State, it appeared not.

Coaches seldom were happy with budget ceilings, particularly when they raised as much money as MSU baseball did for its own cause. It was natural that there would be frustration and bitterness, as there so often had been among MSU's wrestling coaches. If it justified greater budgets, Weaver might not argue, but he was not increasing spending. A new baseball infield was on the way in 1987. Outfield improvements and a new fence were also being planned. Down the road, permanent stands were a priority item. Moveable seats would have to do for now.

Baseball through the '80s at Michigan State was remaining competitive as MSU compensated for bad overall records with break-even Big Ten seasons. The big bats of Mike Eddington, Cordell Ross and Dave Corey were teaming with pitchers like Chris Hayner and Arnie Mathews to keep the team alive.

Michigan State would get another boost in 1987. Baseball scholarships at MSU numbered 11, two beneath the NCAA limit. Kirk Gibson, who had come within a whisker of quitting baseball nine years earlier, struck a deal with the athletic department in the winter of 1987. He would finance a four-year scholarship if Doug Weaver would match it.

There was a handshake. And, at least temporarily, as much peace as there was hope.

Twelve

FIRE AND ICE

It was always safest on East Lansing's winter weekend nights during the 1980s to be one of the 6,255 who already had a Michigan State hockey ticket. If not, the options were fairly clear: Either get in line and wait one's turn for a standing-room pass, or stand in the chill, keeping eyes and ears open for the rare customer who had an extra pair of tickets for sale.

During the coldest season of the year, Munn Arena was playing host to the hottest team on campus. Since coming to East Lansing in 1979, Ron Mason was making hockey at Michigan State a national success stocked by a system of strong recruiting, coaching and budgets, enhanced by a top-caliber facility, and a university that could offer as much appeal to a centerman from Flin Flon, Manitoba, as to a defenseman from Livonia, Michigan.

Once established, as Mason's teams became in the early '80s, the program would become almost self-perpetuating as long as coaches did their homework and paid attention to recruiting. The on-ice instruction was easier once you had good students with upper-crust skills. It was a simple formula successful coaches applied wherever a school and a sport enjoyed annual excellence.

That it was becoming such a prominent part of Michigan State's sports fabric was a surprise 100 years after intercollegiate sports were introduced in East Lansing. There had been a national championship in 1966, and a pair of excellent teams in the mid-'70s, but hockey had become Michigan State's most enduring sports success by the evening of March 29, 1986, when Mike Donnelly, with 2:51 to play, blistered a goal past Harvard goalie Grant Blair that gave Michigan State a 6-5 victory and the 1986 NCAA hockey championship.

The sport had come a great distance in three decades. In 1952, Amo Bessone's second as head coach, 18 people watched Michigan State play Colorado College at the old MSU Ice Arena in Demonstration Hall. Even during the national championship season of 1965-66—MSU finished 16-13 but still won the NCAA title—home attendance at the old arena (capacity 4,174) averaged 1,963.

It was the novelty sport at Michigan State until television and pro hockey's proliferation made it more fashionable entertainment beginning in the 1970s, when fans scrambled for tickets and even found a certain charm in dank, obtuse Dem Hall. It was the only polite way for season-ticket holders to describe an arena where front-row fans were forced to stare through mesh fence that stood above the boards, protecting them from flying pucks and crashing skaters. Plexiglass would not be part of MSU's hockey landscape until Munn Arena opened on November 1, 1974.

John Kobs—better-known as MSU's head baseball coach for 38 years—had been Michigan State's first head hockey coach, directing the Spartans in a 6-3 defeat to the University of Michigan in Michigan State's only game of the 1925-26 season. Because all games prior to 1950 were played out of doors, Michigan State never played a game during the winter of 1930-31 due to balmy weather. Interference from nature was only one of the reasons why Michigan State decided that hockey was a bad bet at a college where students were much more interested in the doings of Jim Crowley's football team.

Not until an artificial ice surface was installed at Dem Hall in 1950 did hockey make a comeback, this time under Harold "Babe" Paulsen, who shook off an 0-14-0 debut to win six games the following season. Paulsen had decided to give up coaching in 1951 when Athletic Director Ralph Young contacted Amo Bessone—head coach at Michigan Tech, a Massachusetts native, graduate of the University of Illinois, and former semi-pro hockey and baseball player—who seemed the best candidate to take over a low-profile sport at Michigan State.

Bessone had little to lose at East Lansing, where the biggest advantage was artificial ice. At Michigan Tech, where he was rink manager as well as hockey coach, he was normally forced to get up at 2 a.m. to flood the rink and make ice at an optimum time. To sleep in peace during the winter, to play hockey with a roof over your head and walls around the rink, was a luxury he could only dream about at Houghton.

Putting together a quality hockey team that could hold its own among the few colleges that played the sport competitively would be a task as sticky as turning on fans to a game that at Dem Hall was not nearly as comfortable as taking in a movie at the Campus Theater. Hockey existed in the '50s because Biggie Munn and the Michigan State braintrust believed it to be part of an all-around sports program a major northern university should provide.

It did not make money. But it would not lose much as long as the overhead was held in check. Michigan State spent nothing on scholarships heading into the 1960s but was staying competitive, finishing as NCAA runner-up in 1959 when North Dakota beat State, 4-3, in overtime to best a team led by Terry Moroney, Dick Hamilton, Joe Polano and Joe Selinger.

It had been a quirkish season—a team built from walk-ons finding a groove. Still, Bessone in the early '60s could see that Michigan State was going nowhere without a better budget and a few scholarships.

"Amo," Munn said, "what are you worried about? Is anybody pressuring you or your job?"

"No," Bessone answered, "but I hate taking a backseat."

Munn coughed up five scholarships, and within three seasons, Michigan State had won a national title and followed with a third-place NCAA finish. Crowds were now picking up. WJIM-TV was, once a winter anyway, giving Bessone a two-minute spot during sports. The *Lansing State Journal* began staffing games. Students discovered that at 25 cents per seat it was the cheapest date on campus.

And Bessone, for all the excuses he had to make when showing recruits Dem Hall, still had to admit it beat getting up at 2 in the morning to flood an outdoor rink.

Recruiting still consisted of whatever Bessone could do with a postage stamp. You did not fly to Toronto to inspect a hot goaltender. You did not tour the Canadian Junior A circuit, trying to talk future pros into dropping their National Hockey League dreams to try it as a college student at some place called Michigan State.

You wrote letters, sent campus brochures, or had a bird dog like

Joe Finegan of Toronto act as scout and spokesman in your behalf. Usually, you never saw your scholarship player until he reported for school.

Michigan State's first genuine Canadian hockey import had been Derio Nicoli, a defenseman and forward from Copper Cliff, Ontario, who played on Bessone's early MSU teams and later helped steer talent from Copper Cliff and Sudbury toward Michigan State. The first heavy talent load arrived following Munn's scholarship shower when Doug Volmar, Doug Roberts, Tom Mikkola and Sandy McAndrew came to East Lansing. Roberts and Volmar would go on to play in the NHL, where no less than Gordie Howe would say that Volmar had the hardest wristshot he had ever seen.

Slowly, the Canadian pipeline began pumping Ontario talent to East Lansing, which Bessone realized was the steadiest ally at a time when Detroit's suburban hockey programs were only beginning to develop better players.

Help would continue to come from Joe Finegan in Toronto, whose son, Dan, had played defense for MSU from 1969-71. It tied Joe all the closer to a head coach who counted on Finegan's eye, as well as his ability to check on grades and character, in getting help from the rich Toronto-Oakville region. It was Finegan who in the winter of 1972 would send three forwards—Steve Colp, Daryl Rice and John Sturges—to take a look at a campus that was only a 5 1/2-hour drive from their homes.

Colp and Rice would settle on Michigan State not because of academics, or Bessone or academic opportunities, but because of the university's feminine charms. They had never met so many attractive young women as during their weekend visit. Sturges, a muscular, blond left-winger who would become the team's resident lady-killer, was also impressed by the social atmosphere at a school where hockey seemed to matter as long as you ignored that barn of an arena inside Dem Hall.

Like Jenison Field House, it was a bizarre place to bring a recruit during the off-season. Fans were seated on three sides of the building, most of them in a dark balcony that offered bloodthirsty front-row customers a position from which they could hang over a railing and verbally abuse enemy players. Fights only heightened madness in the student section, particularly when defenseman Bob Boyd was at his prime before leaving as a junior to sign a World Hockey Association contract in 1973.

Dem Hall—the hockey facility's name remained, officially,

MSU Ice Arena—began filling regularly from 1972-74. It had become the vogue ticket among students who increasingly found an outlet for energy and wackiness not always welcomed by the more chic basketball crowds. Dem Hall only encouraged the outlandish. The loft became to hockey fans what a theater balcony was to movie-goers—a place for mischief.

One bold group of students had taken to threading a rope around a ceiling beam, hanging from it a rubber chicken with the sign "SIEVE" attached. On every MSU goal, the chicken would be hoisted and the group's marksman would blast it several times with a starter's pistol. The gag came to a halt when campus police arrived a few weeks later and arrested the hit man as he dispatched the chicken following a Steve Colp goal.

Dem Hall was into its final days as stage for Michigan State hockey when Colp, Rice, Sturges, Brendon Moroney and a pint-sized centerman from the Detroit Junior Wings named Tom Ross, all turned out for their freshman season in the winter of 1972-73. Across the road, a new $5.6-million hockey arena that would seat 6,255 was only a year from opening. There would be no more hanging from lofts, no more rubber chickens, no more viewing hockey from three sides of a rectangular arena. It would be the finest college hockey facility in the country, and open just as the Colp-Ross-Rice trio was turning MSU into one of the top-scoring teams of all time.

It was scoring that a community lean on hockey sophistication wanted to see from Bessone's team, and scoring in which Bessone's mid-'70s gang specialized. Colp was a superb stickhandler and skater whose finesse game was a notch above most college forwards; Ross played similarly and was expert at flicking loose pucks past a screened or sprawling goaltender.

Rice was less talented, but had a nose for goals. Sturges, too, was not the speediest skater, but had a hard shot and knew the game. Together they were becoming the deadliest power play a college team had concocted. Expert passing, neat stickwork, good shooters—a man-advantage for MSU normally turned into a goal within a minute as Colp, Ross and Rice worked the puck slickly up front, rifling it back to Sturges, Norm Barnes, or later, to Pat Betterly on the points.

Bessone's problem was that better recruiting and scoring were not translating through the early '70s into any particular Michigan State choke-hold on the Western Collegiate Hockey Association

(MSU would move to the Central Collegiate Hockey Association in 1981). Bessone had been turning out an All-American here and there in goalies Rick Duffett and Jim Watt, forward Don Thompson in 1971, and defensemen such as Boyd, and then Barnes, who would go on to play with Philadelphia in the NHL. But there were four consecutive fourth-place finishes from 1971-74, a fall to fifth in '75, followed by a second-place final act in '75-76 that would see seniors Ross, Rice, Colp, Sturges, and right-wing Brendon Moroney nearly put MSU in the NCAA semifinals at Denver.

Ross would finish the '75-76 season with 51 goals, Colp with 40 and Rice with 31 as Michigan State's offense took a team never noted for its muscle to a 23-16-2 record and a WCHA championship game against Minnesota on March 14, 1976. Michigan State had beaten Herb Brooks' team in three out of four regular-season games and now had the edge: Munn Arena ice and a Sunday afternoon mob of 6,605 as two teams who had tied, 2-2, the previous night in a two-game, total-goals-scored series would shoot it out for a spot at hockey's Final Four.

Michigan State throughout the Ross-Colp years had been a team that never worried terribly about being behind. Even when a team like Colorado College hopped off to a 4-0 lead, it was generally a matter of time until the power play heated up, or until Colp and Ross scored a pair of goals each within 10 minutes, to make a game of it.

But spotting Minnesota a 6-2 second-period lead was not what Bessone's team had in mind against a team coached by Brooks and led by a cannon-shooting defenseman named Reed Larson. Michigan State came back with a pair of quick goals to make it 6-4, and late in the third period, got the tying goal to send a 6-6 game into overtime as a crowd not terribly concerned about its sanity continued to chant, "Den-ver, Den-ver."

The contest became more and more strange, even eerie as a balmy March afternoon wore on, and as MSU goalie Dave Versical held Minnesota to its early six goals. Michigan State outshot Minnesota, 17-4, in the first overtime, hitting Gopher goalie Jeff Tscherne with shot after shot, including a goal-mouth backhand from Lansing's Joey Campbell that missed by inches of clearing Tscherne's pads as he lay prone on the ice. It was still 6-6 after the first overtime.

The second overtime was slower, more conservative, a couple of saves at both ends, but still, incredibly, it was 6-6 as the teams skated off in sweat-drenched pads to find energy for a third 10-minute session.

At 6:33 of the third overtime—some four hours after the game's opening faceoff—Pat Phippen took a pass from the right side, set up in the slot, and riveted a shot, stickside, just past Versical's glove. It was as if the Munn Arena crowd had been lobotomized.

"Toughest loss ever," said Bessone. He had painted a half-smile across his face as he sat calmly in his office, trying to fight back the anguish, knowing perhaps that if he did not take this team to a national championship, the chance may never come again while he was coach at Michigan State. He was 59 years old and the team's strength was a gang of departing seniors.

It was Brooks who was going on to Denver—and on to a national championship—that would lead to an appointment three years later as United States Olympic hockey coach, and in four years, make him a national hero as the U.S. team took the gold medal at Lake Placid.

The Minnesota defeat had been a crusher, but Bessone was having problems in 1976 that dwarfed anything happening on the ice. His wife, Mary, was dying from the arthritis that had been torturing her for years. More and more the job and the strain of watching his wife fade away were eating at him, and when she died in September of 1976, there was thought it might bring an end to his career at Michigan State.

Instead, hockey offered him refuge from the emptiness at home. Bessone became even more dependent on a job that could absorb a man once he made it down those steep concrete stairs and into a tunnel leading from the ice, to dressing rooms, to training and equipment areas, and finally, to his office where the usual collection of hockey hangers-on gathered regularly in a cracker-barrel atmosphere to chew the fat and provide company for a coach.

It had always been like that with hockey. It was its own galaxy, tucked away in the Munn Arena labyrinth, almost independent from the MSU athletic headquarters at Jenison Field House. It had its own, cult-like following that took pride in its adoration of a sport that remained a notch beneath football and basketball on the public's interest scale. And it had in Bessone a nationally known college coach who, as time went on, became a kind of enchanting self-caricature with his gruff voice, perpetual cigar and easy humor.

The first name probably helped. At Wisconsin, where more than 8,000 people would fill Dane County Coliseum, students lived for their nightly refrains of "A-mo, A-mo." He drew a reaction wherever Michigan State went—mostly an affectionate response sparked by his longevity, his appearance, his style, and maybe, too, by the fact Michigan State so often crumpled on an opponent's ice. Administrative support had grown better through the '70s as Burt Smith, athletic director from 1972-75, opened up the hockey budget. Scholarships were full and no longer was recruiting dependent on the United States and Canadian postal services. Assistant Coach Alex Terpay was traveling to Sudbury and Toronto to look at the talent MSU previously got only when Finegan or a former player helped with the sales pitch.

Michigan State's problem was in not sticking closely to beaten recruiting paths, and in missing talents even closer to home. On the night in 1975 Versical signed with Michigan State, his Detroit Junior Wings teammate Ken Morrow, a future U.S. Olympic star who would go on to play with the New York Islanders, was ignored. Morrow, who would have happily played at Michigan State, instead signed with then-Bowling Green State Coach Ron Mason.

When Michigan State in 1977, '78 and '79 sank to seasons of 15-21-1, 7-27-1 and 15-21, Bessone knew it was time to get away from a job that had gotten away from the head coach. His knees were hurting so much that it had become difficult to skate at practice. Bad teams set up by poor recruiting had temporarily wrecked hockey at a school that only four years earlier had opened the most impressive college ice facility in the land.

Joe Kearney, Michigan State's athletic director, was being careful with a coach who had spent more than a quarter-century building MSU hockey. Bessone had for two decades endured Dem Hall, bad budgets, sparsely attended Blue Line Club luncheons and the death of a wife, and was not, at age 61, going to be fed to the wolves. Bessone instead acknowledged after a pair of weekend losses to Michigan in December of 1978 that his 28th season as head coach would be his last. He sat down with Kearney later in the season to make it official and to work out a satisfactory arrangement for reassignment.

Kearney's reputation at the University of Washington as a man who hired good head coaches had not, by 1979, been challenged in his three years as Michigan State's AD. Darryl Rogers and Jud Heathcote had completed Big Ten championship seasons, and Kearney understood Michigan State was viewed in the college coaches circle as a gold mine—a can't-miss job that would draw some of the best young coaches in the United States.

He had by March of 1979 settled on two names: Jerry York, head coach at Clarkson (New York) College, and Bowling Green State's Ron Mason, both of whom Kearney would interview during the NCAA hockey championships in Detroit. Each man impressed an athletic director who, when evaluating coaches, went on his own instincts and on references from experts. Kearney was agonizing between Mason and York, but his top hockey advisor—Kearney would only say it was a nationally "astute" hockey man—had said Michigan State could not lose.

Kearney went with Mason, the polished, impressive Canadian who had won more than 70 percent of his games at Lake Superior State and then at Bowling Green. Mason was only 39, but he knew where MSU could shake loose the Canadian talent it had been overlooking for so many years, and he knew when a thoroughbred Detroit-area player was emerging, as opposed to the so-so talents that too often were finding their way from the suburbs to East Lansing. The quantity of inferior hockey players Michigan State had been taking through the mid-to-late '70s remained one of the real mysteries among competing college coaches.

Hockey had become so sophisticated at the college level that most schools, Bowling Green included, kept recruiting files on Grade 10 and Grade 11 talent. Michigan State's recruiting file consisted of a manila folder. It was also known that MSU had been using only about half of its recruiting budget, which helped explain why a school that had every reason to sit among college hockey's elite had instead been stumbling its way to second-division finishes.

College hockey had developed into a sport where talent alone guaranteed nothing. A program needed rigid, off-season conditioning if it wanted to keep up even with second-tier hockey schools whose teams, in the spring of 1979, seemed far ahead of Michigan State and its outdated approaches.

Mason could also see the players needed attitudinal overhauls. They had overrated themselves, believing that by simple virtue of playing in the premier Western Collegiate Hockey Association they were superior athletes with supreme skill. They tended to blame past problems on the coaching staff and on Michigan State's administration. They were not about to blame themselves for problems that were showing up in the classroom, in personal comportment, and on the ice, where Mason's defensive-minded, flow-pattern game would stand in such contrast to the dump-it-in-the-zone style directed by Bessone.

Mason brought to practice in the fall of 1979 as much tyranny as a coach dared in shaping up a team on which egos needed as much work as its hockey concepts. It was not that they were bad kids, but that they perceived themselves as such stars, as athletes who were above the commoners who went to class regularly, and certainly as hockey players who were a notch better than the peasants who played for Central Collegiate Hockey Association schools.

Mason's strategy was to get through the 1979-80 season—MSU would finish 14-24-0, Mason's first losing season as a head coach—and then recruit a core of heart-and-soul talents who would become the framework for his program. Ken Leiter and Mark Hamway, a pair of suburban Detroiters recruited in 1980, were the first high-caliber examples of the talented, solid-citizen types Mason intended to bring to Michigan State.

His 1981 group would be a breakthrough class: Newell Brown, Gary Haight, Gord Flegel, David Taylor and Ron Scott. Mason was still lacking an overall cache of All-American talent, but it was paying to be finicky, paying to recruit in British Columbia, in Saskatchewan, in the state of Washington—wherever Michigan State had a chance to persuade a talented hockey player with salt-of-the-earth tendencies that a campus in East Lansing could enrich his life, athletically, academically and socially.

Mason's third recruiting class in 1982 would be his most talented and start MSU's mid-'80s climb toward a national title. Lyle Phair, Tom Anastos, Dale Krentz, Dan McFall and Kelly Miller were now putting the program on another, more elite level that would make a 15-minute wait in 10-degree temperatures worthwhile to fans begging for standing-room spots at Munn Arena. Mason could see the difference primarily in attitude. These kids were hungry, competitive, confident in their ability, but aware that talent took a player only as far as his effort.

There were very few classroom problems, and even fewer disciplinary hassles as performance was picking up as much off the ice as on it. After a second consecutive losing season in 1980-81—MSU finished 12-22-2 as only Ron Scott, the great goaltender, was keeping State in the games—Mason's team came back in the winter of '81-82 with a 26-14-2 record that included a spot in the NCAA tournament, where MSU lost a two-games, total-goals series at New Hampshire by scores of 3-2 and 6-3.

The NCAA invitation came courtesy of a wild championship in the Central Collegiate Hockey Association playoffs at Detroit's Joe Louis Arena. It had been MSU's first winter in the CCHA after 21 years in the WCHA, and it had become clear that shifting leagues was not nearly the comedown some feared.

It had represented more of an adjustment for Mason than for anyone else at Michigan State. In leaving Bowling Green for MSU, Mason had considered his move to the WCHA as one of the job's best features. It meant a team had an easier path to the NCAA tournament when better-quality competition carried added prestige with NCAA tournament selectors.

The CCHA was still fighting its image as college hockey's step-child league, and Mason could not argue. Bowling Green was a blue-chip hockey school, but from top to bottom, the CCHA was not a hockey league that could compare to the WCHA or to conferences in the East. Its saving grace was, naturally, an economic advantage in playing more regional teams. But that was a plus to be valued more by an athletic director like Doug Weaver—who decided on the shift—than by a head coach aware of the imagery and political problems a CCHA team would have on the national level.

Mason could take comfort only in that WCHA cohorts Michigan Tech, Michigan and Notre Dame also were moving to the CCHA in 1981. The victory over Notre Dame in the 1982 CCHA playoffs, followed by a taste of life in the NCAA tournament, would change everyone's attitude, especially Mason's. Hockey was back as a vibrant sport at Michigan State, and not even the CCHA was hurting perceptions that Mason's team was becoming a national threat.

Fans in East Lansing, who were turning out 240-strong for Friday Blue Line Club luncheons, were saying it, as were the 1,500 who were jamming Long's Convention Center for the post-season banquet. Fans who by nature developed a hero-worship syndrome toward any winning coach, were finding in Mason the greatest thing to hit campus since Earvin Johnson. He had a smooth, sincere air about him—a friendliness that was not blotted out by a coach whose systematic, highly organized, all-business approach to hockey made him a marvel among Michigan State's coaches.

And, also, among his players.

They knew him as a shrewd motivator and coach who had a

carefully calculated reason for doing everything. He was an excellent communicator and his door was always open, but a player wanting a sit-down session with him could expect to have it arranged for the next day—giving Mason time to prepare for a conversation that probably centered on playing time. There were no loose ends with Ron Mason.

Nothing typified the style as much as Mason's pre-game, and between-periods speeches to players. Mason was smart enough to know that teams win on talent and systems, and not on emotion, which became central to his psychological approach. Mason would hold a quick team meeting 15 minutes before faceoff, going over game plans, then offer a final, two-minute address just before player introductions.

He had been an excellent centerman during his college days at St. Lawrence and knew how a 20-year-old's mind worked. He knew, above all, that between periods players needed time to themselves. It was the reason his between-periods talks lasted no more than five minutes: A player required 10 minutes to collect his own thoughts during a game when the mind worked at Indy-car speed.

Mason appreciated also that screaming and thundering at players would in the long run signify the arrival of a second-division hockey club. Good athletes and mature kids rarely needed any verbal brow-beating. The closest Mason came to anything evangelical was during his "Prima Donna" speeches that players came to expect about twice a season if the team were strolling through practices or if February minds had been focused on spring break rather than on a weekend series at Illinois-Chicago.

"You've got the best facility in college hockey," he would say, disgustedly, "you've got all the best equipment, the best skates, free schooling, and meal money on road trips, and then you won't go out there and play the way you're capable."

Shaming them into playing better, he understood, was better than berating them. Appealing to their personal honor and pride was a sure ticket if you were recruiting solid kids. On that score, Mason had no doubts. He had a team that only required an occasional show of muscle, as when a first- or second-line player perceived as dogging it was dropped to fourth line for a week, or as when Lyle Phair and Dale Krentz missed most of a practice week due to illness, recovering in time for Friday night's game. Mason suspected they could have brought their sniffles to practice a bit earlier in the week. They sat out Friday night.

Michigan State would in the 1982-83 season crack the 30-victory mark for the first time in MSU history, and continue to win at least 30 games every year through 1987. Its 30th victory in 1983 would come in the finals of the CCHA tournament at Joe Louis Arena against the No. 1-ranked team in college hockey, Jerry York's Bowling Green squad that had already beaten MSU twice in two regular-season games.

Scott and his 2.64 goals-against average had been so critical to MSU's '82-83 surge that it seemed almost predestined when he stood in the goal mouth, eyeing Bowling Green's great scorer Brian Hills, in overtime of a movie-like championship game at Joe Louis. It was 3-3 when Hills was awarded a penalty shot that could send Bowling Green onto the NCAA tourney and most certainly end Michigan State's season minus any NCAA invitation. It seemed all the more likely that an All-American forward would murder a goalie suffering so badly from strained ankle ligaments that he had been forced to leave midway through the previous day's semifinal game against Ohio State.

"He loves to shoot," Mason told Scott as the Joe Louis crowd screamed. "Take away his shot, Ronnie. Make him deke."

Hills was at full-stride as he crossed into the MSU zone, ready to whistle a shot into whatever corner of the net Scott would show him. But as he got set to shoot, Scott was out on him, forcing him to move to his forehand. Hills deked, shot and missed as Scott gobbled up the puck. When Mark Hamway scored the winner one minute and 43 seconds later, Scott's save earned a few more votes as Michigan State's most dramatic hockey moment in history.

MSU was going for the second consecutive year to the NCAA tournament, and for the second year in a row, MSU was going home following two games as Harvard won a two-game, most-goals series by scores of 6-5 and 3-3, Hamway hitting the pipe with 15 seconds remaining to help Harvard move on with a 9-8 total-goals victory.

There was developing at Michigan State in 1983-84 a mini-dynasty under Mason, where personalities were in their own subtle ways lending flavor to the workmanlike way in which MSU was thrashing everyone in sight.

Mark Hamway, MSU's team captain and right-winger, was not Mason's best player but in his own unique style was undoubtedly State's on-ice, off-ice leader. He did not have great affection for the King's English, using a fair share of "don'ts" and "ain'ts," but players knew one thing about Hamway: He wanted to win and he wanted them all to do well. He never got down on a player, and in the same fashion as Mason displayed a brand of psychology that made teammates embarrassed to play anything less than their best.

Kelly Miller, another descendant of a Lansing hockey family that had played at MSU for decades, was, like Hamway, a winger who specialized in intensity and hard work more than in natural gifts. He was the team over-achiever who impressed everyone with the way he came back quickly from shoulder surgery.

Lyle Phair, a left-winger from Pilot Mound, Manitoba, fit into a 40,000-student community very deftly for a youngster who grew up in a village of a few dozen. He was a study in contrasts: The Canadian Junior veteran and cut-up who would leave his dental plate in the beers of teammates or even in the drinks of girls, was also, in addition to playing a tough left-wing, the most meticulous player on the team. Never an unmade bed. No underwear tossed in a corner. At the campus apartment he shared with teammates, it was Phair who handled all cooking and cleaning.

Phair was the extrovert compared with another Manitoba left-wing, Dale Krentz, who played the strong, silent role as MSU's blue-collar forward. There was with Krentz none of the glitz you got with defenseman Dan McFall, whose strength in the corners and all-around defensive game set the standard by which Mason defensemen would be measured.

In the same way, Craig Simpson, the elegant center from London, Ontario, would do things during his two years at Michigan State that college centers simply were not supposed to do, particularly at age 17. He had a graceful style on ice that matched his off-ice charm with the public—and made him all the more attractive to the National Hockey League's Pittsburgh Penguins, who swept him away as the league's first draft pick in 1985.

No player from the formative years under Mason had as much raw skill, or as many game-day idiosyncrasies, as goaltender Scott, whom Mason had plucked from Guelph, Ontario, in 1981. On weekend road trips, players knew it was only a matter of time before Scott would scream and jump them, trying to pin them in a hockey player's impromptu version of professional wrestling. They knew also that once they retaliated, once they got the upper hand, Scott would shriek: "No, don't hurt me! C'mon, I've got to play goal tonight." It was almost a ritual on road trips.

Scott had other habits he considered sacrosanct. While most players ate their pre-game meal at 2:30 or 3 in the afternoon, he without exception ate at 1:30 sharp. He would sit and talk during his meal, but after the last bite, he was a mute for the rest of the afternoon. Scott would return to his hotel room, turn on the TV, and sit in absolute silence and in deep concentration.

Players could see how the routine obviously affected his subconscious. Not only was Scott a lightning-quick goalie, but he could fixate on a puck, seeing it through a maze of eight players. He could be spellbinding.

It was Mason's personally recruited collection of talents and personalities that would take Michigan State to a 1983-84 record of 34-12-0, another CCHA championship, and this time a longer stay in the NCAA tournament before crashing in the NCAA championships at Lake Placid, New York. Bowling Green's 2-1 victory in the semifinals stuck MSU in the consolation game against North Dakota, which won, 6-5, in overtime.

But Mason learned as quickly as his team got back to the hotel that Michigan State's Final Four trip was anything but a downer for the scads of State fans who had come to New York. A band was playing, people were partying, the team was being treated as if it had won the Stanley Cup. Quite a change from his early days at MSU when Michigan State was lucky if 4,000 fans made it to Munn.

Mason also knew what everyone had in mind for the '84-85 season: A NCAA championship. Mason's recruiting had stocked Michigan State by the autumn of '84 with such awesome front-line talent on offense, defense and in goal that the Spartans were expected to follow their 34-12-0 season and Final Four pilgrimage with something substantially closer to an undefeated season.

The marvel was how close Michigan State actually came to a blitz, taking a 38-4-0 record into the first round of the NCAA playoffs at Munn Arena. Mason never argued that he had in the '84-85 season his most talented, his deepest team of all time. It was a club that never worried about getting behind, never worried about a defeat when it had the muscle and knockout power to control a game almost at will.

It was a season that had rolled along too merrily to think that percentages would not, at one point or another, get involved.

They did a few days before MSU was to open the playoffs at home against Providence College, when Bob Essensa, MSU's brilliant goaltender whose goals-against average was an unbelievable 1.64, had a 2 a.m. spat with his girlfriend and accidentally shoved his arms through a window. Essensa had come within a thousandth of an inch of doing permanent damage to nerves in his arm. MSU's championship plans already were in trouble, even if the Spartans had an experienced alternate goalie in Norm Foster as they got set for another two-game, most-goals-scored series at Munn Arena.

Michigan State won the opener, 3-2, on March 23, 1985, and needed only tie the next day to keep its one-goal advantage and skate off to the NCAA championships at Joe Louis Arena, which was being called "Munn Arena East" because of MSU's annual success in the CCHA and Great Lakes Invitational tournaments.

Foster, though, was unaccustomed to going a second night during a season when Essensa was living a weekly dream. Foster the following game gave up two bad first-period goals, and it was 4-1, Providence, heading into the final period of a series in which Providence goalie Chris Terreri was spitting 83 shots back at the Spartans.

Mason knew it was over when a Tom Anastos shot banged off one post, into the other, and kicked out to Simpson, whose shot also rattled a post. It finished as a 4-2 victory for Providence and a 6-5 total-goals edge that stopped the winningest team in NCAA history from even making the semifinals.

It was also a wretched farewell for Miller, Krentz, Haight, Phair, McFall and all the seniors whose grand ideas of a senior-season NCAA title had been swallowed by Terreri's glove. MSU would rebuild in 1985-86 around Mike Donnelly, Mitch Messier, Don McSween, Kevin Miller (brother of Kelly), Bill Shibicky and a freshman center from Vancouver named Joe Murphy. It would be a competitive team, thought Mason. Young, talented, apt to take its bruises and likely to run into a losing streak somewhere down the line.

Funny feelings began developing at Christmas time, when State won its fourth consecutive Great Lakes Invitational before the usual swarms of 20,000 at Joe Louis Arena. Long winning streaks followed as the team no one expected to dazzle began coming from two or three goals down to win games in which State never felt any pressure. The freshmen, notably Murphy, were playing brilliant hockey, and even though MSU lost to Western Michigan, 3-1, in the CCHA finals at Joe Louis Arena, Mason felt good. MSU was going to the NCAA playoffs with a 35-9-2 record and nothing approaching the pressure or expectations that had saddled onto the Spartans a year earlier.

Michigan State knocked out Boston College with 6-4 and 4-2 victories in the home-ice quarterfinals, and headed to the NCAA championships at Providence, Rhode Island, for a semifinals date against WCHA giant Minnesota.

"They'll come at us crazy out of the chute," Mason had told his team before the game. "Just play 'em tough at our end."

The team did, especially Foster, who made 42 saves in a 6-4 MSU victory that would put State in the finals against a Harvard team that was unaccustomed to the brand of crunching hockey routinely played in the CCHA.

"Play 'em physical from the drop of the puck," Mason said. "Don't let up."

Harvard took a 2-0 lead before Messier's goal at 17:55 made it a 2-1 game heading into the second period. It was 4-3, Harvard, at the end of two periods, and Mason decided it would be wise to tell a lie.

"We play better when we're down a goal than when we're ahead," he told them, although there was no statistical evidence that a third-period deficit had been anything close to an edge for MSU.

Brad Hamilton's goal at 1:06 tied the game, and Brian McReynolds 69 seconds later gave State a 5-4 lead before Harvard tied it at 6:46. It would remain scoreless for the next 10 minutes.

With three minutes to play, Murphy won a draw in the Harvard end, then lost the puck to a Harvard player attempting to clear it. Donnelly intercepted and ripped a slapshot past Grant Blair that would bring a NCAA championship trophy to East Lansing. Michigan State would still need to survive a too-many-men-on-the-ice penalty when Jeff Parker prematurely jumped on the ice to congratulate Bill Shibicky on an empty-net goal that would have wrapped it up.

"My God," Mason thought to himself as a nightmare loomed, "the basketball team gets screwed by a clock at Kansas City, and now this."

A theater-of-the-absurd finish continued when Parker's stick broke, preventing him from clearing the puck during Harvard's last-ditch power play, but on a faceoff in MSU's end, Shibicky followed Mason's instructions to "just get it to the boards" as the clock died.

The next day, a Sunday afternoon, Mason and his team pulled into Munn after a night in which the team had slept, collectively, about 20 minutes. When Mason spotted the huge mob waiting outside Munn, he got a key, threw open the doors, and got on with the kind of spontaneous victory party that had been seven winters in the making.

A few days later, a championship parade snaked its way through East Lansing. Governor James J. Blanchard spoke, a university and community celebrated, and a hockey team realized that a once-forlorn sport at Michigan State owed no more apologies.

Mason's concern heading into the 1986-87 season was consistency. It was difficult in sport, at any level, to avoid a follow-up fade after so much energy—and good fortune—had been expended on the way to a national title.

Of equal concern was MSU's talent loss: Joe Murphy, Craig Simpson and Jeff Parker had foregone their remaining years of eligibility for contracts with the National Hockey League. Losing three players of their caliber was difficult in college, where maturity and a core of returning talent meant everything.

Mason, instead, found that the fire was back in his '86-87 team. Michigan State won the big games. It got leadership from Messier, Don McSween and Shibicky, and steady goaltending from Essensa and Foster.

After finishing second to Bowling Green in the regular-season CCHA schedule, Mason's team came back to whip Western Michigan, 6-3, in the CCHA semifinals at Joe Louis Arena, setting up another championship classic on Saturday night, March 7. Kevin Miller's overtime goal gave MSU a 4-3 victory that pushed the Spartans' record to 30-9-2 and sent them into a home-ice, two-game NCAA opening series against Maine, which fell, 6-2 and 5-3, in the total-goals series.

A team that had Mason fretting in September was on its way to the Final Four at Joe Louis Arena in a marvelous following act to State's '86 championship.

Michigan State would meet Minnesota in the semifinals, just as they had met a year earlier at Providence. Mason would follow the same strategy.

"They'll come at us with everything," he warned his team, a speech they had heard a year before. "Let's play hard and smart in our end."

The Gophers never got a second shot the entire evening, and when Dave Arkeilpane blasted home a bad-bounce Gopher clearing pass with 9:28 to play, Michigan State had broken a 3-3 tie and was on its way to a 5-3 victory that would put the Spartans into their second straight NCAA title game, this time against North Dakota and its great forward Tony Hrkac.

The Spartans were shot off the ice, 5-3, in Saturday night's finale, a game played in the most favorable of settings, at Joe Louis, with more than 17,000 mostly pro-MSU fans jamming the arena along the Detroit River.

Hrkac and North Dakota exploded to a 3-0 lead in the first period and the Spartans never got closer than two goals. Tom Tilley scored a second-period goal for the Spartans, and Kip Miller scored late. But Gino Gasparini's Fighting Sioux destroyed the Spartans, as well as Mason's battle plan. Mason had decided to break up his normal three-line offense and put a pair of checking lines on Hrkac. It left the scoring responsibility to Shibicky, Messier and Brian McReynolds—a shake-up in part forced when left-wing Bobby Reynolds went out with a concussion when torpedoed into the boards during the Minnesota game.

But in the championship showdown, the Shibicky line drew first-period blanks, while Hrkac and his Sioux teammates stormed the Spartans.

Mason thought about it on the way back home. It was a day when any coach had a right to wonder whether it would ever be his turn. And then Mason reminded himself that only 12 months earlier, it had been his turn.

He laughed.

"I'll take that every year," he said.

"Every year."

EPILOGUE

An examination of 40 years of sports history at Michigan State leaves one with two overwhelming reactions:

For all the pain and political tangles, college athletics are enriching and worthwhile. Among the pluses is that sports expose participants and observers to an extraordinary collection of people and personalities. Michigan State has been blessed—and at times cursed—by its own fascinating mix.

A second, more basic response is: Why has a university as enlightened and as filled with human resources as Michigan State encountered such uncommon trouble along the way? Why the extremes? Why were the national football championships followed by years of mediocrity? Why did the football renaissance of the mid-'70s result in a NCAA investigation and a devastating probationary sentence? Why did basketball fortunes of the '70s rise and fall on the recruitment of a single hometown superstar? Why not more consistency at a university where athletic and scholastic achievement should be able to walk hand in hand?

Why was Michigan State so concerned even into the '80s about dredging up teams and programs that would emulate those from 30 and 40 years before? Why not a move to bring people with new vision, energy and purpose to a campus where creative direction ideally should originate?

It is more than a simplistic question of winning and losing. It is, rather, a statement about excellence. Michigan State has not always cashed in on its potential.

The school remains such an appealing physical complex that its followers tend to dismiss the pratfalls and disappointments as the price they pay for autumn walks along the Red Cedar and spring strolls through beautiful Beal Gardens. There has, too, been a widely perceived friendliness to Michigan State that the university must never forsake in the name of athletic achievement or academic self-importance. Perhaps that warmth manifests itself in occasional gaffes by the athletic department—specifically, poor personnel decisions. In many years of observing the Michigan State sports network, and in the months of interviewing that preceded publication of this book, it has been clear that a good many nice people were outmatched by their position.

So, too, Michigan State's devastating NCAA probation sentence in 1976 remains more than a decade later a subject of intense debate in East Lansing. Within the university's highest circle, there remains a belief that had Michigan State been contrite rather than contentious with the NCAA, it might have been punished much less severely. Some maintain that MSU could have gotten off with a year, or at the most, two years, of probation rather than the three-year sentence handed down—a penalty that crushed Michigan State well into the 1980s.

Those who share that opinion may be right. But one wonders if a system fraught with so much looseness, a program in which too many undisciplined boosters were staying too close to the scene, would ever have tightened the slack had a serious penalty not shaken the athletic department to its very foundation. Michigan State has been an acknowledged law-abider ever since.

The university's beauty, though, remains people. Some are part of Michigan State's athletic lore. Others are still there, awaiting their place in Michigan State history. During the months of interviewing for this text, so many stories, about so many of those people, surfaced but never found their way into the context of this book's preceding chapters.

One tale concerned Michigan State President John Hannah's recruitment of Biggie Munn in 1946. Hannah, legend has it, was driving Munn and his assistants, Forest Evashevski and Red Dawson, around campus, showing them Michigan State and its various sights, including Beaumont Tower. Evashevski was seated in the front opposite Hannah. Munn and Dawson were seated in the back when Hannah drove past Beaumont as its carillon rang loudly.

"Aren't those chimes pretty?" Hannah asked Munn.

Munn leaned forward.

"What?"

Hannah raised his voice and repeated:

"Aren't those beautiful chimes?"

"What?" Munn asked, frustrated. "I can't hear you. The goddamn bells are ringing too loud."

A charming friendship was enjoyed by the man who preceded Munn as football coach, Charley Bachman, and by his one-time player and eventual follower to the MSU head coaching job, Muddy Waters. They would sit by the hour in Munn's home talking football, watching films, or in later years, catching a game on television. While one night watching the old *Phillips 66 Game of The Week*, Bachman fell asleep, only to awake as a running back broke off a spectacular run. Bachman, a product of earlier days when he and Waters sat for hours by a projector, momentarily forgot what he was watching.

"Hey," he yelled to Waters. "Run that play back."

Bachman and Notre Dame Coach Knute Rockne were close friends who regularly corresponded and traded thoughts on football. Bachman received over the years scores of letters from Rockne on which were diagrammed plays and priceless notations from one of collegiate sports' alltime legends. Bachman, sadly, lent the letters to an acquaintance some years ago and never recovered them—he in his old age had forgotten to whom he had given Rockne's writings.

Rockne in 1931 had also paid a visit in Florida to the vacationing Bachman, telling his friend that he would soon be giving up coaching at Notre Dame and that he would be recommending one man as his successor: Charley Bachman.

Rockne the next day left Florida to make a speech at Kansas City. On the way from Kansas City to Los Angeles—where he was to appear in a football promotional film—Rockne was killed when his plane crashed in a Kansas field. Bachman was bitter after Hannah moved him aside in 1947 to make room for a young firebrand from Syracuse University named Biggie Munn. He remained bitter and angry through the years, resentful toward a university that had broomed him following 13 season in which his record was 70-34-10.

Waters had taken note of his friend's distress and venom, and vowed if he ever got the MSU job and was ever dismissed, he would never allow himself to be overwhelmed by such poison. To those who marveled at the decency and equanimity with which Waters comported himself after his firing in 1982, the lesson learned from Bachman was appreciated.

Throughout conversations with those who were at Michigan State during the '70s, Kirk Gibson stories abounded, none much better than an episode from a Michigan State ski class in which Gibson enrolled. Tom Smith, who later became MSU baseball coach but was then a full-time physical education instructor, taught the class at the Lansing Ski Club. One of his students came to him following a class and reported that Gibson had run into the student's car.

Smith walked over to inspect the damaged auto and discovered that its left front fender was indeed mangled.

How did the student know Gibson had been responsible?

"I saw him run into it," he told Smith.

"Did he back into it?" Smith asked, noticing no paint damage or metal scrapes. "How did it happen?"

"No, you don't understand," the student explained. "Gibson ran into it—on skis."

Smith later confronted Gibson.

"I barely touched it," Gibson said.

The fender showed otherwise, but the damage, and the response, were vintage Gibson.

It was precisely such stories, precisely such performances over the decades by Michigan State's athletics cast, that have made the university such a fascinating study in human behavior. It remains, first and foremost, a people place. A place where man's brilliance and foibles are there to be studied, enjoyed, celebrated, and sometimes, denounced.

It is a university that has so often done well, but can and must always strive to do much, much better.

SEASON RECORDS

FOOTBALL

1947
CLARENCE L. (Biggie) MUNN
Head Coach

0	Michigan	55
7	Mississippi State*	0
21	Washington State	7
20	Iowa State*	0
6	Kentucky*	7
13	Marquette*	7
28	Santa Clara*	0
14	Temple	6
58	Hawaii	19

7-2-0

1948

7	Michigan*	13
68	Hawaii*	21
7	Notre Dame	26
61	Arizona*	7
14	Penn State	14
46	Oregon State	21
47	Marquette*	0
48	Iowa State	7
40	Washington State*	0
21	Santa Clara	21

6-2-2

1949

3	Michigan	7
48	Marquette*	7
14	Maryland*	7
42	William & Mary*	13

* means home football game

24	Penn State*	0
62	Temple*	14
21	Notre Dame*	34
20	Oregon State	25
75	Arizona	0

6-3-0

1950

38	Oregon State*	13
14	Michigan	7
7	Maryland*	34
33	William & Mary*	14
34	Marquette*	6
36	Notre Dame	33
35	Indiana*	0
27	Minnesota*	0
19	Pittsburgh	0

8-1-0

1951

6	Oregon State*	0
25	Michigan	0
24	Ohio State	20
20	Marquette*	14
32	Penn State	21
53	Pittsburgh*	26
35	Notre Dame*	0
30	Indiana	26
45	Colorado*	7

9-0-0

1952

27	Michigan	13
17	Oregon State	14
48	Texas A&M*	6
48	Syracuse*	7

275

34	Penn State*	7
14	Purdue	7
41	Indiana	14
21	Notre Dame*	3
62	Marquette*	13

9-0-0

1953

21	Iowa	7
21	Minnesota	0
26	Texas Christian*	19
47	Indiana*	18
0	Purdue*	6
34	Oregon State*	6
28	Ohio State	13
14	Michigan*	6
21	Marquette*	15

Rose Bowl

28	UCLA	20

9-1-0
Big Ten: 5-1-0, T-1st

1954
HUGH D. (Duffy) DAUGHERTY
Head Coach

10	Iowa	14
0	Wisconsin*	6
21	Indiana	14
19	Notre Dame	20
13	Purdue*	27
13	Minnesota	19
54	Washington State*	6
7	Michigan	33
40	Marquette*	10

3-6-0
Big Ten: 1-5-0, T-8th

1955

20	Indiana	13
7	Michigan	14
38	Stanford*	14
21	Notre Dame*	7
21	Illinois*	7
27	Wisconsin	0
27	Purdue	0
42	Minnesota*	14
33	Marquette*	0

Rose Bowl

17	UCLA	14

9-1-0
Big Ten: 5-1-0, 2nd

1956

21	Stanford	7
9	Michigan	0
53	Indiana*	6
47	Notre Dame	14
13	Illinois	20
33	Wisconsin*	0
12	Purdue*	9
13	Minnesota	14
38	Kansas State*	17

7-2-0
Big Ten: 4-2-0, T-4th

1957

54	Indiana*	0
19	California	0
35	Michigan	6
13	Purdue*	20
19	Illinois*	14
21	Wisconsin	7
34	Notre Dame*	6
42	Minnesota*	13
27	Kansas State*	9

8-1-0
Big Ten: 5-1-0, 2nd

1958

32	California*	12
12	Michigan*	12
22	Pittsburgh*	8
6	Purdue	14
0	Illinois	16
7	Wisconsin*	9
0	Indiana	6
12	Minnesota	39
26	Kansas State*	7

3-5-1
Big Ten: 0-5-1, 10th

1959

7	Texas A&M*	9
34	Michigan	8
8	Iowa	37
19	Notre Dame*	0
14	Indiana*	6
24	Ohio State	30
15	Purdue*	0
15	Northwestern*	10
13	Miami (Fla.)	18

5-4-0
Big Ten: 4-2-0, 2nd

1960

7	Pittsburgh	7
24	Michigan*	17
15	Iowa*	27
21	Notre Dame	0
35	Indiana	0
10	Ohio State*	21
17	Purdue	13
21	Northwestern	18
43	Detroit*	15

6-2-1
Big Ten: 3-2-0, 4th

1961

20	Wisconsin	0
31	Stanford*	3
28	Michigan	0
17	Notre Dame*	7
35	Indiana*	0
0	Minnesota	13
6	Purdue	7
21	Northwestern*	13
34	Illinois*	7

7-2-0
Big Ten: 5-2-0, 3rd

1962

13	Stanford	16
38	North Carolina*	6
28	Michigan*	0
31	Notre Dame	7
26	Indiana	8
7	Minnesota*	28
9	Purdue*	17
31	Northwestern	7
6	Illinois	7

5-4-0
Big Ten: 3-3-0, T-5th

1963

31	North Carolina*	0
10	So. California	13
7	Michigan	7
20	Indiana*	3
15	Northwestern	7
30	Wisconsin*	13
23	Purdue	0
12	Notre Dame*	7
0	Illinois*	13

6-2-1
Big Ten: 4-1-1, T-2nd

1964

15	North Carolina	21
17	So. California*	7
10	Michigan*	17
20	Indiana	27
24	Northwestern*	6
22	Wisconsin	6
21	Purdue*	7
7	Notre Dame	34
0	Illinois	16

4-5-0
Big Ten: 3-3-0, 6th

1965

13	UCLA*	3
23	Penn State	0
22	Illinois*	12
24	Michigan	7
32	Ohio State*	7
14	Purdue	10
49	Northwestern*	7
35	Iowa	0
27	Indiana*	13
12	Notre Dame	3

Rose Bowl

12	UCLA	14

10-1-0
Big Ten: 7-0-0, 1st

1966

28	N. Carolina State*	10
42	Penn State*	8
26	Illinois	10
20	Michigan*	7
11	Ohio State	8
41	Purdue*	20
22	Northwestern	0
56	Iowa*	7

37	Indiana	19
10	Notre Dame*	10

9-0-1
Big Ten: 7-0-0, 1st

1967

7	Houston*	37
17	So. California*	21
35	Wisconsin*	7
34	Michigan	0
0	Minnesota	21
12	Notre Dame	24
7	Ohio State*	21
13	Indiana*	14
7	Purdue	21
41	Northwestern*	27

3-7-0
Big Ten: 3-4-0, T-5th

1968

14	Syracuse*	10
28	Baylor*	10
39	Wisconsin	0
14	Michigan	28
13	Minnesota*	14
21	Notre Dame*	17
20	Ohio State	25
22	Indiana*	24
0	Purdue*	9
31	Northwestern	14

5-5-0
Big Ten: 2-5-0, 7th

1969

27	Washington*	11
23	S. Methodist*	15
28	Notre Dame	42
21	Ohio State	54
23	Michigan*	12
18	Iowa	19
0	Indiana*	16
13	Purdue	41
10	Minnesota*	14
39	Northwestern	7

4-6-0
Big Ten: 2-5-0, 9th

1970

16	Washington	42
28	Washington State*	14
0	Notre Dame*	29
0	Ohio State*	29
20	Michigan	34
37	Iowa*	0
32	Indiana	7
24	Purdue*	14
13	Minnesota	23
20	Northwestern*	23

4-6-0
Big Ten: 3-4-0, T-5th

1971

10	Illinois*	0
0	Georgia Tech	10
31	Oregon State*	14
2	Notre Dame	14

13	Michigan*	24
28	Wisconsin	31
34	Iowa*	3
43	Purdue	10
17	Ohio State	10
40	Minnesota*	25
7	Northwestern	28

6-5-0
Big Ten: 5-3-0, T-3rd

1972

24	Illinois	0
16	Georgia Tech*	21
6	So. California	51
0	Notre Dame*	16
0	Michigan	10
31	Wisconsin*	0
6	Iowa	6
22	Purdue*	12
19	Ohio State*	12
10	Minnesota	14
24	Northwestern*	14

5-5-1
Big Ten: 5-2-1, 4th

1973
DENNIS E. STOLZ
Head Coach

10	Northwestern	14
14	Syracuse	8
21	UCLA*	34
10	Notre Dame	14
0	Michigan*	31
3	Illinois*	6
10	Purdue	7
21	Wisconsin*	0
0	Ohio State	35
10	Indiana*	9
15	Iowa	6

5-6-0
Big Ten: 4-4-0, T-4th

1974

41	Northwestern*	7
19	Syracuse*	0
14	UCLA	56
14	Notre Dame*	19
7	Michigan	21
21	Illinois	21
31	Purdue*	7
28	Wisconsin	21
16	Ohio State*	13
19	Indiana	10
60	Iowa*	21

7-3-1
Big Ten: 6-1-1, 3rd

1975

0	Ohio State*	21
14	Miami (O.)*	13
37	N. Carolina State*	15
10	Notre Dame	3
6	Michigan*	16
38	Minnesota	15
19	Illinois*	21
10	Purdue	20
14	Indiana	6

47	Northwestern*	14
27	Iowa	23

7-4-0
Big Ten: 4-4-0, T-3rd

1976
DARRYL D. ROGERS
Head Coach

21	Ohio State	49
21	Wyoming*	10
31	North Carolina State	31
6	Notre Dame*	24
10	Michigan	42
10	Minnesota*	14
31	Illinois	23
45	Purdue*	13
23	Indiana*	0
21	Northwestern	42
17	Iowa*	30

4-6-1
Big Ten: 3-5-0, T-7th

1977

19	Purdue*	14
21	Washington State*	23
34	Wyoming*	16
6	Notre Dame	16
14	Michigan*	24
13	Indiana	13
9	Wisconsin	7
49	Illinois*	20
29	Minnesota	10
44	Northwestern*	3
22	Iowa	16

7-3-1
Big Ten: 6-1-1, 3rd

1978

14	Purdue	21
49	Syracuse*	21
9	Southern California	30
25	Notre Dame*	29
24	Michigan	15
49	Indiana*	14
55	Wisconsin*	2
59	Illinois	19
33	Minnesota*	9
52	Northwestern	3
42	Iowa*	7

r

8-3-0
Big Ten: 7-1-0, T-1st

1979

33	Illinois*	16
41	Oregon*	17
24	Miami (Ohio)*	21
3	Notre Dame	27
7	Michigan*	21
29	Wisconsin	38
7	Purdue*	14
0	Ohio State	42
42	Northwestern	7

31	Minnesota*	17
23	Iowa	33

5-6-0
Big Ten: 3-5-0, T-7th

1980
FRANK D. (Muddy) WATERS
Head Coach

17	Illinois	20
7	Oregon	35
33	Western Michigan*	7
21	Notre Dame*	26
23	Michigan	27
7	Wisconsin*	17
25	Purdue	36
16	Ohio State*	48
42	Northwestern*	10
30	Minnesota	12
0	Iowa*	41

3-8-0
Big Ten: 2-6-0, 9th

1981

17	Illinois*	27
13	Ohio State	27
10	Bowling Green St.*	7
7	Notre Dame	20
20	Michigan*	38
33	Wisconsin*	14
26	Purdue	27
26	Indiana*	3
61	Northwestern	14
43	Minnesota*	36
7	Iowa	36

5-6-0
Big Ten: 4-5-0, T-6th

1982

16	Illinois	23
10	Ohio State*	31
22	Miami (Fla.)	25
3	Notre Dame*	11
17	Michigan	31
23	Wisconsin	24
21	Purdue*	24
22	Indiana	14
24	Northwestern*	28
26	Minnesota	7
18	Iowa*	24

2-9-0
Big Ten: 2-7-0, T-8th

1983
GEORGE J. PERLES
Head Coach

23	Colorado*	17
28	Notre Dame	23
10	Illinois*	20
29	Purdue	29
0	Michigan*	42
12	Indiana	24
11	Ohio State	21
34	Minnesota*	10
9	Northwestern	3
6	Iowa*	12
0	Wisconsin	32

4-6-1
Big Ten: 2-6-1, 7th

1984

24	Colorado	21
20	Notre Dame*	24
7	Illinois	40
10	Purdue*	13
19	Michigan	7
13	Indiana*	6
20	Ohio State*	23
20	Minnesota	13
27	Northwestern*	10
17	Iowa	16
10	Wisconsin*	20

Cherry Bowl

6	Army	10

6-6-0
Big Ten: 5-4-0, T-6th

1985

12	Arizona State*	3
10	Notre Dame	27
7	Western Michigan*	3
31	Iowa	35
0	Michigan*	31
17	Illinois*	31
28	Purdue	24
31	Minnesota*	26
35	Indiana	16
32	Northwestern*	0
41	Wisconsin	7

All-American Bowl

14	Georgia Tech	17

7-5-0
Big Ten: 5-3-0, T-4th

1986

17	Arizona State	20
20	Notre Dame*	15
45	Western Michigan*	10
21	Iowa*	24
6	Michigan	27
29	Illinois	21
37	Purdue*	3
52	Minnesota	23
14	Indiana*	17
21	Northwestern	24
23	Wisconsin*	13

6-5-0
Big Ten: 4-4-0

BASKETBALL

FORDDY ANDERSON
Head Coach

1954–55 (13-9 overall; 8-6, 4th in Big Ten)

1955–56 (13-9 overall; 7-7, 5th in Big Ten)

1956–57 (16-10 overall; 10-4, T-1st in Big Ten)

1957–58 (16-6 overall; 9-5, 3rd in Big Ten)

1958–59 (20-4 Overall; 12-2, 1st in Big Ten)

Date	Site	Opponent	Score	
12/ 6/58	H	Detroit	88-51	W
12/ 8/58	H	Butler	72-46	W

12/17/58	A	Notre Dame	....	74-56	W
12/20/58	H	Nebraska	....	80-55	W
12/29/58	*A	Duke	....	82-57	W
12/30/58	*A	North Carolina	...	75-58	W
12/31/58	*A	North Carolina St.	.	61-70	L
1/ 3/59	H	Indiana	....	79-77	W
1/ 5/59	A	Iowa	....	68-80	L
1/10/59	A	Illinois	....	97-96	W
1/17/59	H	MSU Alumni	.....	63-56	W
1/19/59	H	Ohio State	....	92-77	W
1/24/59	H	Minnesota	......	82-76	W
1/31/59	H	Northwestern	.....	81-72	W
2/ 2/59	A	Wisconsin	......	88-57	W
2/ 7/59	A	Purdue	....	81-85	L
2/14/59	H	Michigan	....	103-91	W
2/16/59	A	Northwestern	......	71-68	W
2/21/59	H	Purdue	....	94-87	W
2/28/59	A	Indiana	....	86-82	W
3/ 2/59	H	Wisconsin	....	93-73	W
3/ 7/59	H	Iowa	....	84-74	W
3/13/59	**A	Marquette	....	74-69	W
3/14/59	**A	Louisville	....	81-88	L

*Holiday Tournament at Raleigh, N.C. (Dixie Classic)
**NCAA Mideast Regional at Raleigh, N.C.

LEADERS: Bob Anderegg, (Co-Capt.), F, 19.5 ppg
John Green, (Co-Capt.), F, 18.5 ppg
Horace Walker, F/C, 13.3 ppg

OTHER
LETTERWINNERS: David Fahs, G
Art Gowens, C
Lance Olson, G
Tom Rand, G
Jim Stouffer, G
John Ulmer, Mgr.

1959–60 (10-11 Overall; 5-9, 8th in Big Ten)

1960–61 (7-17 Overall; 3-11, 9th in Big Ten)

1961–62 (8-14 Overall; 3-11, T-9th in Big Ten)

1962–63 (4-16 Overall; 3-11, 9th in Big Ten)

1963–64 (14-10 Overall; 8-6 T-4th in Big Ten)

1964–65 (5-18 Overall; 1-13, 10th in Big Ten)

JOHN BENINGTON
Head Coach

1965–66 (17-7 Overall; 10-4, 2nd in Big Ten)

1966–67 (16-7 Overall; 10-4, T-1st in Big Ten)

Date	Site	Opponent		Score	
12/ 1/66	H	Western Michigan	..	77-55	W
12/ 3/66	H	Miami (Ohio)	......	63-51	W
12/ 5/66	H	South Dakota	......	81-54	W
12/10/66	H	Wichita State	......	103-68	W
12/20/66	*A	Loyola (La.)	....	70-74	L
12/21/66	*A	Tulane	....	76-66	W
12/27/66	*A	Villanova	....	63-66	L
12/28/66	A	Bowling Green	.....	67-75	L
1/ 7/67	A	Illinois	....	76-74	W
1/14/67	H	Iowa	....	79-70	W
1/21/67	A	Michigan	....	59-81	L
1/28/67	H	Wisconsin	....	68-61	W
2/ 1/67	H	Notre Dame	....	85-80	W
2/ 6/67	A	Indiana	....	77-82	L
2/11/67	A	Purdue	....	79-77	W
2/13/67	H	Indiana	....	86-77	W
2/18/67	H	Minnesota	......	67-66	W
2/20/67	A	Ohio State	....	64-80	L
2/25/67	A	Wisconsin	....	64-68	L
2/27/67	H	Ohio State	....	74-63	W
3/ 4/67	H	Purdue	....	75-71	W
3/ 6/67	A	Minnesota	....	67-59	W
3/11/67	H	Northwestern	.....	79-66	W

*Tournament at New Orleans, La.

LEADERS: Matthew Aitch, (Capt.), C, 16.3 ppg
Lee Lafayette, C/F, 14.8 ppg
Steve Rymal, G, 11.4 ppg

OTHER
LETTERWINNERS: John Bailey, G
Art Baylor, F/C
Bob Bouma, Mgr.
Ted Crary, F
Heywood Edwards, C/F
John Headen, Mgr.
John Holms, F
Gerry Geistler, C
Richie Jordan, G
Vernon Johnson, G
Dave Keeler, C
Tom Lick, C
Shannon Reading, G
John Warren, Mgr.

1967–68 (12-12 Overall; 6-8, T-6th in Big Ten)

1968–69 (11-12 Overall; 6-8, T-5th in Big Ten)

GUS GANAKAS
Head Coach

1969–70 (9-15 Overall; 5-9, T-6th in Big Ten)

1970–71 (10-14 Overall; 4-10, T-7th in Big Ten)

1971–72 (13-11 Overall; 6-8, T-5th in Big Ten)

1972–73 (13-11 Overall; 6-8, T-6th in Big Ten)

1973–74 (13-11 Overall; 8-6, T-4th in Big Ten)

1974–75 (17-9 Overall; 10-8, 5th in Big Ten)

1975–76 (14-13 Overall; 10-8, 4th in Big Ten)

JUD HEATHCOTE
Head Coach

1976–77 (12–15 Overall; 9-9, 5th in Big Ten)

1977–78 (25-5 Overall; 15-3, 1st in Big Ten)

Date	Site	Opponent		Score	
11/28/77	H	Central Michigan	..	68-61	W
12/ 2/77	**A	Rhode Island	....	92-64	W
12/ 3/77	**A	Syracuse	....	67-75	L
12/ 8/77	H	Wichita State	......	84-57	W
12/10/77	H	Western Michigan	..	79-57	W
12/19/77	H	Middle Tennessee St.	....	72-51	W
12/21/77	A	Detroit	....	103-74	W
12/29/77	#A	Southern Methodist	....	95-69	W
12/30/77	#A	New Hampshire	...	102-65	W
1/ 5/78	H	Minnesota	....	87-83	W
1/ 7/78	H	Wisconsin	....	74-63	W
1/12/78	A	Illinois	....	82-70	W
1/14/78	A	Northwestern	......	67-63	W
1/19/78	H	Purdue	....	60-51	W
1/21/78	H	Iowa	....	68-58	W
1/28/78	A	Ohio State	....	70-60	W
1/30/78	A	Indiana	....	66-71	L
2/ 2/78	H	Michigan	....	63-65	L
2/ 4/78	H	Indiana	....	68-59	W
2/ 9/78	A	Iowa	....	71-70	W
2/11/78	A	Michigan	....	73-62	W
2/16/78	A	Purdue	....	80-99	L
2/18/78	H	Ohio State	....	79-74	W
2/23/78	H	Northwestern	......	66-56	W
2/25/78	H	Illinois	....	89-67	W
3/ 2/78	A	Wisconsin	....	89-75	W
3/ 4/78	A	Minnesota	....	71-70	W
3/11/78	*A	Providence	....	77-63	W
3/16/78	*A	Western Kentucky	.	90-69	W
3/18/78	*A	Kentucky	....	49-52	L

*NCAA Mideast Regional Games
**Carrier Classic at Syracuse, N.Y.
#Old Dominion Classic at Norfolk, Va.

LEADERS: Greg Kelser, (Co-Capt.), F, 17.7 ppg
Earvin Johnson, G/F, 17.0 ppg
Bob Chapman, (Co-Capt.), G, 12.3 ppg

OTHER
LETTERWINNERS: Mike Brkovich, G/F
Alfred Brown, F
Ron Charles, F
James Coutre, C
Terry Donnelly, G
Sten Feldreich, C
Don Flowers, G
Michael Longaker, G
Nate Phillips, G
Dan Riewald, G
Jay Vincent, F/C

1978–79 (26-6 Overall; 13-5, T-1st in Big Ten)

NCAA TOURNAMENT CHAMPIONS

Date	Site	Opponent	Score	
11/27/78	H	Central Michigan ..	71-54	W
12/ 9/78	H	Cal State Fullerton .	92-89	W
12/13/78	A	Western Michigan ..	109-69	W
12/16/78	A	North Carolina	69-70	L
12/19/78	A	Cincinnati	63-52	W
12/28/78	#A	Washington State ..	98-52	W
12/29/78	#A	Oregon State	65-57	W
12/30/78	#A	Indiana	74-57	W
1/ 4/79	H	Wisconsin	84-55	W
1/ 6/79	H	Minnesota	69-62	W
1/11/79	A	Illinois	55-57	L
1/13/79	A	Purdue	50-52	L
1/18/79	H	Indiana	82-58	W
1/20/79	H	Iowa	83-72	W(OT)
1/25/79	A	Michigan	48-49	L
1/27/79	A	Northwestern	65-83	L
2/ 1/79	H	Ohio State	84-79	W(OT)
2/ 3/79	H	Northwestern	61-50	W
2/ 4/79	H	Kansas	85-61	W
2/ 8/79	A	Iowa	60-57	W
2/10/79	A	Ohio State	73-57	W
2/15/79	A	Indiana	59-47	W
2/17/79	H	Michigan	80-57	W
2/22/79	H	Purdue	73-67	W
2/24/79	H	Illinois	76-62	W
3/ 1/79	A	Minnesota	76-63	W
3/ 3/79	A	Wisconsin	81-83	L
3/11/79	*A	Lamar	95-64	W
3/16/79	*A	Louisiana State	87-71	W
3/18/79	*A	Notre Dame	80-68	W
3/24/79	*A	Pennsylvania	101-67	W
3/26/79	**A	Indiana State	75-64	W

*NCAA Tournament
**NCAA Championship Game
#Far West Classic at Portland, Ore.

LEADERS: Greg Kelser, (Co-Capt.), F, 18.8 ppg
Earvin Johnson, (Co-Capt.), G/F,
17.1 ppg
Jay Vincent, C/F, 12.7 ppg

OTHER
LETTERWINNERS: Randy Bishop, Mgr.
Terry Donnelly, G
Jaimie Huffman, G
Ron Charles, F
Mike Brkovich, G/F
Mike Longaker, G
Rob Gonzales, F
Greg Lloyd, G
Don Brkovich, F
Darwin Payton, Mgr.
Gerald Gilkie, F
Rick Kaye, F

1979–80 (12-15 Overall; 6-12, 9th in Big Ten)

1980–81 (13-14 Overall; 7-11, 8th in Big Ten)

1981–82 (12-16 Overall; 7-11, T-7th in Big Ten)

1982–83 (17-13 Overall; 9-9, T-6th in Big Ten)

1983–84 (16-12 Overall; 9-9, 5th in Big Ten)

1984–85 (19-10 Overall; 10-8, T-5th in Big Ten)

Date	Site	Opponent	Score	
11/24/84	A	Canisius	80-71	W
11/30/84	**H	Western Michigan ..	77-61	W
12/ 1/84	**H	Army	76-64	W
12/10/84	H	St. Peter's	50-38	W
12/12/84	A	Western Illinois	93-61	W
12/15/84	H	Missouri	79-61	W
12/18/84	A	George Washington	68-54	W
12/22/84	A	Illinois-Chicago	81-60	W
12/28/84/	#A	Boston College	78-82	L
12/29/84	#A	San Diego State	77-61	W
1/ 3/85	H	Ohio State	82-79	W
1/ 5/85	H	Indiana	68-61	W
1/10/86	A	Purdue	81-72	W(OT)
1/12/85	A	Illinois	63-75	L
1/17/85	H	Iowa	65-79	L
1/19/85	H	Minnesota	75-81	L
1/24/85	A	Michigan	75-86	L
1/31/85	A	Wisconsin	77-68	W
2/ 2/85	A	Northwestern	68-54	W
2/ 7/85	H	Illinois	64-56	W
2/ 9/85	H	Purdue	65-66	L
2/13/85	A	Minnesota	64-73	L
2/16/85	A	Iowa	57-55	W
2/23/85	H	Michigan	73-75	L
2/27/85	H	Northwestern	61-47	W
3/ 2/85	H	Wisconsin	82-63	W
3/ 7/85	A	Indiana	68-58	W
3/ 9/85	A	Ohio State	79-90	L
3/15/85	*A	Alabama-Birmingham	68-70	L

*NCAA Tournament at Houston, Tex.
**Spartan Cutlass Classic
#Cabrillo Classic at San Diego, Calif.

LEADERS: Sam Vincent, (Co-Capt.), G, 23.0 ppg
Scott Skiles, G, 17.7 ppg
Ken Johnson, C, 10.8 ppg

OTHER
LETTERWINNERS: Richard Mudd, (Co-Capt.), F
Greg Pedro, G
Barry Fordham, F/C
Larry Polec, F
Greg Vanek, F
Darryl Johnson, G
Mark Hollis, Mgr.
Ralph Walker, F
George Johnson, Mgr.
Carlton Valentine, F

1985–86 (23-8 Overall; 12-6, 3rd in Big Ten)

Date	Site	Opponent	Score	
11/23/85	H	Western Illinois	98-63	W
11/26/85	H	Maine-Orono	89-58	W
11/29/85	**H	Central Michigan ..	103-60	W
11/30/85	**H	Western Michigan ..	84-64	W
12/ 4/85	H	George Washington	87-61	W
12/ 7/85	H	Canisius	90-61	W
12/14/85	H	Iowa State	80-82	L(OT)
12/21/85	H	Illinis-Chicago	99-74	W
12/27/85	#A	Massachusetts	93-45	W
12/28/85	#A	New Mexico	76-61	W
1/ 3/86	A	Ohio State	73-84	L
1/ 5/86	A	Indiana	77-74	W
1/ 9/86	H	Purdue	88-83	L
1/12/86	H	Illinois	58-51	W
1/16/86	A	Iowa	71-82	L
1/18/86	A	Minnesota	71-76	L
1/25/86	H	Michigan	91-79	W
1/30/86	H	Wisconsin	83-81	W
2/ 1/86	H	Northwestern	97-69	W
2/ 6/86	A	Illinois	84-80	W
2/ 8/86	A	Purdue	82-88	L
2/13/86	H	Iowa	83-73	W
2/15/86	H	Minnesota	76-66	W
2/20/86	A	Michigan	74-59	W
2/27/86	A	Northwestern	82-48	W
3/ 2/86	A	Wisconsin	84-71	W
3/ 5/86	H	Indiana	79-97	L
3/ 8/86	H	Ohio State	91-81	W
3/13/86	*A	Washington	72-70	W

3/15/86	*A Georgetown	80-68	W	
3/21/86	@A Kansas	86-96	L(OT)	

*NCAA Tournament at Dayton, Ohio
@NCAA Tournament at Kansas City, Kan.
**Spartan Cutlass Classic
#Lobo Classic at Albuquerque, N.M.

LEADERS: Scott Skiles (Co-Capt.), G, 27.4 ppg
Darryl Johnson, G, 16.6 ppg
Vernon Carr, G/F, 13.8 ppg

OTHER
LETTERWINNERS: Mark Brown, G
Barry Fordham, C
Mario Izzo, C
David Mueller, F
Larry Polec (Co-Capt.), F
Jim Sarkine, F
Scott Sekal, F
Carlton Valentine, F
Ralph Walker, F
George Johnson, Mgr.
Tom McCall, Mgr.
Tim MacDonald, Mgr.
Daron Barnes, Mgr.

1986-87 (11-17 overall; 6-12, 7th in Big Ten)

BASEBALL

DANNY LITWHILER
Head Coach

	Overall			Big Ten		Place
1964	22	12	0	8	7	4th
1965	28	11	0	9	6	3rd
1966	24	13	1	8	5	4th
1967	22	23	1	8	10	6th
1968	32	10	1	13	4	2nd
1969	24	17	0	8	8	5th
1970	28	15	2	9	7	3rd
1971	36	10	0	13	3	1st
1972	28	10	1	10	4	2nd
1973	27	20	0	9	9	4th
1974	23	16	1	7	8	6th
1975	28	16	0	11	4	4th
1976	15	23	1	7	5	4th
1977	28	26	0	10	8	4th
1978	32	21	0	11	5	2nd
1979	28	27	0	11	4	1st
1980	15	35	0	3	13	10th
1981	23	28	0	6	8	4th (East Div.)
1982	25	29	0	6	10	3rd (East Div.)

TOM SMITH
Head Coach

	Overall			Big Ten		Place
1983	22	32	0	8	6	2nd (East Div.)
1984	32	26	0	8	9	2nd (East Div.)
1985	22	35	0	2	14	5th (East Div.)
1986	28	26	1	7	9	3rd (East Div.)
1987	33	20	0	6	10	4th (East Div.)

HOCKEY

AMO BESSONE
Head Coach

	W	L	T
1951–52	7	13	0
MHL	5	13	0
1952–53	5	16	0
WIHL	2	16	0
1953–54	8	14	1
WIHL	4	13	1
1954–55	9	17	1
WIHL	5	14	1
1955–56	5	18	0
WIHL	1	17	0
1956–57	7	15	0
WIHL	5	15	0
1957–58	12	11	0
WIHL	9	11	0
1958–59	17	6	1
1959–60	4	18	2
WCHA	4	18	2
1960–61	11	16	0
WCHA	5	15	0
1961–62	13	11	1
WCHA	6	9	1
1962–63	11	12	0
WCHA	6	10	0
1963–64	8	17	1
WCHA	1	12	1
1964–65	17	12	0
WCHA	8	8	0
1965–66	16	13	0
WCHA	9	11	0

1965–66
NCAA TOURNAMENT CHAMPIONS

MSU		OPP.
0	Colorado College	4
3	Colorado College (OT)	4
3	St. Lawrence	5
3	Clarkson	6
6	St. Lawrence	4
11	North Dakota	5
3	North Dakota	5
6	Denver	8
4	Denver	1
4	Colorado College (OT)	5
6	Colorado College	2
5	Minnesota	7
1	Minnesota	5
6	Minnesota-Duluth (OT)	5
5	Minnesota-Duluth	2
5	Minnesota (OT)	6
4	Minnesota	3
8	Michigan	7
4	Michigan	2
3	Wisconsin	1
5	Wisconsin	3
4	Michigan Tech	8
2	Michigan Tech	4
7	Michigan	1
0	Michigan (OT)	1
3	Michigan	2
4	Michigan Tech	3

2	Boston University		1
6	Clarkson		1

1966–67	16	15	1
WCHA	8	11	1
1967–68	11	16	2
WCHA	6	13	1
1968–69	11	16	1
WCHA	7	10	1
1969–70	13	16	0
WCHA	10	12	0
1970–71	19	12	0
WCHA	12	10	0
1971–72	20	16	0
WCHA	15	13	0
1972–73	23	12	1
WCHA	16	9	1
1973–74	23	14	1
WCHA	15	12	1
1974–75	22	17	1
WCHA	19	12	1
1975–76	23	16	2
WCHA	20	12	0
1976–77	14	21	1
WCHA	11	20	1
1978–79	15	21	0
WCHA	12	20	0

RON MASON
Head Coach

	W	L	T
1979–80	14	24	0
WCHA	12	16	0
1980–81	12	22	2
WCHA	7	20	1
1981–82	26	10	1
CCHA	21	10	1
1982–83	30	11	1
CCHA	23	9	0
1983–84	34	12	0
CCHA	21	9	0
1984–85	38	6	0
CCHA	27	5	0
1985–86	34	9	2
CCHA	23	7	2

1985–86
NCAA TOURNAMENT CHAMPIONS

MSU		OPP.
6	Ohio State	2
5	Ohio State	2
1	Western Michigan	5
4	Western Michigan	3
5	Miami	2
7	Miami	2
5	Ferris State (OT)	5
5	Ferris State	3
4	Michigan	5
6	Michigan	2
3	Team Canada	5
5	Team Canada (OT)	4
4	Bowling Green State (OT)	3
5	Bowling Green State (OT)	6
6	Illinois-Chicago	4
2	Illinois-Chicago	3
3	Lake Superior State	7
5	Lake Superior State (OT)	6
6	Ohio State (OT)	5
8	Ohio State	0
2	Northern Michigan	3
2	Michigan Tech (OT)	1
8	RPI	3
4	Western Michigan	2
8	Western Michigan	5
8	Miami	3
6	Miami	3
8	Ferris State	6
9	Ferris State (OT)	9
7	Michigan	5
3	Michigan	5
12	Northern Arizona	2
9	Northern Arizona	3
7	Bowling Green State	4
6	Bowling Green State	4
4	Illinois-Chicago	2
7	Ilinois-Chicago	2
8	Lake Superior State	5
5	Lake Superior State (OT)	4
4	Michigan	2
5	Michigan	2
3	Lake Superior State	2
1	Western Michigan	3
6	Boston College	4
4	Boston College	2
6	Minnesota	4
6	Harvard	5

1986–87	33	10	2
CCHA	23	8	1

INDEX

DATE DUE

OCT 1 0 '00		
	FEB 1 2 2008	
FEB 0 7 01	0007	FEB 1 2 2011
APR 1 8 2002		
APR 2 9 2002		FEB 2 6 2008
MAY 2 6 2005		
	MAR 1 7 2009	
MAY 1 0 2006		
FEB 2 0 2007		MAR 0 2 2009
APR 0 2 2007	2010	
APR 1 7 2007		
JAN 0 7 2008		
FEB 0 3 2008		
MAR 1 6 2010		
		FEB 0 3 2008

Jaguar

Jaguar

ROLAND SMITH

HYPERION BOOKS FOR CHILDREN
NEW YORK

For Marie, as always . . .

First Edition

7 9 10 8 6

This book is set in 14-point Perpetua.

Library of Congress Cataloging-in-Publication Data
Smith, Roland, (date)
Jaguar / Roland Smith. — 1st ed.
p.   cm.
Summary: While accompanying his father on an expedition up the Amazon River to a jaguar preserve in Brazil, fourteen-year-old Jacob must contend with dangerous animals and fortune hunters.
ISBN 0-7868-0282-0 (trade)—ISBN 0-7868-2226-0 (lib. bdg.).
[1. Rain forests—Fiction. 2. Jaguar—Fiction. 3. Adventure and adventurers—Fiction. 4. Amazon River Valley—Fiction. 5. Brazil—Fiction.] I. Title.
PZ7.S65766Jag   1997
[Fic]—DC20   96-36750

CONTENTS

BEFORE . . .

I walked into the den. Pinned up on the wall was a huge map of the Amazon Basin in South America. On the floor were stacks of books, scientific journals, and my father—a field biologist named Robert Lansa, Ph.D., also known as Doc to his friends and to his only son.

Doc sat in front of a laptop computer, staring intently at the screen. He didn't notice I was there. I was used to this.

"What's going on?" I asked.

He grunted and didn't look up.

"What's with the map and stuff?"

"Brazil, field project, preserve, jaguars," he mumbled.

When my mom was alive, she called this kind of response, "Lansa Latin." It had been awhile since I had heard this language. My mom's technique for dealing with it was to leave my father alone and wait for him to snap out of it. I left the room.

I went into the kitchen and opened the refrigerator.

Inside was a carton of sour milk, a block of cheddar cheese with splotches of green fuzz colonizing it, and a new item—a half-empty jug of orange juice. My father must have decided to go on a health kick. I grabbed the OJ and rinsed out a cup from the sink, which we were using as a cupboard.

Translating my father's mumbling was easy. He was looking at a field project that had something to do with a jaguar preserve in Brazil.

The only thing that surprised me about this was the timing. We had only been back in the States for a few months, and the tan I got in Kenya hadn't totally faded yet. We had rented a small house in Poughkeepsie, New York, near my grandfather's retirement home. His name is Tawapu, but we call him Taw. He's a Hopi Indian who spent most of his life riveting steel girders together high above the streets of New York City.

The plan was to stay in Poughkeepsie for at least a year while my father wrote up his research notes on elephants and got them published. It looked as if the plan might change, which was fine with me. Poughkeepsie was an okay city, and I liked the high school I was going to, but after my trip to Kenya, life was a little too tame for my liking. A trip to Brazil would be fantastic!

I waited a couple of hours, then went back into the den. My father was on the phone talking to someone. When he saw me, he covered the mouthpiece.

"Hey, Jake," he said. "I'm going to be hung up here for a while getting this together. I'll tell you all about it when I have it figured out."

This was polite Lansa Latin for "Get out of the den and don't bother me." I nodded and closed the door.

I didn't see my father for several days, but he left signs that he was still alive. I'd get home from school and find human spoor like pizza boxes and coffee grounds on the counter, and every once in a while I'd hear him talking on the phone behind the closed door.

Late on the fourth night he finally emerged from his den. I had just put away my homework and was getting ready to go to bed.

"Hey, Jake," he said. "Shouldn't you be in school?"

"I don't go to night school, Doc."

He wandered over to the window and opened the blind. "Wow, I really lost track of time."

That wasn't all he had lost track of. His long black hair hung down to his shoulders without the benefit of the usual ponytail, and he hadn't shaved for a week. I couldn't tell if he had changed his clothes, because he always wore jeans and denim shirts. He had at least a dozen sets exactly alike.

He turned back from the window.

"You remember Bill Brewster?"

"Sure." Bill was one of my father's oldest friends. They

had spent a lot of time in the field together studying animals. I hadn't seen Bill since my mom's funeral.

"Well, he's in Brazil now, and he's looking for someone to help him set up a jaguar preserve down there."

"And that someone is you."

"Right." He paused. "I won't be gone long."

I stared at him. He hadn't said the magic word—*we*. "How long?"

He looked away—a bad sign. "Not long. A month. . . . Maybe a little longer."

I should have seen this coming. Doc had become increasingly distant over the past few weeks. He'd go out for long walks by himself and spend hours closed up in his den. Some days we didn't say more than a dozen words to each other. I thought he was just concentrating on his book about elephants and didn't have time for me. I realized, now, that it was something else.

"And what am I supposed to do?" I asked.

"It's not like I'll be gone forever."

He had said the same thing when he went to Kenya. I didn't see him for over two years.

"What about my flying lessons?" I had just taken my first solo flight. The plan was for me to get my pilot's license by spring so Doc and I could do some cross-country trips this summer.

He walked back over to the window and looked outside—not that there was anything to see.

"I talked to Pete over at the Home," he continued. "He said you're welcome to stay there until I get back."

"You're joking."

"It's not like it's permanent."

"I thought we were a team," I reminded him, as calmly as I could. "Partners."

He turned back to me. "We are! But you have school."

"I could take correspondence courses."

"It's not the same. And I'll only be gone a little while."

Doc had made up his mind, and I knew there was no point in arguing with him. He was the most pigheaded man on earth, which is one of the reasons he and my mom had broken up before she died. For some reason, Doc had now suddenly turned into a parent. Our partnership was dissolved.

"I'll just stay at the house," I said.

"You're only fourteen, Jake. You can't stay here by yourself."

"I was in Kenya by myself."

"That was different. In this country there are laws about leaving minors by themselves."

"I won't tell anybody."

"Knock it off, Jake. You're going to stay with Taw at the Home."

Definitely a parent.

"That isn't fair."

"I'll only be gone a month," he said. "Maybe a little longer. . . ."

The Home

CHAPTER 1

Taw's retirement home is about ten miles outside Poughkeepsie. Years ago it was a resort hotel. From the outside, it still looked like a hotel, but the image changed when you walked through the front door.

On the main floor was a recreation room with three televisions mounted on brackets hanging from the ceiling. The televisions were tuned to three different channels, and the volume was kept so loud you could hear the soaps and *Oprah* from the front porch. The recreation room also had several tables set up for jigsaw puzzles, cards, and board games. Along one wall was a small library with large-print books. Once a week the local library sent a van over to take the books people had read and replenish the shelves with new titles.

Next to the recreation room was a clinic. In the morning this was the first stop for the *inmates,* as some of the residents called themselves. Before breakfast they lined up for their little white paper cups of brightly colored pills. This morning ritual was called the M&M's—*morning meds*. The nutritionist even put me on M&M's, which consisted of a cup of vitamins—at least I hoped they were vitamins. Then the nurse checked our names off a list. If people didn't show up for their M&M's, an orderly was sent to look for them.

Next to the clinic was a cafeteria. Everyone had an assigned seat so the nurses could make sure they got their "special" meals. The inmates called the cafeteria McDonald's.

Because I was young, the nutritionist let me have almost anything I wanted. At first I took advantage of this. But after a few meals with my tablemates staring enviously at my plate, I asked the cook to make my food at least look like theirs.

Taw was happy to have me around when he remembered who I was, which was only about half the time. Sometimes he thought I was a staff member, and at other times he thought I was an inmate. One time he mistook me for a childhood friend on the Hopi Indian reservation in Arizona—that was an interesting conversation!

Aside from me, the youngest person in the Home was Peter Steptoe. He was a thirty-two-year-old nurse. Peter and I got along very well. He was also very fond of my grandfather.

I guess the Home was pretty nice, but you haven't lived until you've been marooned in a house with fifty surrogate grandparents. Everyone meant well, but they drove me crazy!

My daily routine never varied. I was usually up by six in the morning. After my shower I went down to the clinic, got my M&M's, then ate breakfast with everyone. After breakfast Peter drove me to school, because buses didn't run this far outside the city. After school, Peter picked me up and drove me back to the Home. I held what came to be known as the *Press Conference,* had dinner with everyone, did my homework, and went to bed.

The Press Conference came about because everyone wanted to know what I had done during the day. When I first got to the Home, I would tell anyone who asked about my day. Fifty times! It took hours. If I left anyone out, their feelings got hurt. Peter thought it would save me a lot of time and spare people's feelings if I told everyone about my day at one time. The Press Conference was held in the recreation room every evening just before dinner. I thought the other inmates would get bored with it after a few days, but they didn't. The televisions were turned off and the recreation room was always jammed. Here's how a typical Press Conference went:

ME: Well, let's see. . . . Peter dropped me off at school this morning. I went to my classes and everything went pretty well. In history Mr. Pentegrast showed us a video on the Vietnam War. We played volleyball in PE. My team lost. After school I spent some time in the library doing research on a paper I'm writing on the Amazon rain forest. Peter picked me up and drove me back here. That's about it for today.

[*Hands are raised.*]

ME: Mr. Blondell.

MR. BLONDELL: You saw the video on the Vietnam War. What did you think of it?

ME: It seemed like a tragic waste of human life and money.

ME: Mrs. Mapes.

MRS. MAPES: Didn't you talk to anyone at school?

ME: Well, sure I talked to . . .

MRS. MAPES: Who?

ME: Well, I talked to Patty Teters.

MRS. MAPES: What does she look like?

ME: I don't know. . . . She has brown hair, brown eyes, she's about . . .

MRS. MAPES: Cute?

ME: Well, yeah. I guess so. . . .

MRS. MAPES: You're too young to get involved with anyone. You have your whole life to . . .

You get the idea.

When I first got to the Home, I made a couple of mistakes. The first was doing my homework in the recreation room. I sat down at one of the tables and started to work on a geometry problem, and suddenly there were seven inmates surrounding me asking if I needed any help. My second mistake was saying, "Sure."

They all started helping at once. A disagreement broke out, which quickly escalated into a shouting match, and before I knew it, two of the old guys started swinging at each other. Peter rushed in and broke it up. He suggested that I do my homework in my room to avoid this happening again.

My room was on the second floor, just down the hall from Taw's. It was a nice room with its own bath and a good view of the stream that ran into the lake in back of the Home. The room had an adjustable hospital bed, a nightstand, a dresser, and an oak desk that had seen better days. Hanging above the bed was a cord with a button on the end of it, in case I had a medical emergency. Because the room was temporary, about the only improvement I made was to put up a map of the Amazon Basin.

Doing my homework in the room stopped the fistfights, but it didn't stop the disturbances. After the Press Conference and dinner I'd go up to do my homework. Usually, within ten minutes I'd hear a light tapping on the door:

ME: Hello, Mrs. Bellows. What can I do for you?
MRS. BELLOWS: I know you probably get lonely here. I

just wanted you to know that if you need someone to talk to, I'm here.

ME: That's very nice of you. But right now I better get my homework done.

MRS. BELLOWS: Of course! I just wanted you to know that I'm here in case you need me.

ME: Thanks. I'll find you if I need to talk to someone.

MRS. BELLOWS: Wonderful! You're such a nice young man. Nothing like my own son, who only comes here three times a year to visit.

[*Ten minutes later another tap at the door.*]

ME: Mr. Clausen, what a pleasure.

MR. CLAUSEN: I hope I'm not disturbing you.

ME: I'm just trying to get my homework—

MR. CLAUSEN: That's why I'm here. I used to be an accountant. I'm a whiz at arithmetic, and I just wanted you to know that I'd be glad to help you if you need it.

ME: Thanks for offering. But right now I'm working on my geology.

MR. CLAUSEN: Hmmmm . . . I don't know anything about geology. But when you get to that arithmetic, I'm your man. I'm a whiz at that stuff. I really am!

* * *

It was the same every night—a constant parade of people dropping by. They meant well, but I didn't need any help—the homework was simple. What I needed was to be back in my own home with my father. Or better yet, I needed to be in Brazil. But I had a bad feeling this wasn't going to happen anytime soon. A month went by, and I hadn't heard a word from him.

Saturdays and Sundays were the worst. Peter was off on the weekends, so I didn't have anyone to drive me places. I could have asked one of the other staff members, but I didn't want to impose on them.

It was one of the worst winters in New York history. Two days after my father left, the snow started falling, and it didn't let up through most of February. The snowplows had piled it so high on the side of the roads that you felt as if you were driving through an ice cave. The lake in back of the Home and the stream that fed it were frozen solid. I made one trip out there and nearly froze to death. I hadn't gotten around to buying any winter clothes.

So on weekends I was stuck inside. I usually hung out in my room and read. When the door-knocking got out of hand, I took refuge on the second-floor landing.

The winding stairway leading to the upper floors was seldom used. It was off-limits for inmates unless they were accompanied by a nurse or an orderly. To get to the second and third floors, inmates had to take the elevator. Fortunately, this rule didn't apply to me. When I wanted to be alone, I'd go to the second-floor landing and sit in the window seat, which couldn't be seen from the hallway.

It had a great view of the stream and lake in back of the Home. Peter found me in the window seat one afternoon, reading a book.

"I won't tell a soul," he said.

The next time I retreated to the landing, I found a small reading lamp attached to the wall above the seat. Peter never said a word about it, but I knew he had put it there so I'd be able to use the seat during the evening if I needed to.

When I hid out on the landing, I could still hear people wandering the hallways looking for me.

"Have you seen Jake?"

"No, I was looking for him, too."

"I wonder what he's up to now."

"Heaven knows, but you know young people these days. You can never . . ."

It took me awhile, but I learned to ignore the searchers' voices and concentrate on my books.

Since Doc left, I had read everything I could find on the Amazon. Every week the library van brought me a new pile of books. I read about rain forest ecology, indigenous tribes, Brazilian history, insects, snakes, birds, mammals, and of course jaguars. Actually, there hadn't been a lot written about jaguars, despite the fact that they are the third largest cat in the world, right behind tigers and lions. This is because they live in very isolated areas and are extremely secretive—not unlike my father.

I also read books about the men who had explored the Amazon Basin. My favorite among the explorers was a man named Colonel P. H. Fawcett. In 1953 his papers and journals were published in a book called *Exploration Fawcett*. He spent his entire life looking for the fabled Muribeca gold mines, which some people thought were tied to an ancient civilization and its lost city.

Colonel Fawcett set out on his final expedition to find the lost mines in 1925, accompanied by his eldest son and his son's friend. No one ever heard from them again.

Another book I liked was by Sir Arthur Conan Doyle, of Sherlock Holmes fame. Apparently he and Colonel Fawcett were friends. Conan Doyle wrote a novel called *The Lost World,* which was loosely based on some of the things that Fawcett had seen and heard about during his various expeditions to find the Muribeca gold mines.

* * *

And this is how it went—M&M's, breakfast, school, homework, hiding, and no word from Doc. When he was in Kenya and I was still in New York, he would at least send me a letter once in a while to tell me he was okay. What was he doing down there? I knew he had a tendency to throw himself into a project and forget almost everything else, but this was the first time he had forgotten about me.

CHAPTER 2

By March, I'd had just about enough of the Home. More snow had fallen, and school was closed for a few days. The library van couldn't make it up the driveway, so there were no new books to read. The snow also kept the inmates' relatives away, which made everyone pretty gloomy.

The staff tried to cheer the inmates up by scheduling group games and theatrical skits, but the inmates weren't very enthusiastic.

Even Taw seemed depressed by our snowy isolation. He spent most of his time in his room looking through the spotting scope that Doc had given him for Christmas. I made it a point to drop by his room several times a day and see how he was doing. A couple of times I found him sitting in front of the spotting scope sound asleep, with his long gray braids dangling over his lap.

I was worried about my father. It wasn't like him not to

call or write. Peter guessed that the mail system in Brazil was not very good. "And the snow around here hasn't helped our own mail system," he said. He was probably right, but it didn't lessen my growing concern.

I started to think of ways to get down to Brazil. I had a valid passport, and with the credit card Doc had left me, I could buy a ticket. But there were a number of obstacles standing in my way. One of the problems was Peter. He was responsible for me, and there was no way he would let me go traipsing off to the wilds of Brazil. And if I ran away, he'd go out of his mind with worry—to say nothing of how this would affect the other inmates. I couldn't do this to them.

An even bigger barrier was the fact that I had no idea where Doc was. I knew he had flown to a city called Manaus, but he could be anywhere by now. When I went to Kenya to find Doc after my mother died, I at least had a rough idea of where he was. And what if I managed to fly down to Brazil and he was on his way back to the States?

It seemed that my only choice was to wait and worry. My mood swung between frustration and fury—frustration because there wasn't anything I could do, and fury at Doc for leaving me behind and not staying in touch.

One afternoon I got so fed up I just had to talk to someone about the situation. It was Saturday and Peter was off. My only choice was to try talking to Taw. There was only about a fifty percent chance that he would remember who

I was or hear what I had to say, but I didn't care. I was willing to try anything to get rid of the bitter thoughts stampeding through my head.

I knocked on his door. He didn't answer. I knocked again, then opened the door. As usual, he was sitting at his window looking through the spotting scope. He didn't turn around. I walked over and sat on the bed.

"I need to talk, Taw."

He still didn't turn around.

"I'm getting kind of frustrated living here and I'm worried about Doc. . . ."

I told him about everything that was bothering me. It must have taken me twenty minutes to get to the end. All through it Taw didn't move a single muscle in his thin body. He just continued looking through the spotting scope. I doubted he had heard a single word I said. He probably thought my speech was one of the shows on the downstairs televisions. Despite this, I felt a little better letting it all out like that. I got up from the bed.

"Nice talking to you, Taw."

I started toward the door.

"A buck."

I stopped and turned around. Taw was in exactly the same position. I thought for a moment that I was having an audio hallucination. Then I heard it again.

"A buck."

At first I thought he wanted a dollar. I didn't know why

he needed money. Sometimes it's simpler not to question my grandfather. I took out my wallet.

Taw moved away from the scope and pointed out the window. "Look."

I walked over and looked through the spotting scope. I put my wallet away, feeling a little stupid. A big buck—as in *deer*—was standing by a tree near the frozen lake. He was stretching his neck up to nibble on the last clump of leaves within reach.

"You should stalk him," Taw said.

"What?"

"Like you told me you learned in Kenya."

When I was in Kenya, I was taught to stalk animals by a Masai named Supeet. When I got back to Poughkeepsie, I told Taw about it. At the time I didn't think he was even listening. I hadn't thought about stalking since I got to the Home.

"That was different," I said, turning away from the scope. "For one thing it was a lot warmer and there wasn't two feet of snow on the ground."

"Wear warm clothes."

"In Kenya, I stalked without any clothes," I said. "I was naked."

"Too cold here," he pointed out. "You'll have to wear clothes. Perhaps all you need is a good stalk. I'll watch you through the telescope."

I looked through the scope at the buck again. He was on

the far side of the lake. A light snow was falling, blown by an east wind. I'd have to go around the lake from the west so I could come upwind of him. "It would take a long time," I said.

"I have plenty of time."

"I don't know how close I can get."

"You can try."

I went back to my room, put on white running shoes and three shirts, and grabbed my pillowcase. Next stop was the linen closet, where the nurses kept their laundered, white uniforms. I found a pair of Peter's pants and slipped them over the pants I was wearing. I put my coat on, then found a white lab coat big enough to fit over it. The next item was a pair of disposable surgical gloves, which wouldn't keep my hands warm but would camouflage them to some degree. The final touch was the pillowcase. I found a black marker and put the pillowcase over my head and made two marks over my eyes. I took it back off and cut out holes, then put it back on and looked in the mirror. I looked as if I was ready for Halloween.

The next challenge was to get out of the house without anyone seeing me in this getup. That was relatively easy, because one of the inmates was putting on a piano recital and everyone downstairs was in the recreation room listening.

It wasn't as cold as I thought it would be outside. In fact, when I began high-stepping through the deep snow, I started to get a little hot. I waved at Taw up in his window and hoped that he'd be able to keep track of me as I got closer to the buck.

My plan was to move at a regular pace until I got about 150 yards from the buck. As I made my way around the lake, I performed little experiments while I plowed through the deep snow. It was much more difficult than tracking in Kenya, because I had to lift my foot two feet in the air every time I took a step.

Before I began my true stalk, I stopped and caught my breath. The buck was on the other side of a large tree. If I moved slowly and kept the tree between me and the buck, there was a good chance of getting at least as close as the tree before the buck sensed me.

I started. One slow step at a time, like a blue heron walking in shallow water. At first my legs cramped, but I ignored the pain and eventually it went away. I got into the rhythm of the stalk—a zone where nothing mattered but getting to the buck undetected.

As I drew closer, I concentrated on the buck's ears. They were constantly moving, like twin radar dishes monitoring the snow-covered landscape for incoming threats. The nearer I got, the slower I moved. When the buck looked my way, I stopped in midstep, holding that position until he looked away and started eating again.

When I reached the tree, I stood behind the trunk. I was so close I could hear him pulling the brittle leaves off the branches. He wasn't more than six or seven feet away from me. I rested, then very, very slowly moved out from behind the tree. The buck stopped eating and looked directly at me, with his ears pricked forward. His nostrils flared, and I could see his breath. He didn't know what I was, or how I had gotten there.

"Trick or treat," I whispered and pulled the pillowcase off my head. The buck snorted and wheeled around on his hind legs. He bounded away with the underside of his tail sticking straight up in the air like a white flag.

I should have felt guilty for disturbing his meager winter meal, but instead I was ecstatic. I jumped up and waved the pillowcase in the air, hoping that Taw had seen the whole show. Knowing him, he probably dozed off halfway through, but I didn't care. As Taw predicted, the stalk had made me forget my problems for the first time since Doc had left for Brazil.

I walked back to the Home feeling great. It was nearly dark by the time I got there. Before going inside, I slipped off my wet running shoes and Peter's pants. I ran up the stairs to Taw's room to find out how much he had seen of the stalk. There were about thirty people crammed into his room and more people spilling out into the hallway.

"I couldn't see," Mrs. Mapes complained.

"We need more of them telescopes," Mr. Clausen said.

As I pushed my way into the room, people patted me on the back and congratulated me. Taw was sitting on the bed, smiling. In fact, everyone was smiling and laughing. It was as if the depression of the last week had been miraculously taken away.

"I invited a couple of friends up," Taw said.

"How much of it did you see?"

"We took turns," he said. "They let me look when you stepped out from behind that tree."

Marcy, the duty nurse, pushed her way through the crowd to Taw's bed. "I knocked on your door, Jake, and you weren't there. Then I came down here and discovered what you were up to." She reached into her pocket and pulled out a folded piece of paper. "This fax from your father came while you were out back."

I took the piece of paper. I didn't want to read it in front of the others. I excused myself and went down to the window seat and turned the light on.

Dear Jake,

Sorry I haven't written or called. It's been crazy down here, and I thought I would be coming back up there anyday, so I didn't get in touch. It looks like this is going to take longer than I thought.

There's an airline ticket waiting for you at Kennedy International Airport. The flight leaves on March 21 and returns on March 30. Just go to the Pan Am counter with your passport—you're on Flight 636 to Brasília. You'll have to spend the night in Brasília and catch the afternoon flight to Manaus. You can stay at one of the hotels near the Brasília airport.

The only thing you need to do before you leave is to overnight your passport to the Brazilian embassy for a visa. I've contacted them and they'll stamp it and get it back to you before you take off. I'm sure Peter can give you a hand with this.

We're looking forward to your visit....

Love, Dad

Visit? The dates coincided with my spring vacation. It didn't sound as if Doc was coming home anytime soon. And it was clear that he didn't want me to stay down there with him.

Taw came down the stairs and joined me on the seat. I was surprised to see him on the stairs without a nurse, but I didn't say anything about it. Instead, I showed him the fax.

"We'll miss you," he said.

"I'll only be gone a week."

"When do you leave?" he asked.

"Next Saturday."

He looked at the lamp. "Is this working out for you?"

I stared at him. "Did you put this light here, Taw?"

He nodded.

"I thought Peter put it up for me. How did you . . ."

"Shhhh." He held his finger to his lips. "I'm not supposed to use the stairs without a nurse."

CHAPTER 3

The next five days moved like a glacier. . . .

On Friday I sat in my classes glancing at the clock every ten minutes, imagining where I would be at that time on the next day. After school, Peter picked me up and drove me to the Home. The Press Conference that evening was packed. The great buck adventure had renewed everyone's interest in the youngest inmate. I didn't have much to say about the day, but it didn't matter. What they wanted to hear was the story about how I had learned to stalk animals—for the fifth time that week.

They had a little celebration for me at dinner. Mrs. Clausen made a cake and decorated it with a beautiful jaguar. When we finished, Taw stood up to say something. Everyone got quiet. He looked confused, as if he had forgotten why he was on his feet.

Mrs. Mapes came to his rescue. "What Taw wanted to say,

or suggest, is that you stay in touch with us while you're down there, Jake."

"Dispatches!" Mr. Blondell said. "You know, like corre-spondents sent back to the States during the Vietnam War. Reports about what's going on. When our son was in Vietnam, my wife and I were totally dependent on dis-patches. Without 'em we would have been lost."

"I'm only going to be gone for a week," I said. "And I don't even know if there's a phone where my father's staying."

"There must be a fax machine down there," Mrs. Mapes insisted. "That's how your dad got in touch with you." She handed me a slip of paper with the Home's fax number scrawled on it.

"I'll try," I said. But I doubted Doc had a fax machine handy.

I went up to my room early, telling everyone that I needed to get ready for the trip. It took me less than three minutes to pack. When I finished, I lay down on my bed and thought about Doc. I played with the amulet I always wore around my neck. It was made out of a round, flat stone, about the size of a quarter. There was a hole in the middle and surrounding the hole was an intricately carved snake swallowing its tail. It had belonged to Taw when he was young. He gave it to my father and my father gave it to my mom when they got married. I'd worn it ever since my mom died.

I knew Doc wouldn't have sent for me if he were coming back anytime soon. I tried to come up with various schemes to convince him that I should stay down there, but I knew it was hopeless.

* * *

The next morning I was up before sunrise. Peter was coming to the Home at six to take me to Kennedy Airport. My plane didn't leave until eleven and it was only about a two-hour drive, but I wanted to make a stop on the way.

I took my bag downstairs and put it by the front door, then went into the kitchen to see if I could get something to eat. Peter got there about ten of six and joined me in the kitchen for some scrambled eggs and toast.

"Where's Taw?" he asked.

"Asleep," I said. "I thought about waking him and saying good-bye, but I didn't want to bug him."

Peter smiled. "When I talked to him yesterday, he said he was driving down with us to see you off. On the way back he's going to give me a tour of all the buildings he put together in the city."

"I'm sure he meant well," I told him. "But he probably forgot. He was supposed to give a speech last night and he forgot what he was going to say. He seems to be drifting more these days."

"He's sharper than you think. You better go up and check. He'd be pretty unhappy if we left him behind."

I went up to Taw's room and quietly opened the door. He was sitting in front of the window. As usual, he didn't turn around and he didn't say anything. I knew that when the weather got better, he would spend his days sitting by the stream, just watching it go by. He loved it out there.

I stood for a moment, looking at his long gray hair hanging loose over the back of the chair—the fact that it was unbraided meant that he had just washed it. Maybe he was planning on going with us.

"Good morning, Taw."

"My hair needs braiding," he said, without turning around. I couldn't tell if he was in a cloud or not. As far as I knew, he thought I was one of the aides or nurses.

When I was little, my mom showed me how to braid using Taw's hair. I got the brush, comb, and ties from the top of the dresser. I stood behind him and started combing his hair.

"How's your father?" he asked.

"I don't know. I haven't seen him for a while."

Taw nodded. I made a part down the middle of his head and started braiding.

"Not too tight," he said. "It gives me a headache if it's tight."

"Okay." I finished the first braid and wrapped a rubber band around the end. "I'm going to be gone for a week."

"Peter told me," Taw said. "I'm going to the city with you."

"I'm going to Brazil. Dad's setting up a jaguar preserve."

"I saw a jaguar once."

Probably at the zoo, I thought.

"It was in Arizona on the reservation. I was eight or nine at the time. A hunter had shot it."

I had read that jaguars used to cross the Mexican border

and wander into Arizona. But that was a long time ago, when northern Mexico still had a few jaguars.

"It was in the back of a pickup. The hunter came to the reservation to buy supplies at the store. He had his picture taken with the cat. I touched the jaguar. Its fur was beautiful and soft, but its body was cold and stiff. I thought about how wonderful it would be to see a jaguar alive in the mountains. But I never saw one. No one did."

"That's a great story, Taw."

He nodded.

"I'll miss you," I said.

"Brazil is hot," he said.

"We better go, Taw. Peter's waiting for us."

* * *

When we got to Brooklyn, Peter stopped at a florist shop so I could buy a bouquet of flowers. From there we made our way to the cemetery, stopping at the entrance to get a map so we could find my mom among the thousands of tombstones. The blanket of snow made everything look the same. It took us two complete passes before we found the right spot.

Peter parked his car as close to the site as he could and said he would wait. It was my third visit to my mom's grave.

"I'm going with you," Taw said.

"The snow's pretty deep, Taw."

Instead of responding, Taw got out of the car.

"There's nothing the matter with his legs," Peter said.

Peter was right. Taw had no problem slogging through the snow. When we got to the top of the small rise where my mom's grave was, he wasn't even out of breath. I decided that when I got back, we would go walking whenever we could. It would be good for both of us.

"There it is," I said.

I brushed the snow off the stone. When I saw my mom's name carved in the marble, the familiar lump lodged in my throat and I felt warm tears rolling down my cold cheeks. I split the flowers into two bunches and handed half to Taw. I planted my flowers in the snow. Taw smelled the flowers he was holding, then looked up at the sky.

"Mom's buried here."

"I know, Jake." Taw put his flowers next to mine. "I was thinking. When you come back, maybe we could go to Arizona. I'd like to see the reservation again. I'd like to go back home."

I stared at him. This was the most lucid he had been since I returned from Kenya.

"That would be great. I'd love to go there with you."

"I'll miss you," he said. "Try to stay in touch. It will mean a lot to everyone."

"I'll only be down there for a week," I said.

Taw smiled and put his hand on my shoulder.

When we reached the car, I looked back at my mom's grave. Her flowers were the only color on the snow-covered hillside.

Manaus

CHAPTER 4

I landed in Brasília late Saturday evening. In the crowded terminal, sweaty people pushed and shouted in Portuguese, which I didn't understand a word of.

Peter had booked a room for me at a hotel right next to the airport. I checked in, went up to my room, turned the television on, and fell asleep watching an episode of *Star Trek* in Portuguese.

The next morning I ate breakfast, then went back to the airport and waited for my flight, which left at noon.

When I stepped off the airplane in Manaus, the blast of heat nearly knocked me over. Breathing the air was like inhaling steam. By the time I walked the short distance to the terminal building, I was drenched in sweat.

A mass of people waited inside, holding up crudely drawn signs with last names printed on them. I tried to pick my father out of the crowd, but I didn't see him. I was just about ready to break through the throng and look for him in another part of the airport when I saw a sign that said LANSA. It was held by a man I had never seen before. He was tall, very thin, and completely bald. He wore wraparound sunglasses, a purple tank top, shorts, and sandals, and carried an old crumpled hat in his hand. On his left shoulder was a tattoo of a large blue butterfly. I read the sign again to make sure, then walked over to him, slowly.

"Are you Jake?" he shouted above the noise.

I nodded.

"Follow me." He turned around and started to wind his way through the crowd.

I wasn't sure if I should follow him or not. I turned around and looked for my father again. No luck. When I turned back, the skeleton with glasses was waving impatiently for me to come with him. I followed at a safe distance behind.

When we got outside the terminal, he stopped and put on his old battered hat, which looked as if he had done a headstand in a chicken coop while he was wearing it.

"My name's Buzz Lindbergh," he said, sticking out a hand embedded with years of black grease as permanent as the tattoo on his shoulder. I shook it, then asked him where my father was.

"He couldn't make it. He and Bill had to go downriver and pick up the boat. I expect they'll be back sometime tomorrow."

Hearing Bill's name made me feel a little better. Buzz was obviously connected with the jaguar preserve in some way.

"The limo is over here."

He saw my hesitancy and smiled. "I don't blame you for being a little leery. I don't think I would go with me if I didn't know me! Let's see how I can fix this up. . . ." He thought a minute, then continued. "Bill Brewster and your father have been friends since they were at college together. Your grandfather is named Tawapu—he's a Hopi Indian. He lives in a retirement home in Poughkeepsie, New York. You've been staying there since Doc came down here. You were with your father in Kenya last year. When you got back, you started taking flying lessons. Your . . ."

"Okay," I interrupted. "I'm convinced."

"Good. It's time to go to the warehouse."

"Warehouse?"

"You'll see."

He led me over to an old truck that didn't have a square inch of good metal on it. It was so rusty that the roof over the cab had corroded away, making a permanent sunroof.

"This is the limo?"

"Yep."

There were two boys sitting in what was left of the bed. Buzz pulled a couple of loose bills out of his pocket and handed one to each boy. They grabbed them and ran away.

Jaguar

"Manaus rule number one," Buzz said. "Never leave anything you want to see again without a guard. Two guards, if you can afford them. It's part of the economy down here. Kind of like insurance up in the States. Hop in."

Hopping in was easy. There was no door on the passenger side. I climbed up and sat down. Something sharp poked me. I jumped up and heard my pants tear.

"Sorry about that," Buzz said. "I should have warned you." He grabbed a clipboard off the dash and put it over the exposed spring. I sat back down, hoping I wouldn't get tetanus from the wound in my butt.

Buzz stomped on the gas pedal a few times, as if he were trying to squash a scorpion. "No key," he explained, reaching under the dash and sparking two wires together. The engine coughed, sputtered, then blew out a plume of thick black smoke. "No muffler, either!" he shouted above the racket. We lurched forward and passed a cheerful sign that said WELCOME TO MANAUS!—in several languages.

There was no point in trying to talk to Buzz above the noise. So I held on and tried to remember some of the things I had read about Manaus while I was at the Home.

Manaus is six hundred miles inland from the east coast of Brazil. It sits on the shores of the Rio Negro, close to where the Rio Solimões and Rio Negro join to form the Amazon River. The city was established by Portuguese colonists in the 1600s and was named after a tribe of Indians that lived in the region.

Jaguar

In 1839 Charles Goodyear discovered a way to turn the sap from rubber trees into rubber tires. This discovery turned Manaus into a thriving city in the middle of the jungle. The plantation owners, rubber traders, and bankers got rich from rubber exports and built palaces with their newfound wealth. They also built a beautiful opera house in the center of the city, and stars from all over the world traveled up the Amazon to perform there. It was said that some of the people in Manaus were so rich they sent their dirty clothes to Europe to be laundered.

This prosperity didn't last long. The British came in and managed to smuggle rubber-tree seedlings back to England. They cultivated the trees, then transported thousands of them to Ceylon and Malaysia and set up plantations of their own. The competition caused the rubber market to crash in Manaus, and people stopped sending their laundry to Europe. Manaus had been struggling ever since.

The first thing that surprised me about Manaus was the terrible air pollution. A visible haze of wood smoke and diesel fumes hung like fog in the humid air. My eyes watered as Buzz drove the gauntlet through the heavy traffic.

The streets of the city were packed with cars and motorcycles. The sidewalks were filled with people moving sluggishly through the late afternoon heat.

Buzz drove down to the waterfront, and we passed a huge marketplace. Gangs of children wearing ragged

T-shirts and shorts ran next to the truck with their hands out, begging for money. Dozens of black vultures perched on roofs and trees surrounding the market, waiting for food to drop on the ground.

We stopped at a chain-link gate, and Buzz jumped out and opened it. He drove through and stopped again.

"I'll get it," I told him, and closed the gate behind us.

He drove down a gravel road and stopped in front of a large warehouse, which had more rust on it than the truck he was driving.

"Home sweet home," he said.

A man in filthy clothes sat in a chair, leaning against the warehouse. He had an old side-by-side shotgun cradled in his arms. Buzz said something to him in Portuguese and gave him some money. The man glanced at me through bloodshot, unfriendly eyes, then walked away in the direction we had come.

"Another guard?"

Buzz nodded and slid open a wide, drive-through door. I stepped inside and staggered backward. The warehouse was hot enough to cook a pizza in, and it smelled like rotting fruit.

"I'll open the other side and we'll get a breeze going." Buzz disappeared into the dark interior, and a moment later a crack of broadening light appeared at the far end.

I walked further into the warehouse but stopped when something *plopped* on my head. I reached up to wipe it away, and my hand was smeared with smelly slime. "What the . . ."

"Can't you hear them?"

"Hear what?"

"The bats," Buzz shouted. "They're echolocating off the metal walls."

I listened and heard high-pitched *pinging* sounds echoing through the warehouse. The floor was covered with sticky bat guano. I glanced up, but it was too dark to see any bats in the rafters.

"I should have warned you," Buzz said. "You need to wear a hat in here." He opened a door along one of the walls and flipped a light on. "It's safe in our office."

On the way over, I got hit twice more.

"Wipe your feet before you come in." Buzz pointed to a mat outside the door.

"How many bats are up there?"

"You tell me."

Buzz turned a flashlight on and shone it at the ceiling. I looked up and my mouth fell open. I closed it quickly so something unpleasant wouldn't fall in. Every inch of the roof was covered with squirming little bats. There had to be thousands of them.

"Fruit bats," Buzz said. "We got a heck of a deal on the place."

"I bet."

"Come on in."

I stepped inside. Air-conditioning! It was probably seventy-five degrees in there, but it felt like the arctic compared to the warehouse.

"All the comforts of home," Buzz said.

I looked around. Along one wall were two sets of bunk beds. On the opposite wall there was a small kitchen, with a sink, refrigerator, and stove.

"We do most of our work in here."

"Good idea."

"I'll show you the rest of the place."

He opened a door near the sink and led me down a short hallway to a room about the same size. Satellite photos and maps of the Amazon Basin covered one of the walls. There were several workbenches with tools and radio telemetry gear to track animals. Buzz opened another door and showed me the bathroom.

"You might want to get cleaned up and change your pants."

I'd forgotten all about the tear in my pants. I felt back there and found that the rip was bigger than I thought.

"Yeah," I said. "Good idea."

I was irritated that Doc hadn't met me at the airport. He should have at least called and prepared me for Buzz. The only excuse I could think of was that there wasn't a phone nearby, or perhaps he had left town right after he sent me the fax at the Home.

* * *

I felt somewhat better after taking a shower and changing my clothes. I stopped in the map room and took a closer look at the gear and the maps. One of the maps had a large area marked in red. I assumed this was the jaguar preserve. It was a long way from Manaus. Buzz had said Doc and Bill were bringing a boat upriver. This probably meant they hadn't been to the preserve yet, which meant that Doc had been in Manaus for the past seven weeks, which meant that he could have called me if he had wanted to.

I walked into the bunk room to ask Buzz what was going on, but he wasn't there. I did find a phone and fax machine, though. I picked up the receiver. There was a dial tone. Doc could have easily called or faxed me. I started to get irritated again.

There was a window in the door leading to the ware-house. I cupped my hands around my eyes and looked out. It was too dark to see anything clearly. All I could see were piles covered with plastic tarps to protect them from the rain of bat guano.

I waited for about ten minutes, then decided to find Buzz. Before I left, I put on my baseball cap. The smell in the warehouse wasn't as sour as before, and the tempera-ture had dropped by at least ten degrees.

I walked out the back door. About fifty feet away there was a boat dock sticking out into the Rio Negro. The river had to be half a mile across at this point. The murky gray water flowed slowly. On the other side was a line of green tropical vegetation. I walked around to the front of the warehouse. No sign of Buzz, and the truck was gone. I walked back around to the dock, then went inside to escape the heat.

I found some paper and wrote a dispatch to the Home. There wasn't much to say aside from the fact that I had arrived safely, Manaus was filthy, Doc and Bill were bringing a boat upriver, and the heat was unbelievable. When I finished, I slipped the sheet into the machine and dialed the Home's fax number. The dispatch was on its way. Why hadn't Doc done the same for me?

An hour later I heard the truck pull up, and a few moments later Buzz came in with both arms full of groceries. I got off the bunk and gave him a hand.

"Dinner," he said. "But before we eat, you need to come outside." He looked at his watch. "We only have a couple of minutes. Don't forget your hat."

I followed Buzz outside and down to the dock. The sun was setting, and it had started to cool down some. Buzz kept glancing at his watch, then at the warehouse.

"What are we doing?"

"Five seconds."

"What do you mean, five—"

"Now!"

Thousands of bats poured out through the warehouse door. The noisy black cloud flew right over us and headed across the Rio Negro. It took at least three minutes for the warehouse to empty.

"There will be a few stragglers," Buzz said. "But that about does it. They'll be back early tomorrow morning. You don't want to be in the warehouse when they leave or come back to roost. Your dad says they go out every night to fill up on fruit. Someday I'm going to design an ultralight modeled like a bat."

"What's an ultralight?"

"I'll show you tomorrow. Let's go in and fix some grub."

Buzz was a pretty good cook, and for someone as thin as he was, he had a huge appetite. When we finished eating, I asked him if Bill and my father had been upriver to the place marked on the map.

"Not yet," he said.

"What's their plan?"

"You'll have to ask them. They should be back tomorrow sometime."

It was clear he wasn't going to tell me anything about what was going on. I helped him clean up the mess in the kitchen. When we finished, Buzz got into his bunk.

"We need to get up before the bats flap back to their roost tomorrow morning," he said. "You better get some sleep."

A few minutes later he was snoring. I wondered if that's where he got the nickname Buzz.

CHAPTER 5

I slept pretty well, considering the rattling air-conditioner and my roommate's snoring. Buzz was out of bed half an hour before I was, making coffee and fixing breakfast.

"We better get moving," he said from the kitchen, which was ten feet from my bunk.

I sat up. "What are we doing?"

"I need a hand getting the Morpho out of the warehouse before the bats come back."

"What's a Morpho?"

"It's a beautiful butterfly," Buzz pointed at the tattoo on his shoulder. "As soon as you eat, we'll go out and take a look."

I didn't know why he needed my help with a butterfly or why it was in the warehouse. Maybe he was the project's bug expert. He sort of looked like a praying mantis. I got dressed and ate. When I finished, I followed Buzz out into the dim warehouse. We wove our way through the tarp-covered piles.

"What is all this stuff?"

"Supplies for the expedition," Buzz explained. "If Doc and Bill come back with a serviceable boat, we're in business."

If the truck was their idea of "serviceable," I had some doubts about them making it upriver very far. Doc usually had much better equipment than I had seen so far.

Buzz stopped next to an unusually large tarp. "Grab hold of the corner. I'll get the other side and we'll peel it back together. I don't want to get any bat crap on the Morpho."

I took ahold of the tarp and we rolled it back. Underneath was an airplane. Or what looked like an airplane.

The wings were made out of electric-blue fabric. In the front was a small engine with a single propeller. Just behind and below the engine was a single seat that was no more than eight inches off the ground.

"The Morpho's an airplane?"

"Well, your dad calls it a go-cart with wings. Bill calls it a kite with an engine. They're wrong. It's called an ultralight. I named it after the most beautiful butterfly in Brazil. Unfortunately, you don't see many morpho butterflies around Manaus, because the children catch them and sell their wings to tourists."

"How does it work?"

"Like an airplane! I designed it myself, and I'm rather proud of it. It carries a single pilot and has a range of about a hundred miles. It has a five-gallon gas tank and a cruising speed of fifty-five knots. It weighs 232 pounds when the gas tank is full. The aluminum frame is covered with Dacron. The reason I leave it inside is to keep it out of the sunlight. Too much sun will turn the fabric into blue toilet paper. I'd find myself trying to keep an aluminum ladder airborne."

"What are you using it for?"

"We're going to track the jaguars with it. On the ground we'll be lucky to pick up the radio collar signal from a few miles away. I've been running some tracking experiments in the Morpho, and I've picked up radio signals from as far as fifteen miles away. And of course, tracking by air is more accurate."

I had helped Doc track elephants, and I was familiar with radio tracking techniques. But when we were in Kenya, we had a real airplane, not some cloth-covered toy.

"So you're a field biologist?"

"Nope. I'm a pilot and an ultralight designer. I volunteered for the expedition. I've always wanted to see how an ultralight performed down in the tropics. Give me a hand. We've got to get it out of here before the bats come back."

I took hold of one wing, and Buzz grabbed the other. We pulled the ultralight through the door. It looked even more flimsy in the daylight. It was nothing like the airplane I was taking lessons in back in Poughkeepsie.

"Go ahead and sit in the seat if you want to," Buzz said.

I climbed in—or, more accurately, I crawled in. There was a control stick and a pair of foot pedals, but they looked like something you'd see in a video game arcade. Buzz had designed the cockpit to fit his long legs, and I could barely reach the floor pedals.

The control panel had several instruments: a variometer, which keeps track of vertical airspeed; an altimeter, so you know how high you are; an airspeed indicator; compass; tachometer; and a temperature gauge.

"What's this?" I asked, pointing to an instrument I hadn't seen before.

"That's a global positioning system, or GPS."

"What does it do?"

"It tells you where you're at. When you hit the button, it sends out a signal that bounces off the nearest satellite. It gives your exact longitude and latitude. Once you know that, you can put in the longitude and latitude of your destination and it will plot a course to get you there. I won't be using the GPS to find my way home, though, because I won't be that far away from the base camp. I'll use it to pinpoint the jaguar's location. I'll show you the tracking antennas."

I climbed back out, and he pointed to the end of one of the wings.

"I built antennas right into the wing struts here and on the other side. Coaxial cable runs right down this tube. I can attach my receiver to the panel and listen to the jaguar's signal like I'm listening to a compact disc. When I'm right over the top of the jaguar, I'll hit the GPS button and it'll give me the cat's longitude and latitude.

Takes all the guesswork out of it."

Buzz was very excited about this feature, and I'm sure Doc and Bill were, too. It would make tracking a lot easier.

"I also have a two-way radio, so I can stay in touch with the base camp." He went into the warehouse and came back out carrying a helmet. "Got this from the air force. Go ahead and try it on."

Because of the heat, I didn't really want to, but I slipped it on anyway because I thought Buzz would be disappointed if I didn't. I even flipped the tinted visor down for the full effect.

"Everything hooks up to the helmet," he said. "And I have a switch that toggles between the two-way radio and the telemetry receiver, so I can listen to one or the other."

I took the helmet off and looked at the landing gear more closely. It consisted of two small rubber tires under the fuselage and an even smaller tire underneath the tail.

"I'll replace the landing gear with pontoons when we get where we're going. The only reason I have the wheels on now is that it's easier to pull it out of the warehouse." Buzz glanced at his watch, then looked across the river. "Help me get the Morpho out of the way. Our furry friends will be returning any minute."

We pulled the Morpho further away from the warehouse. A few minutes later the bats started to fly in from across the river. It wasn't as dramatic as when they had left, because they were more spread out. But it was still impressive.

"Bill and your dad insisted that we work around the bats rather than get them out of there."

This didn't surprise me. Doc always thought of the animals first, before his own convenience or comfort.

"I'm going to take the Morpho up for a little spin and run some tests. I could use your help, if you have the time."

What a joke, I thought. "No problem."

"In the map room is a two-way radio. I want to see how far away I can get and still stay in touch."

Buzz squirmed his long body into the cockpit, put on his seat belt, then slipped the helmet over his head. He connected the helmet to the radio outlet, held his thumb up, then started the engine. He swung the Morpho around, pulled the throttle out to full power, and started toward the Rio Negro. It looked as if he was going to run right into the river, but just as he reached the shore, he pulled back on the stick and the Morpho was airborne.

I watched him fly around for a few minutes. The Morpho *did* look like a flying go-cart. Buzz circled over the river a few times as he gained altitude.

I headed back into the warehouse. They had enough supplies in there to last them for months. Doc wasn't just down here to help Bill "get started." I should have realized there was no way he would be satisfied living in Poughkeepsie, New York. He may have come down here with the thought of helping Bill, but he was part of the expedition now. Where did that leave me?

I went into the map room, found the two-way radio, and switched it on.

"Buzz to base . . ." the speaker crackled.

I keyed the microphone. "Base to Buzz."

"How am I coming in? Over."

"Loud and clear. Over."

"Roger. I'll do periodic radio checks during the next hour. Over."

"Roger."

"Out."

I spent the next hour looking through the stuff in the map room and telling Buzz that he sounded just fine.

"I'm heading back in," Buzz announced over the radio. "And we're going to have visitors soon. Your old man is about forty-five minutes out."

"Great!" I said. "I mean . . . roger."

I went outside to watch Buzz bring the Morpho in for a landing. He came in low over the water, flying very slowly. When he got over shore, he pulled the nose up slightly and the Morpho touched down like a butterfly landing on a flower.

Buzz was drenched in sweat. "Hot up there in the wild blue," he said.

"So you saw Doc?"

"Yep. He should be here anytime."

I helped him put the Morpho back in the warehouse and cover it with a tarp. He went into the bunk house to take a shower, and I went out to the dock to wait for Bill and my father.

About half an hour later, an old boat came chugging up to the dock. Bill Brewster stood on the bow, waving. He was much stockier than Doc and had kept his long black beard, despite the heat. Doc was in the wheelhouse steering the boat. When they were close enough, Bill threw me a rope, and I tied it to one of the cleats. My father shut the engine off and jumped down to the dock. He was wearing his denim uniform and had his hair pulled back in a pony-tail. He came over and gave me a hug.

"Sorry I wasn't at the airport," he said. "Duty called." He made a gesture toward the boat.

Bill joined us and clapped me on the back. "Hot enough for you, Jake?"

"Too hot!" I said, smiling. The smile was involuntary. I wanted to be somber and surly, so Doc would know I wasn't happy about the way he had treated me. But it was just too good to see him.

"You look good, Jake!" Doc said.

"A little pale," Bill added.

"It's been snowing in Poughkeepsie."

"I wouldn't mind lying down in a snowbank for a month," Bill said.

Doc looked tired, but he was in very good spirits. I hadn't seen him this happy in years. He was either very pleased to see me, or was just happy to be back in the field, or both.

"You call this a boat?" Buzz came up behind us.

"It's the best we could do," Bill said.

"Who's the captain?"

"We flipped a coin," Bill said. "I lost."

"Or maybe you won," Doc said.

"Good point! There are a few minor mechanical problems," Bill admitted. "But nothing you can't fix, Buzz."

"I'd like to remind you that I'm an aeronautical engineer. Not a grease monkey."

Bill laughed. "I stand corrected. But we still need you to fix this pile of junk."

"Then you can give me a hand with the tools."

"I'll give you a hand, too," Doc offered.

"Forget it, Doc," Buzz said. "No offense, but you're not exactly a mechanical genius. Bill and I can handle this ourselves. Anyway, you need to pick up Flanna."

Doc acted as if his feelings were hurt, but he knew as well as they did that he was a complete klutz when it came to anything mechanical. Bill and Buzz headed toward the warehouse to get the tools.

"Who's Flanna?"

"Flanna Brenna. She's our botanist. And she's probably a wee bit upset. I was supposed to pick her up yesterday. I think you'll like her."

"What's going on, Doc?"

"I'll tell you all about it on the way to pick up Flanna."

* * *

The truck was so loud we could barely hear each other. Doc drove us out of Manaus and up into the hills. The roads, if you could call them that, were terrible. The vegetation got thicker and greener the farther away from the city we got.

"Most of this is secondary growth," Doc shouted above the racket. "You don't see primary rain forest until you get way up the Amazon. And even then you have to hike in a couple of miles from the river, because everything along the shore has been cut at one time or another."

"Why do they cut it?"

"Firewood, lumber, settlements, oil, gold . . . You name it! They're gobbling up the rain forest big time."

We were in the truck for at least two hours before Doc finally came to a stop, at what looked like a dead-end road. We got out and looked around. There was no one waiting for us there.

"This is bad," he said. "Flanna must have gotten tired of waiting, so she went back into the forest. We'll have to go find her. Want to go for a hike?"

"Sure." I went back to the truck and drank some water from the jug had we had brought with us. Doc did the same.

"The trail's over here." He pushed through a stand of thick green vegetation. "It will open up when we get under the canopy."

It took us awhile to get through the tangle of plants. Doc went first. He didn't seem to be following any kind of trail that I could see, but I was confident that he knew what he was doing. He might get confused driving a car or walking in a city, but put him in the middle of nowhere and he could navigate like an animal that had lived there its whole life.

When we finally broke through the ground cover, we stopped and looked up. We were surrounded by huge trees. Their massive trunks were wrapped with thick vines. The lowest branches were at least a hundred feet above us. Shafts of sunlight battled their way through the canopy to the ground, which was much more open than I had thought it would be. The forest was filled with sounds of animals I couldn't see.

"It's like a cathedral," I whispered.

"That's a good description. This is the only untouched rain forest for a hundred miles. Relatively untouched—people are beginning to encroach on the outer edges. It's hard to keep them out."

We started walking again and continued until we came to a narrow stream. Doc sat down on a rotting log covered with a thick cushion of moss. I sat next to him.

"I guess I better tell you what's going on," he said.

I nodded. He unlaced his boots, peeled his socks off, and let his feet dangle in the water.

"I'm not exactly sure where to begin."

"Why don't you start by telling me about the jaguar project?" I suggested, trying to make this as easy as possible for him.

"It's Bill's project, not mine. I just came down here to help him get it started. It's a little more involved than that now."

Translated, he was much happier down here than he was in Poughkeepsie and he didn't want to go back.

"Bill has been trying to put together a jaguar preserve for over twenty years. And it looks like he's about ready to pull it off. Just a couple more hurdles."

"Such as?"

"It boils down to this. There's a rich industrialist from the States who's getting a million acres from the Brazilian government in payment for a debt they owe him. His name's Woolcott."

I'd heard the name before. He owned an oil company or something in the States.

"Anyway, Woolcott loves jaguars almost as much as he loves money. The government gave him his choice of a million-acre tract of land. He has a dozen to choose from and two months to decide which one he wants—and, more important, what he wants to do with the land. He can either set up a preserve and write off the debt, or he can suck out every last resource in the million acres and leave behind a garbage dump. Of course his advisers are telling him to go for the garbage-dump idea. He'll get all his money back and probably a lot more.

"But Woolcott's getting older and he doesn't need any more money. This is where Bill comes in. Bill pitched him the jaguar preserve idea. Woolcott liked it. In fact, he liked it so well that he told Bill to pick one of the tracts of land right on the spot. Bill did."

"So what's the problem?"

"Bill picked the area without knowing if it would support jaguars. And the deal is that he has to show reasonable progress within two months or Woolcott will pick one of the other sites and suck it dry."

"How does he define 'reasonable progress'?"

"Woolcott's been kind of vague about that. We know he wants radio-collared jaguars on the ground and enough tracking data to prove that the spot is a viable location for the preserve. In other words, the preserve has to be up and running within two months."

I thought about the terrible warehouse they were stuck in, the old truck they drove, and the decrepit boat they hoped would get them up the Amazon.

"Who's paying for all this?"

"Bill is. Flanna and I have put money in, too. We're on a pretty tight budget."

"Why doesn't Woolcott pay for it? He could probably fund the whole expedition with the change in his pocket."

"He says he's gone as far as his advisers will let him. If we show progress, he'll not only donate the land but set up an endowment fund that will pay for operating the preserve."

"So this is sort of a test or something?"

"That's one way of looking at it. Woolcott is pretty eccentric and impulsive."

Just like you, I thought. "Where does this leave me?"

Doc looked away. Not good. I felt the guillotine sliding down the greased grooves toward my neck.

"I'm not exactly sure," he said. "I mean, I've thought a lot about it. That's why I wanted you to come down here. I wanted to talk to you face-to-face."

We might as well get right to it, I thought. I took a deep breath. "I think I should stay down here with you," I said.

"I know." No eye contact. This was not going the way I wanted it to go. "But this isn't the best place for you to be right now. We don't know exactly what we're facing up-river, and it could be dangerous."

"I walked halfway across Kenya looking for you! I think I've proven I can take care of myself."

"You could have been killed in Kenya! I have enough on my mind without worrying about your safety. To say nothing of the fact that you have school."

I knew this excuse was going to come up. "Doc, I can't live in a retirement home until I go to college. It won't work."

"I know, I know. . . . I've been checking into some things. If you can just hang in there until the end of the school year, there's a summer camp in Colorado that—"

"What are you talking about?" I shouted, losing my cool completely. "I don't want to go to a summer camp. I want to be with you! How long are you staying down here?"

"I'm here for the duration," Doc said quietly.

"What's that mean?"

"I don't know."

"What happens in the fall after this so-called summer camp?"

"There are some good boarding schools. . . ."

I got up from the log and walked away. It was either that or start crying in front of him. How could he do this to me without even asking? What about what I wanted? I heard Doc call, but I kept walking. I'd figured I would lose the first round, but I thought I'd at least be able to spend the summer down here with him. He was talking about us being separated for a year or two! He was no longer help-ing an old friend out. This was as much his project as it was Bill's now.

Doc's voice got further and further away. He probably wished now that he hadn't taken his boots and socks off. Having to put them back on had given me a big head start. I found what looked like a trail and followed it. I had no idea where I was going, and I didn't really care.

Without any warning, something appeared right in front of me. Something large. I couldn't see clearly because my eyes were blurred with tears. I staggered backward, fell on my butt, turned over, and started crawling as fast as I could, back the way I had come. It had to be some kind of animal. Doc would be sorry now!

"I'm sorry. . . . I'm sorry. . . . I thought you were Bob."

I stopped crawling. Wild animals don't usually apologize before they attack you. Bob? It was a woman's voice. I turned around and looked. She had curly red hair sticking out from a yellow hard hat and was hurriedly undoing a climbing harness around her waist. Attached to the harness was a rope that was tied off up in the canopy somewhere. When she got untangled, she ran over to me.

"I'm so sorry. . . ."

I stood up and brushed myself off. "Who's Bob?"

"Aren't you Jake?"

I nodded.

"I was referring to your father."

My father, Dr. Robert Lansa, despised being called Bob. Everyone knew this. That's why he adopted the nickname Doc. When my mom was alive, he didn't even let her call him Bob.

I stared at the woman. She was about my height and had green eyes. She wore a pair of khaki shorts, a green sleeveless leotard, and a pair of heavy climbing boots. She had a slight but very athletic body. In other words, she was beautiful.

"I'm Flanna Brenna," she said.

"The botanist."

"Right."

I had a feeling that she was more than a botanist. I heard Doc running up the path behind me. He stopped when he got to us, slightly out of breath. Flanna smiled brightly when she saw him. He smiled back at her. She was definitely more than a botanist. I guess Doc forgot to tell me about this part of the expedition.

"I'm afraid I nearly scared your son half to death, Bob. I thought it was you. You look just alike from a hundred feet up."

"Jake, this is Dr. Flanna Brenna."

"We already introduced ourselves, *Bob.*"

CHAPTER 6

Flanna led us down the trail to her camp, which turned out to be 150 feet up in the canopy.

"I'll lower the gear down." She strapped her harness on, attached a rope hanging from a tree, and began her ascent, using some kind of clamping device that held her in place until she pulled herself up further. She made it look as easy as climbing a ladder, which I'm sure it wasn't.

I could tell that Doc wanted to explain the situation to me, but I was too mad even to look at him. I was convinced that Flanna was the main reason he didn't want me with him in Brazil. It had very little to do with how dangerous it was down here.

Flanna crawled around through the canopy like a monkey. Despite my feelings about her, I was pretty impressed with her abilities. She gathered her equipment and lowered it down to us one bunch at a time.

"Flanna has her doctorate in tropical ecology," Doc said.

"She's been down here for three years studying the medicinal uses of rain forest plants. She had a grant from a large pharmaceutical company in the States, but that ran out about three weeks ago. So she threw in with us."

I didn't say anything to him. Flanna must have come down here right after she got her doctorate. She was definitely under thirty, which would make her about fourteen or fifteen years younger than Doc. I had read about the medicinal uses of rain forest plants. Many of the lifesaving drugs we use originated from plants found in the tropical rain forest. Many scientists believe that the cure for almost every disease could be found in the rain forest. It was just a matter of finding the right plant before it was lost forever because of deforestation.

"Jake, I should have told—"

I interrupted him. "I don't want to talk about this right now."

"Okay," he said quietly.

"That's it!" Flanna yelled down to us. A few seconds later, she dropped from the canopy like a spider on the end of a silk thread. We each took some of the gear and headed out of the forest. I walked ahead so I wouldn't have to talk to either of them. I was angry and confused. I needed time to think—a lot of time. It was nearly dark when we got back to the truck. We put Flanna's stuff in the back and climbed into the cab. Flanna sat between me and Bob.

* * *

When we got back to the warehouse, we found Bill and

Buzz drinking beer and playing cards at the kitchen table.

"I see the crew is hard at work," Doc said.

"We need some parts for the engine, which we can't get until tomorrow," Bill said. "Pull up a chair, Doc."

"Not tonight."

"Flanna?"

"No thanks."

"That leaves you, Jake. You interested in joining our friendly little game?"

I was in no mood for cards, and watching them reminded me of my future with the inmates back at the Home. I shook my head.

"Flanna and I are going to walk into town and get something to eat," Doc said. "Anyone want to come?" He looked at me.

"I'm going to take a shower and go to bed," I said.

I found some clean clothes and went into the bathroom for a quick shower. When I came back, Bill and Buzz were still playing cards and barely noticed me. Flanna and Doc were gone. I walked outside and wandered down to the river.

It was a nice evening despite the humidity. Thick clouds had moved in, and lightning flashed on the other side of the river.

I thought of sending another dispatch to the home:

This afternoon my father told me he was sending me to summer camp. In the fall I'll be attending a boarding school. I had the pleasure of meeting his new girlfriend, Flanna Brenna. She's a knockout and young enough to be my sister. I hope things are well with all of you. Everything down here is absolutely perfect! Jake.

I tried to sort out my feelings. Doc and my mom had been divorced for a couple of years when she died. She remarried as soon as the divorce was final. The guy's name was Sam and he was a real jerk, but he and my mom got along pretty well. I put up with him for her sake.

Doc and my mom rarely got along. She loved living in New York City. Doc hated big cities—New York most of all. She was a professor and loved the university atmosphere. Doc thought university people were the most boring blowhards on earth. His idea of bliss was wandering around the middle of nowhere observing wild animals, or, as my mom used to say, "He's a man who needs to be out in the wilderness howling at the moon."

I didn't mind that Doc had a girlfriend. Flanna was obviously intelligent and independent, and could climb a rope better and faster than anyone else I had ever seen. What bothered me was the fact that he hadn't told me about her. After our experiences in Kenya, I thought he had become my partner. I thought that he had given up on being my parent. This is one reason he had insisted that I call him Doc, not Dad. I must have been mistaken.

Parents split up. Families split up. But partners stay together. Or so I thought. A partner should at least tell you when he finds a girlfriend. Doc was acting like a parent who didn't want to be a parent.

What was I acting like? I didn't want to think about this. I also didn't want to be in Manaus anymore. I couldn't stand the thought of five more days of Doc and Flanna having meaningful eye contact with each other. Five more days of knowing that I would be back in the Home in five more days.

Doc had the next few years of my life planned out for me. Three months of summer camp with other kids whose parents didn't want them around. Then off to boarding school, for nine months with kids in the same situation.

If Doc didn't want me with him, I guess it didn't matter how I spent the next few years. In the morning I would tell him that I wanted to catch the next flight back. No sense sticking around.

* * *

Flanna slept on a cot in the map room. The rest of us slept on the bunk beds. Well, I didn't exactly sleep. I spent most of the night lying on my cot listening to the others sleep.

I was grateful when Bill finally stumbled out of bed and started clanging around in the kitchen, trying to get the coffee going. I got up and helped him. Buzz and Doc weren't far behind. Flanna joined us just as Bill was pouring the coffee. She was the only one who looked relatively rested. Buzz and Bill were feeling the effects of their poker game, and Doc looked as if he had spent the night as wide awake as I had.

"So what's the matter with the boat?" Doc asked.

"I think it's the fuel system," Buzz said. "We'll take it apart this morning as soon as this coffee starts to work."

"When will we be able to leave?" Flanna asked.

"As soon as the boat's in shape, we're ready to go."

"We'll wait until next Sunday," Doc said, glancing at me.

"You don't have to wait for me," I said. "If you're ready to go sooner—"

"We'll wait," Bill interrupted.

"Actually, I was going to check and see if I can get an earlier flight back," I said. I looked at Doc. "I don't see any point in sticking around any longer."

This emptied the kitchen pretty quickly. Flanna remembered something important she had to do in the map room. Buzz and Bill took their cups of coffee to the boat to work on the engine. I think Doc wanted to go somewhere, too, but he didn't have any choice.

"I know you're unhappy with me, Jake—"

"You came down here knowing that you weren't coming back," I interrupted. "You put me in a retirement home, for crying out loud! You didn't write, you didn't call. You have a girlfriend who isn't much older than I am, and you're taking her up the Amazon and sending me back to summer camp and boarding school! I'm not unhappy, Doc. I'm furious!"

Doc glanced at the map room door. "Maybe we should go outside," he said quietly.

I wanted to suggest another place he could go all by himself, but instead I got up and went outside. Doc was right behind me. We went out the back door of the warehouse. Bill was just about to board the boat, carrying a gas can in one hand and his coffee in the other. Buzz was about twenty feet behind him carrying a heavy tool box.

"Okay," I said. "We're outside. Where do you want to go?"

Suddenly a blast knocked us both off our feet. Fiery debris slammed into the metal warehouse. I lay there with the wind knocked out of me as bats poured out through the open door.

After I regained my breath and some of my senses, I looked to see if Doc was okay. He was running toward the boat, now engulfed in black smoke. Someone was on the ground in front of the boat—on fire! I ran after Doc. I got there just in time to see his shirt ignite as he tried to help whoever it was on the ground. I tore my shirt off and wrapped it around Doc, smothering the flames. It was way too late for the other person.

I was afraid there might be another explosion. "Come on, Doc! We've got to get out of here!" I pulled him away from the boat.

"Who was it?" he screamed. "Who was it?"

I didn't know.

CHAPTER 7

It was Bill Brewster.

Buzz had somehow been blown free of the wreckage. His leg was badly broken, but he didn't have any burns. Doc's right hand and forearm were covered with ugly blisters. I was fine. Flanna and I tried to make Doc and Buzz comfortable while we waited for the ambulance and fire department, which seemed to take forever.

Flanna was very calm. She helped me get Doc into the air-conditioned kitchen and convinced him to lie down on the bunk and rest. Then we went back outside with a stretcher they had for moving tranquilized jaguars. We got Buzz onto it and carried him inside. Flanna told me to make Buzz as comfortable as I could. She went to work on Doc's hand and forearm, smearing on a salve of her own concoction. When she was done, she cut off Buzz's pant leg. The flesh was terribly discolored, and the leg was twisted at an unnatural angle.

Buzz lifted his head to assess the damage. "Looks like I

busted a strut," he said, then passed out.

"I'm afraid I don't have anything in my bag of tricks for a broken leg," Flanna said. "We'll just have to wait for the ambulance."

Only when she had done everything she could do, did Flanna break down. She held Doc's good hand and cried without making a sound.

The ambulance pulled up outside. I ran out and told the driver where we were. He and his partner brought a stretcher in. Flanna barked something at them in Portuguese, and one of them shrugged his shoulders.

"They only sent one ambulance," she said. "We'll take your father in the truck, if I can figure out how to get it started."

"I can show you," Doc said, weakly, and added, "Jake, you better stay here."

I was about to protest, when Flanna put a hand on my shoulder. "He's right, Jake. We can't leave our equipment untended. Every thief in Manaus will know we're at the hospital."

"Fine," I said.

"I'll call you from the hospital and tell you how things are going," Flanna said.

Buzz was placed on the stretcher and rolled out the door. Flanna and I helped Doc out of his bunk. He was in a lot of pain. Flanna managed to get the truck started as I helped Doc into the passenger seat.

"I'll be fine," he said.

I watched them drive away. The boat was still burning. Bill Brewster's body was hidden behind a veil of black smoke. I couldn't believe he was dead.

Suddenly a man walked out from the side of the warehouse.

"Can I help you?" I asked.

He stared at the burning boat. "Look's like you're the one that needs help."

He sounded like an American.

"What are you doing here?"

"I saw the smoke."

He had silver-gray hair cut so short it looked as if it had been painted on his head. His eyes were pale blue and his face was tanned and wrinkled, as if he'd spent many years in the tropics. He wore black jeans, white tennis shoes, and a starched white shirt. I guessed him to be in his late fifties, but he was in very good shape.

"What happened here?" he asked.

"Who are you?"

"My name is Jay Silver, but you can call me Silver. You must be Doc's son."

"Jake," I said. "You know my father?"

"Not very well," he admitted. "We only met once. So what happened?"

I had no idea what had happened. And I wasn't in the mood to have a conversation with a complete stranger. I was worried about Doc's injuries, and his best friend had just been killed. Who was this guy?

"The boat blew up," I said. "Bill Brewster's dead."

"And your dad?"

"His hand got burned."

"And the tall guy. I forget his name. . . ."

"Buzz," I said. "His leg's broken. They're at the hospital."

"You have no idea how this happened?"

I shook my head. "Bill and Buzz were going to do some work on the fuel system. But they didn't make it to the boat before it blew up."

"Did they work on the fuel system earlier?"

"I don't know. They were working on the engine yesterday. Why?"

"Things usually don't just blow up on their own. I'm just curious about how it happened."

A fire engine pulled up, followed by two police cars and a van. The firefighters got out of their truck, took one look at the fire, then got back in their truck and just sat there.

"What are they doing?"

"The cab's air-conditioned," Silver said. "I imagine they'll just wait for the boat to burn itself out. It's too late to save it."

A uniformed policeman got out of one of the cars and came over to us. He nodded at Silver as if he knew him, then started jabbering at me.

"I'll take care of this," Silver said, and launched into an

explanation in what sounded like perfect Portuguese.

The policeman took a pad out and jotted down some notes. When Silver was finished, the officer asked him a few questions, then saluted and walked back to his car.

Now it was my turn to ask what was going on.

"They're going to go to the hospital and talk to your father."

One of the police cars drove away.

"What about Bill?" It didn't seem right to leave him lying there.

"The firefighters will take care of him as soon as the fire burns itself out."

I heard the phone ringing and ran inside to pick it up. It was Flanna. She said they were wrapping my father's hand and putting a cast on Buzz's leg. She thought they would be back at the warehouse later that afternoon. I thanked her and went back outside.

Silver was gone.

* * *

I couldn't look when the firefighters zipped what remained of Bill's body into the black plastic bag and put it into the van. I'd known Bill Brewster my whole life. He and Doc had gone to school together, had worked as curators for the New York Zoological Society, and had been field partners all over the world. Now he was gone.

I watched as the police poked around the wreckage for a few minutes, then left without trying to ask me any more questions. The fire engine and van drove away right behind them.

I walked down to the water. There was nothing left of the boat except charred wood. The dock was gone as well.

Bill's death was going to be very hard on Doc. There was no one closer to my father than Bill Brewster. I had no idea what was going to happen to the expedition now that he was gone. And then there was Doc's and Buzz's injuries. The only way I could help Doc was to do whatever he wanted me to do. If this meant going back to the Home, going to summer school, or even to boarding school, I would do it. And I'd try to do it cheerfully, without complaint.

I pulled the back door wide open, so the bats could come home if they wanted to.

Flanna didn't drive up in the old truck until late that evening. Doc wore a sling, and his arm was wrapped in thick bandages. Buzz's leg was in a cast, and he had been given a pair of crutches to get around on. I helped Flanna get them inside. They immediately lay down on their cots without a word and went to sleep.

"They're on pain medication," Flanna said, tiredly. "Are you all right?"

"I guess," I said, but I wasn't sure. "Did the police figure out what happened?"

"They think it was an accident. Something to do with a fuel leak. We're lucky it didn't happen when we were on our way upriver."

Not lucky for Bill, I thought.

"I think I'll go to bed, too." Flanna said, wearily. "Good night, Jake."

"Good night."

CHAPTER 8

I was the first one awake the next morning. I got out of bed quietly and went outside, so I wouldn't disturb anyone. The bats still had not come back. I wandered around for about an hour, then went back inside to see if anyone was awake.

Doc was sitting on his bunk with a cup of coffee in his good hand. Buzz sat at the kitchen table with his cast resting on a chair. Flanna was making breakfast. The mood inside was very somber. I helped Flanna finish breakfast and brought plates over to Doc and Buzz. Neither one of them was very hungry.

"I guess the big question is, what are we going to do now?" Doc said.

No one offered any answers.

Doc continued, "I'll take Bill's remains back to the States."

"So the expedition's off," Buzz said.

"Right," Doc said. "We don't have a boat and we don't have the money or the time to get another one. And with Bill gone, what's the point?"

No one had an answer for this, either.

There was a loud screeching noise out in the warehouse that startled all of us. Before I could get up to see what had caused it, there was a knock on the door. I opened it. It was Jay Silver. The screeching came from a large red-and-yellow macaw sitting on his shoulder. I let him and his bird in.

"Sorry," he said. "Scarlet doesn't like bats."

"Scarlet?"

"My macaw."

"But the bats are gone."

"They seem to have come back."

I stuck my head out the door. The bats were flying back into the warehouse.

I closed the door. "He's right."

Doc didn't look at all thrilled to see Silver.

"I just dropped by to see how you were doing," Silver said.

"Very thoughtful," Doc said, flatly.

"I don't believe I've had the pleasure, ma'am," Silver said. Scarlet almost lunged off his shoulder toward Flanna when he addressed her. "I'm afraid Scarlet isn't very fond of women."

"My name's Flanna Brenna. And you are?"

"Jay Silver."

"This is my son, Jake," Doc added.

"We met yesterday," I said.

Doc was surprised to hear this.

"I just wanted to make sure you were okay," Silver said. "And to tell you that I was sorry to hear about Bill."

There was an awkward silence and a lot of tension in the room, which I didn't understand.

"What will you do now?" Silver asked.

"We were just discussing that when you came in," Doc said.

"And?"

"We've decided to call the expedition off."

"I'm sorry to hear that," Silver said. "It's a shame after all the work you've put in."

"What's a shame," Doc said, "is that my best friend died twenty-four hours ago in a senseless accident. He and his dream were turned to ashes at the same exact moment."

"I know this is a difficult time for you, Dr. Lansa," Silver said, calmly. "But let me be frank. . . . I didn't know Bill well, but I can't imagine that he would want to see his dream abandoned like this."

"You didn't know him at all," Doc said. "What are you getting at, Silver?"

"I have a boat and it's still available."

"Forget it!"

Doc's hostility didn't seem to faze Silver.

Doc stared at the floor. After a long time he looked up at

Silver again. "I'm sorry, Silver. I don't mean to be so . . . Well . . ."

"I understand completely, Dr. Lansa."

"No you don't," Doc said. "You're the third skipper that's approached us since the boat blew up. At least you had the courtesy of waiting a day. The other two approached us while we were at the hospital. If my hand wasn't burned to a crisp, I would have slugged them."

"Who were they?" Silver asked.

"How would I know?" Doc said, irritably.

"It's not surprising, Dr. Lansa. You have an exploration permit to go upriver, and those are hard to come by."

"*Bill* had a permit! A lot of good it will do him now."

"The name on the permit could be changed," Silver said.

"I'd have to fly all the way to Brasília and see if I could get it transferred to me. This would take time. Too much time. And that's not the only problem.

"Buzz can't fly because of his leg. I can't fly with this bum hand. Without the ultralight, we would never be able to gather enough tracking data to prove that we can do this job. Not in the deadline that they've set for us.

"The other problem is the funding. We don't have enough money to hire you and your boat."

"I'm sure we can work something out," Silver said.

"That wouldn't solve the ultralight problem," Doc said.

"Perhaps your son could learn to fly the ultralight," Silver said.

My father laughed, which sort of hurt my feelings, but I understood why he laughed. It was a pretty wild suggestion.

"First of all, he's not a pilot. Second, he has to go back to the States in a couple of days and finish three years of high school. Third, I couldn't possibly put him in that kind of danger."

"Well," Silver said, "I'm just trying to come up with alternatives. My boat is fast. I think we can make up the time you'll lose getting the permit transferred. As far as your son becoming an ultralight pilot, that's your call. It's just an idea."

He opened the door and started to leave, then stopped and turned back.

"Still seems like a shame to give up after all the sacrifices that have been made." He continued through the door and closed it quietly behind him. Scarlet screeched again.

"Can you believe that guy?" Doc asked.

No one responded.

"Do you know him very well?" Flanna asked.

"Hardly at all. He was just one of the people who offered to take us upriver."

"Why didn't you let him?"

"There must have been a dozen skippers that offered their services. We turned all of them down. Bill and I decided that we would be better off getting our own boat." Doc shook his head. "Actually, we almost went with Silver. He was definitely a cut above most of the other skippers we talked to, but he was just too good to be true.

"We did some asking around about him. Silver's an ex-mercenary, soldier of fortune type, hired gun—whatever you want to call it—and we simply didn't trust him. He has other reasons for going upriver, but I have no idea what they are."

Flanna stirred her coffee slowly. "Still," she said, quietly, "Silver made some good points."

"About what?" Doc asked.

"About Bill and the jaguar preserve."

"Such as?"

"There have been a lot sacrifices made for this preserve. Bill was your best friend, you knew him better than any of us did. Do you think he would want you to give up?"

Doc rubbed the bandages on his arm. He didn't say anything for a long time.

"He wouldn't want that," Doc finally said. "But he would also know it was impossible to continue for the reasons I gave Silver."

Flanna looked at Buzz. "How dangerous are ultralights?"

Buzz grinned. "I think they're safer than driving around Manaus. Especially in our truck."

Doc frowned.

"How long would it take you to teach someone to fly the ultralight?" Flanna asked.

"Impossible!" Doc said. "You'll be too busy doing a botanical survey. That's part of Woolcott's conditions."

"How long?" Flanna persisted.

"A week," Buzz said. "Maybe a little longer. Depends on the student."

Flanna looked at me, then back at Doc. "I bet Jake would make an excellent ultralight pilot."

"No way," Doc sputtered.

"You told me he was a great pilot. You went on and on about it. Remember? You said that he was much more comfortable behind the controls than you were—"

"Yeah, but . . ."

"You and I could fly to Brasília today and meet with Woolcott. With his help we can probably get the expedition permit transferred. If Silver and Jake were ready, we could be on our way within a week."

I was thrilled that Doc had bragged about my flying, but I didn't say a word. In fact, I tried not to show any emotion, but at that moment I wanted to hug Flanna.

Doc looked at Buzz for help. "Jake has only flown by himself once in his life."

"To be honest with you, Doc, that's a big plus," Buzz replied. "One of the toughest things to do is teach a conventional pilot to fly an ultralight. The feel of the controls is totally different. I'd rather teach someone who has never flown. And besides, the helmet is almost a perfect fit. We'll have to do something about those foot pedals, though."

"You're not helping, Buzz," Doc said.

"I'm just telling it like it is."

"Jake doesn't even have a pilot's license."

"He doesn't need one to fly an ultralight. I'm sorry, Doc, but Flanna's right. If at all possible, Bill would want us to set up the preserve. And this is definitely a possibility. My busted strut will be healed up in a couple of months. Just in time to ride upriver with Woolcott and his team. I could take over for Jake then."

"Face it, Bob," Flanna said. "If you go back to the States and bury Bill without at least trying to fulfill his dream, you'll regret it for the rest of your life. Bill didn't want a tombstone. He wanted a jaguar preserve."

Doc looked at me. "I know I don't have to ask this, but are you game?"

He was right. He didn't have to ask.

Doc, Flanna, and I took the old truck down to the moorage to find Silver's boat and talk to him. His boat was called the *Tito*, and on the outside it looked as neat and well preserved as Silver was. As we walked up to the boat, we heard Scarlet scream. A second later, Silver came down from the wheelhouse with Scarlet perched on his shoulder.

"Welcome aboard." He didn't seem at all surprised to see us.

We climbed on board. Scarlet eyed Flanna suspiciously. Doc eyed Silver suspiciously.

"A change of mind, Dr. Lansa?"

"Maybe," Doc said. "If you have time, we'd like you to show us around."

"My pleasure."

The *Tito* was half again as big as the boat Doc and Bill had bought. The teak decks were bright with fresh varnish, and the brass fittings glittered in the morning sunlight. Silver took us below deck and showed us four roomy sleeping compartments.

"I'd recommend that you use these compartments for storage, not sleeping. Your equipment will be much safer down here."

"Where will we sleep?" Flanna asked.

"On deck. We'll put up mosquito netting. It's cooler up there, anyway."

He showed us the engine room, then took us up to the galley, which was good sized. It even had a large walk-in cooler. The last stop was the wheelhouse, or pilot house, where the boat was controlled. To get to it, we had to climb a steep metal stairway.

"As you can see," Silver explained, "I have pretty good equipment."

I pointed to the door opposite the bridge and asked him what it was.

"Those are my quarters."

I expected him to open the door and let us look inside, but apparently it wasn't part of the tour.

Doc and Flanna seemed impressed with the boat, and I know I was. I was also impressed with Silver. He was calm and competent. We went back down to the deck.

"How much would you charge to take us upriver?" Doc asked.

"How long do you need me?"

"I'm not exactly sure. Could be several months. Longer if things work out like we hope."

"I'll charge you a thousand bucks a month, and you pay for everything—provisions, fuel, boat repairs, and so on. And I want to be paid for three months up front, before we leave."

"I guess I don't understand," Doc said. "That's about a quarter of what the other skippers wanted, and their boats weren't half as nice as yours."

Silver shrugged his shoulders. "I have simple needs," he said.

"That doesn't really explain it, does it?"

"You're right," Silver admitted. "I want to go upriver, and I can't without an exploration permit. I wouldn't get a hundred miles before I got turned back."

"But why do you want to go upriver?"

"Like I told you before, Dr. Lansa. You're going to an area of the Amazon I've never been to before. I just want to take a look around. I'm not a conservationist like you are. I'm just curious. I'll let you talk about it privately." He climbed back up to the wheelhouse.

"I told you he was too good to be true," Doc said.

"I agree," Flanna said. "But if he gets us to the preserve safely, what difference does it make?"

Doc looked around the deck as he thought about it. "I guess if we can get the permit, and if Jake can learn to fly the Morpho, we'll give it a go. But those are a lot of ifs."

CHAPTER 9

Doc and Flanna got tickets to leave for Brasília that afternoon. Doc also arranged to have Bill's remains flown back to his family in the States. Silver offered to drive them to the airport in his Landrover, which was a lot nicer than our truck.

Doc's final words to Buzz were: "By the time I get back, if I'm not convinced that Jake can fly that contraption of yours safely, then the deal's off."

"Yes, sir!" Buzz saluted, and almost fell over because of the crutches.

Doc shook his head in despair. We watched them drive away, then Buzz turned to me. "We don't have much time to accomplish this mission." I followed him back into the warehouse. "I'm afraid I'm not going to be much help with this bum leg, Jake. Go ahead and take the tarp off and pull the Morpho outside."

I managed to get it through the door without ripping a wing off.

"Are you ready?"

I looked at the Morpho, not sure if I would ever be ready and hopeful that I wouldn't let Buzz down by flying it into the ground. "I guess so," I said, and ran back in and got the helmet. When I got back outside, I slipped it on my head.

Buzz looked at me quizzically for a few moments. "I don't think you'll need that. Unless you have a tendency to bump your head a lot."

"I don't think I should fly without a helmet."

"I don't think you should, either. But you're not even close to flying yet. Bring the big toolbox out here."

I ran back inside and lugged the toolbox back out. I figured he had a few adjustments to make before I took off. I was badly mistaken.

"The first thing you're going to do is to take this thing apart," Buzz said. "Every wire, nut, bolt, and cotter pin. Then you're going to put it all back together again, and I want it to look just like it does now."

I thought he was joking. It would take hours to get it apart, and I wasn't sure if I could ever put it back together again.

"I'm not a mechanic," I said.

"And you won't be a mechanic when you finish, either. But you'll understand how the Morpho works. And if something shakes loose in the wild blue, you'll know what it is and whether it's going to make you fall out of the sky. I'll tell you the names of the things as you take them apart. Then you'll tell me the names when you put them back together. We'll make a game out of it. I hope for your sake that you're better with tools than your old man. Get ready to have your mind bent."

Not only did my mind get bent, but my knuckles got bruised and my eyes blurred over with sweat from the stifling heat.

It took me hours to get the ultralight apart. And Buzz was the reason. Every time I unhooked or unscrewed something, he'd ask what it was and what it did. If I didn't know, I'd guess. If I was wrong, which I often was, he'd tell me the proper name and function. Periodically he'd point at something with his crutch from the growing pile of nuts, bolts, and tubing, and ask me what it was. If I didn't answer correctly, he'd make me reassemble the connecting pieces until I could tell him exactly what it was and what it did.

"Were you in the army?" I asked.

"Fat chance. They said I was too thin. Guess I wasn't a big enough target."

"I think you missed your calling as a drill sergeant."

I don't know how long it took. When the sun went down, I thought Buzz would call it a day. But no, he had me run an extension cord and hook up a light, so I could continue.

Silver dropped by a couple of times and watched for a while. He said that he had a crew coming in the next day to rebuild the dock. As soon as it was finished, he planned to move his boat down from the moorage.

Finally I pulled out the last cotter pin and unscrewed the

last nut. My hands were swollen, I was hungry, and I couldn't remember being more exhausted. Buzz nodded, turned off the light, and hobbled back into the bunk room.

All I wanted to do was get something to eat and climb into bed, but Buzz had other ideas. We began ultralight ground school. The first lecture was on weather flying. Buzz went on for over two hours. The bottom line was not to take off in the Morpho unless the weather was perfect and looked as if it would stay perfect throughout the flight.

When he was finished with the lecture, I stumbled into the bathroom. When I got out, Buzz was in his bunk sound asleep, snoring away. I grabbed some food, collapsed on my own bunk, and almost dozed off in midchew.

A few hours later, I felt something hard poking me in the back. It was Buzz's crutch. He was a cruel man.

"Rise and shine, Ace!"

It took me all that day and half the night to get the ultralight back together again. Every time I made a mistake, Buzz made me back up a few steps and start again. A couple of times I got so mad at him that I had to walk to the dock to calm down. That didn't seem to offend Buzz in the least. Silver and his hired help were making much better progress on the dock than I was on the ultralight. I envied them because they got to work in the water, where it was relatively cool.

When I finally got the Morpho back together, I held up the last cotter pin and ceremoniously snapped it through the end of the last bolt.

Buzz looked at his watch. "That didn't take you as long as I thought it would."

I wasn't sure if he meant that as a compliment or not.

"So you understand how it works now?"

"Yes," I said, weakly.

"Do you think you could repeat the assembly?"

"I think so," I said, praying he wouldn't ask me to do it again.

"I think you can, too. Let's go in and get some sleep."

The phone was ringing when we got inside. Buzz picked it up. It was Doc.

"I've never seen anything like it," Buzz said into the phone. "Jake's a natural born pilot. It's incredible!" He winked at me and held his finger to his lips. "That's great! When do you think you'll be back? . . . Silver finished the dock today. He'll bring his boat over tomorrow. . . . He seems okay to me. I don't think you'll have any problems with him. . . . Okay. Bye." He hung up the phone.

"Flanna and Doc met with Woolcott today. He was very sorry to hear about Bill and he thinks they should continue with the expedition. He's going to help them get the permit transferred."

"What were you saying about Silver?" I asked.

"Doc just wanted to know what I thought of him. He's just being cautious."

"What was that stuff about my being a 'natural born pilot'? I haven't even flown the Morpho yet."

"Just wanted to bolster his spirits a bit. He was very pleased."

* * *

The next morning I was up before the crutch poked me. Today was the day I'd be flying, or so I thought. I made a pot of coffee for Buzz, then went outside to look at the Morpho. I sure hoped I had put it together right.

About half an hour later, Buzz joined me outside. "You have one more little chore before you climb into the cockpit."

I frowned.

"You need to learn how to pack the Morpho's parachute."

I didn't even know it had a parachute.

Buzz hobbled back inside and pointed at one of the boxes. I opened it and pulled something out that looked like a backpack. He told me to haul it outside and pull the chute out of the pack. There were actually two parachutes in the pack, a primary chute and a smaller, backup chute in case the first one malfunctioned.

"This is a ballistic parachute," he said. "There's an explosive charge in the pack. When you pull the string, it shoots the parachute out away from the ultralight so it doesn't get tangled up in the wings."

"You mean you don't bail out?"

"Nope. If you get in trouble, you pull the cord and you and the Morpho float to the ground like a dry autumn leaf. Ideally."

"Have you ever had to use a parachute?"

"One time," he said. "And I got hung up in an oak tree and nearly broke my neck."

This was not encouraging. "The rain forest is nothing but trees," I pointed out.

"I know," he said. "You probably won't need the chute. And if you do, you'll have to be very careful."

Great!

Buzz had me pack and repack the chute until I could have done it with blindfolds on.

"I think you have that down," he finally said. "*Now* you can put the helmet on."

I spent most of the day doing "touch-and-goes." This exercise consisted of flying the Morpho down the flat area in back of the warehouse, never getting more than about ten feet off the ground.

"The idea is to get used to the throttle and other controls," he said. "I want you to be able to land with your eyes closed."

The ultralight's engine was very loud despite the advanced muffler system Buzz had put on it. And at only ten feet off the ground, the Morpho was very difficult to control. I felt that I was going to crash at any moment. By late afternoon, Buzz was satisfied that I could take the ultralight off and land it. Every muscle in my body ached, and I didn't know if this was from being jarred every time I landed or if the soreness was caused by tension.

"I think you've had enough for today," he said.

"Tomorrow we'll put the pontoons on and see how you do with water landings."

"You know, Buzz, Doc's going to be back here in a few days and expects me to know how to fly this thing."

Buzz laughed. "Believe it or not, you've already learned the hardest part—getting the ultralight up and getting it back down safely. The actual flying part is easy."

Silver and his men finished the dock that evening, and he said that he would bring the *Tito* over the next day.

Early the following morning Buzz told me how to attach the pontoons to the Morpho's landing gear.

Landing and taking off from the water was much harder than landing and taking off from land. The water caused a lot more drag on the ultralight, and I had to get more speed before I could take off. When I landed, I had to watch out for the current and the crosswind so I wouldn't flip the Morpho over. I found that if one float started to come up off the water, I had to lean my weight toward it to get it back down on the surface. After twenty touch-and-goes, I was drenched. I taxied over to the dock where Buzz was standing and shut the engine down.

He looked up at the sky. "I guess it's time to hit the wild blue yonder. But first you've got to change into some dry clothes. At two thousand feet it can get darn cold when you're wet."

"Two thousand feet?"

He nodded. "Thereabouts," he said. "I want you to do

some lazy circles. Just keep the warehouse in sight, and I'll keep in touch with this handheld radio."

After I changed my clothes I topped the fuel tank off with gas, buckled myself into the seat, and flipped the visor down on my helmet.

"Okay," he said over the radio. "Let her rip."

I took a deep breath and started the engine. When the oil pressure was right, I pulled the throttle all the way out. In seconds I was airborne, but instead of reducing power and landing again, I pulled the control stick toward me and I was off. At first I was very nervous, but this feeling was soon replaced with exhilaration. I was actually flying the Morpho, and it was awesome.

"What's your altitude?" Buzz said.

I looked at the altimeter. "About a thousand feet."

"Good. Bring her around counterclockwise, keeping the same pitch, then level out at two thousand feet. You're doing great."

I could see for miles, although the view was obscured somewhat by a thick haze of smoke from all the wood burning. In the distance, miles from the river, I saw the leading edge of the rain forest.

I took the ultralight up to two thousand feet and leveled it off. Buzz was a little speck standing near the dock. I was going fifty knots. At that speed, the controls were very responsive. To turn left, all it took was a little pressure on the stick and rudder pedal.

I felt every puff of wind and the different temperatures as I flew through the thermals. Buzz had me fly half a dozen wide loops around the warehouse, then told me to come in for a landing before I forgot how to get down. The landing was a little rough, but I got down safely and taxied over to the dock.

"Not bad," Buzz said. "Not bad at all."

"It was wonderful!"

He smiled. "Let's check this machine over, refuel, and then you can get back up there again."

At the end of the day, after we put the ultralight into the warehouse, I was still flying even though I was on the ground. Buzz was very pleased with how I had done.

CHAPTER 10

I spent the next day practicing different maneuvers in the Morpho with Buzz watching. That evening he and Silver drove off in the Landrover on what Buzz called a "secret mission." They didn't get back until late.

The next morning Buzz announced that we were going to play hide-and-seek.

"What do you mean?"

"Simple," he explained. "Last night we scattered half a dozen radio collars around the countryside. You're going to find them with your receiver and the global positioning system. When you get the collar's position, radio it in to me and I'll verify it and give you the frequency of the next collar."

I took off. When I got to two thousand feet, I leveled out and entered the number of the first collar on my receiver. As I flew in slow, wide circles, I listened carefully for the collar's signal. Halfway through the loop I heard a very faint *beep* . . . *beep* . . . *beep* as the antennas picked up the signal. All I had to do now was to follow the beeping until I thought I was over the top of it. I had radio-tracked from an airplane when I was in Kenya, but I hadn't been flying the airplane at the same time. Doing both wasn't easy. I managed to lose the signal twice before I figured out which direction it was coming from. The beeping got louder the closer I got to the collar. Then it began to fade, and I knew I had passed over the top of it. I swung the ultralight around. When I thought the signal was loudest, I punched the button on the GPS and radioed the longitude and latitude to Buzz.

"Close enough," he said, and gave me the frequency of the next collar.

It took me the rest of the day to find the remaining collars. I had to fly back to the warehouse five times and refuel.

That evening Silver offered to collect the collars and hide them by himself. Buzz gratefully accepted. His leg had been bothering him all day from bouncing around in the Landrover the night before.

Buzz and I hit our bunks pretty early, but for some reason I couldn't fall asleep. I hadn't sent a dispatch to the Home since I learned that I might be staying down here. I kept putting it off because I didn't know what to say. Taw would be sorry to hear about Bill and disappointed that I wasn't coming back in a few days.

I lay in the dark for a long time thinking about Doc, Flanna, the expedition, and flying. I was excited about going with them, but I wished that Doc had wanted me to go instead of being forced into it by Bill's death. Why didn't he get in touch with me while I was at the Home? Why didn't he tell me about Flanna? A little voice went off in my head—*for the same reason you don't want to tell Taw you're not coming back home.* I realized that it was difficult to tell people things that they don't want to hear. Maybe this was the reason Doc hadn't contacted me.

I got up and slipped outside, thinking that a short walk might help me sleep. There was a light coming from the *Tito*'s wheelhouse. I wandered over to see what Silver was up to. I stepped aboard and called out his name, but he didn't answer.

I climbed the steep stairs to the wheelhouse. He wasn't there, nor was Scarlet, but the door to his cabin was slightly ajar. I knocked and called his name again. Nothing. I opened the door the rest of the way.

"Silver?"

The only light in his cabin came from a small lamp on the desk. I stepped inside. His cabin was twice the size of the cabins below deck. There was a simple bed, an oak desk, and a large map table. Along one wall were floor-to-ceiling shelves overflowing with books. I was happy to see them and I hoped he would let me borrow a few for the long trip up the Amazon. He had some of the same books about explorers I had read back at the Home. He also had books on history, animals, and several works on the indigenous people of the Amazon. Some of the volumes looked very old, with tattered leather covers. I pulled one out and looked at the yellowed pages. It was written in Portuguese.

I was going to pull another book off the shelf when it occurred to me that Silver might not want me snooping around in his private quarters. I decided I better get out of there, but as I was turning to leave, the framed photographs above Silver's desk caught my attention. I went over for a closer look. A much younger version of Silver looked out from the photos. He had dark, close-cropped hair and was wearing military fatigues. The photos must have been taken during the Vietnam War. There were other soldiers in the photos with Silver—probably buddies of his in the same platoon. Below these photos were several color snapshots of Silver playing with a young Indian boy. The boy was about two years old. Silver was smiling in every shot and seemed to be really happy.

I heard a noise behind me. Before I could turn around, someone shoved me into the bookshelves, then grabbed me and slammed me down on the floor. I caught a glimpse of his face in the dim light. He had a small scar on the left side of his face. That's the last thing I remember before I blacked out.

* * *

I don't know how long I was out, but when I came to, I was still on the floor and Silver was kneeling next to me. I had a splitting headache and my vision was fuzzy.

I started to sit up, but Silver gently pushed me back

down. "You better stay where you are for a minute."

"What happened?"

"Looks like we had a little break-in. How many were there?"

"Just one, I think."

"Did you happen to see what he looked like?"

"Not really. It was pretty dark. I think he had a scar on his face."

Silver nodded. "Can you sit up? Real slow." He helped me into a sitting position. The room spun around, and it was all I could do not to throw up. "You must have disturbed his little party."

I looked around the room. It was a mess. The mattress on Silver's bed had been shredded. Every book was pulled off the shelf; all the drawers had been opened and dumped on the floor.

I took a deep breath. "I didn't disturb his party," I admitted. "He disturbed mine." I explained what I had been doing in his cabin and apologized for going in there without asking.

Silver didn't seem upset about it.

"Did he take anything?" I asked.

"Nothing important. Do you think you can stand?"

He helped me to my feet and assisted me out into the wheelhouse, where the light was better.

"That's quite a bump," he said, looking at the back of my head.

"I'll be all right. Do you need some help cleaning up?"

"No, I'll take care of it. You need to get some rest."

He walked with me to the warehouse, stopping outside the door. "Can you make it from here?"

"Sure."

"One more thing," Silver said. "Why don't we keep this between you and me? No use upsetting Buzz and your father. They have enough to worry about as it is."

He was right. The incident would just confirm Doc's belief that it was too dangerous for me down here. I told him that I wouldn't tell anyone and apologized again for going into his cabin.

"No harm done. Well, except for your head."

* * *

Buzz woke me with a poke from his crutch. "We have work to do, Ace."

I'd only slept about four hours, and my head felt as if it were going to burst. I didn't really feel like flying, but I knew I had to. I stumbled into the bathroom and took a long shower. The bump on the back of my head was very tender. I walked back to the bunk room. Buzz had managed to cook breakfast, despite his crutches. He was obviously feeling better than he had the day before. I sat down at the table and started eating. Buzz was standing behind me drinking a cup of coffee.

"What happened to your head?" he asked in alarm.

"I went out for a walk last night and bumped it on something."

"That's more than a bump. Are you going to be okay?"

"I'll be fine." Eventually, I thought.

"Our friend Silver told me he did a great job hiding those collars last night. It's not going to be as easy today," he warned.

Nothing was going to be easy today. I finished breakfast and climbed into the Morpho.

Buzz was right: finding the collars wasn't easy. It took more than three hours to find the first two. As I was flying around trying to pick up the signal from the third collar, a call came over the radio.

"Morpho, this is base," Buzz said. "Please return immediately. Over."

"What's up? Over."

"Just get back here," Buzz said. "And you better make the best landing of your life. Over and out."

I wondered what was going on. I turned the Morpho around and headed back. From a distance I saw four people standing on the dock, but it wasn't until I got closer that I recognized them—Buzz, Silver, Flanna, and my father. I hadn't expected Doc and Flanna back so soon. I wondered if it meant they hadn't gotten the expedition permit.

I flew over them and waggled my wings. They waved back. Buzz was right: I needed to make a perfect landing; otherwise Doc might call the whole expedition off. I only wished that my head felt better.

I followed the river downwind and banked the Morpho

to the left for my final approach. I eased the power off and gently pulled the nose back until the Morpho began to stall. The Morpho shuttered slightly. A second later, the pontoons skimmed the surface of the water with hardly a skip. I breathed a deep sigh of relief.

"Not bad, Ace," Buzz said over the radio.

I taxied over to the dock. Silver grabbed the wing and held the ultralight steady while I unbuckled the belt and got out.

"That was pretty good," Doc said. "I really didn't think you'd be able to pick it up that quickly."

"He had a great instructor," Buzz said humbly.

"Did you get the permit?" I asked.

"We did. Looks like you'll be tracking jaguars in a few weeks."

* * *

It took all of the next day to get the supplies loaded on the boat. I spent that time dismantling the Morpho, so we could get it on board. When Doc saw me taking it apart, he threw a minor fit because he thought there would be no one to put it back together once we got there. Buzz assured him that his son had *not* inherited his lack of mechanical ability. Doc calmed down about it, but he was still skeptical.

That evening I sent a fax to the Home:

> *Dear Taw,*
> *There's been a terrible accident down here. Doc and*

Bill's boat exploded in Manaus and Bill was killed. Doc's hand and arm were burned in the fire, but he'll be fine. The expedition's pilot, Buzz Lindbergh, broke his leg when the boat blew up. They've asked me to fly the airplane they're using to track the jaguars—at least for the time being. So it looks like I won't be coming back to Poughkeepsie for a while.

We're leaving tomorrow for the preserve. Unfortunately, I won't be able to send any more dispatches for the time being because I'll be on a boat going up the Amazon River.

I'll miss you! When I get back, we'll take that trip to Arizona you were talking about.

Please give my love to all the other "inmates" and tell them that when I get back, we'll have a Press Conference they'll never forget.

All my love, Jake

P.S. Tell Peter to go for walks with you every day. You need to be in good shape for our trip to Arizona!

The next morning Doc and Buzz looked at a map and picked a tentative base camp.

"I'll bring Woolcott up there in a couple of months," Buzz said. He turned to me. "And Jake, you better take good care of my baby."

I told him I would.

Just as the sun was coming up, we said good-bye to Buzz and started the long journey up the Amazon River.

The River

CHAPTER 11

As soon as we were under way, Silver came down from the wheelhouse and laid down some rules. The first was that we were to keep a loaded shotgun nearby at all times. Flanna didn't like this idea at all, and Doc wasn't far behind her. He had never been fond of guns.

"Guns are nothing but trouble," Flanna said.

"The shotgun is to stop trouble, not start it," Silver said.

"Don't you think you're being a little paranoid?" Doc asked.

Silver was clearly irritated by their reaction. He leaned on the rail and looked across to the far shore as if he was thinking of an appropriate response.

"While you're down here telling us to arm ourselves like we're in the middle of a war zone," Flanna said, "who's steering the boat? We won't need the shotgun if we sink."

Silver turned and looked at her. "The boat is on automatic pilot," he said calmly.

"And does the automatic pilot tell you when a floating log is going to ram the boat?" Flanna asked.

"No," Silver said. "Scarlet does that for me. Her eyesight is much better than mine. And yours, I might add. She'll let me know if something's coming along."

"Oh, that's great," Doc said in disgust. "You want us to carry shotguns, and we have a macaw for a first mate."

"Okay, Doc," Silver said quietly. "I guess it's time we got down to it. And I'm glad it's happening now rather than further upriver, where we might not have time for this type of discussion.

"As you know, we're going into uncharted territory. Outside of the fact that it will be hot, and filled with nasty insects, poisonous snakes, and debilitating diseases, I don't know what to expect."

"I've been upriver before," Doc reminded him.

"That was a long time ago, Dr. Lansa. Things have changed a great deal. The interior has been opened up and it's filled with men who will murder you for a hundred dollars, or for pleasure, if the mood strikes them. There's virtually no law enforcement, and what little there is, is so corrupt that it would be better to have no law at all. It's worse than the Wild West ever was."

My father thought about this for a few moments. "If it's as bad as you say, why didn't you have us hire a crew to protect us?"

"Because that's the worst thing we could possibly do!"

Silver said. "The reason most expeditions fail is because they take too many people. More mouths to feed, more personality conflicts, more disagreements about what to do when things go bad. Once the preserve is set up, you can bring in as many people as you want. But for now there's a world of difference between four people and half a dozen people. Believe me, I know! I've done this before. Which brings me to the most important point of this conversation and perhaps the foundation of your and Dr. Brenna's little problem."

"And what's that?"

"I'm the captain of this boat. Period! I'm in charge of getting us to the preserve, and you're in charge of getting the preserve going."

Scarlet let out an ear-piercing scream.

"Excuse me," Silver said, and climbed up to the wheelhouse.

"He's crazy," Doc said. "And I must have been crazy to think this was going to work."

The boat lurched to the right. A few seconds later, we passed a very large tree floating just below the surface of the water. None of us would have seen it until after it had put a hole in the boat the size of a washing machine. I looked at Flanna and Doc.

"How did Silver time that?" Flanna asked, clearly impressed with Scarlet's seamanship.

"You were with him for a week, Jake," Doc said. "Do you trust him?"

I thought about Silver helping me on the day of the explosion and after the break-in. Other than this I had had very little contact with him. He kept to himself most of the time. "I don't know," I said. "I guess he's trustworthy."

Silver climbed back down to the deck. "Where were we?"

Doc shook his head. "I'll admit that I haven't been upriver in a while, but I still don't like the shotgun idea."

"I'm not asking you to shoot anybody," Silver said. "I just want you to keep the shotgun close by, to discourage those who might want to shoot you."

Doc looked at Flanna. She nodded. "All right, Silver," he said. "You're the captain."

"Good. It will take us three weeks to get to the site if everything goes well, but things rarely go well in this country." He climbed back up to the wheelhouse.

* * *

The days on the river were long, hot, and pretty boring. It rained nearly every day. Dark clouds swooped in, dumping inches of rain, then disappeared as quickly as they had come.

Doc was not in the best mood. His hand and arm were not healing properly, and I think he was in constant pain. And this wasn't his only problem. Bill's death was eating away at him. The way he usually dealt with tragedy was to throw himself into a frenzy of work.

The first few days on the river he was able to keep the

demons of grief away by staying busy. He set up our living quarters on deck by hanging the hammocks and mosquito netting. He did an inventory of all our supplies and calculated how long they would last us. After this, he worked on the telemetry gear we would use to track jaguars. He rebuilt receivers, cataloged collar frequencies, and set up a tracking database on his laptop computer. But then there was nothing else for him to do. He spent a good portion of the day in his hammock watching the shore go by, which had changed a great deal since his last trip.

Doc was horrified by the amount of rain forest destruction we saw on the way upriver. Twenty years ago, he and Bill had spent six weeks along the Amazon as graduate students. Many of the lush green places they had visited were gone now—replaced by mining, timber, and oil operations. Silver didn't say anything, but I could see that he was as appalled by the destruction as we were. Every once in a while I would catch him staring at the devastated landscape and shaking his head in quiet dismay.

"The search for gold is the worst," Flanna told me. "Even a vague rumor of gold brings thousands of people into the rain forest. They knock the trees down, burn the vegetation, cut roads, build crude shantytowns, and kill every animal they can find for food and to sell their skins. When they abandon an area, there's nothing left but an ugly scar that won't heal for a hundred years, if at all."

She went on to explain how they find the gold.

"Prospectors follow a small tributary up to the head-waters, then pan their way downstream until they find gold. They then work their way back up until they find the source of the gold by digging alongshore. When they find the source, they follow it to the rock formation and dig around the formation until they find the vein.

"But that's not the worst of it. The trees are cut, the rivers polluted, and the Indians who have the misfortune of living near the mining camps are either killed or turned into slave laborers."

"This doesn't sound much different from what happened to the Indians in North America," I said.

"It's exactly the same," Silver agreed. "And it will probably never change."

As we got further away from Manaus, I thought we would start seeing animals along the river, but about the only animals we saw were vultures roosting in the trees near the shantytowns.

Every few days we made a brief stop at a fuel barge to fill the *Tito*'s gas tanks. Silver said that when we got further upriver, fuel would be harder to find and much more expensive.

There were a lot of other boats on the river besides ours—barges with ramshackle houses built on them like floating villages; small fishing boats; large supply boats; ferries carrying travelers; floating brothels that moved prostitutes from one town to the next; and produce boats that carried fruits, vegetables, meat, and fresh eggs from their onboard chicken coops.

There were also patrol boats, which stopped us several times to check our passports and make certain that our expedition permit was in order. Sometimes the patrols were stationed at a fuel barge, and they checked us out when we came in to fill up. Other times they made us stop in midriver, much to Silver's irritation. We would have to head toward shore and throw the anchors out. The officers came aboard and looked through everything we had under Silver's ever-watchful eye.

Flanna said they had started the permit system to stop foreigners from plundering the rain forest without giving anything back to the country. Silver's opinion was that government officials used the permits as a way of making sure they got a cut of the action before people left town with the goods.

During the day, Silver kept the boat moving up the middle of the river. Doc offered to take over the helm so Silver could rest, but Silver told him that he and Scarlet had everything under control. Toward evening he would find a good spot about thirty feet from shore and throw out the anchors. We stayed away from shore to keep the insects from eating us alive.

When we anchored for the evening, we'd go for a swim, then Flanna and Doc would slather themselves with insect repellent and take Silver's inflatable Zodiac to shore to look around. Silver didn't like the idea, but they reached a compromise by agreeing to take the shotgun with them. I went with them a couple of times, but stopped when it dawned on me that they might want to be alone with each other. They always left the shotgun in the Zodiac, but I didn't tell Silver this.

I was beginning to really like Flanna, despite my misgivings about her and Doc's romance—if you could call it that. Doc hadn't been in what I would call a romantic mood since Bill's death. I could see at times that his attitude hurt Flanna's feelings, but she didn't push the issue and gave him plenty of space. She was smart enough to know that this was the only way to handle my father. She changed Doc's bandages twice a day, ignoring his complaints while she smeared her special salve on his tender skin. She was friendly to me without being overly friendly, which I appreciated. I guess she knew how to handle me as well.

She told me she had been born in Ireland but raised in Oregon. Her interest in botany came from her parents, who owned a large plant nursery outside Portland. They wanted her to become a botanist and take over the nursery one day. She wanted to become a doctor and travel.

"I split the difference with them," she said. "I became a botanist, but I specialize in medicinal rain forest plants."

"Where did you learn to climb?"

"We had giant oak trees on our property. When I was a kid, I spent more time in them than I did on the ground. When the trees got too manageable for me, I took up rock climbing, learned to use ropes, and adapted the techniques for canopy exploration."

Most evenings our first mate, Scarlet, would leave her perch in the wheelhouse and spend the night in the forest. "Shore leave," Silver called it. He didn't know where she went or what she did on these nocturnal flights. And he didn't care, as long as she was back before sunrise. "And sober," he added.

He and Scarlet had been mates for ten years. He bought her from an Indian when she was no bigger than the palm of his hand. "'Ugliest chick you've ever seen," he said. "I didn't even know what kind of parrot she was until she grew up. I hand-fed her every two hours for weeks."

Silver stayed pretty much to himself. He spent his days in the wheelhouse and his nights in his cabin. We hadn't had any conflicts since the first day out, but there was always some underlying tension in the air. He was different from what he had been onshore—kind of edgy and somewhat nervous. A couple of times, late at night, I heard him leave the wheelhouse and come down to the deck. I watched him through the mosquito netting as I lay in my hammock. With his shotgun cradled in his arms, he would take about ten steps, then stop and stand perfectly still as if listening for something. I had no idea what he was up to. The only sounds were the steady hum of insects and the water lapping against the boat.

One evening, after Flanna and Doc had rowed to shore, I went up to the wheelhouse to talk with Silver. I found him in his cabin sitting at his map table, staring at a chart. I started the conversation by asking him about Colonel Fawcett and his search for the lost Muribeca mines.

"Colonel Fawcett was a courageous man and a great explorer," Silver said. "But he was chasing after something that never existed. The fruitless search killed him, his son, and his son's friend. It's a tragedy that's as old as the rain forest."

What I really wanted to talk to him about were the snapshots of him and the young Indian boy. In these photos Silver looked happy and relaxed, as if he were at peace with himself and the world. It was a very different portrait from the tense and suspicious Silver that I had come to know. I walked over to the desk where the photos were hanging.

"What else can I do for you, Jake?" Silver asked.

"I was wondering about these photographs. You were in Vietnam?"

"Three tours of duty. Special Forces."

"And these other photographs of you with the young boy?"

"That was a long time ago," he said, with a faraway look in his eyes. "That boy is my son, Tito."

"Like your boat."

He nodded. "His mother—my wife—was Alicia. She was a Huaorani woman from Ecuador and we lived together along the Rio Curaray."

"What happened?"

"I'm not sure," he said. "I had to go away on a job. I was

away for three months. When I got back, they were gone. That was ten years ago. Alicia's family might have come by and convinced her to live with them elsewhere. They weren't very fond of me—not that most native people have any reason to love whites. Or maybe she joined a different group of Indians and disappeared into the forest with them. She missed her people," he paused for a moment. "Tito would be a little younger than you now."

"Did you look for them?"

"For a very long time, but I never found them. It's like they disappeared from the face of the earth. I still ask around, of course. And I named my boat after Tito, thinking that one day a young man would come up to me and tell me that his name is the same."

I wondered if this was his real reason for traveling upriver.

"That's when I got Scarlet. I was bringing her back as a gift for little Tito."

He looked back at his chart. I waited around for a few moments, hoping he would tell me more, but he didn't. I left him alone.

CHAPTER 12

The days and nights flowed into each other, and I lost track of how long we had been on the river. One afternoon, earlier than usual, Silver steered the boat toward shore and let the anchors down.

"What's the problem?" Doc asked.

"I don't know," Silver said. "But we're losing oil pressure." He went below to the engine room and came back up a couple of hours later covered in grease and sweat. "We'll have to pull in somewhere and find a mechanic."

* * *

The next morning Silver brought the *Tito* into a good-sized moorage near a mining settlement. Silver grabbed his shotgun and jumped down to the dock.

"Don't leave the boat," he said. "There's nothing but trouble here."

I watched him as he strode purposefully along the dock. Everyone he encountered along the way made room for him to pass. When he got to the end of the dock, he took a well-beaten path cut into a steep bank, which I assumed led to the town.

Along the bank were several small shacks with rusty tin roofs. Laundry flapped in the wind. Gangs of children wearing nothing but ragged T-shirts played in the black mud alongshore and threw sticks and rocks at any mangy dog that was fool enough to get within range. The air was foul. It smelled like rotting meat and fruit mixed with oil and urine.

I wasn't tempted to leave the boat, nor were Flanna and Doc. They dozed in their hammocks. I wondered how anyone could live in a place like this.

After about an hour of staring at the sad scenery, I got kind of bored and found the binoculars. I wanted to see if I could spot Silver coming down the jungle path before he got to the dock.

I focused the lenses on the hillside, looking for a likely opening in the thick growth, when I saw a man watching *us* through binoculars! As soon as he saw me, he took the binoculars away from his face and I saw the scar. I could have sworn it was the same man who had broken into Silver's cabin.

I almost shouted out to Doc and Flanna, but caught myself. They didn't know anything about the break-in. It was Silver's and my little secret. If Doc found out about it at this late date, he would be very upset with both me and Silver. The expedition didn't need this kind of problem.

The man started up the path in the same direction Silver had gone. I needed to warn Silver that the man was here. I looked back at Doc and Flanna—both of them were sound asleep. I jumped to the dock and ran.

The path was steep and muddy. I was out of breath when I got to the top. No sign of the man. I continued on, and half a mile later I got to the town. Nothing could have prepared me for what I saw. There were hundreds of men standing and trudging through deep, smelly mud. Most of them carried guns or machetes. There were no real streets—just dozens of shacks with narrow spaces between them. Silver was wrong: it wasn't like the Wild West; it was like another planet.

I'd never be able to find Silver in a place like this. I couldn't even ask anyone, because I didn't speak Portuguese. My best bet was to wait for Silver and catch him on his way down. I looked one more time at the men milling and standing around, wondering why they stayed in this miserable place. That's when I saw the man again. At least I thought it was the same man. He was walking up a narrow trail that ran along the hill behind the town. I'd never catch him before he reached the top, but I might be able to get an idea of where he was going. I jogged over to the trail and started up.

A constant string of exhausted-looking men passed me on their way down the path. They were completely covered with dried mud. What were they doing up there? I wondered. When I got to the top, I found out.

The trail came to an end near the edge of a giant pit. The hole was five times the size of a football field and at least three hundred feet deep. Hundreds of men swung picks and shoveled rocks from patches of ground measuring about ten feet square. The rocks were put into large burlap bags. The men without shovels or picks hefted the bags to their shoulders, then waited in line to climb up a series of rickety ladders leading to the top of the pit. When they reached the top, they dumped their bags into wooden sluice boxes, then climbed back down into the pit and started all over again.

They were mining for gold, and each tiny patch of ground was a claim. The men carrying rocks were probably laborers, working for pennies a day. As I watched, a man on a ladder lost his load. This started a chain reaction, and half a dozen men fell several feet to the rocky ground. The work didn't stop; in fact, it barely paused. The ladder was straightened, and within seconds it was filled with men carrying bags that weighed more than they did.

It was the most depressing thing I had ever seen. I didn't care anymore whether I found the man with the scar. I just wanted to get back to the boat. I hoped Silver would return soon so we could leave.

As I walked back through town, I saw a group of men standing in a circle around an Indian, shouting and laughing at him. One of the men punched the Indian in the face, and he fell to the ground. When I saw this, something snapped inside me. It was almost as if the man had punched me instead of the Indian.

"Leave him alone!" I shouted. I broke through the circle and faced the man who had slugged the Indian. He looked at me and laughed. I hit him in the stomach as hard as I could. The man was stunned, but not from the punch. I tried to help the Indian off the ground, but someone pulled me away from him. The man I hit shouted at me in Portuguese, then slapped me. I tried to get away, but the man who held me was too strong. The man slapped me again. He was about to slap me a third time, when a loud explosion erupted—his hand stopped in midswing.

It was Silver. He pumped another shell into the shotgun, leveled the barrel at the man's chest, and said something to him. The man said something back. Silver tightened his finger on the trigger. The man held up both hands and said something else. He turned to me and smiled, then ruffled my hair, as if the whole thing were a big joke. Silver didn't smile. The man holding me loosened his grip.

"They were beating up the Indian," I said. I looked for the Indian, but he had slipped away.

"They've been known to do that," Silver said. He didn't take the gun off the man. "I thought I told you to stay on the boat."

"I know, but I saw—"

"What's going on, Jake?" It was Doc, out of breath from running up the path.

"What are you doing here?" Silver asked him.

"I woke up and Jake was gone, so I went to look for him."

"And who's guarding the boat?"

"Flanna's down there."

"That's just great!" Silver said. "A woman who hates guns is guarding my boat."

The crowd that had gathered began to break up. Silver lowered his gun and the man walked away. Sorry, no bloodshed today, I thought.

Silver shoved the shotgun into Doc's good hand. "When you two finish sightseeing, come on back and we'll continue our cruise." He walked away, trailed by a nervous little man carrying a toolbox.

Doc looked around the town. "What were you doing up here?"

"Just wanted to stretch my legs."

"You couldn't have picked a more depressing spot."

"You haven't seen anything," I said, and told him about the gold pit outside town and the Indian getting punched.

"That's a good way to get killed, Jake. We better get back to the boat before Captain Bligh leaves without us. I wouldn't want to be marooned here."

"Tell me about it, mister!" a man said behind us.

We turned around. The man was a little over five feet tall. He had long, curly black hair, a scraggly beard, and no front teeth.

"Didn't mean to eavesdrop," he said. "Americans?"

Doc nodded.

"Thought so. And you're new in town?"

"Just passing through."

"Are you going up- or downriver?"

"Up."

"Oh." He looked disappointed, then a thought occurred to him. "But you're coming back down. What goes up must come down." He laughed at his joke.

"We've got to get going," Doc said. We started for the path, and the man joined us.

"My name's Fred Stoats."

"Nice to meet you, Fred," Doc said. We kept walking.

"I've been stuck here for two years. Had a claim . . . Had three claims, in fact, but I lost them. Been haulin' rock sacks out of the hellhole like a monkey ever since. Trying to get enough cash together to go downriver. Got to get back to the good old U.S. of A. and see my wife and little girl. She's real sick."

Doc stopped. "Who's sick? Your wife or your little girl?"

"Little girl. Little Mary, we call her. Has cancer. I miss her."

Doc looked at him, trying to figure out if he was telling the truth.

"You need help on your boat?" Fred asked.

"I don't think so." Doc started walking again. He didn't buy Fred's story, and neither did I.

"That was a real nice thing you done for Raul," he said to me.

"Who?"

"The Indian. His name's Raul."

"Oh." We got to the top of the trail.

"Those guys were giving him a rough time because of the jaguar," Fred added.

This stopped us in our tracks.

"What jaguar?" Doc asked.

"Boy, you guys *are* new in town! The jaguar that's been killin' the dogs at night. The jaguar that everyone's tryin' to get their hands on for the reward and pool money."

Fred had a captive audience now. Doc's eyes were lit up like flares. We weren't going anywhere.

Fred went on to explain that one of the store owners was offering fifty dollars for the jaguar's skin. This same owner had set up a betting pool. For a dollar you could bet on the jaguar's weight. The man with the closest guess would get all the money in the pool.

"How long has the jaguar been around here?" Doc asked.

"About two months. They've tried everything to kill that devil. They've tethered goats as bait and sat in shooting blinds all night, set snares. . . . They even put out poisoned meat. Nothing's worked, although we did lose a few dogs with that poisoned-meat idea. Nobody's even seen the jaguar. It comes in like fog and leaves like smoke."

"What makes you think it's a jaguar?" Doc asked.

"Ha! Come with me." He led us back into town, and we followed him as he zigzagged between several hovels. "There!" he said, pointing to the ground.

Doc squatted down and looked at the print in the mud. "That's a jaguar, all right."

"That's fresh from last night."

"So what about this Raul?"

"The rumor is that he's pretty good at tracking cats. I don't know if it's true, but that's what people say. Problem is that Raul doesn't want anything to do with it. Money doesn't mean a thing to him, and he thinks the jaguar should be left alone. Those men were just trying to convince him to give them a hand when your boy came along."

"I'd like to talk to Raul," Doc said.

Fred picked at something in his beard for a moment. "Well, I could take you to him," he said. He looked at his wrist as if he were checking the time. The only problem was, he didn't have a watch on. "I've got an important appointment in a few minutes. I sure hate to miss it. I'm meetin' a guy who might just be my ticket out of here."

Doc dug into his pocket and pulled out a twenty-dollar bill. Fred snatched it out of his hand and stuffed it into his pocket before Doc could change his mind. "Raul lives down in the Indian camp. It's not far."

He led us to a trail on the other side of town. The Indians' living conditions were worse than those in town, which was hard to believe. Despite the heat, people huddled near smoking fires to keep the insects away. Potbellied children ran around completely naked. I noticed ugly red scars on their legs and arms and asked Fred what they were.

"Piranha bites," he said. "They don't eat you up like in the movies, but they can sure take out a divot of flesh if they're hungry."

"Why don't these people live in town with everyone else?"

"They have their ways and we have ours. Living separate keeps the fights down, somewhat."

It was clear that we weren't welcome. Men and women with dull, hostile expressions watched us walk by. Most of them had tattoos all over their bodies, including their faces. Almost everyone we passed had golf-ball-sized wads of tobacco or something stuffed in their cheeks. Many of them spit strings of brown juice when we walked by.

"Don't pay attention," Fred said. "It's just their way."

We came to a stop outside a lean-to built next to a tree.

"Raul!" Fred shouted, adding something in Portuguese. "He don't speak any English and only a little Portuguese."

Raul crawled out of the lean-to and sat on his haunches, looking up at us. His right eye was swollen shut. He didn't seem to recognize me. Like the other Indians, he had black tattoos on his arms and face. On either side of his upper lip he had three tattooed lines that looked like cat whiskers. Two young girls, no more than six or seven years old, peeked at us from behind the tree the lean-to was against. A couple of people sauntered over to see what was going on. They were soon joined by several others.

"Tell him that I would like his help catching the jaguar," Doc said. "Tell him that I won't kill the jaguar. I'll use a drug to make the cat go to sleep. When the jaguar wakes up, I'll let him go someplace a long way from here where it will be safe."

"That's a mouthful," Fred said, picking at his beard and looking at his wrist.

"I'll give you more money when we leave," Doc told him.

Fred pantomimed as he talked, to make sure that Raul understood. Fred seemed to have some difficulty explaining the tranquilizing and waking-up part, but managed to get through it. Raul watched him impassively. A couple of times he glanced at Doc and me.

Fred finally came to the end of his speech. Raul stared off into the distance. We waited for what seemed like a long time. No one said anything—even the spitting stopped.

Raul turned his head toward Doc and said something. He then called one of the girls out from behind the tree and whispered in her ear. She and her friend ran off giggling.

Fred shook his head. "He said, 'No.'"

"Are you sure you explained it to him right?"

"Clear as a bell. He doesn't want to help you. We better go."

Doc didn't want to leave. "Tell him that the jaguar will die unless he lets me tranquilize it."

"I already did that," Fred insisted.

"Do it again!"

Fred rolled his eyes, then said a few more words. Raul shook his head, then climbed back into his lean-to. "Sorry," Fred said. "But I still get my money."

"You'll get it."

We walked back through the camp. The spitting started up again, and people began muttering things and snickering as we passed. I felt very uncomfortable. The Indians probably had the same feeling every day as they walked through the mining town on their way to the gold pit.

When we got back to the town, Doc gave Fred a five dollar bill. "You sure you don't need any help on your boat?" Fred asked. "I'd sure like to get out of here."

"I'm afraid not."

"Oh, well," Fred said. "Maybe I got the weight right on that cat. You know, it's just as well you didn't get that jaguar. Catching it alive wouldn't set well with most of the people around here."

Doc and I headed to the trail leading to the docks. About halfway down, we heard someone shouting behind us. It was the two little girls that had been with Raul. They ran up to us. One of them had her hands behind her back. She brought one hand forward and presented me with a piece of string.

"What's this?"

She brought her other hand forward and released a large metallic-blue butterfly. It was beautiful. The two girls giggled and ran back up the path. Doc and I watched the butterfly flutter back and forth, trying to get free.

"Morpho butterfly," Doc said.

I reached into my pocket with my free hand and took out my pocketknife. Doc helped me cut the string, and the morpho danced away into what was left of the forest.

CHAPTER 13

I was about ready to go up and look for you," Flanna said, when we got on board.

Doc told her what had happened.

"Are you sure this Fred explained the situation?"

Doc's understanding of Portuguese wasn't very good, but he said he thought that Raul understood. Silver came up from below for a second and got something out of the wheelhouse, then went back below without saying a word to us.

"How's the engine?" Doc asked.

"Silver and the mechanic have been arguing ever since they got down there. I feel sorry for the little man. Silver thinks we'll be under way again sometime tomorrow morning."

"Silver won't kill him. He needs him to fix the engine." Doc sat down on his hammock. Flanna took out her kit and started to change his bandage.

"I've got to do something about this jaguar," Doc told her. "The problem is time. If only we could capture it quickly. We'd learn so much by tracking it at the preserve— the jaguar would be like a guide. It's so frustrating!"

Doc wasn't frustrated. He was stimulated. This was the happiest he had been since we left Manaus.

"There's no time to put out a live trap, and I suspect the locals would tamper with it anyway," he continued. "They want the skin."

"Did you offer Raul money?"

"He doesn't seem to be interested in money."

"Perhaps I could go up and talk to him," Flanna suggested. "I know a few words of several dialects. Tranquilizing an animal is a very difficult concept to get across. He may have misunderstood."

"It might be worth a try," Doc said. "Let's get something to eat, then we'll go back up to the camp."

We didn't have to go back to the Indian camp, because Raul came to us. And he didn't come sauntering down the dock; he came from the river in a dugout canoe. While we were eating, we heard a tapping sound on the starboard side. At first we thought it was engine-repair noise from down below. The tapping got more insistent, and I took a look over the side. Raul was standing in the canoe, knocking on the hull as if it were the front door of a house.

"We have visitors," I announced.

The canoe had two other men in it. They lifted Raul onto

their shoulders so he could reach the rail. Flanna and I helped him the rest of the way up.

When he got on deck, he glanced nervously toward the dock and whispered something.

"He says that he came from the water so he wouldn't attract attention," Flanna translated. "His Portuguese is excellent."

Doc quickly pulled the mosquito netting down, and Raul began to relax, somewhat.

Raul talked quietly for several minutes. Flanna listened, asked questions, commented, smiled, and even laughed a couple of times. When he was finished, she said, "I'll give you the short version. Raul is certain he can help you capture the jaguar. He didn't tell you that this afternoon because he was afraid that some of the hunters in town might try to stop him if they knew. But before he agrees, he has a couple of conditions."

"Fantastic!" Doc said. He was very excited and it was good to see.

"The first is that he wants to look at the tranquilizer darts and have you explain how they work."

"No problem."

"After you've captured the jaguar, he wants to take it to town and have it weighed."

"Why?"

"I didn't quite understand this part, but I think he wants to pacify the people in town who've entered the betting pool."

"Okay," Doc said, but he didn't like the idea. I'm sure his preference was to take the jaguar and run.

"And finally," Flanna continued, "Raul wants to go with us to the preserve and see the jaguar set free."

Doc and I were both surprised by this.

"Doesn't he trust us?" Doc asked.

"I don't think it's that."

"Does he understand that we'll be at the preserve for at least a couple of months?"

"Yes, and he still wants to go."

Doc had to think about this one for a while. "Silver's not going to like the idea, but he's not in charge of the expedition. Tell Raul that if we don't get the jaguar, he doesn't go with us."

Flanna explained.

Raul nodded, then said, "I get jaguar." I guess he spoke a little English, too.

Doc got out his tranquilizing equipment.

"You'll have to do the honors, Jake. I can't do it one-handed."

Flanna explained how it all worked as I put the darts together. The darts used for cats are about three inches long. The shaft, where the drug is held, is made out of a hollow aluminum tube threaded on the inside on both ends. The tubes are reusable. I put a rubber plunger into one end of the shaft. I then took a brass gunpowder cap about the size of a .22 and seated it in the plunger. I screwed a cap over the top of this. The end cap has a tuft of cotton sticking out from it, which is how the air rifle pushes the dart out of the barrel.

I flipped the shaft over, ready to put the tranquilizer drug into it. Flanna showed Raul the little bottle of drugs and tried to explain how it worked. He looked at the bottle carefully, obviously confused by this part of the procedure. Doc told me how much of each type of drug to put into the shaft. When it was full, I screwed the needle onto the end.

Doc showed Raul the dart rifle. Doc held his hand over the barrel and dry-fired it to prove to Raul that it was harmless without the dart in it. Raul put his own hand over the end of the barrel and nodded for Doc to pull the trigger. He smiled when he felt the puff of air come out. He said something to Flanna and she laughed.

"He said it works like a blowgun."

"Exactly."

When the demonstration was finished, Raul climbed back over the side and got into the canoe. He said that he would return sometime before sunrise the next morning.

"What are we going to tell Silver?" I asked.

"Nothing at this point," Doc said. "We'll worry about it later, *if* we capture the jaguar. The chances of that are pretty slim."

* * *

Raul showed up about half an hour before sunrise, carrying a small, dirty cotton bag over his shoulder. He handed the bag up to me and said something to Flanna.

"These are his things for the trip upriver," Flanna said.

The bag was nearly empty. I guess he believed in traveling light. I put it under my hammock.

Raul brought three canoes and three men to help us. We lowered the equipment to them quietly so we wouldn't wake Silver. I was afraid Scarlet would hear us and call out, but she must have gone on another shore leave.

Once we were in the canoes, they pushed off and started paddling against the current. It was a very dark night, and I could hardly see anything ahead of us, but the men paddling didn't seem to have a problem navigating through the darkness. The insects swarmed all around us, despite the insect repellent we had smeared on. We paddled upriver a couple of miles until we came to a small tributary. We followed the tributary for another mile, then stopped. Raul got out and motioned for us to stay in the canoes. He went off into the forest and was gone for about half an hour. By the time he returned, it was light out. He spoke to Flanna in a soft whisper.

"He says that the jaguar is a female."

"How does he know that?" Doc asked.

Flanna shrugged her shoulders. "He wants us to follow him with the rifle and darts. When we have the jaguar, he'll call the other men and they'll bring the rest of the equipment."

Raul moved through the forest with the grace of a deer.

His toes were splayed out and twisted from a lifetime of walking barefoot over uneven terrain. He came to a small open area and stopped. He whispered to Flanna.

"He wants to know who is going to dart the jaguar."

"Jake's the shooter," Doc said. "I can't do it with my bum hand."

Doc had taught me to use the dart rifle when I was a little kid.

"Okay," Flanna said. "We're to wait here and stay out of sight. Raul will position Jake up ahead and call the jaguar to him."

"He's going to call the jaguar?" Doc asked, in surprise.

"That's what he says."

"This I've got to see. You have everything, Jake."

I slipped a loaded dart into the breech of the rifle. "I'm ready."

"You'll only get one chance."

I nodded and followed Raul deeper into the forest. He stopped at the base of a huge tree and positioned me near the trunk behind a tangle of vines. He pointed to a spot about twenty feet away. I guessed this is where he thought the jaguar was going to appear. I lay down in a prone position. When I was comfortable, I flipped the safety off and brought the butt of the rifle up to my shoulder.

Raul moved off to my right, disappearing from view. For a long time nothing happened. Sweat trickled down my face. Insects buzzed all around me, and it took all my willpower to resist swatting them away. I heard a bird call to my right. I wondered when Raul was going to start. The bird called again, and I realized that Raul had already started! I didn't know what kind of bird he was imitating, but the call certainly sounded genuine.

Several minutes passed. My neck began to cramp. I started to wonder how Raul knew where the jaguar was going to appear. What if the cat came up behind me? Or over to my left? *Stop it, Jake! Think like you're stalking. Breathe. Concentrate on the spot. There's nothing but the spot. . . .* I saw a leaf move in the clump of palms in front of me. There was a shift in the forest, as if the volume had been turned down. The jaguar was here. She wanted the bird. I saw her head first—yellow fur spotted with black rosettes, bright golden eyes. Her stocky, powerful body moved low to the ground as she placed each foot with infinite care before taking the next step. I didn't move. I took long, slow breaths. I wanted to put the dart in her thick haunch muscle. *Wait for the rosette to come to you. Wait. . . .*

Pop! I hadn't consciously pulled the trigger. The sound startled me. When the dart hit, she jumped straight up and let out a chest-rattling roar. She bit angrily at the dart in her haunch, tearing it out of her leg. She licked her wound, then walked away. I waited. Five minutes passed. Someone touched me on the shoulder. Raul. I stood up and worked the kink out of my neck. Doc and Flanna came over.

"Nice shot, Jake." Doc looked at his watch. "We'll give

her a few more minutes to make sure she's completely out." Flanna told Raul what we were doing.

We found her about fifty yards away, lying on her side.

Raul's men came up with the medical kit and the stretcher to carry her back to the boat. Doc checked the jaguar's breathing and squeezed some ointment into her open eyes, so they wouldn't dry out. He looked at her teeth.

"I'd say she's four or five years old. If it is a she." He lifted her hind leg. "Damn!"

"What?"

"She has milk, which means she has cubs somewhere."

Flanna explained the situation to Raul. He nodded and took off into the forest with one of his men. About ten minutes later, Raul came back alone.

"He found the cubs," Flanna said. "He thinks there are two of them."

He led us to the den, which was under a tree near a small stream. Doc bent down and shone his flashlight inside. "Two sets of eyes. I'd guess they're three or four months old—close to being weaned. She's probably been bringing dog meat back to them for weeks. It's going to take awhile to get them out of here. Maybe we should take their mom back to the boat before she comes out of the drug, then come back and get them. We can bring some crates back to put the cubs in. I don't think they'll leave the den, but someone should stay here and make sure."

Flanna spoke to Raul, and he told one of his men to guard the den.

We carried the female to the canoes and paddled back to the mining settlement. As soon as we arrived the word went out and a stream of people ran down the path to see the jaguar.

Doc wanted to get her right on the boat and put her into the cage we had assembled the night before, but Raul stopped him and pointed up the path.

"You made a deal," Flanna reminded Doc.

"I know, but it doesn't make sense. The best thing for the jaguar is to get her right onto the boat." He looked at Raul. It was clear that Raul expected Doc to take the jaguar up to town. Doc sighed. "We'll have to hurry," he said. "She'll be waking up pretty soon."

Silver came walking down the dock with his shotgun. He looked at the jaguar. "I saw the cage on deck this morning," he said. "I should have known it was something like this."

He only knew one third of it.

"We have to take her up to be weighed," Doc said. He explained the deal he had made with Raul, leaving out the part about Raul coming with us.

Silver shook his head. "You know, Doc, this isn't a movie and the men up in town aren't actors. They're very real and they're not going to be happy about Doctor Dolittle taking their fun away."

"I know."

"Well, as long as you know. At least the engine is working, so we can get out of here reasonably quickly. Let's get this over with."

"You're coming with us?" Doc asked.

"Dead passengers would be very bad for my reputation."

"Who'll guard the boat?" Flanna asked.

"Our friendly little mechanic is still down there. He knows better than to let anyone on board, and I haven't paid him yet, which should keep him on our side for the time being."

We walked up the path with a parade of people behind us. There was a huge crowd waiting inside the store, spilling out into the street. We had to push our way through the entrance and up to the weight scale. Behind the scale was a long blackboard with names and numbers. Hanging on a hook above the board was a three-gallon bucket filled with money. The store owner came over and looked at the jaguar. He jumped backward.

"He just discovered that your jaguar is still alive," Silver said, grinning. He seemed to be enjoying himself.

The owner started shouting at Raul.

"He's not pleased about losing out on the skin," Silver interpreted. "And he's blaming Raul because he led you to the jaguar. Bad day in Mudville. Go ahead and put her on the scale and let's get out of here."

Doc and I put her on the scale, and the owner moved the counterweights to balance the arm. He took his time about it, nudging the smallest weight on the arm little by little. The room got very quiet. Most of the men stared intently at the scales, hoping their number would come up. Fred Stoats stared at Flanna with his toothless mouth hanging open. The owner was finally satisfied with the weight and wrote it down on a piece of paper. He announced the weight in Portuguese, then turned to the board and ran his finger down the list of names and numbers, stopping at seventy-two kilos.

"Raul," the owner said, quietly.

Fred Stoats tore up his mark and threw it on the floor in disgust. He leaned over and hissed in my ear: "You should have taken me upriver! You're going to regret it now." He stamped out of the store.

"You better get your jaguar out of here, Doc," Silver said. "I have a feeling that things are about to get very ugly."

No wonder Raul had insisted we take the jaguar up to be weighed. He was more interested in money than we had thought.

Doc and I rolled the jaguar onto the stretcher. Raul stepped forward and gave the store owner his mark, then held his hand out for the bucket. The owner took the bucket down, but hesitated in handing it over to him.

Silver said something to the owner. I don't know what it was, but men immediately got as far away from Silver as they could. The owner's face turned bright red.

"Do you have the cat?" Silver asked, without taking his

eyes off the owner. Flanna and I picked the stretcher up.

"We're all going to leave together," Silver said. "You and your pet first, then me and your friend, Raul, with his bucket of money." He said something to the owner and punctuated it by pumping a shell into the chamber of his shotgun. The owner very reluctantly handed the bucket to Raul. "The party's over. Let's move out."

I backed out the door with the stretcher. Doc was behind me, clearing the way. When we got outside, I turned around so I could see where I was going. We walked over to the path and started down.

"Doc," Silver yelled. "Why don't you run ahead and get the mooring ropes untied. As soon as they gather their wits, they'll be coming down. I'd like to be gone when they get there."

Doc ran ahead of us. I glanced behind. Silver was walking backward down the trail. Raul walked next to him with his bucket. A group of men were following, but they kept their distance. The jaguar lifted her head for a second, then put it back down. She was coming out of the drug. When we got down to the dock, we started moving faster. By the time we got to the boat, Doc had the lines untied. We got the jaguar aboard. Silver scrambled up to the wheel house, ignoring the mechanic's complaints about getting his money. The engine came to life, and we started backing out.

When we got far enough away from the dock, Silver swung the bow around and started upriver at a pretty good clip. We put the jaguar in the cage. After a while, Silver came down from the wheelhouse to take a look at our new passenger.

The jaguar snarled at him. "She doesn't look very grateful, Doc."

Doc looked up at him. "Thanks for your help, Silver."

"All part of the service." Silver grinned. "To tell you the truth, I sort of enjoyed it, but let's not do it again. We'll drop Raul and the mechanic off upriver. Raul is going to have to stay out of town, but he'll be able to go anywhere he wants with the money he won."

"He's coming with us," Doc said.

Silver stopped grinning. "Why?"

"He wants to see the jaguar set free. Also, he happens to be the best cat tracker I've ever seen. I need him."

"Doc, Indians are the most unreliable people on earth. He won't stick around. He'll just take off one day without a word. They always do."

I thought about Silver's wife, Alicia, and his son, Tito.

"He can leave whenever he wants," Doc said.

"So now I have an Indian and a jaguar to worry about. What's next?"

"Three jaguars," I said.

Doc told him about the two cubs. When he finished, it started to rain.

Silver looked up at the sky. "I should change the boat's name to *Silver's Ark*." He walked back up to the wheelhouse.

"He took that better than I expected," Doc said.

* * *

The jaguar cubs were much bigger than Doc had predicted. They put up quite a fight as I used a noose pole to pull them out of the den. I was surprised to see that one of them was black and one was spotted.

"Black jaguars aren't that unusual," Doc said. "The black fur is called melanism. It's just a color phase. If the sun hits the fur just right, you can still see the outlines of spots."

We paddled back to the boat and handed the crates up to Silver and Flanna. When we got back on board, we helped the mechanic into one of the canoes. Raul then took his bucket of money and lowered it over the side to one of the men, and said something to him.

Silver looked very surprised.

"Raul told his friend to give the money to the people in the Indian camp," Flanna explained.

"I wouldn't have bet on that," Silver said. He said something to Raul in Portuguese, then went back up to the wheelhouse.

Flanna smiled. "Our captain just told Raul that he was welcome on his boat anytime."

"I guess there's hope for this expedition yet," Doc said. "Let's get a cage put together for the cubs."

"Why don't we put them in with their mother?" Flanna asked.

"It would be too crowded. They're ready to be weaned, anyway."

We assembled another cage and set it right next to the female's cage, so the cubs could at least see their mother.

"Our biggest problem is going to be feeding them," Doc said. "Their favorite food is the peccary and capybara, but they'll eat just about anything they can catch—turtles, deer, monkeys, sloths, snakes, lizards, caiman, birds, opossum, fish, and even snails and insects."

"Perhaps Raul is as good a hunter as he is a tracker," Flanna said.

"Let's hope so."

That night, Doc's mood was still upbeat. He had three jaguars, and he hadn't even gotten to the preserve yet.

Flanna removed his bandage. "I think the burns are finally starting to heal," she told him. "There'll be some small scars, but I think they'll go away with time."

I stood up suddenly, startling both Doc and Flanna.

"Did something bite you?" Doc asked.

"No, just feeling restless. I think I'll go up and talk to Silver for a while."

In all the excitement I had forgotten to tell Silver about the man with the scar. I climbed the stairs to the wheelhouse. He was standing at the helm with Scarlet perched on his shoulder.

"What's up?" He, too, seemed pretty cheerful.

"I forgot to tell you that I thought I saw the man with the scar in town yesterday. At least I think it was him. He was standing near the trail, looking at the *Tito* through binoculars."

Silver didn't say anything for a few moments. "Facial scars are almost as common as ears in this country. And it's very unlikely that the same guy would be way up here."

"Maybe he followed us."

"He already went through the boat. Why would he follow us? Forget about it, Jake."

"What about him watching us through binoculars?"

"I'm sure someone in town checks out every new boat that comes in. It's not the same guy."

I didn't push the issue any further, but there was a definite change in Silver's mood. The cheerfulness of a few seconds ago was gone.

"Is there anything else?" he asked, staring out the window.

"I guess not," I said, and left him alone.

When I got back to my hammock, there was something sitting on my pillow. It was wrapped in a green leaf.

"What's this?"

"I don't know," Doc said. "Raul put it there."

I looked over at Raul. He was watching the jaguars.

I opened the leaf. Inside was a large yellowed canine tooth. It had a small hole drilled in one end of it. I showed it to Doc.

"Jaguar," Doc said.

I looked back at Raul. He was watching me and said something to Flanna.

"He says it's to make you strong."

I smiled at him. He nodded and turned back to the

jaguars. I took off my snake amulet, ran the leather thong through the tooth, then put it on. I went over to Raul and showed him the tooth around my neck. He nodded with approval. I pulled out my pocketknife and gave it to him. He tried to give it back, but I folded his rough, copper-colored fingers around the knife and shook my head.

That night, Silver didn't let the anchors down. When Doc asked him why, Silver said he wanted to push upriver to make up for the lost time.

CHAPTER 14

The next few days were relatively calm. Raul spent most of his time sitting in a folding chair staring at the shoreline. I gave him a pair of binoculars to use. He could hardly keep them away from his eyes. At night he slept on the hard deck, just out of reach of the young jaguars. When Raul wasn't looking through the binoculars, he was looking over Doc's shoulder, while Flanna tried to explain what Doc was doing. Raul was enthralled with anything that had to do with technology, like Doc's laptop computer and the radio collars. Flanna joked that if we were on the boat much longer, Raul might become a computer nerd.

Raul also spent a lot of time with Silver up in the wheelhouse talking late into the night. They seemed to enjoy each other's company, which surprised all of us.

Doc's mood held up. He was excited about the preserve and the work ahead. He spent hours looking at the jaguars, and they spent hours looking at us. He built special radio collars for the two cubs. The battery pack was smaller, and the collars were made out of light canvas instead of the heavy canvas he was using on the big jaguars. His plan was to put the collars on when we got to the refuge.

"The reason I'm using the light canvas is because the cubs are still growing," he explained. "We'll try to recapture them in a couple of months and put on bigger collars. If we fail to capture them, these light collars will rot and fall off before they constrict their necks."

We named the jaguars. Well, actually Doc let me name them. The black cub was Wild Bill, after Bill Brewster. The spotted cub was Taw. And I named their mother, Beth, after my mom. Doc thought the names were perfect.

When we anchored at night, Raul gathered food for the jaguars. Sometimes he'd spear fish in the shallow water alongshore. Other times he'd go deep into the forest to hunt. He had made a bow as tall as he was and several arrows that were nearly as long as the bow. He rarely came back empty-handed. Once he brought back two howler monkeys. Another time he brought back a capybara—a rodent the size of a small dog. On his last hunting trip he hit the jackpot and bagged a tapir, which provided several hundred pounds of meat. Flanna and I had to help him carry the tapir back to the boat and put it into the cooler. Doc thought it would keep the jaguars' stomachs full until we got to the preserve.

The farther upriver we got, the fewer settlements there

were. We also started seeing a lot more wildlife, especially in the early morning and late evening. We saw troops of howler and woolly monkeys scurrying through the canopy alongshore. Giant river otters slid off the muddy banks and swam out to the boat to check us out. Flanna said the otters were called "jaguars of the river" because of their voracious appetites and skill at catching fish. Once in a while we saw an anaconda swim by, or passed a tree boa sunning itself on a branch. And of course there were countless birds darting in and out of the green tangle of trees and plants growing onshore. I think my favorite animals were the *boutos,* or Amazon dolphins. They had pinkish skin and long beaks and rode our bow waves for miles as we made our way upriver to the preserve.

One night while we were anchored, Silver took the Zodiac out by himself. He took off upriver with Scarlet flying above him and screaming her lungs out. He didn't get back until long after dark. We were all worried about him.

When we asked him what had taken him so long, he said that he had had a little motor trouble. "Took awhile to get it going. No big deal."

Before Silver went up to the wheelhouse, Doc asked him when he thought we were going to arrive at the preserve.

"Within a week," he said, confidently.

The next morning Silver pulled the anchors up very early. We had gone maybe ten miles upriver when he slowed the *Tito* down, took a hard left, and gunned the engine. Raul fell out of his chair. At first we thought Silver had done it to avoid a floating tree, but nothing passed by us and he continued heading toward the shore.

Doc and I climbed up to the wheelhouse to find out what was going on.

"What are you doing, Silver?" Doc asked.

"Shortcut," Silver said, continuing his heading. "And I thought we had an agreement that I was the captain."

"I'm not disputing that," Doc said. "I just want to know what's going on."

We were about thirty feet from shore. Silver slowed the boat down, then dropped the bow anchor to hold us in place.

"You see that tributary?" He pointed to an opening alongshore. It was barely wide enough for the *Tito* to squeeze through.

Silver went into his cabin and brought a map out. "Let's pretend for a moment that the Amazon River is an interstate freeway, because in a sense that's what it is. It's the main highway through the Amazon Basin. Now, up here, right along the highway, is your preserve." He pointed to a large area marked in red. "And here is where you wanted to set up your base camp." There was a black *X*. "Are you with me?"

"I'm with you," Doc said. "But I still don't know where you're going."

"If you had the choice of releasing jaguars in the center of a national forest or near a freeway off-ramp, which would you choose?"

"The center, of course."

"Well, I think I have a way of getting us right to the center. You can't get there overland. There are too many swamps and other obstacles. I suspect the jaguars you want to catch and collar aren't living next to the freeway, either. They're here." He pointed to the center of the preserve.

"So how do we get there by boat?"

Silver pointed to a squiggly blue line.

"That tributary doesn't even reach the border of the preserve!" Doc protested.

"I think it does."

"You said you hadn't been in this area before. How could you possibly know that?"

"I don't," Silver admitted. "But I think it's worth a try."

"Based on what?"

"A hunch, Doc. Do you ever get those?"

Doc nodded. He was the king of hunches. "But we're supposed to meet Buzz and Woolcott up here." Doc pointed to the agreed-upon spot for the base camp.

"We have several weeks before we have to be there. If I'm right, by the time they show up, we'll have already explored the interior of the preserve. Your three cats will be miles away from civilization and safe. And I'll bet you'll have several more jaguars radio-collared."

Doc looked at the entrance to the narrow tributary. "It

doesn't look wide enough for the boat."

"It's tight," Silver admitted. "But it gets wider about a mile in. I took the Zodiac up there last night. If I'm wrong and the tributary stops, we'll turn around and continue with our original plan. We'll only lose a few days, which I think we can afford, since you already have three jaguars in hand."

"Let's get Flanna up here," Doc said.

When she got there, Silver explained the plan again. Flanna was willing, but she was suspicious of Silver's motivation. "Why would you risk your boat to do this?"

"First of all," he said, "we're not going to lose the boat. If it doesn't work out, we will lose some time and some blood—the insects are really bad up there. Second, I want to see if I'm right. And third, even if I'm wrong, I want to see what's up there."

"Curiosity," Flanna said.

Silver nodded.

* * *

It was worse than any of us could have imagined. Silver was right: the tributary did get wider about a mile up, but not by much. The branches from the trees on both sides scraped the side of the boat. Twice, snakes dropped onto the deck. Raul scooped them into the water as casually as if he were dropping a banana peel overboard.

In some places the branches met in the middle overhead, nearly blocking out all the sunlight. The main channel twisted and turned in impossible ways. We hit so many floating trees that Scarlet gave up warning Silver altogether.

But the worst of it was the insects. Black clouds of gnats, mosquitoes, and blackflies engulfed the boat. They were so thick on the outside of our mosquito netting that we couldn't see through it.

The jaguars started to go crazy. We had to leave the safety of our mosquito netting and put netting over their cages. When the net was set, Doc used two cans of repellent to kill the insects trapped inside.

Throughout the day we lay in our hammocks trying not to scratch the red, itchy welts covering our bodies. The only one who didn't seem bothered by our situation was Raul. He sat in a folding chair and flipped through *National Geographic* magazines as if he were on the deck of a luxury liner.

That night, Silver turned on bright floodlights and continued up the tributary.

The next morning, Doc and I made a dash for the wheelhouse to bring Silver some food and see if he needed us to take over the helm, so he could rest. He looked absolutely terrible. His face was swollen with bites, and he was so exhausted he could barely keep his eyes open. Even Scarlet looked tired.

"We need to turn back," Doc said.

Silver nodded wearily. "I think you're right. But the only way we can do it is to back our way out of here, which isn't going to be easy. I can steer the boat from the deck wheel, but someone's going to have to sit in the stern and give me directions."

Doc went first. He wore a long-sleeve shirt, gloves, and a special hat with mosquito netting to protect his face and neck. We also put netting around the deck wheel to shield Silver from the insects, which made it very difficult for him to see out.

Doc shouted out instructions: *Hard right! Center! That's good! Left! Stop! Center!* for two hours. It was very slow going. As Flanna got ready to relieve Doc, we heard a loud screeching sound and the engine came to a sudden stop.

Silver swore and disappeared below deck to the engine room. He came back up with very bad news.

CHAPTER 15

"We no longer have a reverse gear," Silver said.

"Can it be fixed?" Flanna asked.

"I'm afraid not. At least not here."

"So what do we do?" Doc asked.

"Follow the tributary and hope there's a place to turn around up ahead."

"And if there isn't?"

"There has to be."

Silver climbed up to the wheelhouse and started the boat back up the tributary.

* * *

By the next morning nothing had changed. If anything, the tributary had narrowed. Doc and I went up to the wheelhouse to relieve Silver at the helm. He had been up all night, and he didn't resist when Doc suggested that we take over for a while.

I led Silver to the cot in his cabin. Scarlet followed us

and landed on her perch.

"This is all my fault," Silver said.

I told him that it wasn't, but I don't think he heard me before he fell asleep.

Doc was sitting in the captain's chair with his good hand resting on the helm. Insects bounced against the windshield, trying desperately to get inside for a bite to eat.

"I'm sorry I got you into this, Jake," Doc said. "I should have insisted that you go back."

"I didn't want to go back."

"I know."

I had been waiting to ask him this question for weeks. And I knew that now wasn't the best time to get into it with him, but he was the one who brought it up. "Why didn't you want me down here with you?"

"Because of situations like this," Doc said, pointing up ahead. "The danger . . ."

"There's more to it than that!"

Doc nodded. "You're right," he said, softly. "There's a lot more."

I waited and I started to feel guilty for pushing the issue. Doc was tired and he was scared. *I* was scared. "Maybe we should talk about this later," I said.

"No. You've been waiting long enough. I just don't know if I can explain it. I'm not sure if I understand what's going on myself."

"You don't have to, Doc."

"I'll try," he said. "When we came back from Kenya and moved to Poughkeepsie, I thought that everything would be fine. That I'd work on my field notes and you'd go to school. In the summer, maybe we'd take off and go someplace and come back in the fall so you could go back to school. That was the plan, anyway. But after a month I started to feel restless, and I knew it wasn't going to work." He looked at me. "To tell you the truth, Jake. If Bill hadn't called with this field project, I would have tried to get a project of my own."

"You mean you would have left me behind?"

"Yes," he said. "I think I would have."

I let this sink in for a minute, and it didn't feel very good. "I thought we were partners."

"This is where it gets confusing for me. I was trying to be a good father and a good field biologist. I now realize that doing both at the same time may not be possible.

"Your mom understood this. That's why she stayed at the university and didn't go into the field. She was the one making sure you got to school, that you went to the doctor and dentist, and that you had someone to talk to when you had a problem. She loved you very, very much. You are who you are because of Beth, not because of me. I let you down, Jake. And I let her down, too."

I started to protest, but he stopped me.

"If we get out of this, we're going back to Poughkeepsie."

"But your work . . ."

"No," he interrupted. "It's time I started acting like your

father. The work can wait. You'll be out of high school in three years. That leaves plenty of time for me to get back into the field. Beth wanted you to have a formal education. You can't get one down here. I want to complete what she started. I owe her that. You're the best work we ever did. Beth saw to that, and I wish she were here so I could tell her."

I started to cry. I couldn't help myself. My father joined me.

"If only Silver could see us now," I said.

Doc laughed and wiped his tears away. "Yeah, he'd be real impressed."

"I don't think you'll be happy in Poughkeepsie," I said.

"Poughkeepsie looks pretty good right now."

I had to agree with him on this, but I knew Doc well enough to realize that his resolve could change overnight. All it would take was another field project, another animal in trouble, and he would be gone.

"What about Flanna?"

"I'm sorry I didn't tell you about her before you got down here. I should have. In fact, Flanna asked me to, but I didn't know what to say, or how you would take it. It was selfish of me."

"So you love her?"

"I think so, but I don't know where it's going to take us. She's a remarkable woman. I'm not sure she deserves to be stuck with someone like me."

"She could do a lot worse."

"She could also do a lot better."

"I like her," I told him, and I meant it.

"I'm glad to hear that, Jake."

A few hours later, Doc asked me to go below and get one of the handheld global positioning units we had on board. I brought it up and turned it on, but I had to wait for an opening before I could get a hit off one of the satellites orbiting thousands of miles above us. After I got the reading, Doc had me take the wheel, so he could calculate where we were on the map.

"Silver's hunch was right," he said. "We're miles from where the tributary ends on the map. We've crossed the preserve boundary and we're headed toward the center in a roundabout way. Not that it will do us much good."

"I think it will open up," Silver said from behind us.

We turned around. He didn't look much better after four hours of sleep.

"What makes you think so?" Doc asked.

"Because I was right about the tributary leading to the center of the preserve," he said, but he didn't look all that confident.

We stared at the map as if it might help us in some mysterious way.

* * *

That afternoon, Silver called all of us into the wheelhouse to discuss our options. As we talked, he continued to steer the boat upstream.

Doc wanted to know if we could widen the channel and make our own turnaround.

"We'd bottom out in the shallows," Silver said.

"What about taking the Zodiac back down to the river and getting help?" Flanna suggested.

"We're beyond help up here," Silver said. "Any boat big enough to pull us out would find itself in the same situation as we are." He paused, as if he were reconsidering the idea. "I guess we could start ferrying people down to the river. The Zodiac will carry three of us. It would be a hellish trip, but at least . . ."

Scarlet screamed and started hitting the window with her beak. Silver quickly reduced power. All of us looked out the window, trying to see what she was so upset about. We couldn't see anything. Just the same narrow channel crowded with vegetation and trees. There was nothing blocking our way.

"What's gotten into you?" Silver asked. Scarlet started screaming even louder and hit the glass so hard I thought it would break. Silver slid the side window open and Scarlet took off through it as if she were being chased by a harpy eagle. She flew straight down the channel and disappeared around the bend.

"I guess she didn't like the idea of us using the Zodiac to get out of here," Silver said. "I can't say that I blame her."

I stared out through the open window and what I *didn't*

see amazed me. "The insects are gone," I said. They weren't totally gone, but there were several million fewer than there had been a few minutes earlier.

Flanna put her hand outside. When she pulled it back in, there were only half a dozen gnats and mosquitoes crawling on it. "Now that's what I call an improvement," she said.

Silver eased the boat around the next bend. "Well, I'll be . . ."

About three hundred yards in front of us was an opening with bright light shining through it. We stared in stunned silence as it drew nearer. When we passed through, we found ourselves on a small lake. Silver cut the engine and started the anchors down.

Everyone stepped out of the wheelhouse. In front of us was a sheer, rocky wall about thirty feet high. A waterfall poured down from the top. Clinging to the side of the wall was a flock of red and yellow macaws. When they saw the boat, they took off, disappearing into the green canopy surrounding the little lake. All but one, that is . . . Scarlet still clung to the wall, wondering why her new friends had abandoned her. To the left of the wall was a sandy beach.

Flanna, Doc, and I hugged each other.

"I knew it was here!" Silver said. "I just knew it!"

The only one of us who didn't seem surprised or moved by the discovery was Raul. He went to the back of the boat to get the binoculars and started scanning the shore.

Silver checked one of the anchor cables. "It's deep," he

said. "It must be some kind of natural sinkhole."

Doc went to the wheelhouse and brought back the map and the global positioning system. He got a reading immediately and marked a small red circle on the map. The lake was almost exactly in the center of the preserve.

He looked up at Silver. "That was some hunch," he said.

Silver was too excited to respond.

The Preserve

CHAPTER 16

T he jaguars are free," Doc said. "Over."

"Roger. I'm switching to telemetry mode. Out." I dropped the Morpho's left wing and started slowly circling eight hundred feet above the canopy. I dialed in Beth's frequency. When I picked up the steady *beep . . . beep . . . beep* from her radio collar, I marked her position with the GPS and wrote the location down in the notebook Doc had given me. Next I dialed in Wild Bill's collar, then Taw's. The three jaguars were together under the umbrella of rain forest canopy.

I flipped the switch back to radio. "They're all coming in loud and clear."

"Great!" Doc said. "Raul and I are going to do some exploring. We should be back later this afternoon, or early this evening. Out."

It was a beautiful day despite the intense heat. As I flew back toward camp, I again tried to see the tributary we had taken

to get to the lake. It was nowhere in sight. The canopy completely covered it. No wonder it wasn't shown on the map. We
all referred to it as the tunnel now. None of us were looking
forward to going back through it when the time came.

We had been at the lake for two weeks. It took us three days
to set up camp, and five days for me to get the Morpho back
together. It would have taken a lot longer if Silver hadn't
helped me.

The spot we picked for camp was about two hundred feet
in from shore under the rain forest canopy. We put up four
tents—one for Doc and Flanna, one for me, a cook tent, and
a tent for our gear. Silver slept on the boat in his cabin.
The boat was anchored on the far side of the lake, near the
tunnel, so I'd have enough room to take off and land the
Morpho. Silver used the Zodiac to get to it.

Raul built a lean-to out of large palms near the edge of
camp. We told him that we had a tent for him, but he
wasn't interested. There was another thing he wasn't interested in, either—clothes. The first day we got to the lake,
he took his off and hadn't put them on since. The only thing
he wore was the cotton bag slung over his shoulder. It was
a little strange having him running around naked, but we
got used to it after a few days.

Raul continued to give me little presents. There was a
flat rock next to the waterfall that I sat on during the heat
of the day to cool off, and, from time to time, he would

leave me gifts up there. So far he had given me the jaguar tooth, various feathers, a turtle skull, a blue stone, and a dried piranha jaw. I never thanked him for the gifts. Instead, I'd leave a gift for him on the rock in exchange. I had given him the pocketknife, a mini-flashlight, a pair of pliers, and a five-dollar bill, which was worthless, but it's all I had at the time.

Flanna was in botanical heaven. We hadn't been out of the boat for ten minutes before she was up in a tree, crawling around in the canopy looking things over. She set up a canopy research station about half a mile from camp. She spent all day up there and, sometimes, all night.

Doc had slipped back into his usual intense self. He was up before the howler monkeys let loose with their morning serenade. He would slurp down a cup of coffee, pack his gear, and disappear into the rain forest with Raul at his side. Going back to Poughkeepsie was the furthest thing from his mind, which didn't surprise me.

With Raul's help, he had already captured one anteater, three monkeys, two capybaras, one paca, one tapir, and a number of other small mammals. Most of the animals were radio-collared and set free. The animals that were too small to be radio-collared were either tagged or tattooed. Doc wanted to know what types of animals were out in the forest, how they utilized the forest, and how they interacted with one another.

He was also running telemetry trials—trying to determine the effectiveness of radio tracking from the ground with a handheld antenna and receiver. One problem with air-tracking is that on some days you simply can't fly because of weather or mechanical problems. Doc found out that the new ground tracking equipment we had would pick up a collar from about five miles away, and sometimes further, depending on the terrain and where the animal was hanging out. He was quite pleased with the results, because it meant we could effectively track on the ground when the Morpho couldn't fly.

At night, Doc would come stumbling back into camp totally exhausted and spend hours entering data into his laptop computer.

Flanna and I were concerned about how hard he was pushing himself. He wasn't drinking enough water or eating enough food, he slept about four hours a night, and he paid absolutely no attention to our advice. He wanted this preserve for the animals and the rain forest, but, most of all, he wanted it for Bill Brewster. He wasn't about to let his human frailties stand in the way of fulfilling his friend's dream. The dream was driving him to his limits.

After his initial excitement over finding the lake, Silver became edgy again. He wanted everyone to keep the shotguns handy, but Flanna and Doc absolutely refused this time around. They were no longer on the boat, and Silver was no longer their captain. Silver stuck very close to camp during the first few days. At night I'd see him sitting on the deck of the boat, staring out across the lake.

After about a week his attitude changed. He began taking short trips into the rain forest by himself. As the days went by, the trips got longer and longer. He became almost as driven as Doc, but I had no idea why. He would leave for a day or two at a time, come dragging back into camp covered in sweat and grime, then take the Zodiac out to the boat. When I asked him where he went, he'd say he was just out for a relaxing little stroll. He didn't look relaxed to me.

And Scarlet? She spent most of her time with her new feathered friends doing whatever macaws do in the rain forest. The only time she came to camp was when the flock visited the lake, and she never stayed long. When the flock flew away, she was right in the middle of it.

As for me, I spent as much time as possible flying above the canopy in the Morpho. I took the ultralight up twice a day, weather permitting, to get locations on the collared animals.

Doc had waited to release the jaguars until he had a better understanding of the area. Now that they were free, tracking would be a lot more interesting.

* * *

This was by far the clearest day I had flown, and I wasn't eager to get back to camp. Every time I went up, I'd try to pick a different route back to the lake, but I didn't detour too much out of the way because we were low on gas and couldn't afford to waste it.

Landing in the lake was easy compared to landing on the river. There was very little crosswind and the current was slow. The only thing I had to watch out for was the pair of dolphins that showed up periodically in the lake. Fortunately, they had learned to dive into the depths when they heard the Morpho's engine.

I taxied to the beach, cut the engine, then jumped out and pulled the Morpho up on the sand. I put a tarp over it to protect the fabric from deteriorating in the sun.

I didn't expect anyone to be at camp, but now that the jaguars had been set free, it seemed more deserted than normal. Up until today, the cats had kept me company during the long wait between flights.

I went over to Doc's tent and transferred the coordinates from the morning's flight into his logbook. When he got back this evening, he would enter the data into his computer. This was all I had to do until late afternoon, when I'd take my second flight.

I put my shorts on, grabbed a towel, and headed down to the rock. When I got there, I found yet another gift from Raul. It was some kind of nutshell with geometric designs carved in it. He must have carved it with the knife I'd given him. I felt in my pocket and found an automatic pencil. It wasn't much, but it was better than a five-dollar bill. I was running out of things to leave for him.

I lay back and let the mist from the waterfall cool me off.

Doc had been so preoccupied we hadn't had a chance to

continue the conversation we had in the boat on the way through the tunnel, but I had thought about it a lot. There was no way he was going to be satisfied in Poughkeepsie. Wandering around wild places was as important to his life as breathing was to other people. *"He's a man who needs to be out in the wilderness howling at the moon."* In Poughkeepsie, people were arrested for that kind of behavior.

I had no doubt that when Woolcott saw what Doc had accomplished in such a short time, Bill's dream was going to come true. Then what? Doc would say good-bye to Brazil and Flanna, and he and I would live happily ever after in our ranch house in Poughkeepsie? I didn't think so. No, Doc was going to have to come up with a different solution. And the only way I could see to resolve the problem was to have me stay down here with him. At least I hoped that's the way it would turn out.

Then there was Taw—I'd miss him. And I'd promised him the Arizona trip. I didn't know if he was serious about this, or whether he would even remember that he wanted me to go there with him. But if this was something he wanted to do, I'd feel bad about letting him down.

* * *

Late that afternoon I took off in the Morpho again. Surprisingly, Beth was no longer near her cubs. She was at least five miles away from them, and seemed to be moving even farther away. Doc said Taw and Wild Bill were big enough to be on their own, but he thought Beth would stick close to them for a few weeks or months.

I flew over them again and double-checked the readings. The cats had definitely split up. I tried to get Doc on the radio, but he didn't answer. He must have turned his handset off.

I turned the Morpho around and flew back to the lake.

Doc and Raul didn't get back to camp until after dark. I told Doc about the jaguars not being together anymore.

"That's interesting," he said wearily, looking at the logbook. He got his laptop out of the tent and retrieved a fresh battery from the charger plugged into the small generator we had brought with us.

"How about some food, Bob?" Flanna said.

"I'm not really hungry."

"I think you should eat, anyway," she said, firmly.

"I'm not hungry!"

"Suit yourself."

Doc took a deep breath. "I'm sorry, Flanna. I didn't mean to snap at you. I guess I'm just tired."

"You need to take a couple of days off," she said. "Your arm was badly burned and you've been under a lot of stress. You're pushing yourself too hard."

"The arm is just fine." He held it up and flexed his fingers. The bandage had been off for a week.

Flanna looked at him doubtfully.

"Raul found some old jaguar sign today," Doc said. "We're going to head out tomorrow and see if we can find it. . . . Or him. Raul says it's a male. We'll only be gone a few days. . . ."

"A few days!" Flanna was irritated, and I didn't blame her. Doc was in no shape to go traipsing off into the forest for several days.

"It might only take a couple of days," he said. "We need to get more jaguars collared."

"You're being foolish, Bob!" Flanna was really mad now, and I admired her for it. "You should take a week off and do nothing but sleep."

"I'll rest after we leave here," he said. "I feel just fine." He got up and went into his tent. Flanna followed him.

I heard them talking late into the night. I hoped that Flanna would talk some sense into him.

CHAPTER 17

S he hadn't. The next morning Doc was up at his usual time, stuffing his pack with gear. He didn't look healthy. "Doc, are you feeling all right?"

"I'm fine," he said, and tried to smile. "If the weather isn't right, don't go up."

"Flanna's right," I said. "You should wait until you're stronger."

"Jake, I have to do this. I promise I'll take it easy out there. Don't worry about me."

"Right." An idea occurred to me. "Why don't you let me go with you? I could carry some of the gear—lighten your load."

"You need to stay here and keep track of the jaguars. I'm concerned that Beth isn't near her cubs. Something isn't right."

"What will you do if she stays away from them?"

"Probably nothing."

"Then why don't you let me go with you?"

"Jake, your job is to fly the Morpho. I'll be fine." He gave me a halfhearted hug and slipped his pack over his shoulders. A few moments later, he and Raul disappeared behind a veil of green vegetation.

Flanna came out of the tent after he had left. "Your father is the most pigheaded man I've ever known!"

I laughed.

"What's so funny?" she snapped.

"You sound exactly like someone else I used to know." I don't know how many times I had heard my mom say the same thing, with exactly the same level of exasperation.

She took a deep breath. "He's a maniac!"

"But you gotta love him."

"That's the worst part! He's been running a fever for the past week. He thinks he can *work* his way through it." She shook her head. "Oh, well, we tried. . . . Are you ready to learn something about climbing trees?"

"Absolutely!"

"Great. When you come back from your morning flight, I'll show you my web."

"What web?"

"You'll see."

* * *

Wild Bill and Taw were in the same areas I had found them in the day before. Beth was another story. I circled around and around trying to pick up her signal, with no luck. I began to wonder if her collar had malfunctioned. I flew around some more, then started to get low on gas. I continued to monitor her frequency as I flew back toward the lake. About halfway there, I picked up a faint signal. It grew louder the closer I got to the lake, and still louder as I passed over the lake. What was she up to? I finally flew over the top of her several miles west of the lake. At this rate she would be out of the Morpho's range in a few days. I hoped she would settle down.

By the time I landed, I was nearly on empty. I reminded myself to be more careful in the future. Doc wouldn't be very happy if I had to tell him that I lost the Morpho because I ran out of gas. To say nothing about what Buzz would say when we finally saw him again.

Silver was standing on the shore. He must have just gotten back from one of his strolls. He looked worn out, but he helped me put the Morpho away.

"So you let the jaguars go?"

"Yesterday, and Beth is in a traveling mode." I told him where she was.

"What's it like on that side of the lake?"

"What do you mean?"

"I don't know," he said. "Did you see any unusual land formations, other lakes? Things like that."

I shook my head. "Just green canopy. Are you looking for something in particular?"

"Nah. I'm just interested in the geography of this place.

If you're over there again, keep your eyes open and let me know if you see anything."

"Sure."

I told him that Doc and Raul had taken off for a few days. He seemed too tired to care one way or the other. He got into the Zodiac and headed out to the *Tito*.

Before I visited Flanna, I went up to the rock to make sure Raul had picked up the mechanical pencil. I didn't want it to rust while he was away. It was gone.

* * *

I took the trail to Flanna's treetop kingdom. In the few areas where the sunlight found its way through the thick canopy, there were patches of dense tropical growth. But very little sunlight made it to the ground. Most of the light was blocked a hundred feet above, where the lowest tree branches hung.

I came across a river of red flower petals crossing the trail in front of me. A two-inch-wide column of leaf-cutting ants were carrying petals to their underground nest. I had read that their nests were gigantic, holding up to five million workers. The entrances to the same nest can be separated by as much as fifty yards. The ants don't eat the leaves or petals. They use them to cultivate subterranean fungus gardens.

I stepped over the column and continued on. The huge tree trunks I passed were covered with moss and plants. Aerial roots twisted around each other and dangled to the ground.

When I got to the site, I didn't see Flanna. I put my head

all the way back and tried to find her in the dark canopy, but I couldn't spot her. I called out.

"I'll be there in a second!" Flanna called back.

A few moments later, she dropped to the ground on the end of a rope. She had on a yellow hard hat, gloves, a pair of protective goggles hanging around her neck, and a machete hanging from a belt around her waist. It reminded me of old photos I had seen of Taw in his steelworking outfit—minus the machete.

Flanna gave me about an hour of climbing instructions before she let me put the harness on.

"How do you get the first rope up in the tree?" I asked.

"If there are good vines around the trunk, I free-climb. If not, I use a bow and arrow.

She brought out a compound bow and a quiver of arrows. "I don't use the points, of course."

She took an arrow, removed the point, and put on a different attachment. She tied some heavy fishing line to the attachment, then strung the bow. Leaning back, she took aim and sent the arrow up into the canopy. It went over the top of a branch and got tangled.

"Now for the hard part." She pulled on the line until the shaft was free, then carefully fed more line and lowered the arrow an inch at a time until it was back on the ground. "All you do is tie your rope onto the fishing line and pull it up over the top of the branch. Of course, it always gets hung up. It took me over four hours to get the first rope set.

After that, it usually goes pretty smoothly. Are you ready?"

"I guess so."

She gave me a hard hat, gloves, and goggles. "You won't need the goggles until we get into the canopy. A lot of people don't use them, but I don't like worrying about my eyes when I'm up there."

I started to pull myself up the rope. She had a special clamping devise that held you in place, while you got your next handhold. It was a lot harder than I expected. I had to pause every few feet to catch my breath. Flanna paused along with me, but it was clear she didn't need to.

The first hundred feet or so there was nothing to see but the vine-covered trunk. This changed dramatically when we passed through the lower story of the canopy. It was a different world—a world that couldn't be seen from below or from up above, flying the Morpho.

The canopy was alive with plants and animals: spiders, scorpions, centipedes, lizards, frogs, snakes, and little, colorful birds. We stopped to look at a three-toed sloth hanging upside down. Its long hair was tinted green and blended perfectly with the moss-covered branch it clung to.

I saw a gigantic spider web with several large shapes wrapped in silk.

"Bats and birds," Flanna said.

What kind of spider eats bats and birds? I thought. "How big is it?"

"You don't want to know."

There were dozens of beautifully colored orchids and other plants I couldn't identify.

"Most of these plants are different types of lichens and bromeliads. They're air plants," Flanna said. "There's no soil up here. They get their nutrients from small particles of dust dissolved in rain."

She went on to explain that some types of bromeliads have leaves that overlap, forming bowls that store water.

"Like this one." She carefully parted the leaves of a large plant. At the base was a little pool of water, and sitting in the middle of the pool was a bright red frog no bigger than my thumb. "Poison arrow frog. It's called that because it secretes a toxin that some tribes distill and put on the end of darts and arrows. The frog's bright color warns potential predators that they're in for a surprise if they try to make a snack out of it."

A little further on, I saw a fierce-looking insect about an inch long, covered in what looked like body armor.

"It's called a paraponera ant. It's also known as a bullet ant, because that's what it feels like when it stings you."

It was bigger than any ant I'd ever seen. It looked like a little tank.

"Listen," Flanna said. She broke off a long twig and poked the ant. It spun around with its large jaws wide open and let out a threatening screech. The noise was exactly what Scarlet would sound like if she were only an inch long.

We finally reached the branch that the ropes were tied to. "We'll rest here."

The branch was three feet around and covered with a virtual garden of large-leafed plants, orchids, bromeliads, and ants! As soon as I sat down, the ants started snapping at me. I scooted further down the branch to get out of their way and came to a carpet of thick moss that continued up the trunk of the tree. After checking to make sure there wasn't anything hiding in it that would bite me, I leaned back. It was as comfortable as an easy chair.

I looked up. About thirty feet above me were several ropes leading off in different directions.

"That's my web," Flanna said. "That's how I get around from tree to tree."

Now that I was sitting, I could feel the tree swaying back and forth. It was a little unnerving.

"You'll get used to the motion in a minute," Flanna said. "It's like being on the deck of a boat. You just have to learn to move with it."

"As long as you don't fall out," I said.

"Yeah, that can hurt."

"What kind of tree is this?"

"Brazil nut. Are you hungry?"

Without waiting for an answer, Flanna stood up on her toes as casually as if she were standing on a city sidewalk. She reached to the next branch and pulled off a pod about the size of a soccer ball. She set it down in front of me and sliced it open with one swing from her machete. Inside were twenty or thirty of the most delicious Brazil nuts I had ever tasted.

There was a sudden motion above us, and Scarlet landed on the branch.

Flanna didn't act surprised. "She always seems to show up when I have food."

"I thought Scarlet hated you."

"Not anymore." She gave Scarlet a Brazil nut. "She drops by every day. Her friends are still a little shy." She pointed up.

The flock was about fifty feet above us.

Flanna explained that despite the heavy rainfall in the Amazon Basin, three quarters of the yearly precipitation comes from the moisture released into the air by the plants.

"If enough trees are removed, the precipitation cycle will be broken, and the result will be extended dry periods that will kill the canopy and the animals that live here."

I realized that the jaguars were only a small part of why the rain forest needed to be preserved. The important part was here in the canopy, where, Flanna said, three quarters of the forest animals lived—many of them never touching the ground.

I also realized that Flanna was as committed to her work in the treetops as Doc was to his work on the ground.

"Now that I have you captive," Flanna said, "perhaps we should talk about your maniac father and me."

I liked Flanna, but I didn't know if I was ready to talk about this with her.

"If you're uncomfortable, we don't have to. . . ."

"No," I said. "Go ahead." But it did seem a little odd, sitting up in a tree talking about my father with his girlfriend.

"I guess one thing you should know is that if you and he go back to Poughkeepsie, I'd like to go with you," Flanna said.

"What about your work down here?"

"It might be nice to go back to the States for a while."

"Sounds like you and Doc have talked about this."

"A little," she said. "He's determined to go back so you can go to school."

This was bad news. I thought that he would change his mind once he got into the project.

"I don't know what the big deal is," I said. "You both have Ph.D.'s. Why can't you teach me what I need to know?"

Flanna laughed. "I used the same argument on him."

"And?"

"And he said no."

"Pigheaded!"

"Exactly! But don't give up hope. If we both keep working on him, maybe we can get him to change his mind."

"That would be a first," I said. "But I'm glad to know you're on my side."

Flanna smiled.

"Are you ready to go higher?"

* * *

I spent the rest of the afternoon with her. We crossed over to three different trees. To accomplish this, we hung upside down and pulled ourselves along the outstretched ropes. The only thing stopping us from a 150-foot drop was a small, stainless-steel pulley.

Just as I was about to climb down and go back to camp, the wind picked up and thick dark clouds moved in over the canopy.

"Looks like the afternoon flight is scratched," I said.

"I was kind of hoping this wouldn't happen your first time up," Flanna said.

"A little storm isn't going to bother me."

Flanna raised her eyebrows. "We better find a good place to ride this out."

We climbed up to one of her observation platforms, which were pretty luxurious. They were made out of plywood covered with thick foam rubber for comfort, and plastic to keep the foam rubber dry. A waterproof tarp hung over the top and mosquito netting was draped around the sides to keep the insects out.

"The platforms are designed for long stays," Flanna said, as we climbed in. "I once spent three weeks on a platform. After a while I felt like I had been transformed into a bromeliad. I just lay there and watched the canopy life pass in front of me. It was the most wonderful experience I've ever had."

The rain started to fall in huge, cold drops. It felt and sounded as if we were sitting under a glacial waterfall, but the worst was yet to come. The wind started gusting through the canopy, and the tree began whipping back and forth like a telephone line in a hurricane. I was sure that it was going to snap in two at any moment.

Fortunately, the storm passed as quickly as it had come. When it was over, I couldn't tell whether I was shivering from the cold rain or from terror.

"That wasn't as bad as I thought it would be," Flanna commented.

I realized something else that day. Flanna was the toughest human I had ever met in my entire life. She and Doc were perfect for each other.

CHAPTER 18

I took off in the Morpho early the next morning, eager to find out if Beth had wandered farther away. Before checking her, though, I flew to the east and checked on Wild Bill and Taw. They were both in the same areas as the day before. I quickly went through frequencies of the other animals Doc had collared. The paca's signal was in almost the same location as Wild Bill's. If the signal was in the same spot during the afternoon flight, it could mean that Wild Bill had gotten a little fresh paca for breakfast.

I flew back over the lake to the west and picked up Beth's signal almost immediately. She hadn't moved very far, which was good news. But it still didn't explain why she had left her cubs. Perhaps it was just time for her to move on with her life, and time for them to move on with theirs.

It was such a beautiful morning! The clear sky was almost

turquoise, and the canopy was bright green without a spot of mist hanging over it. Somewhere below, Doc and Raul were wandering around looking for jaguars. I hoped Doc was taking it easy, but I kind of doubted it.

I decided to do a little exploring of my own and continued flying west. The canopy stretched below me like a green ocean. I flew in a straight line for ten minutes, then banked to the right and started back to the lake. As I completed my turn, I saw something I hadn't seen on the way out. It was a small hill or a mound, slightly higher than the surrounding canopy. If the light hadn't been just right, I would have missed it completely. I didn't know if it was unusual enough for Silver, but it was the only odd formation I'd seen so far. I flew over the top and got the coordinates with the GPS.

When I got back to the lake, Silver was in camp drinking a cup of coffee. He looked well rested and I knew it wouldn't be too long before he took off again for one of his strolls. I told him about the mound and gave him the information from the GPS. He wanted to know how tall the mound was, how big around it was, and what it was covered with.

"I don't know," I said. "It was sort of a little hill covered with trees. I almost missed it."

"Well, maybe I'll go check it out."

"What are you looking for, Silver?"

"Nothing, really," he said, innocently. "I'm just trying to

keep busy while we're here. Not much for a landlocked skipper to do."

"You could help Doc," I suggested.

"I think Raul is doing just fine in that department."

He was probably right. I got my towel and went up to the rock.

And that's when I found the golden jaguar. It was in exactly the same spot where I had left the pencil. The figurine was small, about the size of my thumb, but very heavy. The jaguar was crouching, as if it were about to pounce on something. Tiny rosettes dotted its golden body.

At first I wondered if I had missed it the day before. But I knew I hadn't. I couldn't possibly have overlooked something like this. My second thought was that it wasn't really made out of gold and that Silver had put it there as some kind of a joke. But Silver wasn't a practical joker. Perhaps Doc and Raul had come back while I was out flying. But where did Raul get something like this? If it was made out of gold, it was worth a lot of money.

I walked back to camp. Silver was still there, drinking another cup of coffee. I heard Flanna rummaging around inside her and Doc's tent.

"Have you seen Doc and Raul?"

"I thought you said they were out looking for jaguars," Silver said.

"I was just wondering if they got back while I was up in the Morpho."

Flanna came out of her tent. I asked her if she had seen them.

"No," she said. "What makes you think they're back?"

"Nothing," I said. "I was just wondering."

I walked back down to the water. Silver followed me.

"What's going on, Jake?"

"I'm not sure."

"Something on your mind?"

I nodded and opened my hand, showing him the jaguar. When he picked it up, his hand trembled slightly.

"Where did you get this?"

I pointed to the rock and explained how Raul and I had been leaving gifts for each other.

"Raul didn't leave you this." He looked around the perimeter of the lake. "And he didn't leave you the other things. I should have known!"

"What are you talking about?"

"We're not alone."

"What do you mean?"

"There must be an uncontacted tribe in the area. A small band of Indians that nobody knows about. Isolated for years."

"Wow!"

"This is a very bad situation, Jake."

"Why?"

He raised his voice. "Because they're very unpredictable, that's why."

"But the gifts," I said. "Why would they——"

"No more gifts! In fact, I don't want you to go up to the rock anymore. Just stay away from it. It will only encourage them. Maybe we'll get lucky and they'll leave us alone."

"What about Doc and Raul?"

"What about them?"

"Are they in any danger?"

Silver thought about this for a few moments. "I don't think so, but we'll all have to be more careful from now on."

"I better tell Flanna," I said, turning to go.

"Wait."

I thought Silver was going to tell me not to, but instead he followed me up to camp.

I went over the story again and showed the jaguar to Flanna. She agreed with Silver that I shouldn't go up to the rock anymore.

"I want you to carry a gun," Silver said to her.

"Forget it, Silver! I agree that we should discourage contact, but that doesn't include shooting at them. So far, they've done nothing wrong. We're the ones that don't belong here."

"What does that mean?"

"We're the worst thing that could ever happen to these people. As soon as Bob and Raul get back, we should leave."

"I think you're overreacting," Silver said. "This site is perfect. Why should we leave?"

"It *was* perfect. And I'm not overreacting. You know as well as I do what happens when we come in contact with these people. We win. They lose."

Flanna walked off into the rain forest, leaving Silver standing there shaking his head.

"Now that's an opinionated woman," he said.

I thought about the Indians I had seen in Manaus and at the camp in the mining town. Flanna was right. Nothing good could come from our having further contact with them.

"I'd like to see the other things they left," Silver said.

I went into my tent and brought out the small box I was using to keep the gifts in. He picked up each one and looked at it closely.

"Mind if I borrow these things?" he asked. "I have some old books back in my cabin. I might come across something in one of them that describes gifts like these."

That seemed very unlikely, but I told Silver I didn't mind. I put the golden jaguar in the box and gave it to him.

CHAPTER 19

Two days passed and still no sign of Doc and Raul. Flanna and I were very worried about them. Silver said that our anxiety was a result of our knowing that we weren't alone. I'm sure this was part of it, at least for me. I'd look around at the thick forest cover and wonder if someone was watching us. What did he think of us? Had he left another gift on the rock? Was he wondering why I hadn't taken it and left something in exchange? I had to stop myself from checking the rock a dozen times a day.

The other part of our anxiety was Doc's rundown condition when he left camp. He had said they would be back in a few days. In Doc's warped sense of time, this could mean anything from a week to several weeks. The only thing that brought us comfort was the fact that Raul was with him.

So we waited. Silver stayed close to camp, but he didn't talk to us much. I carried the shotgun when he was around

but stashed it when I was with Flanna, because I knew it
made her uncomfortable.

I continued to make my telemetry flights. Wild Bill and
Taw had moved, but they were still east of the lake. Beth had
stayed within a five-mile radius west of the lake. The hunting
must have been good there.

When I wasn't flying, I helped Flanna in the canopy. She
was serious about leaving as soon as Doc got back. We had
taken down most of her web, leaving only two research
platforms.

We talked a lot about what had happened to Brazil's
indigenous peoples. Millions had been killed over the
years—entire tribes wiped out by rain forest exploitation.
She said the most effective means of getting rid of them had
been to go into their villages and cough on them.

"For them a flu virus, or measles, can be as bad as the
bubonic plague or AIDS," she told me. "The diseases of civilization are the same bullets that killed hundreds of thousands of North American Indians. Down here, those that
survive the diseases are contaminated by Western civilization. They work in the mines and oil fields for a few pennies
a day and the privilege of living in total squalor."

On the morning of the third day, Doc returned.

Flanna and I were up in the canopy. I was lying face down
on one of the observation platforms, looking through the
foliage, when I caught a slight movement on the ground
below. I found the binoculars and shifted over to the right

of the platform so I'd have a clearer view. All I could see was a pair of muddy boots lying on the ground. The wind moved the branch I was trying to see around, and I got a glimpse of a pair of torn Levi's blue jeans.

"It's Doc!" I yelled, scrambling for my rope.

By the time I reached the ground Flanna was already there and out of her harness. She was cradling Doc's head in her lap. His eyes were closed and his lips were swollen and cracked. He was having trouble breathing.

"We have to get him back to camp," Flanna said. "He's burning up."

I ran. When I got to camp, I yelled for Silver, but he didn't answer. I didn't wait around to find out why. I grabbed the jaguar stretcher and ran back into the forest.

* * *

Flanna thought Doc had malaria, but she wasn't certain. She said it wasn't the first time, which was news to me.

"It could be a flare-up," she said. "Stress can bring it out again. Or else he hasn't been taking his antimalaria pills and he's been infected."

That wouldn't surprise me.

Whatever he had was very serious. We put him on a cot in his tent. He had a raging fever and was nearly comatose. Flanna dribbled water into his mouth and sponged him down, trying to cool him off. She force fed him a huge dose of antimalaria pills.

"This won't work unless it's malaria," she said. "I guess all we can do is try to keep him comfortable and hope the fever breaks."

I wandered in and out of the tent all afternoon and evening, bringing water up from the lake to cool Doc down. We hadn't seen Silver all day. He couldn't have picked a worse time to go out for one of his strolls.

That night I came back from the lake with yet another load of water. When I got to the tent, Flanna was in tears.

"I don't know what to do, Jake. I think he's getting worse!"

The man lying on the cot did not look like my father. In the dim lantern light he looked like the ghost of Robert Lansa. It took all my strength to hold back my own tears. My father couldn't die like this.

Flanna wiped her tears away. "No sign of Silver yet?"

I shook my head. I thought he'd be back by evening, but he hadn't shown up. Nor had Raul. What had happened to them out there? Raul wouldn't leave Doc like this.

"There's nothing we can do for him here," Flanna said. "He needs medical attention. We have to get him to a doctor."

"How?"

"The boat," she said.

"What about Silver and Raul?"

"We'll come back for them."

A trip down the tunnel right now would probably kill Doc.

"Who would pilot the boat?" I asked. "I don't know how

to do it. If we ran aground in the tunnel, all of us would die, including Silver and Raul. The boat's our only way out of here."

"You're right," she said. "But we need to do something."

I had never felt more helpless.

"Do you want me to take over?" I asked. She hadn't left Doc's side in twelve hours.

"No. I'm fine," she said. "I just wish Silver would get back here!"

"I'm sure he'll be back tonight or tomorrow morning," I said, but I wasn't at all certain. Something might have happened to him, too.

I left the tent and walked down to the beach. I was hoping to see a light on in Silver's boat, but it was dark and the Zodiac was still on the beach. The moon was full, and I could see the *Tito* clearly bobbing near the tunnel's entrance.

I sat down and thought about ways to help my father. In the morning I could try to find Silver. But where would I start looking? I couldn't track him the way Raul could.

Maybe the tribe could help us, I thought. They might know what Doc's problem was. Then again, they might be responsible for his problem and Raul's disappearance.

I began to wonder if there really was an uncontacted tribe. Raul wasn't with Doc, which meant that he could have left the golden jaguar. That still didn't explain where he had gotten the figurine.

I glanced over to the rock. I could see it clearly in the

moonlight. What if there was another gift up there? Perhaps it would explain what was going on. What would be the harm in just looking?

I climbed up to the rock and turned my flashlight on. In the beam was a rusty pair of eyeglasses. I picked the frames up. The lenses were missing. Raul didn't wear glasses, nor did anyone else in our group. And I doubted that the tribe had an optometrist living with it. Where would they get a pair of glasses? I was even more confused.

I looked out across the lake. The full moon reflected off the surface, and I was reminded of something I had read when I was in Poughkeepsie.

I ran over to the Zodiac, started it up, and sped across the lake to Silver's boat.

His cabin was unlocked. I went inside and switched on the light and found the book I was looking for. It took me awhile to find the right page:

> **A river running through the forest beside the city fell over a big fall whose roar could be heard for leagues, and below the fall the river seemed to widen out into a great lake empty- ing itself they had no notion where.**

The tunnel, I thought. The lake wasn't "great" and the waterfall couldn't be heard for "leagues," but who knows what kind of changes had taken place here since 1753, when this description was written? The lake the book was talking about was supposed to be near the lost mines of Muribeca.

I looked over at Silver's desk and was surprised to see a radio collar lying on it. What was even more surprising was that the transmitter had been cut away from the collar. Why would he do that?

Sitting next to the collar was my box of gifts. I opened it. Inside was the golden jaguar, various feathers, the turtle skull, the blue stone, the dried piranha jaw, and a new item—an old rusty compass. I picked it up and turned it over. There was an engraving on the back. It read: COLONEL P. H. FAWCETT, 1924.

I knew why Silver wanted to come up here.

I took the Zodiac to shore. Before going in to check on Doc, I went to the supply tent. One of the receivers and handheld antennas was missing.

Silver had cut the radio collar transmitter off and left it on the rock as a gift. Right now he was out in the forest tracking the Indian who had taken it, hoping he would lead him to the place where he had found the golden jaguar.

> **Colonel Fawcett was a courageous man and a great explorer. But he was chasing after something that never existed. The fruitless search killed him, his son, and his son's friend. It's a tragedy that's as old as the rain forest. . . .**

Jaguar

Silver had lied to me. He had lied to all of us.

Flanna was sitting in the chair next to Doc's cot, asleep. I touched her on the shoulder, and she woke up with a start.

"Why don't you go to my tent and rest," I whispered.

"Are you sure?"

"Yeah. I'm wide awake," I said, which wasn't an exaggeration.

"I'll be back soon. Just keep putting the cold compresses on."

"Is he any better?"

"I don't know. He's been talking, but none of it makes sense. Delirious ramblings."

I watched Doc all night. Every once in a while he would start mumbling, as if he were having a nightmare. I couldn't understand what he was saying. About two in the morning he sat straight up in bed and yelled, "Watch out, Beth! You're smarter than that!"

I was so startled I almost fell over backward. As soon as he said it, he lay back down, and didn't say another thing the rest of the night.

CHAPTER 20

F lanna came in just after sunrise. I debated telling her about Silver, but had decided against it. It wouldn't do her any good to know about what he was up to. Right now the important thing was to find him and convince him to take Doc out of here.

"No change," I said.

"Why don't you go rest?"

"Okay," I said, but I had no intention of resting. I walked out of the tent.

During the night I had gotten the frequency of the collar Silver had taken out of Doc's logbook. My plan was to take the Morpho up, mark the signal on the GPS, then go in on foot. The trick would be talking Silver into coming back with me.

I suspected he had been looking for the lost mines of Muribeca for years. This would explain a lot of different things. . . . The books in his library, his eagerness to take us upriver for next to nothing, and his insistence on going through the tunnel.

The most important question was one I didn't like thinking about. Did Silver blow up the boat in Manaus so he could take us upriver? Was he responsible for Bill Brewster's death? If so, what would stop him from killing me when he found out I knew all about his scheme?

I went down to the lake, uncovered the Morpho, and took off. I picked up the signal from the missing collar almost immediately. The Indian was west of the lake near the mound, which I figured must have something to do with the lost mines. I flew over the top of the signal and marked it with the GPS.

I flew straight back to the lake without bothering to check the collared jaguars. They could wait, my father couldn't.

I pulled the Morpho on shore and started to put the tarp over it.

"Nice landing, Ace."

I turned around. A man was standing behind me. He was carrying an automatic rifle and had a scar on his face— although the scar was hard to see in the midst of all the insect bites. I hoped he had enjoyed his trip up the tunnel.

My shotgun was about ten feet away from me.

"Don't." He picked up the shotgun and threw it into the lake.

So much for that idea. "What do you want?" I asked.

He didn't answer. I heard someone coming down the path leading to the camp. It was Fred Stoats from the mining town!

"What's going on in camp?" the man asked him, without taking his eyes off me.

"I didn't see anybody, Tyler," Fred said.

"What do you mean, you didn't see anybody?"

"I'm telling you the truth!" Fred insisted.

"What are you doing up here, Fred?" I asked.

He smiled a toothless grin. "I told you that you should have taken me upriver with you."

"But how—"

"Shut up!" Tyler said, and knocked me down with the butt of his rifle. "Tie him up."

Fred flipped me over and tied my hands behind my back. Tyler pointed his rifle at me. "Where's Colonel Silver?"

Colonel? "He's not here," I said.

"I'm about out of patience."

"You better tell him," Fred said to me.

"He left a couple of days ago and we haven't seen him. I have no idea where he went."

"We'll see about that," Tyler said. "So who's up in camp?"

I didn't see any point in lying about this. "Flanna Brenna and my dad. They're in a tent. That's why he didn't see them. My dad's sick and Flanna is taking care of him."

"We'll see about that, too," Tyler said. "Get on your feet."

I stood up.

"What do you want me to do, Tyler?" Fred asked.

"How about keeping your mouth shut for ten minutes? That would be very helpful."

I had a feeling that Tyler wasn't exactly fond of Fred Stoats.

"We're going to walk up to your camp very quietly," Tyler said. "When we get there, I want you to call them. If you pull any crap, I'll pull this trigger and that'll be all she wrote. Do you understand the plan?"

I nodded. I could hear my heart beating in my chest.

"Good. Let's go."

When we got there, Tyler had me drop to my knees. He put the barrel of his gun against my head.

"Okay, call them out."

"Flanna?" I said. My mouth was so dry I could barely speak.

"Louder." He bumped my head with the barrel.

"Flanna!"

She came right out and froze when she saw me. "What—"

"Just come on over here, honey, and join the party. Or I'm going to make a real mess of this boy's head."

Flanna walked over to me very slowly, and Tyler motioned for her to join me on the ground. Fred tied her hands behind her back.

"You're the man from the hospital," she said.

"You know him?" I asked in shock.

"He's one of the men who offered to take us upriver after the accident."

"Shut up!" Tyler shouted, pointing the rifle at her. He looked at the tent. "Dr. Lansa!"

"He's sick," Flanna said. "He can't even walk!"

"Fred, go over and take a look."

Fred went into the tent and came right back out. "She's telling the truth. He looks real bad."

"Are there any weapons in there?"

Fred went back inside and came out shaking his head. "The tent's clean."

Tyler pointed the rifle at me. "Where's the Indian?"

"What Indian?"

"Don't get cute. The one who helped you catch that jaguar downriver."

"He didn't come up here with us."

"I believe that's the first truthful thing you've said today, boy. An Indian with a bucketful of money would have much better sense than to come up here. Fred, go search the other tents."

"What's this all about?" Flanna asked.

"My advice for both of you is to just stay quiet for the time being," Tyler said. "I'm very tired."

Fred came back from searching the tents. "Just supplies," he said.

"Go out to Silver's boat and see what you can find."

Tyler didn't say anything else until he heard the Zodiac start up.

"Okay," he said. "I'm going to ask again. Where's Colonel Silver?"

"I already——"

"Not you! Her."

"I don't know," Flanna said. "He left a couple of days ago. We've been waiting for him to come back so we can get out of here."

"Why would you want to get out of here?"

"Because Bob's sick. We need to get him to a doctor."

"And Silver doesn't know he's sick?"

"He got sick after Silver left," I said.

Tyler sat down about ten feet away from us and just looked at us through tired eyes. I didn't know about Flanna, but this really frightened me. Not that I wasn't scared before, but there was something even more menacing about him just sitting there staring at us.

I heard the boat start up and come across the lake. A few minutes later, Fred came back into camp. He had my box of gifts with him.

"What's this?"

"I found it in Silver's cabin."

Tyler flipped the box over on the ground and looked at the contents. The golden jaguar wasn't there. I guess Fred decided not to share that little item. Tyler picked the old compass up and read the back. He smiled.

"Jake, do you have any idea where Colonel Silver found this?"

I shook my head.

"I see." Tyler stood up. "Pick that stuff up, Fred."

As Fred bent down to pick up the gifts, something bright and shiny fell out of his shirt pocket. Uh-oh, Fred. He tried to cover it up with his hand before Tyler saw it, but he was too late.

"Let's see it, Fred."

Fred handed him the figurine. Fred looked as if he was about to throw up.

Tyler looked at the jaguar closely. "I wish you hadn't done that, Fred."

"I was going to show it to you," Fred said. He started to back away.

Tyler shot him in the chest. Fred flew backward, hitting the ground about ten feet away.

Flanna and I just stared.

"As you can see," Tyler said, "I'm a very serious man, and I want some very serious answers. The next person to go will be your father, Jake. Then I'll kill Flanna. Then I'll kill you. Do you understand?"

I nodded.

"Good. Now, tell me where Silver is."

I didn't know what to do. If I didn't tell him how to find Silver, then he might just kill us all and wait for Silver to come back to camp. Of course, he might just kill us, anyway.

He started walking toward Doc's tent.

"Wait!"

He stopped and turned back around.

"Silver's looking for the lost mines of Muribeca!"

He smiled. "He hasn't found them yet?"

"I don't think so."

Flanna was totally shocked.

"What about this?" He tossed the jaguar up into the air and caught it.

I told him about the gifts, the tribe, and the radio collar.

"The colonel was always a clever one."

"What are you going to do?"

"Well, the first thing I'm going to do is to take a little nap. The colonel is not the kind of man you want to approach when you're tired. It took us three tries to find the right tributary, and I didn't have a nice boat like yours. You can imagine what that was like. And then there was Fred—not the best traveling companion. The only reason I let him go with me was because Silver sabotaged my boat and I needed another. Fred helped me steal one."

"What about us?" Flanna asked.

"For now, I'm going to tie you to separate trees. I can't have you running around while I'm trying to take a nap. And I don't want you putting your heads together and making big plans. Believe me, it's for your own protection."

CHAPTER 21

Tyler crawled into the hammock outside the cook tent and fell asleep with his rifle resting on his chest. Flanna was about fifty feet away from me, tied to another tree. I could see her struggling to get loose, but it didn't do her any good.

Tyler didn't wake until late afternoon. The first thing he did was to check on Doc. When he came out, he looked at Flanna and said, "He's alive, but he doesn't look good."

He went into the cook tent and came back out eating something.

"I guess I'm about ready to move out." He walked over and untied me. "I want you to get the map and show me where that collar is. Then I want you to get the telemetry gear and show me how it works."

I brought out a map and showed him the last telemetry location. Then I brought out a receiver and a collar and showed him how to track with it.

"What's the frequency of the collar I'm after?"

I gave him the number and he dialed it in and held the antenna up. He didn't pick up the signal.

"You're too far away," I said. "You'll have to get within five miles before you pick it up."

He wasn't happy about this. "Any reason why I should trust you?"

"No," I said. "But I could care less what happens to Silver. He set us up!"

Tyler laughed. "That's the spirit."

"Now, what's going to happen to us?"

"I'm going to tie you back up. Then I'm going to find my old friend Silver."

"What about my father?"

"I'm afraid he's on his own."

"We can't just leave him in the tent by himself," Flanna shouted.

"Well, that's exactly what we're going to do," Tyler said.

He tied me to a tree and walked out of camp. I heard the Zodiac start and go across the lake.

"You should have told me about Silver," Flanna said.

"I didn't put it together until last night, but you're right. I should have told you."

I looked over at Doc's tent. There was a movement inside. A moment later, Doc came stumbling outside and fell down.

"Dad!"

"Bob!"

He slowly got to his feet and stood there for a moment trying to get his balance. I heard the Zodiac start back up and come across the lake.

"What's going on?" Doc asked.

"There's no time to explain," Flanna said. "You need to go back into the tent and act as if you're dead."

Doc hesitated.

"Just do what Flanna said!" I shouted.

He turned around and stumbled back inside. A minute later, Tyler came back into camp carrying a backpack slung over his shoulder.

"If Silver happens to show up while I'm gone, tell him that I fixed all the boats just like he fixed mine. If he wants the missing parts, he can come and find me. I got them right here." He patted the pack.

"And Jake, this little tracking thing better work. If it doesn't . . . Well, I'm sure you can put two and two together. Have a good day."

Tyler walked out of camp. Flanna and I just stared at each other. She waited about ten minutes, then yelled to Doc that it was all right to come out. He came out of the tent and walked over to me on shaky legs.

"What's going on?" he asked.

He was in bad shape, and I was afraid he would pass out before he could cut me loose.

"You need to get a knife to cut the ropes," I said very slowly.

He nodded and stumbled over to the cook tent and came back with a knife. Without a word, he cut through my ropes. As soon as I was free, he collapsed. I went over to Flanna and cut her rope. Then we both ran back over to Doc.

"I didn't have time to tell you," she said. "But before that maniac came into camp, your father was showing some signs of improvement." She cradled Doc's head in her lap. "I'm afraid he's relapsed. What's going on, Jake?"

"You know as much as I do. Silver's looking for the Muribeca gold mine, and Tyler's looking for him."

"We need to find a place to hide before Tyler gets back."

"He won't be back for a while."

"As soon as he finds Silver, he'll—"

"He's not going to find him," I told her. "I gave him Beth's radio frequency, not the Indian's. She'll hear Tyler coming a mile away. He'll never get close to her."

"But he'll be back eventually."

"Hopefully I'll be able to find Silver before Tyler returns." I tried to sound confident.

"What do you mean?"

"I'm going to go out and look for him."

"I don't think that's a good idea, Jake."

"Why not?"

"What if Silver doesn't want to help us? He's up to his neck in this. There's no telling what he'll do."

I hadn't quite worked through this part of the plan, but I didn't want to debate it with her. There wasn't enough time. Finding Silver was our only hope.

"Maybe we should get Doc back into the tent," I said. "We can talk about this later."

"You're right."

We carried him back into the tent.

"I'll go down and get more water," I said.

I ran to the lake and got into the Zodiac. Tyler had taken the spark plug out of the engine, so I had to paddle out to the boat. I found Silver's underwater flashlight, a box of shotgun shells, and some dry rags. I wanted to try to find the shotgun Tyler had thrown into the lake. If he returned while I was gone, I hoped Flanna would have a change of heart about using it.

I got back into the Zodiac and paddled out to where I thought Tyler had tossed the shotgun. I stripped my clothes off and dove in. The bottom was deeper than I expected. I also had thought that it would be flat and sandy in the middle, as it was alongshore, but instead it was covered with huge blocky stones. I ran out of breath and had to come back up for air.

I dove again. Just as I reached the bottom, something very large came at me from behind one of the stones. A dolphin! I was so startled I nearly sucked in a lungful of water. The dolphin passed within inches of me and disappeared into the gloom.

I shone my flashlight in the dolphin's wake and saw something glittering in the light. I knew it wasn't the shotgun, but I grabbed it anyway, then swam to the surface for air.

I held onto the side of the Zodiac with my left hand and caught my breath. I opened my right hand and stared in amazement. It was another golden jaguar, about three times the size of the first one. I realized that the stones beneath the lake might not be just big rocks but the ruins of a city—perhaps the fabled lost city connected with the Muribeca gold mines. The rest of the city was probably all around us, buried under centuries of tropical decomposition. Silver didn't have to look further than our own backyard for his precious treasure.

There was no time to celebrate my discovery. We still needed to get Doc out of here, and our only hope of achieving this was being stalked by a psychopath. I had to find Silver before Tyler did.

I dove again without success. I resurfaced and looked up at the sky. Dark, ugly clouds were starting to move in, and the trees around the lake were beginning to sway.

One more dive, I told myself. I saw the dolphin again, but it kept its distance. I searched until my lungs felt as if they were going to burst. Then I saw the shotgun. It was lying at the bottom near a particularly large stone. I grabbed the gun and swam back to the surface.

I climbed into the Zodiac and paddled to shore. When I got there, I took the shotgun apart and dried it off with the rags. When I finished, I ran back to camp.

Flanna was in the tent with Doc. Quietly, I put the shotgun and box of shells outside the entrance, then went inside with the bucket of water.

"How is he?"

"Not good." She dipped a cloth into the bucket and started sponging him down.

I slipped back outside and went over to the tent where we had our gear stored and grabbed two bundles of climbing rope. I hoped it was enough to do the trick.

I ran back down to the lake, started the Morpho, and took off. Before I left the area, I flew over camp and waggled my wings. Flanna came out of the tent to see what was going on. Wish me luck, Flanna, I thought, and I headed west.

CHAPTER 22

When I got to a thousand feet above the canopy, I leveled off. The wind was really blowing, and I had to fight the stick all the way. This was not the best weather to be flying in. My only consolation was that I wouldn't be flying for long.

I picked up the signal and flew until I was right over the top of it. Here we go, I thought. I switched the engine off.

It got very, very quiet. I pushed the nose forward into a dive. When the altimeter reached two hundred feet, I flipped the red switch. There was a loud *pop* and, a second later, a hard upward jerk as the parachute filled with air. I braced myself as I floated down to the canopy. Sorry, Buzz.

The initial impact wasn't as bad as I had expected. The Morpho settled onto the top of the canopy and hesitated there for a moment. There was a loud cracking sound, and I dropped about twenty feet, then came to a bone-wrenching stop. I breathed a deep sigh of relief. So far so good.

I looked around for a branch that I could get a rope around, but it was hard to see in the dim light. There was a gust of wind and I was suddenly jerked upward. The wind had filled the parachute again! The left wing smashed into a branch and bent like a piece of baling wire. Then the right wing crumpled. I looked down. I was swinging freely about 150 feet above the ground. My only hope of getting out of this alive was to swing over and try to get ahold of one of the vines running up a tree trunk. I tied my two ropes together and let one end drop. The Morpho slipped another ten feet, then caught again. This was probably the dumbest thing I had ever done.

I started to swing the Morpho back and forth. I reached out for the nearest vine, but missed it by a good five feet. Two more swings, I thought, and my momentum will get me close enough to grab it. My next grab was closer, but not close enough. I knew I wasn't going to be able to reach the vine on the next pass unless I took off my safety belt and leaned out. I quickly tied the rope around my wrist, unsnapped my belt, and squatted with my legs on the seat. I waited until the very last second. Then, just as the Morpho reached the end of its swing, I lunged for the trunk.

I clung to the vines with all my strength. I heard a loud tearing sound and turned my head. The Morpho dropped from sight. Now all I had to do was to get to the ground, which seemed relatively easy compared to what I had just been through.

There was a loud screeching noise, and Scarlet grabbed onto the trunk about two inches from my face. I nearly fell out of the tree.

"What are you doing here?" I shouted.

Her eyes dilated and the featherless area around her beak turned bright pink. All I needed now was to have an enraged macaw tear my ear off.

"It's okay, Scarlet," I said quietly, trying to calm her down. "We'll be fine."

Either she had followed the Morpho, or Silver wasn't far away. She screeched again and flew off. I was happy to see her go.

I tied the rope around the thickest vine I could reach and tested it by jerking on it. I let myself down the rope very slowly, making sure I always had something to grab onto in case the vine didn't hold.

At one point I grabbed a thick glob of spider web and pulled my hand away as if I had stuck it into a fire. I'm not fond of spiders—especially big spiders that eat bats and birds. Fortunately, I didn't disturb the spider or even see it. If I had, I probably would have had a heart attack.

When my feet finally touched the ground, I collapsed and nearly wept with gratitude. I closed my eyes. When I opened them, Silver was standing right in front of me, with Scarlet perched on his shoulder.

"That was quite an entrance," he said.

I looked up at him and didn't say anything.

He looked at the rope. "I take it that the canopy landing wasn't an accident."

At least I wouldn't have to go looking for him, I thought. I felt a mixture of relief and hatred.

"What are you doing here, Jake?"

I stood up. My legs were shaking so badly I had to hold onto the tree to steady myself. "What are *you* doing here?"

"I heard the ultralight's engine cut out and I knew there was a problem."

"That's not what I meant!" I shouted. "You're out here looking for the lost mines of Muribeca. That's why you offered to take us upriver. That's why you insisted on going through the tunnel. That's why you told me not to leave any more gifts on the rock. I know about the transmitter you left."

He looked at me calmly. "You've summed that up nicely," he said. "Now, tell me why you're out here."

"Doc's sick and he needs help."

"What happened?" He looked genuinely concerned.

I told him how Doc had come stumbling back into camp alone. "If you weren't out here looking for that stupid mine, we could have been through the tunnel by now."

Silver frowned and shook his head. "There's no way I could have known, Jake. I'm sorry."

This threw me off a little. He seemed sincere.

"And now your friend Tyler is here," I said.

He tensed. "Where?"

"On a wild jaguar chase with Beth. At least I hope that's where he is. He thinks he's tracking you."

"I need to know everything Tyler said, everything he did."

When I finished explaining, he sat down and leaned against the tree. Suddenly he looked very tired. "Tyler's wanted in almost every country south of the Mexican border, including Brazil. You're lucky he didn't kill you."

"I think he was going to get around to it."

"No doubt."

Silver went on to explain that he and Tyler had been in Vietnam together. When the war ended, he talked Tyler into coming to Brazil to look for the lost mines of Muribeca.

"We followed Fawcett's supposed journey into the Matto Grosso. To fund our expeditions, we hired ourselves out to the highest bidder. Some of the bidders were pretty unpleasant people."

"You were mercenaries?" I said.

"Hired guns," he said, sadly. "It took ten years for us to realize that Matto Grosso was a dead end. Tyler got fed up with the search and found a different way of finding gold. He got into drug running and gun smuggling. We parted ways. I moved to Ecuador, met Alicia, and we had Tito. I was never going to look for the mine again, but then my family disappeared. I bought a boat and spent years looking for them. I finally gave up, and after a while, I started looking for the mines again. I had nothing else to do.

"I figured out that the mines and the lost city were somewhere around here, but I didn't have the money or the permit to get into this area.

"Then Bill and your father showed up. I offered my services, but they turned me down and got their own boat. Tyler found out that I had new information about the mines. He came to Manaus and said he wanted in. I insisted that there was no new information, but of course he didn't buy that story.

"He was desperate . . . on the run, no money. I told him that I didn't have the cash for an expedition or the permit to go into this area and explore. I made a mistake and told him about Bill's permit. The next thing I know the boat blows up."

"He blew the boat up?"

"I'm not sure. But he's an expert at that sort of thing. It would have been easy for him. I think his plan was to steal a boat and offer to take you upriver, which is why I approached your father so soon after Bill's death. Tyler can be very charming when he needs to be."

That wasn't the Tyler I knew.

"So he followed us," I said.

"No, he went ahead of us. When he broke into the cabin, he found a map. There were four different tributaries marked as possible routes to the lake. He waited in the mining town, and I think his plan was to follow us to the right tributary. While you were out catching your jaguar, I found his stolen boat and wrecked his engine. After a week at the lake, I thought we were safe."

"So you knew he was in town all along?"

"I'm afraid so, Jake."

I told him about Tyler and Fred's false starts up the other tributaries.

"That explains the delay," he said.

"You picked a bad time to leave camp."

He nodded. "I knew Flanna wanted to get out of here because of the tribe. I wasn't about to leave without finding out if the Muribeca mines were here. I had to go before Doc came back."

"Did you find the mines?"

"I did. And you're the one that pointed me in the right direction. The Muribeca mines are in the mound you saw from the air."

"What are you going to do about it?"

"Nothing."

I was shocked. This isn't what I had expected.

"I've been thinking a lot the last few weeks," he said. "Mostly about my son, Tito, and the whole problem down here with the Indians. What if he was living in the rain forest like these people are—happy, content with his life? Then some greedy jerk like me comes along and takes it all away from him. It's not right, and I'm ashamed to admit that this thought never entered my mind before I met you and Doc and Flanna. I know where the gold is and that's going to have to be enough."

"How long will it be 'enough?' " I asked.

"Hopefully, for the rest of my life," he said. "I think I'm cured."

I hoped he was right.

"Our big problem now is Tyler," Silver continued.

"I think we should just leave him here," I said.

"Unfortunately, we can't do that. He's an expert in jungle survival. Eventually, he'll stumble onto the tribe and kill them one by one until he gets what he wants. He's done this kind of work in the past for oil and mining companies that found the indigenous population incompatible with their plans. It's one of the many things he's wanted for. I can't let that happen."

"You're going to kill him?"

"Not unless I have to," he said.

"Then . . ."

"I'll try to catch him and turn him over to the authorities."

"What's going to stop him from telling everyone about Muribeca?"

"His greed will stop him. Tyler's not stupid. One way or another he'll get out of prison and come back here. He won't tell anyone about this place until he's gotten his share. If and when he gets out, I'll be waiting for him. Now, at that point I might have to kill him." He smiled. "My new mission is to make sure that the Muribeca mines remain a myth. I was thinking that your dad might want to hire me to be the security force for the preserve."

"If he lives, I'll put a word in for you. What are we going to do now?"

"We have three problems to take care of. Your dad, Tyler, and our friend Raul."

"Raul?"

"I know where he is. In fact, I saw him about two hours ago. He's been captured by our uncontacted friends. He's not hurt and he doesn't look terribly upset about his situation, but we can't just leave him here. I don't know what their plans are for him. When you crashed through the canopy, I was waiting for it to get dark, so I could cut him loose."

CHAPTER 23

The tribe's encampment was well hidden in a small clearing. By the time we got there, it was almost dark. There was a single, horseshoe shaped structure made out of poles and covered with dry leaves. The roof was shaped like a dome and quite tall. There were several separate compartments facing the center of the horseshoe, with small cooking fires burning outside them. Raul was sitting down, facing one of the poles.

We were about a hundred yards away, hiding under a fallen tree. Scarlet sat on the tree preening herself.

"What if Scarlet screams?" I asked.

"Scarlet and I have been together a long time," Silver said. "She knows when to be quiet."

He set up a small tripod and a spotting scope. I looked through it. Raul's hands and feet were tied around the pole with vines. Silver was right about him not being too upset about his situation. A woman came over to him and started feeding him out of a large gourd. He was smiling and gulping down the food like a baby bird.

"Are you sure we should free him?" I whispered.

"I told you he didn't seem too upset." Silver smiled. "That's the same woman who was feeding him this afternoon. I think we should at least get him out of there and ask him what happened and what he wants to do.

"The problem's going to be getting in there without disturbing them," Silver continued. "I don't want to get into a 'situation'—someone might get hurt in the process."

"So what are we going to do?" I asked.

"I thought I'd wait until they were all asleep, sneak in, and cut him loose. I don't know what else to do."

"Let me go in," I said.

"I don't think . . ."

"I can do it!" I told Silver about how I had learned to stalk in Kenya.

He listened patiently. "That's quite a story, but—"

"If you get caught, we're dead. You're the only one that can get us out of here. I can do this, Silver."

He gave in. "I hope you're right."

We waited and watched. Silver said there were only about twenty of them.

"Four or five of them are little kids, and there are two babies. There might have been a lot more of them at one time. They could be the few survivors of the lost city, which is around here somewhere, or they might be just a tribe that wandered into the area one day and stayed."

I was tempted to tell him about the ruins under the lake, but I held back.

"So Fawcett was here?"

"You saw the compass?"

I nodded.

"He was here all right. He either lied in his letters to his wife about being in Matto Grosso, or he came up here after he was supposed to have disappeared. I don't know if he and his son and their friend were killed here, or whether they decided to stay. He found it, and that might have been enough for him."

I told him about the glasses.

"In the photos I've seen of Fawcett, he never had glasses on. Maybe they belonged to his son, or his son's friend."

After it got dark, it became difficult to pick out details in the village. All we could do was look for movement. We continued to wait. I thought about Doc and wondered how he was doing. I would have given almost anything to be going down the tunnel right now, but we couldn't leave Raul and we still had to do something about Tyler. If we survived, I would have a heck of a dispatch to send back to the Home.

"You about ready?" Silver whispered.

I nodded and started to take my clothes off.

"What are you doing?"

"This is how I do it." I finished undressing and started smearing dirt all over my body.

"What if you step on a snake?"

"I won't."

He handed me his knife, and I started toward the encampment.

When I got to the open end of the horseshoe, I slowed way down. I could hear people snoring. A child coughed and I froze in midstep. My biggest fear was having Raul cry out when I got to him. I had a plan for that, and I hoped it would work.

Raul was slumped over, sleeping. His forehead was resting against the pole. When I got to him, I reached toward his head very, very slowly, then clamped my hand over his mouth. He jerked awake and made a muffled sound that I was sure they would hear. When Raul recognized me, he relaxed. There was some movement in the hammocks, and I held my breath. I sat perfectly still for about five minutes. When it was clear that no one was going to get up, I quietly sliced through the vines around Raul's feet and wrists. He followed me step for step out of the compound.

"Impressive," Silver said, when we got back.

I put my clothes back on, while Raul and he whispered to each other in Portuguese.

"We have a problem," Silver said. "It seems that our friends down there have your female jaguar's collar."

"How did they get that?"

"Your father and Raul stumbled across a jaguar pit when they were out poking around. Apparently the tribe set it for her and she fell right into it. She's dead."

In his delirium, Doc had been calling out the jaguar's name, not my mom's!

"They were on their way back when your father collapsed. Raul left him in the forest and was on his way to camp to get help, when he got caught by the tribe. They hauled him to the village, and he couldn't make them understand that your dad needed help. Raul assumed that Doc had died in the forest. It's a miracle that he made it back to camp."

"So Tyler is heading right toward the village?"

"Right," Silver said. "I figure our best chance is to go out and try to intercept him before he gets here. At least we know where he's headed. Unfortunately, we don't know which direction he'll be coming from."

I thought about this for a minute. "So there's a pit not too far from here?"

"Yeah," Silver said. "But what's that have to do with anything?"

"Does Raul know where the collar is?"

Silver asked him. "He says that it's hanging from one of the beams on the right side of the compound. What do you have in mind?"

"Let me see if I can get the collar first."

Silver and Raul spoke again.

"Raul says his bag is hanging next to the collar. He'd like to have it back if you can manage it."

"I'll see what I can do."

I took my clothes off again.

CHAPTER 24

I had no problem retrieving the collar. It was hanging right where Raul said it would be, alongside Beth's drying skin and Raul's cotton bag. I hoped Wild Bill and Taw would fare better than their mother had in the new preserve.

It was still dark when we got to the jaguar pit, so we rested until daylight. The pit was about ten feet square. There were sharpened branches embedded in the bottom. I lowered myself down with a rope and took the branches out along with the other sticks and leaves that had fallen in when Beth fell through.

When I climbed back out, Raul wanted to know how much Tyler weighed and how much gear he was carrying. I gave him my best guess.

We went to work. Raul kept undoing everything we did. Finally, Silver and I backed off and let Raul do it by himself. He worked quickly, but it was still taking longer than Silver wanted.

Raul laid heavier sticks around the edges of the pit and light sticks in the middle. I guessed this was to make sure that the animal, or in this case the maniac, would be in the middle when the top collapsed.

Raul made a few final touches to the ground around the pit and announced that it was ready.

We hid ourselves fifty feet away. About twenty minutes later, Tyler showed up. He had the earphones on and the receiver strapped to his belt. He held the antenna above his head, and turned it back and forth very slowly, trying to locate where the signal was coming from. The collar was hanging in a tree in back of the pit. At this range he wouldn't be able to locate where the signal was coming from. All he would know was that it was very close.

Without hesitating, Tyler stepped onto the top of the pit. I expected it to collapse, but it didn't. He continued walking and still it didn't cave in.

Raul made an odd sound. Tyler froze when he heard it. Then the ground gave way and he disappeared. We stayed in our hiding place. Silver waited for the dust to settle before he said anything.

"Tyler?" he shouted.

"I should have known!" Tyler shouted back.

"I'm going to toss you a rope," Silver continued. "I want you to climb out very slowly. When you get out of the pit, I want you to keep both your hands on the rope and just follow it until I tell you to stop. If you take one hand off the rope, I'll blow you back into the pit. Understand?"

"Yes, sir," Tyler said.

Silver threw the rope into the pit. The other end was tied to a tree in back of where we were taking cover.

"Nice and easy."

"I'm coming out." Tyler's head appeared above the edge.

"Just follow the rope," Silver said.

When Tyler was well away from the pit, Silver told him to stop. He said something to Raul in Portuguese. Raul reached into his bag and pulled out some rope.

"One hand at a time, Tyler. You know the routine."

Tyler put one of his hands behind his back. Raul put a loop around it and waited for Tyler's other hand. The second hand shot back like a bolt of lightning and grabbed Raul before any of us knew what was happening. There wasn't time for Silver to get a shot off before Raul and Tyler were tangled up on the ground. Silver fired into the air and Scarlet flew off screaming, as if the shot had been meant for her.

"The next one's in your head, Tyler!" Silver shouted.

Tyler let Raul go.

"Let's try this again," Silver said, calmly. "Get on your belly, Tyler, and put both of your hands behind your back."

Tyler rolled over and put his hands behind his back. Raul tied him up without any problems this time. When he was finished, Silver told Tyler to get to his feet.

During the tussle a few items from Raul's bag had spilled out onto the ground. Raul gathered them up and put them back into the bag.

"Well, colonel," Tyler said. "It looks like you found the mother lode."

"There's nothing here," Silver said.

Tyler laughed. "With all due respect, sir, you're a damn liar!"

"Have it your way, Tyler. Let's go."

Raul led the way, with Tyler just behind him. Silver and I followed.

Tyler didn't say one word during the entire trip back to camp, nor did Silver. When we got there, I called out to Flanna, but she didn't answer. I looked into the tent. It was empty. The shotgun was still leaning outside the entrance.

"She probably took Doc and found someplace to hide," I said, hoping she hadn't gone looking for me.

"I see she didn't take the shotgun, either," Silver said. "She's going to have to get over that one of these days or she's going to get hurt." He said something to Raul and he ran off. "He'll find her."

I looked over to the other side of camp and saw Fred's body. Silver followed my gaze and shook his head.

"First we'll secure our prisoner," he said. "Then I'll bury his friend. Then we'll start packing and get—"

Tyler threw his arm around my neck and lifted me off the ground. In his free hand he held a small pocketknife just below my eye. It was the same knife I had given to Raul. It must have fallen out of Raul's bag during the scuffle, and Tyler picked it up.

Silver looked as shocked as I felt.

"Let him go, Tyler."

"No, sir. And you're not going to shoot me because you'll kill the boy, too. Now, there was a time when that might not have bothered you very much, but I suspect you've gone a little soft over the years."

Silver just stared at him.

"Colonel, if you don't put the gun down, I snap his neck like a twig. You know I can do it because you taught me how."

I saw the frustration in Silver's eyes. He lowered the shotgun to the ground.

"Now step away from it, colonel."

Silver took a few steps backward. Tyler moved forward without releasing his grip on my neck. I couldn't breathe. In one motion he flung me to the side and scooped the shotgun off the ground, bringing it level with Silver's chest.

I glanced at the shotgun by the tent.

"Don't even think about it, son," Tyler said. "Now, just scoot on over there next to the colonel." I got up and walked over to Silver. "I guess this is it, colonel. . . ."

Silver looked at me. "I'm sorry, Jake."

I heard a sharp *thwack* and Tyler dropped the shotgun, staggered, then fell over backward with an arrow sticking out of his chest.

Flanna stepped out from behind a tree on the far side of camp with another arrow already strung in her compound bow.

"Unbelievable," Silver said.

Flanna walked over to us. "Are you okay, Jake?"

I managed to say that I was fine. "How did you know—"

"I heard the shotgun go off. A few moments later, Scarlet came screaming into camp. I figured Silver wouldn't be far behind, so I hid behind the tree."

"With a compound bow?" Silver asked.

"I didn't know whose side you were on," she said.

"Yours," he said. He walked over to Tyler and picked up the shotgun.

"Is he dead?" Flanna asked.

Silver felt for a pulse. "I'm afraid so."

Flanna dropped the bow and started to cry. Silver handed the shotgun to me, then walked over and held her until she recovered.

"How's Doc?" I asked.

"I think he'll be fine if we can keep him horizontal for a few days," Flanna said. "I managed to get him up in the canopy and put him onto one of the platforms so he'd be safe if Tyler came back. When I left, he was yelling at me to give him a rope and let him down, so I guess he's feeling a lot better."

She went on to explain that Doc had regained consciousness the night before. He told her about his dream about Beth being killed in the pit.

"I knew Tyler was headed right for you. I was just about ready to leave and see if I could find you when I heard the shotgun."

Silver looked at her. "I suppose now I'm indebted to you for life or something," he said.

Flanna smiled. "You better believe it."

"There are worse fates, young lady."

We all walked to the tree where Doc was held prisoner.

"We're all fine," I yelled up to him.

"Glad to hear it," he yelled back. "Get me a rope and I'll come down."

I looked at Flanna. She shook her head.

"Sorry, Doc. We're kind of busy down here. You just take it easy and we'll get you down as soon as we can."

"I promise I'll take it easy. Just get me down from here. Jake . . . ? Jake . . . ? Are you there? Flanna?"

We walked back to camp.

We buried Fred Stoats and Tyler in the same grave. Tyler would not have been very happy about this, but in my opinion they deserved to spend eternity with each other.

It took us the rest of the day and half the night to pack our gear and get it out to the *Tito*.

By the next morning we were ready to leave. Flanna went off to retrieve Doc and the remaining canopy platform. I went down to the lake and found Silver on the shore, standing in front of a huge pile of maps and old journals.

"What are you doing?" I asked.

"Destroying the trail." He lit a match and dropped it into the pile. He watched the flames for a moment, then reached into his pocket and pulled out the golden jaguar.

"I believe this is yours."

I reached into my own pocket and gave him the second golden jaguar.

"Another gift?" he asked.

I shook my head and told him about the ruins beneath the lake.

"Why don't you keep the jaguars?" I said. "You spent a long time looking for them."

Silver looked at the figurines. "If I keep them, people will wonder where I found them—and maybe they'll come looking. I don't want that to happen."

He smiled and threw them into the center of the lake.

"That's where they belong," he said.

I climbed up to the rock next to the waterfall for the last time. Below me, Silver stared at the burning pile. He looked happy and relaxed, as if he was at peace with himself and the world. It reminded me of the snapshot of him and Tito. He may not have found his son, but it looked as if he had recaptured that same contentment, at least for the moment.

Flanna brought Doc down to the beach. Other than being weak from his illness and irritated at being kept prisoner in the tree for two days, he was in good shape.

Raul took them out to the boat in the Zodiac, then came back and picked up Silver and me.

Silver climbed up to the wheelhouse and started the engine. We heard a loud scream and Scarlet came soaring in from the rain forest. Shore leave was over.

CHAPTER 25

Our new camp wasn't nearly as nice as the lake camp, but it was a lot more peaceful.

Flanna set up another web in the canopy while the rest of us helped Doc catch jaguars. Over the next six weeks we caught and collared two females. We named one of them Beth.

Tracking was much more difficult and time-consuming because we had to do it on the ground. Silver and I took care of this part of the project, while Raul and Doc conducted a mammal survey to see what was living in the forest.

While we were having dinner one evening, a small airplane landed on the river and taxied over to Silver's boat. We all walked down to the water to see who it was.

The first man out of the airplane was dressed in a white suit with a white Panama hat on his head. He was rather short and pudgy and had a white mustache that curled up at the ends.

"He looks like Mr. Monopoly," I said.

Doc laughed. "In a way he is."

The man walked over to us.

"Jake, I'd like you to meet Mr. Woolcott."

Two other men got out of the airplane wearing conservative business suits, which is not the best attire for the tropics. They looked very uncomfortable. The last person out of the plane was the pilot—Buzz Lindbergh. He looked very comfortable in shorts and a purple tank top. He limped over and gave us all a hug.

"How's the leg?" Doc asked.

"I'm still a little gimpy, but it looks like I'm going to survive! How's the Morpho?" This was directed at me.

"We'll talk about it later," Doc said, quietly. "Let's go up and get Woolcott situated."

All evening long, Doc and Flanna went over the data they had gathered about the flora and fauna of the preserve. The next morning we attached antennas to their airplane. Buzz and Doc took Woolcott for a tour of the preserve as they tracked jaguars.

When they got back, Doc said that he had picked up signals from both Wild Bill and Taw. They seemed to be doing just fine.

"We have to leave early tomorrow morning," Woolcott said. "I'd like to meet with everyone before then."

We gathered together back at camp that evening.

"I'll make this real simple," Woolcott said. "I like what

you've done and I want to fund this preserve. I'll set up an endowment. That way we'll be able to keep it going a long time after we're all dead and buried."

We were all thrilled. Bill's dream had come true.

"Now I assume," Woolcott continued, "that you'll be able to stay on and run it, Dr. Lansa."

"I don't know," Doc said. He looked at me and Flanna. "I was planning to go back to Poughkeepsie."

"We need to talk about this," Flanna said.

AFTER . . .

The recreation room was full. I held the Press Conference after dinner, because I knew it would take awhile to tell the inmates everything that had happened. Well, not everything. I had to leave a few details out, like actually finding the lost mines of Muribeca. If I told them about that, some of the inmates might have checked out of the Home and headed down to Brazil that evening.

When I finished, there were a lot of questions. Over the next few weeks I knew there would be many more.

"What will you do now?" Mr. Blondell asked.

"I have a couple more weeks of school, then Taw and I are going to take a little trip."

"What about the preserve?" Mr. Clausen asked. "Will you go back down there?"

"Oh, I'm sure I'll go back at some point," I said.

"Is your father going to marry this Flanna girl?" Mrs. Mapes asked.

"I don't know. Maybe someday."

"It's getting late," Peter said. "Jake just got home this morning. He needs to rest."

Taw and I took the elevator up to the second floor. I walked him to his room.

"I'm glad you came back," he said.

"So am I, Taw."

"You'll like Arizona. It's beautiful."

"I'm looking forward to it."

I walked back to my room and looked at the jaguar tooth that Raul had given me and thought about my last night at the preserve.

Flanna had talked my father into staying down there and managing the preserve. Doc said that he wanted me to stay there with him and that he would look into correspondence courses for me.

He was surprised when I told him the next morning that I wanted to fly back to Manaus with Buzz and Woolcott—and from there, catch the first flight back to the States.

"I thought we had it all worked out last night? You're going to stay down here with us."

"I just need to go back for a while," I said. "Taw wants me to go to Arizona with him."

Jaguar

I said good-bye to Silver, Raul, and Flanna. Doc walked me down to the airplane.

"So how long will you be gone?"

"I'll only be gone a month," I said. "Maybe a little longer. . . ."

ABOUT THE AUTHOR

ROLAND SMITH is a research biologist who has been caring for exotic animals for over twenty years. He is also the author of many books for children, including *Sea Otter Rescue, Inside the Zoo Nursery*, and *Journey of the Red Wolf*, as well as the novel *Thunder Cave*, which was named a Notable Trade Book in the Field of Social Studies for 1996. Mr. Smith lives in Stafford, Oregon, with his wife, Marie.